AFGHANISTAN

A "SPY" GUIDE

VOLUME 1

STRATEGIC INFORMATION AND POLITICAL DEVELOPMENTS

International Business Publications, USA
Washington, DC USA - Afghanistan

AFGHANISTAN

A "SPY" GUIDE

VOLUME 1 STRATEGIC INFORMATION AND POLITICAL DEVELOPMENTS

UPDATED ANNUALLY

We express our sincere appreciation to all government agencies and international organizations which provided information and other materials for this guide

Cover Design: **International Business Publications, USA**

2018 Edition Updated Reprint International Business Publications, USA
ISBN 1-4330-0004-0

For additional analytical, business and investment opportunities information,
please contact Global Investment & Business Center, USA
at (703) 370-8082. Fax: (703) 370-8083. E-mail: ibpusa3@gmail.com
Global Business and Investment Info Databank - www.ibpus.com

Printed in the USA

For additional analytical, business and investment opportunities information,
please contact Global Investment & Business Center, USA
at (703) 370-8082. Fax: (703) 370-8083. E-mail: ibpusa3@gmail.com
Global Business and Investment Info Databank - www.ibpus.com

AFGHANISTAN

A "SPY" GUIDE

VOLUME 1
STRATEGIC INFORMATION AND POLITICAL DEVELOPMENTS

TABLE OF CONTENTS

STRATEGIC AND DEVELOPMENT PROFILES

BASIC PROFILE

Capital and largest city	Kabul 34°32′N 69°08′E
Official languages	• Pashto • Dari
Ethnic groups	Pashtun, Tajik, Hazara, Uzbek, and others
Religion	Islam
Demonym	Afghan
Government	Unitary presidential Islamic republic
• President	Ashraf Ghani
• Chief Executive Officer	Abdullah Abdullah
Legislature	National Assembly
• Upper house	House of Elders
• Lower house	House of the People
Formation	
• Hotak Empire	April 1709
• Durrani Empire	October 1747
• Emirate	1823
• Recognized	19 August 1919
• Kingdom	9 June 1926
• Republic	17 July 1973
• Current constitution	26 January 2004
Area	
• Total	652,864 km^2 (252,072 sq mi) (40th)
• Water (%)	negligible
Population	
• 2016 estimate	34,656,032 (40th)
• Density	49.88/km^2 (129.2/sq mi) (150th)
GDP (PPP)	2017 estimate
• Total	$70 billion
• Per capita	$1,888
GDP (nominal)	2017 estimate
• Total	$21 billion
• Per capita	$572
Gini	29 low
HDI (2014)	▲ 0.465 low · 171st
Currency	Afghani (Afs) (AFN)
Time zone	D† (UTC+4:30 Solar Calendar)
Drives on the	right
Calling code	+93
ISO 3166 code	AF
Internet TLD	.af افغانستان.

Afghanistan officially the **Islamic Republic of Afghanistan**, is a landlocked country located in the centre of Asia, forming South Asia, Central Asia and the Middle East. With a population of about 29 million, it has an area of 647,500 km^2 (250,001 sq mi), making it the 42nd most populous and 41st largest nation in the world. It is bordered by Pakistan in the southeast, Iran in the west, Turkmenistan, Uzbekistan and Tajikistan in the north, and China in the far northeast. The territory that now forms Afghanistan has been an ancient focal point of the Silk Road and human migration. Archaeologists have found evidence of human habitation from as far back as 50,000 BC. Urban civilization may have begun in the area as early as 3,000 to 2,000 BC.

The country sits at an important geostrategic location that connects the Middle East with Central Asia and the Indian subcontinent, which has been home to various peoples through the ages. The land has witnessed many military conquests since antiquity, notably by Alexander the Great, Chandragupta Maurya, and Genghis Khan. It has also served as a source from which local dynasties such as the Greco-Bactrians, Kushans, Saffarids, Ghaznavids, Ghorids, Timurids, Mughals and many others have established empires of their own.

The political history of modern Afghanistan begins in 1709 with the rise of the Pashtuns, when the Hotaki dynasty was established in Kandahar followed by Ahmad Shah Durrani's rise to power in 1747. The capital of Afghanistan was shifted in 1776 from Kandahar to Kabul and part of the Afghan Empire was ceded to neighboring empires by 1893. In the late 19th century, Afghanistan became a buffer state in the "Great Game" between the British and Russian empires. Following the third Anglo-Afghan war and the signing of the Treaty of Rawalpindi in 1919, the nation regained control over its foreign policy from the British.

After the 1978 Marxist revolution, the Soviet Union began a 10-year war in which over a million Afghans lost lives. The mujahidin insurgency generated by the Marxist government and the Soviet invasion signaled the first sustained entry of Islam into Afghan politics as the religion served as a force to unify the tribally divided multiethnic population.

This was followed by the Afghan civil war (1992–1996), the rise and fall of the extremist Taliban government and the 2001-present war. In December 2001, the United Nations Security Council authorized the creation of the International Security Assistance Force (ISAF) to help maintain security in Afghanistan and assist the Karzai administration. While NATO and other countries are rebuilding war-torn Afghanistan, insurgent groups such as the Taliban and Haqqani network are actively involved in a nationwide Taliban-led insurgency, which includes countless assassinations and suicide attacks against civilians, Afghan authorities and western forces. According to the United Nations, the insurgents were responsible for 75% of civilian casualties in 2010 and 80% in 2011.

STRATEGIC PROFILE

The name Afghanistan literally translates to *Land of the Afghans*. Its modern usage derives from the word *Afghan*. The Pashtuns appear to have begun using the term Afghan as a name for themselves from the Islamic period onwards. According to W.K. Frazier Tyler, M.C. Gillet and several other scholars, *"The word Afghan first appears in history in the Hudud-al-Alam in 982 AD."* The last part of the name *Afghanistan* originates from the Persian word *stān* (*country* or *land*). The English word *Afghanland* that appeared in various treaties between Qajar-Persia and the United Kingdom dealing with the lands between Persia and British Raj inhabited by Pashtun tribes (modern Southeastern Afghanistan) was adopted by the Afghans and became *Afghanistan*.

However, Afghanistan was pronounced by its current name from the 18th century onwards when Ahmed Shah Abdali formed the new government, and was officially named as Afghanistan during the ruling of Abdur Rahman Khan. Before the 18th century, Afghanistan was always known as Khorasan, as today's Afghan territory forms the major regions of the Great Khorasan.

Afghanistan (officially the **Islamic Republic of Afghanistan**; is a landlocked country at the crossroads of Asia. Generally considered a part of Central Asia, it is sometimes ascribed to a regional bloc in either the Middle East or South Asia, as it has cultural, ethno-linguistic, and geographic links with most of its neighbors. It is bordered by Iran in the west, Pakistan and India in the south and east, Turkmenistan, Uzbekistan and Tajikistan in the north, and the People's Republic of China to the east. The name Afghanistan is derived from Persian, meaning "land of the Afghans"

Afghanistan is a mosaic of ethnic groups and cultures, and a crossroads between east and west. An ancient land that has often been plundered, and also a focal point of trade, the region of present-day Afghanistan has seen several invading forces come and go, including Aryan nomads, the Mede and Persian Empires, Greeks, Arabs, Turks, and Mongols. Modern Afghanistan arose as an independent state in 1919, when foreign intervention ceased following the Anglo-Afghan wars. The country's recent history has seen it ravaged by the Soviet Invasion of Afghanistan, the Afghan Civil War, the rise and fall of the Taliban, and the United States invasion of Afghanistan in 2001.

As a result of these traumatic events, Afghanistan is in a rebuilding phase, as it attempts to reconcile the devastation that constant warfare has created, with a new government that seeks to unify and rebuild Afghanistan. Afghanistan faces numerous problems, ranging from its devastated economy, the return of millions of refugees, continued warlordism, drug trafficking, and a new government that is struggling with the political forces trying to define the sort of country Afghanistan will become in the 21st century.

Background:	Afghanistan was invaded and occupied by the Soviet Union in 1979. The USSR was forced to withdraw 10 years later by anti-communist mujahidin forces supplied and trained by the US, Saudi Arabia, Pakistan, and others. Fighting subsequently continued among the various mujahidin factions, but the fundamentalist Islamic Taliban movement has been able to seize most of the country. In addition to the continuing civil strife, the country suffers from enormous poverty, a crumbling infrastructure, and widespread land mines.

GEOGRAPHY

Location:	Southern Asia, north and west of Pakistan, east of Iran
Geographic coordinates:	33 00 N, 65 00 E
Map references:	Asia
Area:	total: 647,500 sq km land: 647,500 sq km water: 0 sq km
Area - comparative:	slightly smaller than Texas
Land boundaries:	total: 5,529 km border countries: China 76 km, Iran 936 km, Pakistan 2,430 km, Tajikistan 1,206 km, Turkmenistan 744 km, Uzbekistan 137 km

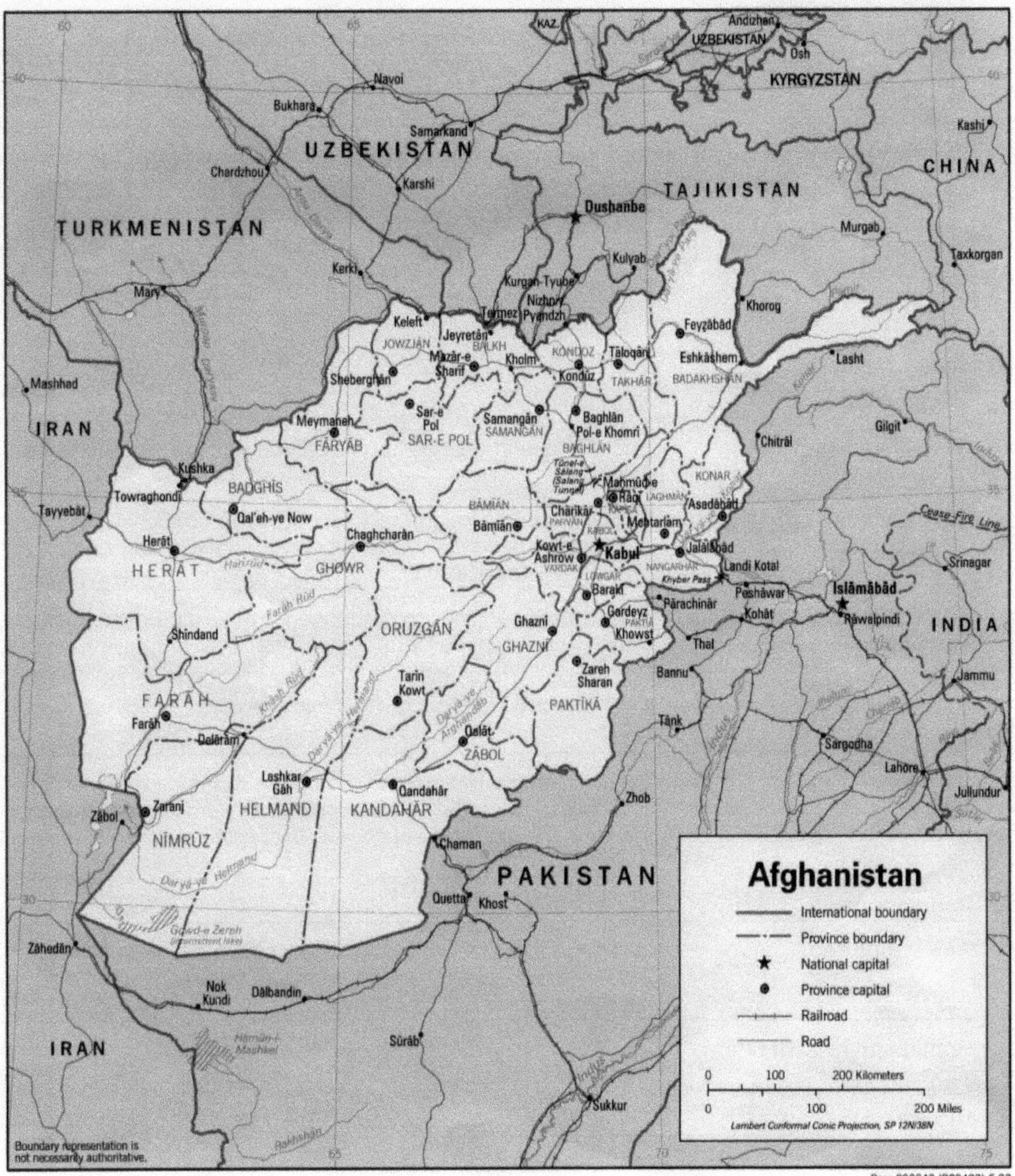

Base 802043 (R00493) 6-93

Coastline:	0 km (landlocked)
Maritime claims:	none (landlocked)

Climate:	arid to semiarid; cold winters and hot summers
Terrain:	mostly rugged mountains; plains in north and southwest
Elevation extremes:	lowest point: Amu Darya 258 m highest point: Nowshak 7,485 m
Natural resources:	natural gas, petroleum, coal, copper, chromite, talc, barites, sulfur, lead, zinc, iron ore, salt, precious and semiprecious stones
Land use:	arable land: 12% permanent crops: 0% permanent pastures: 46% forests and woodland: 3% other: 39%
Irrigated land:	30,000 sq km
Natural hazards:	damaging earthquakes occur in Hindu Kush mountains; flooding; droughts
Environment - current issues:	soil degradation; overgrazing; deforestation (much of the remaining forests are being cut down for fuel and building materials); desertification
Environment - international agreements:	party to: Desertification, Endangered Species, Environmental Modification, Marine Dumping, Nuclear Test Ban signed, but not ratified: Biodiversity, Climate Change, Hazardous Wastes, Law of the Sea, Marine Life Conservation

Geography - note:	landlocked; the Hindu Kush mountains that run northeast to southwest divide the northern provinces from the rest of the country; the highest peaks are in the northern Vakhan (Wakhan Corridor)
Population:	26,813,057
Age structure:	0-14 years: 42.2% (male 5,775,921; female 5,538,836) 15-64 years: 55.01% (male 7,644,242; female 7,106,568) 65 years and over: 2.79% (male 394,444; female 353,046)
Population growth rate:	3.48% note: this rate reflects the continued return of refugees from Iran
Birth rate:	41.42 births/1,000 population
Death rate:	17.72 deaths/1,000 population
Net migration rate:	11.11 migrant(s)/1,000 population
Sex ratio:	at birth: 1.05 male(s)/female under 15 years: 1.04 male(s)/female 15-64 years: 1.08 male(s)/female 65 years and over: 1.12 male(s)/female total population: 1.06 male(s)/female

Infant mortality rate:	147.02 deaths/1,000 live births

PEOPLE

Life expectancy at birth:	total population: 46.24 years male: 46.97 years female: 45.47 years
Total fertility rate:	5.79 children born/woman
HIV/AIDS - adult prevalence rate:	less than 0.01%
HIV/AIDS - people living with HIV/AIDS:	NA
HIV/AIDS - deaths:	NA
Nationality:	noun: Afghan(s) adjective: Afghan
Ethnic groups:	Pashtun 38%, Tajik 25%, Hazara 19%, minor ethnic groups (Aimaks, Turkmen, Baloch, and others) 12%, Uzbek 6%
Religions:	Sunni Muslim 84%, Shi'a Muslim 15%, other 1%
Languages:	Pashtu 35%, Afghan Persian (Dari) 50%, Turkic languages (primarily Uzbek and Turkmen) 11%, 30 minor languages (primarily Balochi and Pashai) 4%, much bilingualism
Literacy:	definition: age 15 and over can read and write total population: 31.5% male: 47.2% female: 15%

GOVERNMENT

Country name:	conventional long form: Islamic State of Afghanistan; note - the self-proclaimed Taliban government refers to the country as Islamic Emirate of Afghanistan conventional short form: Afghanistan local long form: Dowlat-e Eslami-ye Afghanestan local short form: Afghanestan former: Republic of Afghanistan
Government type:	no functioning central government, administered by factions
Capital:	Kabul
Administrative divisions:	30 provinces (velayat, singular - velayat); Badakhshan, Badghis, Baghlan, Balkh, Bamian, Farah, Faryab, Ghazni, Ghowr, Helmand, Herat, Jowzjan, Kabol, Kandahar, Kapisa, Konar, Kondoz, Laghman, Lowgar, Nangarhar, Nimruz, Oruzgan, Paktia, Paktika, Parvan, Samangan, Sar-e Pol, Takhar, Vardak, Zabol; note - there may be two new provinces of Nurestan (Nuristan) and Khowst
Independence:	19 August 1919 (from UK control over Afghan foreign affairs)

National holiday:	Independence Day, 19 August (1919)
Constitution:	none
Legal system:	a new legal system has not been adopted but all factions tacitly agree they will follow Shari'a (Islamic law)
Suffrage:	NA; previously males 15-50 years of age
Executive branch:	**chief of state:** President of the Islamic Republic of Afghanistan Ashraf GHANI Ahmadzai (since 29 September 2014); CEO Abdullah ABDULLAH (since 29 September 2014); First Vice President Abdul Rashid DOSTAM (since 29 September 2014); Second Vice President Sarwar DANESH (since 29 September 2014); note - the president is both chief of state and head of government **head of government:** President of the Islamic Republic of Afghanistan Ashraf GHANI Ahmadzai (since 29 September 2014); CEO Abdullah ABDULLAH (since 29 September 2014); First Vice President Abdul Rashid DOSTAM (since 29 September 2014); Second Vice President Sarwar DANESH (since 29 September 2014) **cabinet:** Cabinet consists of 25 ministers appointed by the president, approved by the National Assembly **elections/appointments:** president directly elected by absolute majority popular vote in 2 rounds if needed for a 5-year term (eligible for a second term); election last held in 2 rounds on 5 April and 14 June 2014 (next to be held in 2019) **election results:** percent of vote in first round - Abdullah ABDULLAH (National Coalition of Afghanistan) 45%, Ashraf GHANI (independent) 31.6%, Zalmai RASSOUL 11.4%, other 12%; percent of vote in second round - Ashraf GHANI 56.4%, Abdullah ABDULLAH 43.6%
Legislative branch:	**description:** bicameral National Assembly consists of the Meshrano Jirga or House of Elders (102 seats; 34 members indirectly elected by district councils to serve 3-year terms, 34 indirectly elected by provincial councils to serve 4-year terms, and 34 nominated by the president of which 17 must be women, 2 must represent the disabled, and 2 must be Kuchi nomads; members serve 5-year terms) and the Wolesi Jirga or House of People (249 seats; members directly elected in multi-seat constituencies by proportional representation vote to serve 5-year terms) **note:** the constitution allows the government to convene a constitutional Loya Jirga (Grand Council) on issues of independence, national sovereignty, and territorial integrity; it can amend the provisions of the constitution and prosecute the president; it consists of members of the National Assembly and chairpersons of the provincial and district councils; no constitutional Loya Jirga has ever been held, and district councils have never been elected; the president appointed 34 members of the Meshrano Jirga that the district councils should have indirectly elected

	elections: the Wolesi Jirga's five-year term expired in 2015, but the president extended its term by decree until elections can be held **election results:** results by party - NA; seats by party - NA
Judicial branch:	upper courts were non-functioning as of March 1995 (local Shari'a or Islamic law courts are functioning throughout the country) the constitution establishes a nine-member Stera Mahkama or Supreme Court (its nine justices are appointed for 10-year terms by the president with approval of the Wolesi Jirga) and subordinate High Courts and Appeals Courts (note - nine supreme court justices were appointed in the interim in January 2005 pending National Assembly selection of the constitutionally mandated justices); there is also a minister of justice; a separate Afghan Independent Human Rights Commission established by the Bonn Agreement is charged with investigating human rights abuses and war crimes
Political parties and leaders:	note - includes only political parties approved by the Ministry of Justice: Afghan Millat [Anwarul Haq AHADI]; De Afghanistan De Solay Ghorzang Gond [Shahnawaz TANAI]; De Afghanistan De Solay Mili Islami Gond [Shah Mahmood Polal ZAI]; Harakat-e-Islami Afghanistan [Mohammad Asif MOHSINEE]; Hezb-e-Aarman-e-Mardum-e-Afghanistan [Iihaj Saraj-u-din ZAFAREE]; Hezb-e-Aazadee Afghanistan [Abdul MALIK]; Hezb-e-Adalat-e-Islami Afghanistan [Mohammad Kabeer MARZBAN]; Hezb-e-Afghanistan-e-Wahid [Mohammad Wasil RAHEEMEE]; Hezb-e-Afghan Watan Islami Gond; Hezb-e-Congra-e-Mili Afghanistan [Latif PEDRAM]; Hezb-e-Falah-e-Mardum-e-Afghanistan [Mohammad ZAREEF]; Hezb-e-Hambastagee Mili Jawanan-e-Afghanistan [Mohammad Jamil KARZAI]; Hezb-e-Hamnbatagee-e-Afghanistan [Abdul Khaleq NEMAT]; Hezb-e-Harakat-e-Mili Wahdat-e-Afghanistan [Mohammad Nadir AATASH]; Hezb-e-Harak-e-Islami Mardum-e-Afghanistan [Ilhaj Said Hssain ANWARY]; Hezb-e-Ifazat Az Uqoq-e-Bashar Wa Inkishaf-e-Afghanistan [Baryalai NASRATEE]; Hezb-e-Istiqlal-e-Afghanistan [Dr. Gh. Farooq NIJZRABEE]; Hezb-e-Jamhoree Khwahan [Sibghatullah SANJAR]; Hezb-e-Kar Wa Tawsiha-e-Afghanistan [Zulfiar OMID]; Hezb-e-Libral-e-Aazadee Khwa-e-Mardum-e-Afghanistan [Ajmal SOHAIL]; Hezb-e-Mili Afghanistan [Abdul Rasheed AARYAN]; Hezb-e-Mili Wahdat-e-Aqwam-e-Islami Afghanistan [Mohammad Shah KHOGYANEE]; Hezb-e-Nuhzhat-e-Mili Afghanistan [Ahmad Wali MASOUD]; Hezb-e-Paiwand-e-Mili Afghanistan [Said Mansoor NADIRI]; Hezb-e-Rastakhaiz-e-Islami Mardum-e-Afghanistan [Said ZAHIR]; Hezb-e-Refah-e-Mardum-e-Afghanistan [Mia Gul WASEEQ]; Hezb-e-Risalat-e-Mardum-e-Afghanistan [Noor Aqa ROEEN]; Hezb-e-Sahadat-e-Mardum-e-Afghanistan [Mohammad Zubair PAIROZ]; Hezb-e-Sahadat-e-Mili Wa Islami Afghanistan [Mohammad Usman SALIGZADA]; Hezb-e-Sulh-e-Mili Islami Aqwam-e-Afghanistan [Abdul Qahir SHARYATEE]; Hezb-e-Sulh Wa Wahdat-e-Mili Afghanistan [Abdul Qadir IMAMEE]; Hezb-e-Tafahum-e-Wa Democracy Afghanistan [Ahamad SHAHEEN]; Hezb-e-Wahdat-e-Islami Afghanistan [Mohammad Karim KHALILI]; Hezb-e-Wahdat-e-Islami Mardum-e-

	Afghanistan [Ustad Mohammad MOHAQQEQ]; Hezb-e-Wahdat-e-Mili Afghanistan [Abdul Rasheed JALILI]; Jamahat-ul-Dahwat ilal Qurhan-wa-Sunat-ul-Afghanistan [Mawlawee Samiullah NAJEEBEE]; Jombesh-e Milli [Abdul Rashid DOSTAM]; Mahaz-e-Mili Islami Afghanistan [Said Ahmad GAILANEE]; Majmah-e-Mili Fahaleen-e-Sulh-e-Afghanistan [Shams ul Haq Noor SHAMS]; Nuhzat-e-Aazadee Wa Democracy Afghanistan [Abdul Raqeeb Jawid KUHISTANEE]; Nuhzat-e-Hambastagee Mili Afghanistan [Peer Said Ishaq GAILANEE]; Sazman-e-Islami Afghanistan-e-Jawan [Siad Jawad HUSSAINEE]; Tahreek Wahdat-e-Mili [Sultan Mahmood DHAZI] (30 Sep 2004)
Political pressure groups and leaders:	Jamiat-e Islami (Society of Islam) [former President Burhanuddin RABBANI]; Ittihad-e Islami (Islamic Union for the Liberation of Afghanistan) [Abdul Rasul SAYYAF]; there are also small monarchist, communist, and democratic groups
International organization participation:	AsDB, CP, ECO, FAO, G-77, IAEA, IBRD, ICAO, ICCt, ICRM, IDA, IDB, IFAD, IFC, IFRCS, ILO, IMF, Interpol, IOC, IOM, ISO (correspondent), ITU, MIGA, NAM, OIC, OPCW, OSCE (partner), SAARC, SACEP, UN, UNCTAD, UNESCO, UNIDO, UPU, WCO, WFTU, WHO, WIPO, WMO, WToO, WTO (observer)
Diplomatic representation in the US:	**chief of mission:** **chief of mission:** Ambassador Sylvanus Adiewere NSOFOR (since 29 November 2017) **chancery:** 2341 Wyoming Avenue NW, Washington, DC 20008 **telephone:** [1] (202) 483-6410 **FAX:** [1] (202) 483-6488 **consulate(s) general:** Los Angeles, New York, Washington, DC
Diplomatic representation from the US:	**chief of mission:** **chief of mission:** Ambassador W. Stuart SYMINGTON (since 1 December 2016) **embassy:** Bibi Mahru, Kabul **mailing address:** U.S. Embassy Kabul, APO, AE 09806 **telephone:** [00 93] 0700 108 001 **FAX:** [00 93] 0700 108 564
Flag description:	hree equal vertical bands of black (hoist), red, and green, with a gold emblem centered on the red band; the emblem features a temple-like structure encircled by a wreath on the left and right and by a bold Islamic inscription above

ECONOMY

Afghanistan is gradually recovering from decades of conflict. Before 2014, the economy had sustained nearly a decade of strong growth, largely because of international assistance. Since 2014, however, the economy has slowed, in large part because of the withdrawal of nearly 100,000 foreign troops that had artificially inflated the country's economic growth. Despite improvements in life expectancy, incomes, and literacy since 2001, Afghanistan is extremely poor, landlocked, and highly dependent on foreign aid. Much of the population continues to suffer from shortages of housing, clean water, electricity, medical care, and jobs. Corruption, insecurity, weak governance, lack of infrastructure, and the Afghan Government's difficulty in extending rule of law to all parts of the country pose challenges to future economic growth. Afghanistan's living standards are among the lowest in the world.

The international community remains committed to Afghanistan's development, pledging over $83 billion at ten donors' conferences between 2003 and 2016. In October 2016, the donors at the Brussels conference pledged an additional $3.8 billion in development aid annually from 2017 to 2020. Despite this help, the Government of Afghanistan will need to overcome a number of challenges, including low revenue collection, anemic job creation, high levels of corruption, weak government capacity, and poor public infrastructure.

In 2017 Afghanistan's growth rate was only marginally above that of the 2014-2016 average. The drawdown of international security forces that started in 2012 has negatively affected economic growth, as a substantial portion of commerce, especially in the services sector, has catered to the ongoing international troop presence in the country. Afghan President Ashraf GHANI Ahmadzai is dedicated to instituting economic reforms to include improving revenue collection and fighting corruption. However, the reforms will take time to implement and Afghanistan will remain dependent on international donor support over the next several years.

GDP (purchasing power parity):

$69.51 billion (2017 est.)
$67.81 billion (2016 est.)
$66.25 billion (2015 est.)
note: data are in 2017 dollars
country comparison to the world: 100

GDP (official exchange rate):
$21.06 billion (2016 est.)

GDP - real growth rate:
2.5% (2017 est.)
2.4% (2016 est.)
1.3% (2015 est.)
country comparison to the world: 129

GDP - per capita (PPP):
$1,900 (2017 est.)
$2,000 (2016 est.)
$2,100 (2015 est.)
note: data are in 2017 dollars
country comparison to the world: 211

Gross national saving:
22.7% of GDP (2017 est.)
25.5% of GDP (2016 est.)
21.4% of GDP (2015 est.)
country comparison to the world: 68

GDP - composition, by end use:
household consumption: 108.6%
government consumption: 12.8%
investment in fixed capital: 18.2%

investment in inventories: 0%
exports of goods and services: 6.6%
imports of goods and services: -46.2% (2014 est.)

GDP - composition, by sector of origin:
agriculture: 22%
industry: 22%
services: 56%
note: data exclude opium production (2015 est.)

Agriculture - products:
opium, wheat, fruits, nuts; wool, mutton, sheepskins, lambskins, poppies

Industries:
small-scale production of bricks, textiles, soap, furniture, shoes, fertilizer, apparel, food products, non-alcoholic beverages, mineral water, cement; handwoven carpets; natural gas, coal, copper

Industrial production growth rate:
2.4% (2014 est.)
country comparison to the world: 116

Labor force:
7.983 million (2013 est.)
country comparison to the world: 62

Labor force - by occupation:
agriculture: 78.6%
industry: 5.7%
services: 15.7% (FY08/09 est.)

Unemployment rate:
35% (2008 est.)
40% (2005 est.)
country comparison to the world: 208

Population below poverty line:
35.8%

Household income or consumption by percentage share:
lowest 10%: 3.8%
highest 10%: 24% (2008)

Budget:
revenues: $1.992 billion
expenditures: $6.636 billion (2016 est.)

Taxes and other revenues:
9.5% of GDP (2016 est.)
country comparison to the world: 214

Budget surplus (+) or deficit (-):
-22.1% of GDP (2016 est.)
country comparison to the world: 218

Public debt:
8.3% of GDP (2016 est.)
9.3% of GDP (2015 est.)
country comparison to the world: 199

Fiscal year:
21 December - 20 December

Inflation rate (consumer prices):
6% (2017 est.)
4.4% (2016 est.)
country comparison to the world: 183

Commercial bank prime lending rate:
15% (31 December 2016 est.)
15% (31 December 2015 est.)
country comparison to the world: 45

Stock of narrow money:
$6.644 billion (31 December 2014 est.)
$6.192 billion (31 December 2013 est.)
country comparison to the world: 93

Stock of broad money:
$6.945 billion (31 December 2014 est.)
$6.544 billion (31 December 2013 est.)
country comparison to the world: 118

Stock of domestic credit:
$-240.6 million (31 December 2016 est.)
$-240.6 million (31 December 2016 est.)
country comparison to the world: 191

Current account balance:
$999 million (2017 est.)
$1.372 billion (2016 est.)
country comparison to the world: 38

Exports:
$619.2 million (2016 est.)
$580 million (2015 est.)
note: not including illicit exports or reexports
country comparison to the world: 171

Exports - commodities:
opium, fruits and nuts, handwoven carpets, wool, cotton, hides and pelts, precious and semi-precious gems

Exports - partners:
Pakistan 46.3%, India 37.6%

Imports:
$6.16 billion (2016 est.)

$7.034 billion (2015 est.)
country comparison to the world: 114

Imports - commodities:
machinery and other capital goods, food, textiles, petroleum products

Imports - partners:
Iran 19.3%, Pakistan 18.3%, China 16.7%, Kazakhstan 9.5%, Uzbekistan 6.1%, Turkmenistan 5.4%, Malaysia 4% (2016)

Reserves of foreign exchange and gold:
$6.477 billion (31 December 2016 est.)
$6.232 billion (31 December 2015 est.)
country comparison to the world: 87

Debt - external:
$1.28 billion (FY10/11)
$2.7 billion (FY08/09)
country comparison to the world: 163

Exchange rates:
afghanis (AFA) per US dollar -
67.87 (2016 est.)
67.87 (2016 est.)
67.87 (2015)
61.14 (2014 est.)
57.25 (2013 est.)

ENERRGY

Electricity access:
population without electricity: 18,999,254
electrification - total population: 43%
electrification - urban areas: 83%
electrification - rural areas: 32%

Electricity - production:
1.034 billion kWh (2015 est.)
country comparison to the world: 149

Electricity - consumption:
4.741 billion kWh (2015 est.)
country comparison to the world: 124

Electricity - exports:
0 kWh (2016 est.)
country comparison to the world: 99

Electricity - imports:
3.779 billion kWh (2015 est.)
country comparison to the world: 48

Electricity - installed generating capacity:
599,100 kW (2015 est.)
country comparison to the world: 139

Electricity - from fossil fuels:
44.7% of total installed capacity (2015 est.)
country comparison to the world: 161

Electricity - from nuclear fuels:
0% of total installed capacity (2015 est.)
country comparison to the world: 36

Electricity - from hydroelectric plants:
55.1% of total installed capacity (2015 est.)
country comparison to the world: 33

Electricity - from other renewable sources:
0.2% of total installed capacity (2015 est.)
country comparison to the world: 160

Crude oil - production:
0 bbl/day (2016 est.)
country comparison to the world: 102

Crude oil - exports:
0 bbl/day (2014 est.)
country comparison to the world: 86

Crude oil - imports:
0 bbl/day (2014 est.)
country comparison to the world: 89

Crude oil - proved reserves:
0 bbl (1 January 2017 es)
country comparison to the world: 102

Refined petroleum products - production:
0 bbl/day (2014 est.)
country comparison to the world: 111

Refined petroleum products - consumption:
130,000 bbl/day (2015 est.)
country comparison to the world: 76

Refined petroleum products - exports:
0 bbl/day (2014 est.)
country comparison to the world: 129

Refined petroleum products - imports:
127,200 bbl/day (2014 est.)
country comparison to the world: 52

Natural gas - production:
189 million cu m (2015 est.)
country comparison to the world: 77
Natural gas - consumption:
816 million cu m (2015 est.)

country comparison to the world: 104
Natural gas - exports:
0 cu m (2013 est.)
country comparison to the world: 59
Natural gas - imports:
0 cu m (2013 est.)
country comparison to the world: 81

Natural gas - proved reserves:
49.55 billion cu m (1 January 2017 est.)
country comparison to the world: 64

Carbon dioxide emissions from consumption of energy:
7.4 million Mt (2013 est.)
country comparison to the world: 115

COMMUNICATIONS

Telephones - main lines in use:	50,000
Telephones - mobile cellular:	600,000
Telephone system:	*general assessment:* very limited telephone and telegraph service *domestic:* telephone service is improving with the licensing of four wireless telephone service providers by 2005; approximately 3 in 10 Afghans own a wireless telephone; telephone main lines remain limited with only 0.1 line per 10 people *international:* country code - 93; five VSAT's installed in Kabul, Herat, Mazar-e-Sharif, Kandahar, and Jalalabad provide international and domestic voice and data connectivity
Radio broadcast stations:	AM 21, FM 23, shortwave 1 (broadcasts in Pashtu, Afghan Persian (Dari), Urdu, and English)
Radios:	167,000
Television broadcast stations:	at least 10 (one government run central television station in Kabul and regional stations in nine of the 30 provinces; the regional stations operate on a reduced schedule; also, in 1997, there was a station in Mazar-e Sharif reaching four northern Afghanistan provinces)
Televisions:	100,000
Internet country code:	.af
Internet Service Providers (ISPs):	76
Internet users:	25,900 in March 2003, 'af' was established as Afghanistan's domain name; Internet access is growing through Internet cafes as well as public "telekiosks" in Kabul

TRANSPORTATION

Railways:	total: 24.6 km broad gauge: 9.6 km 1.524-m gauge from Gushgy (Turkmenistan) to Towraghondi; 15 km 1.524-m gauge from Termiz (Uzbekistan) to Kheyrabad transshipment point on south bank of Amu Darya
Highways:	total: 21,000 km paved: 2,793 km

	unpaved: 18,207 km
Waterways:	1,200 km note: chiefly Amu Darya, which handles vessels with DWT up to about 500
Pipelines:	petroleum products - Uzbekistan to Bagram and Turkmenistan to Shindand; natural gas 180 km
Ports and harbors:	Kheyrabad, Shir Khan
Airports:	46
Airports - with paved runways:	total: 10 over 3,047 m: 3 2,438 to 3,047 m: 4 1,524 to 2,437 m: 2 under 914 m: 1
Airports - with unpaved runways:	total: 36 Over 3047 m: 1 2,438 to 3,047 m: 7 1,524 to 2,437 m: 13 914 to 1,523 m: 4 under 914 m: 11
Heliports:	2

MILITARY

Military branches:	Afghan National Army (includes Afghan Air Force)
Military manpower - military age:	22 years of age
Military manpower - availability:	males age 15-49: 6,645,023
Military manpower - fit for military service:	males age 15-49: 3,561,957
Military manpower - reaching military age annually:	males: 252,869
Military expenditures - dollar figure:	$NA
Military expenditures - percent of GDP:	NA%

TRANSNATIONAL ISSUES

Disputes - international:	most Afghan refugees in Pakistan have been repatriated, but thousands still remain in Iran, many at their own choosing; Coalition and Pakistani forces continue to patrol remote tribal areas to control the borders and stem organized terrorist and other illegal cross-border activities; regular meetings between Pakistani and Coalition allies aim to resolve periodic claims of boundary encroachments; regional conflicts over water-sharing arrangements with Amu Darya and Helmand River states
Refugees and internally displaced	IDPs: 200,000-300,000 (mostly Pashtuns and Kuchis displaced in south and west due to drought and instability) (2005)

persons:	
Illicit drugs:	world's largest producer of opium; cultivation dropped 48% to 107,400 hectares in 2005; better weather and lack of widespread disease returned opium yields to normal levels, meaning potential opium production declined by only 10% to 4,475 metric tons; if the entire poppy crop were processed, it is estimated that 526 metric tons of heroin could be processed; source of hashish; many narcotics-processing labs throughout the country; drug trade source of instability and some antigovernment groups profit from the trade; 80-90% of the heroin consumed in Europe comes from Afghan opium; vulnerable to narcotics money laundering through informal financial networks

IMPORTANT INFORMATION FOR UNDERSTANDING MODERN AFGHANISTAN

PROFILE

OFFICIAL NAME: Islamic State of Afghanistan

Geography
Area: 647,500 sq. km. (249,935 sq. mi.); slightly smaller than Texas.
Cities: *Capital*--Kabul (1,780,000; UN est.). *Other cities* (1988 UN est.; current figures are probably significantly higher)--Kandahar (226,000); Herat (177,000); Mazar-e-Sharif (131,000); Jalalabad (58,000); Konduz (57,000).
Terrain: Landlocked; mostly mountains and desert.
Climate: Dry, with cold winters and hot summers.

People
Nationality: *Noun and adjective*--Afghan(s).
Population: 28,513,677. More than 3.5 million Afghans live outside the country, mainly in Pakistan and Iran, although over two and a half million have returned since the removal of the Taliban.
Annual population growth rate : 4.92%. This rate does not take into consideration the recent war and its continuing impact.
Main ethnic groups: Pashtun, Tajik, Hazara, Uzbek, Turkmen, Aimaq, Baluch, Nuristani, Kizilbash.
Religions: Sunni Muslim 80%, Shi'a Muslim 19%, other 1%.
Main languages: Dari (Afghan Persian), Pashto.
Education: Approximately 4 million children, of whom some 30% are girls, enrolled in school during 2003. *Literacy*--36% (male 51%, female 21%), but real figures may be lower given breakdown of education system and flight of educated Afghans.
Health: *Infant mortality rate* --165.96 deaths/1,000 live births. *Life expectancy* --42.27 yrs. (male); 42.66 yrs. (female).

Government
Type: Islamic Republic.
Independence: August 19, 1919.
Constitution: January 4, 2004.
Branches: *Executive*—president (chief of state). *Legislative*—bicameral National Assembly (House of the People--249 seats, House of the Elders--102 seats). *Judicial*—Supreme Court, High Courts, and Appeals Courts.
Political subdivisions: 34 provinces.
Suffrage: Universal at 18 years.

Economy
GDP : $4.7 billion.
GDP growth : 7.5%.
GDP per capita : $164.83.
Natural resources: Natural gas, oil, coal, copper, chromite, talc, barites, sulfur, lead, zinc, iron, salt, precious and semiprecious stones.
Agriculture (estimated 52% of GDP): *Products*--wheat, corn, barley, rice, cotton, fruit, nuts, karakul pelts, wool, and mutton.
Industry (estimated 26% of GDP): *Types*--small-scale production for domestic use of textiles, soap, furniture, shoes, fertilizer, and cement; hand-woven carpets for export; natural gas, precious and semiprecious gemstones.

Services (estimated 22% of GDP): Transport, retail, and telecommunications.
Trade (2002-03 est.): *Exports*--$100 million (does not include opium): fruits and nuts, hand-woven carpets, wool, cotton, hides and pelts, precious and semiprecious gems. *Major markets*--Central Asian republics, Pakistan, Iran, EU, India. *Imports*--$2.3 billion: food, petroleum products, machinery, and consumer goods. *Major suppliers*--Central Asian republics, Pakistan, Iran.
Currency: The currency is the afghani, which was reintroduced as Afghanistan's new currency in January 2003. At present, $1 U.S. equals approximately 45 afghanis.

PEOPLE

Afghanistan's ethnically and linguistically mixed population reflects its location astride historic trade and invasion routes leading from Central Asia into South and Southwest Asia. While population data is somewhat unreliable for Afghanistan, Pashtuns make up the largest ethnic group at 38-44% of the population, followed by Tajiks (25%), Hazaras (10%), Uzbek (6-8%), Aimaq, Turkmen, Baluch, and other small groups. Dari (Afghan Farsi) and Pashto are official languages. Dari is spoken by more than one-third of the population as a first language and serves as a lingua franca for most Afghans, though Pashto is spoken throughout the Pashtun areas of eastern and southern Afghanistan. Tajik and Turkic languages are spoken widely in the north. Smaller groups throughout the country also speak more than 70 other languages and numerous dialects.

Afghanistan is an Islamic country. An estimated 80% of the population is Sunni, following the Hanafi school of jurisprudence; the remainder of the population--and primarily the Hazara ethnic group-- predominantly Shi'a. Despite attempts during the years of communist rule to secularize Afghan society, Islamic practices pervade all aspects of life. In fact, Islam served as a principal basis for expressing opposition to communism and the Soviet invasion. Islamic religious tradition and codes, together with traditional tribal and ethnic practices, have an important role in personal conduct and dispute settlement. Afghan society is largely based on kinship groups, which follow traditional customs and religious practices, though somewhat less so in urban areas.

HISTORY

Afghanistan, often called the crossroads of Central Asia, has had a turbulent history. In 328 BC, Alexander the Great entered the territory of present-day Afghanistan, then part of the Persian Empire, to capture Bactria (present-day Balkh). Invasions by the Scythians, White Huns, and Turks followed in succeeding centuries. In AD 642, Arabs invaded the entire region and introduced Islam.

Arab rule gave way to the Persians, who controlled the area until conquered by the Turkic Ghaznavids in 998. Mahmud of Ghazni (998-1030) consolidated the conquests of his predecessors and turned Ghazni into a great cultural center as well as a base for frequent forays into India. Following Mahmud's short-lived dynasty, various princes attempted to rule sections of the country until the destructive Mongol invasion of 1219 led by Genghis Khan.

Following Genghis Khan's death in 1227, a succession of petty chiefs and princes struggled for supremacy until late in the 14th century, when one of his descendants, Tamerlane, incorporated Afghanistan into his own vast Asian empire. Babur, a descendant of Tamerlane and the founder of India's Moghul dynasty at the beginning of the 16th century, made Kabul the capital of an Afghan principality.

In 1747, Ahmad Shah Durrani, the founder of what is known today as Afghanistan, established his rule. A Pashtun, Durrani was elected king by a tribal council after the assassination of the

Persian ruler Nadir Shah at Khabushan in the same year. Throughout his reign, Durrani consolidated chieftainships, petty principalities, and fragmented provinces into one country. His rule extended from Mashad in the west to Kashmir and Delhi in the east, and from the Amu Darya (Oxus) River in the north to the Arabian Sea in the south.

EUROPEAN INFLUENCE

During the 19th century, collision between the expanding British Empire in the subcontinent and czarist Russia significantly influenced Afghanistan in what was termed "The Great Game." British concern over Russian advances in Central Asia and growing influence in Persia culminated in two Anglo-Afghan wars. The first (1839-42) resulted not only in the destruction of a British army, but is remembered today as an example of the ferocity of Afghan resistance to foreign rule. The second Anglo-Afghan war (1878-80) was sparked by Amir Sher Ali's refusal to accept a British mission in Kabul. This conflict brought Amir Abdur Rahman to the Afghan throne. During his reign (1880-1901), the British and Russians officially established the boundaries of what would become modern Afghanistan through the demarcation of the Durand Line. The British retained effective control over Kabul's foreign affairs.

Afghanistan remained neutral during World War I, despite German encouragement of anti-British feelings and Afghan rebellion along the borders of British India. The Afghan king's policy of neutrality was not universally popular within the country, however.

Habibullah, Abdur Rahman's son and successor, was assassinated in 1919, possibly by family members opposed to British influence. His third son, Amanullah, regained control of Afghanistan's foreign policy after launching the third Anglo-Afghan war with an attack on India in the same year. During the ensuing conflict, the war-weary British relinquished their control over Afghan foreign affairs by signing the Treaty of Rawalpindi in August 1919. In commemoration of this event, Afghans celebrate August 19 as their Independence Day.

REFORM AND REACTION

King Amanullah (1919-29) moved to end his country's traditional isolation in the years following the third Anglo-Afghan war. He established diplomatic relations with most major countries and, following a 1927 tour of Europe and Turkey--during which he noted the modernization and secularization advanced by Ataturk--introduced several reforms intended to modernize Afghanistan. Some of these, such as the abolition of the traditional Muslim veil for women and the opening of a number of co-educational schools, quickly alienated many tribal and religious leaders. Faced with overwhelming armed opposition, Amanullah was forced to abdicate in January 1929 after Kabul fell to forces led by Bacha-i-Saqao, a Tajik brigand. Prince Nadir Khan, a cousin of Amanullah's, in turn defeated Bacha-i-Saqao in October of the same year and, with considerable Pashtun tribal support, was declared King Nadir Shah. Four years later, however, he was assassinated in a revenge killing by a Kabul student.

Mohammad Zahir Shah, Nadir Khan's 19-year-old son, succeeded to the throne and reigned from 1933 to 1973. In 1964, King Zahir Shah promulgated a liberal constitution providing for a two-chamber legislature to which the king appointed one-third of the deputies. The people elected another third, and the remainder were selected indirectly by provincial assemblies. Although Zahir's "experiment in democracy" produced few lasting reforms, it permitted the growth of unofficial extremist parties on both the left and the right. These included the communist People's Democratic Party of Afghanistan (PDPA), which had close ideological ties to the Soviet Union. In 1967, the PDPA split into two major rival factions: the Khalq (Masses) faction headed by Nur Muhammad Taraki and Hafizullah Amin and supported by elements within the military, and the

Parcham (Banner) faction led by Babrak Karmal. The split reflected ethnic, class, and ideological divisions within Afghan society.

Zahir's cousin, Sardar Mohammad Daoud, served as his Prime Minister from 1953 to 1963. During his tenure as Prime Minister, Daoud solicited military and economic assistance from both Washington and Moscow and introduced controversial social policies of a reformist nature. Daoud's alleged support for the creation of a Pashtun state in the Pakistan-Afghan border area heightened tensions with Pakistan and eventually resulted in Daoud's dismissal in March 1963.

DAOUD'S REPUBLIC (1973-78) AND THE APRIL 1978 COUP

Amid charges of corruption and malfeasance against the royal family and poor economic conditions created by the severe 1971-72 drought, former Prime Minister Daoud seized power in a military coup on July 17, 1973. Zahir Shah fled the country, eventually finding refuge in Italy. Daoud abolished the monarchy, abrogated the 1964 constitution, and declared Afghanistan a republic with himself as its first President and Prime Minister. His attempts to carry out badly needed economic and social reforms met with little success, and the new constitution promulgated in February 1977 failed to quell chronic political instability.

Seeking to exploit more effectively mounting popular disaffection, the PDPA reunified with Moscow's support. On April 27, 1978, the PDPA initiated a bloody coup, which resulted in the overthrow and murder of Daoud and most of his family. Nur Muhammad Taraki, Secretary General of the PDPA, became President of the Revolutionary Council and Prime Minister of the newly established Democratic Republic of Afghanistan.

Opposition to the Marxist government emerged almost immediately. During its first 18 months of rule, the PDPA brutally imposed a Marxist-style "reform" program, which ran counter to deeply rooted Afghan traditions. Decrees forcing changes in marriage customs and pushing through an ill-conceived land reform were particularly misunderstood by virtually all Afghans. In addition, thousands of members of the traditional elite, the religious establishment, and the intelligentsia were imprisoned, tortured, or murdered. Conflicts within the PDPA also surfaced early and resulted in exiles, purges, imprisonments, and executions.

By the summer of 1978, a revolt began in the Nuristan region of eastern Afghanistan and quickly spread into a countrywide insurgency. In September 1979, Hafizullah Amin, who had earlier been Prime Minister and Minister of Defense, seized power from Taraki after a palace shootout. Over the next 2 months, instability plagued Amin's regime as he moved against perceived enemies in the PDPA. By December, party morale was crumbling, and the insurgency was growing.

THE SOVIET INVASION

The Soviet Union moved quickly to take advantage of the April 1978 coup. In December 1978, Moscow signed a new bilateral treaty of friendship and cooperation with Afghanistan, and the Soviet military assistance program increased significantly. The regime's survival increasingly was dependent upon Soviet military equipment and advisers as the insurgency spread and the Afghan army began to collapse.

By October 1979, however, relations between Afghanistan and the Soviet Union were tense as Hafizullah Amin refused to take Soviet advice on how to stabilize and consolidate his government. Faced with a deteriorating security situation, on December 24, 1979, large numbers of Soviet airborne forces, joining thousands of Soviet troops already on the ground, began to land in Kabul under the pretext of a field exercise. On December 26, these invasion forces killed

Hafizullah Amin and installed Babrak Karmal, exiled leader of the Parcham faction, bringing him back from Czechoslovakia and making him Prime Minister. Massive Soviet ground forces invaded from the north on December 27.

Following the invasion, the Karmal regime, although backed by an expeditionary force that grew as large as 120,000 Soviet troops, was unable to establish authority outside Kabul. As much as 80% of the countryside, including parts of Herat and Kandahar, eluded effective government control. An overwhelming majority of Afghans opposed the communist regime, either actively or passively. Afghan freedom fighters (mujahidin) made it almost impossible for the regime to maintain a system of local government outside major urban centers. Poorly armed at first, in 1984 the mujahidin began receiving substantial assistance in the form of weapons and training from the U.S. and other outside powers.

In May 1985, the seven principal Peshawar-based guerrilla organizations formed an alliance to coordinate their political and military operations against the Soviet occupation. Late in 1985, the mujahidin were active in and around Kabul, launching rocket attacks and conducting operations against the communist government. The failure of the Soviet Union to win over a significant number of Afghan collaborators or to rebuild a viable Afghan army forced it to bear an increasing responsibility for fighting the resistance and for civilian administration.

Soviet and popular displeasure with the Karmal regime led to its demise in May 1986. Karmal was replaced by Muhammad Najibullah, former chief of the Afghan secret police (KHAD). Najibullah had established a reputation for brutal efficiency during his tenure as KHAD chief. As Prime Minister, Najibullah was ineffective and highly dependent on Soviet support. Undercut by deep-seated divisions within the PDPA, regime efforts to broaden its base of support proved futile.

THE GENEVA ACCORDS AND THEIR AFTERMATH

By the mid-1980s, the tenacious Afghan resistance movement--aided by the United States, Saudi Arabia, Pakistan, and others--was exacting a high price from the Soviets, both militarily within Afghanistan and by souring the U.S.S.R.'s relations with much of the Western and Islamic world. Informal negotiations for a Soviet withdrawal from Afghanistan had been underway since 1982. In 1988, the Governments of Pakistan and Afghanistan, with the United States and Soviet Union serving as guarantors, signed an agreement settling the major differences between them. The agreement, known as the Geneva accords, included five major documents, which, among other things, called for U.S. and Soviet noninterference in the internal affairs of Pakistan and Afghanistan, the right of refugees to return to Afghanistan without fear of persecution or harassment, and, most importantly, a timetable that ensured full Soviet withdrawal from Afghanistan by February 15, 1989. About 14,500 Soviet and an estimated one million Afghan lives were lost between 1979 and the Soviet withdrawal in 1989.

Significantly, the mujahidin were party neither to the negotiations nor to the 1988 agreement and, consequently, refused to accept the terms of the accords. As a result, the civil war continued after the Soviet withdrawal, which was completed in February 1989. Najibullah's regime, though failing to win popular support, territory, or international recognition, was able to remain in power until 1992 but collapsed after the defection of Gen. Abdul Rashid Dostam and his Uzbek militia in March. However, when the victorious mujahidin entered Kabul to assume control over the city and the central government, a new round of internecine fighting began between the various militias, which had coexisted only uneasily during the Soviet occupation. With the demise of their common enemy, the militias' ethnic, clan, religious, and personality differences surfaced, and the civil war continued.

Seeking to resolve these differences, the leaders of the Peshawar-based mujahidin groups established an interim Islamic Jihad Council in mid-April 1992 to assume power in Kabul. Moderate leader Prof. Sibghatullah Mojaddedi was to chair the council for 2 months, after which a 10-member leadership council composed of mujahidin leaders and presided over by the head of the Jamiat-i-Islami, Prof. Burhanuddin Rabbani, was to be set up for 4 months. During this 6-month period, a Loya Jirga, or grand council of Afghan elders and notables, would convene and designate an interim administration which would hold power up to a year, pending elections.

But in May 1992, Rabbani prematurely formed the leadership council, undermining Mojaddedi's fragile authority. In June, Mojaddedi surrendered power to the Leadership Council, which then elected Rabbani as President. Nonetheless, heavy fighting broke out in August 1992 in Kabul between forces loyal to President Rabbani and rival factions, particularly those who supported Gulbuddin Hekmatyar's Hezb-i-Islami. After Rabbani extended his tenure in December 1992, fighting in the capital flared up in January and February 1993. The Islamabad Accord, signed in March 1993, which appointed Hekmatyar as Prime Minister, failed to have a lasting effect. A follow-up agreement, the Jalalabad Accord, called for the militias to be disarmed but was never fully implemented. Through 1993, Hekmatyar's Hezb-i-Islami forces, allied with the Shi'a Hezb-i-Wahdat militia, clashed intermittently with Rabbani and Masood's Jamiat forces. Cooperating with Jamiat were militants of Sayyaf's Ittehad-i-Islami and, periodically, troops loyal to ethnic Uzbek strongman Abdul Rashid Dostam. On January 1, 1994, Dostam switched sides, precipitating large-scale fighting in Kabul and in northern provinces, which caused thousands of civilian casualties in Kabul and elsewhere and created a new wave of displaced persons and refugees. The country sank even further into anarchy, forces loyal to Rabbani and Masood, both ethnic Tajiks, controlled Kabul and much of the northeast, while local warlords exerted power over the rest of the country.

RISE AND FALL OF THE TALIBAN

The Taliban had risen to power in the mid 90's in reaction to the anarchy and warlordism that arose after the withdrawal of Soviet forces. Many Taliban had been educated in madrassas in Pakistan and were largely from rural southern Pashtun backgrounds. In 1994, the Taliban developed enough strength to capture the city of Kandahar from a local warlord and proceeded to expand its control throughout Afghanistan, occupying Kabul in September 1996. By the end of 1998, the Taliban occupied about 90% of the country, limiting the opposition largely to a small mostly Tajik corner in the northeast and the Panjshir valley.

The Taliban sought to impose an extreme interpretation of Islam--based upon the rural Pashtun tribal code--on the entire country and committed massive human rights violations, particularly directed against women and girls. The Taliban also committed serious atrocities against minority populations, particularly the Shi'a Hazara ethnic group, and killed noncombatants in several well-documented instances. In 2001, as part of a drive against relics of Afghanistan's pre-Islamic past, the Taliban destroyed two Buddha statues carved into cliff faces outside of the city of Bamiyan.

From the mid-1990s the Taliban provided sanctuary to Osama bin Laden, a Saudi national who had fought with the mujahideen resistance against the Soviets, and provide a base for his and other terrorist organizations. Bin Laden provided both financial and political support to the Taliban. Bin Laden and his Al-Qaida group were charged with the bombing of the U.S. Embassies in Nairobi and Dar Es Salaam in 1998, and in August 1998 the United States launched a cruise missile attack against bin Laden's terrorist camp in southeastern Afghanistan. Bin Laden and Al-Qaida have acknowledged their responsibility for the September 11, 2001 terrorist attacks against the United States.

Following the Taliban's repeated refusal to expel bin Laden and his group and end its support for international terrorism, the U.S. and its partners in the anti-terrorist coalition began a military campaign on October 7, 2001, targeting terrorist facilities and various Taliban military and political assets within Afghanistan. Under pressure from U.S. military and anti-Taliban forces, the Taliban disintegrated rapidly, and Kabul fell on November 13, 2001.

Afghan factions opposed to the Taliban met at a United Nations-sponsored conference in Bonn, Germany in December 2001 and agreed to restore stability and governance to Afghanistan--creating an interim government and establishing a process to move toward a permanent government. Under the "Bonn Agreement," an Afghan Interim Authority was formed and took office in Kabul on December 22, 2001 with Hamid Karzai as Chairman. The Interim Authority held power for approximately 6 months while preparing for a nationwide "Loya Jirga" (Grand Council) in mid-June 2002 that decided on the structure of a Transitional Authority. The Transitional Authority, headed by President Hamid Karzai, renamed the government as the Transitional Islamic State of Afghanistan (TISA). One of the TISA's primary achievements was the drafting of a constitution that was ratified by a Constitutional Loya Jirga on January 4, 2004.

AFGHANISTAN LEGAL SYSTEM

GOVERNMENT – THE EXECUTIVE BRANCH

The Executive Branch of the Afghan government consists of a powerful and popularly elected President and two Vice Presidents.

The constitution involves a strong presidential system. The President of Afghanistan is elected directly by the Afghan people to a five-year term, and can be elected no more than twice.

The president must be Muslim, an Afghan citizen born of Afghan parents, and should not be guilty of war crimes. The president is the commander-in-chief of the armed forces.

Presidential responsibilities include:

- Determining policies with the approval of the National Assembly.
- Appointing the nation's ministers, the attorney general, the director of the central bank, and the justices of the Supreme Court with the approval of the main legislative body, the Wolesi Jirga.
- Appointing the nation's first and second vice presidents.

GOVERNMENT – THE LEGISLATIVE BRANCH

A National Assembly consisting of two Houses, the House of People (Wolesi Jirga) with 249 seats, and the House of Elders (Meshrano Jirga) with 102 seats, forms the Legislative Branch.

There is an independent Judiciary branch consisting of the Supreme Court (Stera Mahkama), High Courts and Appeal Courts. The President appoints the nine members of the Supreme Court with the approval of the Wolesi Jirga.

COMPOSITION OF THE NATIONAL ASSEMBLY

"The National Assembly of the Islamic Republic of Afghanistan as the highest legislative organ is the manifestation of the will of its people and represents the whole nation. Every member of the

National Assembly takes into judgment the general welfare and supreme interests of all people of Afghanistan at the time of casting their vote." *Constitution of the Islamic Republic of Afghanistan (Article Eighty-One)*

The National Assembly, as envisaged in the Constitution, consists of two houses: the Wolesi Jirga (the House of the People) and theMeshrano Jirga (the House of Elders).

Article Ninety of the Afghan Constitution stipulates that the National Assembly shall have the following duties:

- Ratification, modification or abrogation of laws or legislative decrees;
- Approval of social, cultural, economic as well as technological development programs;
- Approval of the state budget as well as permission to obtain or grant loans;
- Creation, modification and or abrogation of administrative units;
- Ratification of international treaties and agreements, or abrogation of membership of Afghanistan in them;
- Other authorities enshrined in this Constitution.

THE WOLESI JIRGA (HOUSE OF PEOPLE)

The Wolesi Jirga has 249 seats with members directly elected by the people.

Sixty-eight women were elected to the seats reserved under the Constitution, while 17 of them have been elected in their own rights.

Each province was given proportionate representation in the Wolesi Jirga according to its population. Each member of the Wolesi Jirga will enjoy a five year term expiring on the twenty-first of June of the fifth year (June 21, 2010).

An aspiring candidate for the Wolesi Jirga must fulfil the following criteria:

- Be at least 25 years of age
- Be a citizen of Afghanistan
- Be registered as a voter
- Be running as a representative in only one province
- Pay a registration fee of 15,000 Afghanis (approximately US$300) which will be refunded provided the candidate wins at least three percent (3%) of the vote
- Submit a nomination form along with photocopies of 500 voter ID cards supporting the candidacy

In addition, no candidate can have been charged with crimes against humanity.

THE MESHRANO JIRGA (HOUSE OF ELDERS)

The Meshrano Jirga consists of a mixture of appointed and elected members (total 102 members). Sixty-eight members were selected by 34 directly elected Provincial Councils, and 34 were appointed by the President.

President Karzai's appointments were vetted by an independent UN sponsored election board and included 17 women (50 %), as required by the Constitution.

Each provincial council has elected one council member to serve in the Jirga (34 members), also each district council (34 members). Representatives of provincial councils will serve a term of four years, while representatives of district councils will serve a term of three years. Sebghatulla Mojadeddi was appointed President of Meshrano Jirga.

An aspiring candidate for the Meshrano Jirga must fulfil the following criteria:

- Be at least 35 years of age
- Be a citizen of Afghanistan

In addition, no potential member of the Meshrano Jirga can have been charged with crimes against humanity

Sessions of the National Assembly

Both Houses of the National Assembly will convene two regular sessions for the term of nine months annually. The sessions are held concurrently, but separately, unless:

- The legislative term or annual sessions are inaugurated by the President;
- It is deemed necessary by the President.

The speaker of the Lower House shall preside over the joint sessions of the National Assembly. The sessions are open, except when the Speaker of the National Assembly or ten members of the House request its secrecy and it is granted by the National Assembly.

The President can order extraordinary sessions of the National Assembly during recess.

The Secretariat of the National Assembly

Upon commencement of their work period, each of the two houses of the National Assembly elects one member as the Speaker for the term of the legislature, and two members as, first and second deputies, and two members as secretary and assistant secretary for a period of one year.

These individuals shall form the administrative teams of the Lower House as well as the Upper House.

The Lower House has the authority to establish a special commission on the proposal of one third of its members to review, as well as, investigate the actions of Government.

THE LEGISLATIVE PROCESS

Any law has to be approved by both Houses of the National Assembly (NA) and endorsed by the President.

Proposal for drafting a law is made by the Government or members of the NA, or if related to regulating judiciary, by the Supreme Court through the Government. It is first submitted to the Wolesi Jirga (the Lower House), which has one month to either approve or reject it by two-third.

The proposal is then submitted to the Meshrano Jirga (the Upper House), which will decide its approval or rejection in fifteen days.

In case the President rejects what the National Assembly has approved, he/she shall send it back, within fifteen days from the date it was presented to the Lower House outlining the reasons for rejection and, expiration of the period. If the House of People re-approves it with two thirds of all the votes, the draft will be considered endorsed and enforceable.

Proposals for drafting the budget and financial affairs law shall be made only by the Government.

While deciding about the proposed laws, the National Assembly shall give priority to treaties and development programs if the government considers them to be urgent.

The state budget and development program of the government shall be submitted, through the Upper House to the Lower House. If it is approved by the Lower House, it will be implemented without being submitting to the Upper House, after endorsement by the President.

In case of discussing urgent matters such as the annual budget, or development program, or issues related to the national security, territorial integrity and independence of the country, the sessions of the Assembly shall not end until a decision is made.

If one House rejects decisions of the other, a joint commission comprised of an equal number of members from each House will be formed to solve the difference. The decision of the commission shall be enforced, after endorsement by the President. In case the joint commission can not solve the difference, the decision will be considered rejected. In such cases, the Lower House will pass it with two-thirds majority in its next session, and will have it endorsed by the President.

THE CONSTITUTION

The present Constitution of the Islamic Republic of Afghanistan was agreed upon by more than 500 delegates representing Afghan men and women from across the country at the Constitutional Loya Jirga (December 13, 2003 - January 4, 2004). The Constitution was formally ratified by President Hamid Karzai at a ceremony in Kabul on January 26, 2004.

The key points of the Constitution are as follows:

- Afghanistan is an Islamic republic with Islam as its "sacred religion";
- Followers of other religions are free to perform religious ceremonies in accordance with the provisions of the law;
- No law shall be contrary to the beliefs and practices of Islam;
- Men and women have equal rights and duties before the law;
- Afghanistan will have a presidential system of government;
- The president is responsible to the nation and the lower house, or Wolesi Jirga;
- The president will be directly elected by the Afghan people with two vice-presidents, who are nominated by presidential candidates when standing for election;
- A national assembly will consist of two houses: a Wolesi Jirga or "house of people" and a Meshrano Jirga or "house of elders";

- The Wolesi Jirga will be directly elected by the Afghan people;
- The Wolesi Jirga has the authority to impeach ministers;
- The president will appoint ministers, the attorney general and central bank governor with the approval of the Wolesi Jirga;
- Ministers should not hold foreign passports but the Wolesi Jirga should vote whether to approve appointments of ministers holding dual nationality;
- Former king Mohammad Zahir Shah is to be accorded the title "Father of the Nation" for his lifetime ;
- Pashto and Dari are the official languages with other minority languages to be considered official languages in the areas in which they are spoken.

THE JUDICIARY

The Judiciary in Afghanistan is composed of the Supreme Court, Courts of Appeal and Primary Courts. Travelling courts may be established when needed, on recommendation by the Supreme Court and approval of the President.

The Judiciary is empowered to resolve disputes between and among individuals, legal entities including the state in accordance with law.

Cases are resolved in courts taking into consideration the quality and nature of the case in two stages, primary and appeal. The Supreme Court deals with the referred cases of Courts of Appeal only in terms of accurate application of law(to see if any provision of law is breached or accurately applied), unless it has been authorized by law to resolve a case taking into consideration the quality and nature of the case.

Cases in court are handled as follows:

- At the primary stage, with participation of three judges. Except less than three judges may decide a case when they are not available.
- At the appeal stage, three judges shall decide any case.
- At the cessation stage, shall take place by two or more persons

The courts are required to resolve cases in accordance with the constitution and other laws of the Islamic Republic of Afghanistan. If there is no clear legal provision for the case, the case shall be handled in accordance with articles 130 and 131 of the constitution.

Trials in the Afghanistan courts happen in open procedure in which everybody may attend, subject to law. The court may convene the trials in a close procedure only if they are legally required or that it is deemed necessary. Making notice of the final decision shall always be open to public.

The courts shall be duty bound to rely on the reasons, grounds and legal provisions for a decision to issue.

THE SUPREME COURT

The Supreme Court constitutes the highest authority of the judiciary of the Islamic Republic of Afghanistan.

The Supreme Court is composed of nine persons appointed by the president in an agreement with Wolusi Jirga (house of people) in accordance with article one hundred seventeen and one hundred eighteen of the Constitution. The president shall appoint one of the members as the chief of the Supreme Court.

Supreme Court Dewans

The Supreme Court consists of the following Dewans:

- General Criminal Dewan
- Public Security Dewan
- Civil and Public Rights Dewan
- Commercial Dewan

Each Dewan is headed by a member of the Supreme Court as selected on rotation basis by the chief justice for the period of one year.

Powers of heads of Dewans

Each head of the Supreme Court Dewans has the following powers and duties:

- Leading relevant Dewan's activities.
- Holding and presiding over relevant Dewan's sessions.
- Arranging affairs, coordinating judicial experiences of the Dewans and submission of report to the Supreme Court.

Judicial advisors

The Supreme Court has judicial advisors and their total number is not to be more than thirty six persons. Their duties consist of analyzing and studying the cases filed and provide a report to the judicial meeting for decision to be made.

Judicial powers and duties of the Supreme Court

The Supreme Court has the following jurisdictions and duties within the scope of interpretation of laws and judicial issues:

- Assessment on conformity of laws, decrees, legal documents, international contracts and conventions with the Constitution and their interpretation based on the government or courts demand in accordance with law.
- Propose for draft law on regulating the judicial affairs to the national assembly through government.
- Revising the rulings of courts due to presence of new reasons based on complaint by the AGO or by party to the claim according to the mentioned provisions and arrangement in the law.
- Resolving Courts' Conflict of Jurisdiction and submitting jurisdiction of resolving a case from one court to the other based on proposal by the AGO or party to the claim when reasonable grounds arise.
- Studying reasons and making decision on extraditing criminals to foreign states in accordance with law.

- Studying reasons of a charge made and making decision on submitting the Afghan citizen to the foreign state in the light of article 28 of the Constitution.
- Ensuring uniformity in judicial treatment.
- Taking measures on criminal and disciplinary offences by judges.
- Evaluating the courts inquiries on judicial issues and providing responses accordingly.

Powers of the head of Supreme Court (chief justice)

The Chief Justice represents the Judicial Authority of Islamic Republic of Afghanistan and has the following jurisdiction and duties:

- lead the judicial and administrative activities of the Supreme Court;
- preside over the meetings of the Supreme Court;
- chair the judicial sessions of the relevant Dewans of the Supreme Court as needed;
- issue orders on the inspection of courts' activities;
- issue orders on resolving cases resulting from crimes and judicial and administrative
- violation by judges;
- monitor the implementation of courts final decisions;
- monitor and control appropriate expenditure of the judicial budget;
- delegate all or some of his/her powers to one of the members of the Supreme Court when sick, on leave, absence and other reasons;
- monitor activities the General Administration Office of the judiciary;
- provide reports on judicial and administrative activities of the judiciary to the president;
- propose on pardoning, mitigation of imprisonment and other punishments of judges to the president's office;
- other assigned powers in accordance with the provisions of this and other laws.

THE COURT OF APPEALS

The Court of Appeals is established in all the provinces in accordance with this law. The Court of Appeals is composed of chief of the court, heads of Dewans and other judicial members. Head of the Court of Appeals shall be selected from among the judges who have enough qualification, experience and competency. Head of the General Criminal Dewan is the deputy head of court of appeals.

Structure of Dewans of Courts of Appeal

The Courts of Appeal contains the following Dewans:

- General Criminal Dewan
- Public Security Dewan
- Civil and Family Dewan
- Public Rights Dewan
- Commercial Dewan
- Juveniles Dewan

There can not be more than six judicial members within each Dewan of the Court of Appeals.

The Supreme Court may as needed establish other Dewans within the structure of the Court of Appeals with the approval of the President.

Powers of the Court of Appeals

- The Court of Appeals oversees the rulings and decisions of the lower courts, in situations according to the provisions of the related laws.
- The Court of Appeals while resolving cases reconsiders the whole legal process. It may correct, overturn, amend, confirm or repeal the rulings and decisions of the lower courts.

Duties and Powers of head of the Court of Appeals

The head of the Court of Appeals has the following responsibilities and powers:

- lead and organize activities of the respective Dewans
- preside over the judicial meetings of the Dewans, when necessary
- assign member of one Dewan to another on temporary basis.
- assign one of the judges of the court of appeals to the primary courts when necessary.
- delegate the authority of resolving a certain case from one Dewan to another, when necessary.
- coordinate judicial experiences of respective Dewans.
- preparation of activity reports of Dewans and courts and delivery of the reports to the Supreme Court.

THE PRIMARY COURTS

In the jurisdictional area of each Court of Appeals, there are these primary courts:

- Central provincial primary court
- Juveniles Court
- Commercial Primary Court
- District Primary Court
- Family Issues primary court

The Supreme Court may establish more courts in the centres of provinces when required after approval of the president.

Primary Court Structure

A Central Primary Court comprises of the following Dewans:

- General Criminal Dewan
- Civil Dewan
- Public Rights Dewan
- Public Security Dewan
- Traffic Criminal Dewan

The Dewans of Central Primary Court shall have one head and no more than four members.

Resolving cases by Dewans of primary courts

Central provincial primary courts have the relevant Dewans to resolve cases in primary level in accordance with law:

- Resolving general criminal cases by General Criminal Dewan.
- Resolving civil disputes between natural persons by Civil Dewan.
- Resolving civil disputes between natural and legal individuals/entities or among legal entities by Public Rights Dewan.
- Resolving criminal cases of public security and interest, drug trafficking and other crimes by Public Security Dewan in accordance with law.
- Resolving traffic criminal cases by Traffic related Crimes Dewan.

Leading Court and Dewans

There is a head for the central provincial primary court to lead and manage the judicial and administrative activities of the Dewans and to attend their meetings when required.

JUVENILE COURT

There is a juvenile primary court in the centre of every province. The juvenile primary court is made up of a head and four members. In case the head is absent due to any reason, his/her powers and duties shall be transferred to one of the judicially experienced judges. The method to resolve juveniles' offences is to be determined by a special regulation.

THE COMMERCIAL COURT

A commercial court is to be established in centre of every province. This court shall have a chief and four other members. In provinces where commercial court is not available, dealing with commercial cases is the jurisdiction of the civil Dewan of the provincial central primary court.

Resolving special cases

Based on the case, the commercial, public rights and public security cases within the judicial jurisdiction of a Court of Appeals shall be initiated in the commercial court and in the relevant Dewans of the provincial central primary court.

DISTRICT PRIMARY COURT STRUCTURE

The District primary court shall consist of a chief and two members. In the areas where there are no members available, the cases shall be decided by fewer than three. The chief of the district primary court shall lead the court. In his/her absence, the responsibilities and powers shall be transferred to the most judicially experienced judge on the court.

District Primary Court Jurisdiction

District Primary courts shall deal in primary stage with all ordinary criminal, civil and family cases which are legally presented to them.

Responsibility

The chief of each Primary Court, heads of Dewans and their judicial members shall be responsible for deciding cases in a timely manner according to the law, correct application of the law, and for explaining the ground for their decision.

Finality of Decision

The decisions of the primary courts are absolute and final in the following situations:

- When both parties agree upon the issued decision of the court.
- When the time for appealing has expired.
- When the disputed property is worth up to 100,000 Afgs.
- When the order for a cash fine of 50,000 Afgs is issued
- Other situations set forth in law.

REGISTRATION OF DOCUMENTS AND DEEDS BRANCHES

In the structure of every Court of Appeals, there is a Directorate of Documents and Deeds Registration (DDDR). There shall be a head in charge of a directorate and shall lead and manage the activities of the directorate. In the districts where there is no such directorate for legal documents registration, the district courts shall have the authority to perform these duties. Duties and powers of the DDDR's are regulated through special legislation.

REGISTRATION OF DOCUMENTS AND TRADEMARKS

Registration of commercial documents and trade marks shall be the jurisdiction of the commercial court.

CONDITIONS OF BEING A JUDGE

On the recommendation of the Supreme Court and with approval of the president, any qualified person meeting following requirements shall be appointed as a judge:

- Upon appointment as judge, hold the citizenship of Islamic Republic of Afghanistan for at least ten yeas.
- Not be convicted of any crime or intentional misdemeanour by absolute and final decision of an authorized court.
- Hold the BA degree from any faculties of law or Shari a or above it or holds diploma on Religious Studies from an officially recognized centre or equivalent.
- Not have any illness or disability which impedes a judge performance of duties.
- Has completed the age of 25 upon appointment.
- Have passed the practical stage of judicial training course successfully.

OATH TAKING

Before occupying the position as judge, a person must swear in front of chief and members of Supreme Court as follow:

"I swear by the name of the Almighty Allah that I perform my duty with full trust and dignity and impartiality, respect and implement provision of Islamic shariah, constitution of Afghanistan and other laws of the country , respect confidentiality of my duty ,will not commit any crime , violation of other rights, injustice and bribery directly and in directly."

GOVERNMENT AND POLITICAL CONDITIONS

On October 9, 2004, Afghanistan held its first national democratic presidential election. More than 8 million Afghans voted, 41% of whom were women. Hamid Karzai was announced as the official winner on November 3 and inaugurated on December 7 for a five-year term as Afghanistan's first democratically elected president. On December 23, 2004, President Karzai announced new cabinet appointments, naming three women as ministers.

An election was held on September 18, 2005 for the "Wolesi Jirga" (lower house) of Afghanistan's new bicameral National Assembly and for the country's 34 provincial councils. Turnout for the election was about 53% of the 12.5 million registered voters. The Afghan constitution provides for indirect election of the National Assembly's "Meshrano Jirga" (upper house) by the provincial councils and by reserved presidential appointments. The first democratically elected National Assembly since 1969 was inaugurated on December 19, 2005. Younus Qanooni and Sigbatullah Mojadeddi were elected Speaker of the Wolesi Jirga and Meshrano Jirga, respectively.

The government's authority is growing, although its ability to deliver necessary social services remains largely dependent on funds from the international donor community. Between 2001-2005, the United States committed over $9 billion to the reconstruction of Afghanistan. At an international donors' conference in Berlin in April 2004, donors pledged a total of $8.2 billion for Afghan reconstruction over the three-year period 2004-2007. At the end of January 2006, the international community gathered in London and renewed its political and reconstruction support for Afghanistan in the form of the Afghanistan Compact.

With international community support, including more than 40 countries participating in Operation Enduring Freedom and NATO-led International Security Assistance Force (ISAF), the government's capacity to secure Afghanistan's borders to maintain internal order is increasing. The government continues to work closely with Coalition Forces in rooting out remnants of Al-Qaida and the Taliban in the south and southeast. ISAF is providing security in Kabul, the North, and the West. An expansion into the South is underway and should be completed by the end of summer 2006. As of February 2006, some 26,500 Afghan National Army (ANA) soldiers had been trained along with some 60,000 police, including border and highway police.

Disarmament, Demobilization, and Reintegration (DDR) has also helped to further establish the authority of the Afghan central government. Disarmament and demobilization of 63,000 official military personnel was completed in June 2005. Many of these are still undergoing reintegration. Also in June 2005, a follow-on program targeting illegal militias, Disarmament of Illegal Armed Groups, was rolled out and is ongoing.

Principal Government Officials

NATIONAL UNITY GOVERNMENT

Portfolio	Name	Years	Status
President	Mohammad Ashraf Ghani	2014-present	Chosen by electorate
First Vice President	Abdul Rashid Dostum	2014-present	Chosen by electorate
Second Vice President	Sarwar Danish	2014-present	Chosen by electorate
Foreign Affairs Minister	Salahuddin Rabbani	2015-present	Approved by Parliament

National Defense Minister	Mohammed Masoom Stanekzai	2015-present	Acting Deference minister, Couldn't secure enough votes from parliament.
Interior Affairs Minister	Nur ul-Haq Ulumi	2015-present	Approved by parliament
Finance Minister	Eklil Ahmad Hakimi	2015-present	Approved by Parliament
Economy Minister	Abdul Sattar Murad	2015-present	Approved by Parliament
Justice Minister	Abdul Basir Anwar	2015-present	Approved by Parliament
Information and Culture Minister	Abdul Bari Jahani	2015-present	Approved by Parliament
Education Minister	Assadullah Hanif Balkhi	2015-present	Approved by Parliament
Higher Education Minister	Farida Momand	2015-present	Approved by Parliament.
Trade and Commerce Minister	Humayoon Rasaw	2015-present	Approved by Parliament
Water and Energy Minister	Ali Ahmad Osmani	2015-present	Approved by Parliament
Transportation and Aviation Minister	Muhamadullah Batash	2015-present	Approved by Parliament.
Public Works Minister	Mahmoud Baligh	2015-present	Approved by Parliament
Women's Affairs Minister	Dilbar Nazari	2015-present	Approved by Parliament
Haj and Islamic Affairs Minister	Faiz Mohammad Osmani	2015-present	Approved by Parliament
Public Health Minister	Ferozuddin Feroz	2015-present	Approved by Parliament
Agriculture Minister	Assadullah Zameer	2015-present	Approved by Parliament
Mines Minister	Daud Shah Saba	2015-Present	Approved by Parliament
Ministry of Communications and Information Technology	Abdul Razaq Vahidi	2015-present	Approved by Parliament
Rural Rehabilitation and Development Minister	Nasir Ahmad Durrani	2015-present	Approved by Parliament
Minister of Labor, Social Affairs, Martyrs and Disabled	Nasreen Owryakhel	2015-present	Approved by Parliament
Border Affairs and Tribal Affairs Minister	Mohammad Gulab Mangal	2015-present	Approved by parliament
Housing and Urban Development Affairs Minister	Sayed Mansur Naderi	2015-present	Approved by Parliament
Counter Narcotics Minister	Salamat Azimi	2015-present	Approved by Parliament
Refugees and Repatriation Minister	Sayed Hussain Alemi Balkhi	2015-present	Approved by Parliament

Chief of the National Directorate of Security	Rahmatullah Nabil	2015-present	Approved by the parliament
National Security Advisor	Mohammad Hanif Atmar	2015-present	Appointed by Ashraf Ghani

Afghanistan maintains an embassy in the United States at 2341 Wyoming Avenue, NW, Washington, DC 20008 (tel: 202-483-6410; email: info@embassyofafghanistan.org).

ECONOMY

Currency	Afghani (AFN)
Fiscal year	21 March - 20 March
Trade organizations	SAARC, ECO, negotiating SCO and WTO accession
	Statistics
GDP	$33.55 billion (est.) $69 billion (PPP) (2014 est.)
GDP rank	108th (nominal) / 96th (PPP)
GDP growth	3.2%
GDP per capita	$2,000
GDP by sector	agriculture: 20% industry: 25.6% services: 54.4%
Inflation (CPI)	7.4%
Population below poverty line	36%
Labor force	7.512 million
Labor force by occupation	agriculture 78.6%, industry 5.7%, services 15.7% (
Unemployment	38%
Main industries	small-scale production of textiles, soap, furniture, shoes, fertilizer, apparel, food-products, non-alcoholic beverages, mineral water, cement; handwoven carpets; natural gas, coal, copper
Ease-of-doing-business rank	160th
	External
Exports	$ 2.76 billion
Export goods	opium, fruits and nuts, Afghan rugs, wool, cotton, hides and pelts, and gemstone
Main export partners	India 31.9% Pakistan 28.5% Tajikistan 7.5% United States 6.2%
Imports	$6.39 billion
Import goods	machinery and other capital goods, food, textiles and petroleum products
Main import partners	Pakistan 28% United States 18.6% Russia 7.6% India 6.3% Kazakhstan 4.5% China 4.3% 4.3%
	Public finances
Public debt	$1.28 billion
Revenues	$1.58 billion
Expenses	$50.000 billion

The **economy of Afghanistan** has improved significantly since 2002 due to the infusion of billions of dollars in international assistance and investments, as well as remittances from Afghan expatriates.The help that came from expatriates and outside investments saw this significant increase when there was more political reliability after the fall of the many terrorist groups in the early 2000s such as the Taliban. The recent improvement is also due to dramatic improvements in agricultural production and the end of a four-year drought in most of the country.

The government of Afghanistan claims that the country holds up to $3 trillion in proven untapped mineral deposits, which could make it one of the richest mining regions on earth. However, due to the conflicts, it remains one of the least developed countries in the world, ranking 175th on the United Nations' Human Development Index. The nation's GDP stands at about $34 billion with an exchange rate of $19.85 billion, and the GDP per capita is about $1,150.

About 35% of its population is unemployed and 36% live below the national poverty line, suffering from shortages of housing, clean drinking water, and electricity. The Karzai administration along with international donors have remained committed to improving access to these basic necessities by prioritizing infrastructure development, education, housing development, jobs programs, medical care, and economic reform.

In the 1930s, Afghanistan embarked on a modest economic development program. The government founded banks; introduced paper money; established a university; expanded primary, secondary, and technical schools; and sent students abroad for education.

Historically, there has been a dearth of information and reliable statistics about Afghanistan's economy. The 1979 Soviet invasion and ensuing civil war destroyed much of the country's limited infrastructure and disrupted normal patterns of economic activity. Gross domestic product had fallen substantially because of loss of labor and capital and disruption of trade and transport. Continuing internal strife hampered both domestic efforts at reconstruction as well as international aid efforts. However, Afghanistan's economy has grown at a fast pace since the 2001 fall of the Taliban, albeit from a low base. In 2003, growth was estimated at close to 30%, and the estimated growth rate for 2004 was 7.5%.

AGRICULTURE

The main source of income in the country is agriculture, and during its good years, Afghanistan produces enough food and food products to provide for the people, as well as to create a surplus for export. The major food crops produced are: corn, rice, barley, wheat, vegetables, fruits, and nuts. In Afghanistan, industry is also based on agriculture, and pastoral raw materials. The major industrial crops are: cotton, tobacco, madder, castor beans, and sugar beets. The Afghan economy continues to be overwhelmingly agricultural, despite the fact that only 12% of its total land area is arable and less than 6% currently is cultivated. Agricultural production is constrained by an almost total dependence on erratic winter snows and spring rains for water; irrigation is primitive. Relatively little use is made of machines, chemical fertilizer, or pesticides.

Overall agricultural production dramatically declined following severe drought as well as sustained fighting, instability in rural areas, and deteriorated infrastructure. The easing of the drought and the end of civil war produced the largest wheat harvest in 25 years during 2003. Wheat production was an estimated 58% higher than in 2002. However, the country still needed to import an estimated one million tons of wheat to meet its requirements for the 2003 year. Millions of Afghans, particularly in rural areas, remained dependent on food aid.

Opium has become a source of cash for many Afghans, especially following the breakdown in central authority after the Soviet withdrawal, and opium-derived revenues probably constituted a major source of income for the two main factions during the civil war in the 1990s. Opium is easy to cultivate and transport and offers a quick source of income for impoverished Afghans. Afghanistan was the world's largest producer of raw opium in 2005. Much of Afghanistan's opium production is refined into heroin and is either consumed by a growing regional addict population or exported, primarily to Western Europe.

TRADE AND INDUSTRY

Afghanistan is endowed with natural resources, including extensive deposits of natural gas, petroleum, coal, copper, chromite, talc, barites, sulfur, lead, zinc, iron ore, salt, and precious and semiprecious stones. Unfortunately, ongoing instability in certain areas of the country, remote and rugged terrain, and inadequate infrastructure and transportation network have made mining these resources difficult, and there have been few serious attempts to further explore or exploit them.

The most important resource has been natural gas, first tapped in 1967. At their peak during the 1980s, natural gas sales accounted for $300 million a year in export revenues (56% of the total). Ninety percent of these exports went to the Soviet Union to pay for imports and debts. However, during the withdrawal of Soviet troops in 1989, Afghanistan's natural gas fields were capped to prevent sabotage by the mujahidin. Restoration of gas production has been hampered by internal strife and the disruption of traditional trading relationships following the collapse of the Soviet Union. Trade in smuggled goods into Pakistan once constituted a major source of revenue for Afghan regimes, including the Taliban, and still figures as an important element in the Afghan economy, although efforts are underway to formalize this trade.

TRANSPORTATION

In the 1960s, the United States helped build a highway connecting Afghanistan's two largest cities. It began in Kabul and wound its way through five of the country's core provinces—skirting scores of isolated and otherwise inaccessible villages; passing through the ancient market city of Ghazni; descending through Qalat; and eventually reaching Kandahar, founded by Alexander the Great. More than 35% of the country's population lives within 50 kilometers of this highway, called, appropriately, modern Afghanistan's lifeline. In 1978, the Soviet Union invaded. By the time its forces withdrew more than a decade later, more than 1 million Afghans had been killed and 5 million had fled. Civil war followed. The Taliban emerged, controlling all but the remote, northern regions. Afghanistan was terrorized by this group, which was dogmatically opposed to progress and democracy. More than two decades of war had left the Kabul-Kandahar highway devastated, like much of the country's infrastructure. Little could move along the lifeline that had provided so many Afghans with their means of livelihood and their access to healthcare, education, markets, and places of worship.

Reviving the Road: Restoration of the highway has been an overriding priority of President Hamid Karzai. It is crucial to extending the influence of the new government. Without the highway link, Afghanistan's civil society and economy would remain moribund and prey to divisive forces. The economic development that the highway makes possible will help guarantee the unity and long-term security of the Afghan people. The restored highway is a visually impressive achievement whose symbolic importance should not be underestimated. It marks a palpable transition from the recent past and represents an important building block for the future. Recently, an official in Herat likened the ring road to veins and arteries that nourish and bring life to the "heart" of Kabul and the body of the country. The highway will not end in Kandahar: there are plans to complete the circuit, extending it to Herat and then arcing it back through Mazar-e Sharif to Kabul. The route is sometimes referred to as the Ring Road.

Landlocked Afghanistan has no functioning railways, but the Amu Darya (Oxus) River, which forms part of Afghanistan's border with Turkmenistan, Uzbekistan, and Tajikistan, has barge traffic. During their occupation of the country, the Soviets completed a bridge across the Amu Darya. The United States, in partnership with Norway, has agreed to reconstruct this bridge, which will stretch more than 650 meters over the Amu Darya/Pyandzh River between Afghanistan and Tajikistan, near Pyanji Poyon (Tajikistan) and Shir Khan Bandar (Afghanistan). The bridge is set for completion in 2007.

Afghanistan's national airline, Ariana, operates domestic and international routes, including flights to New Delhi, Islamabad, Dubai, Moscow, Istanbul, Tehran, and Frankfurt. A private carrier, Kam Air, commenced domestic operations in November 2003. Many sections of Afghanistan's highway and regional road system are undergoing significant reconstruction. The U.S. (with assistance from Japan) completed building a highway linking Kabul to the southern regional capital, Kandahar. Construction is soon to begin on the next phase of highway reconstruction between Kandahar and the western city of Herat. The Asian Development Bank is nearing completion on a road reconstruction project between Kandahar and Spin Boldak, located at the southeastern border with Pakistan.

HUMANITARIAN RELIEF

Many nations have assisted in a great variety of humanitarian and development projects all across Afghanistan since the fall of the Taliban in 2001. The United Nations, World Bank, Asian Development Bank and other international agencies have also given aid. Schools, clinics, water systems, agriculture, sanitation, government buildings and roads are being repaired or built.

DE-MINING

Afghanistan is one of the most heavily mined countries in the world; mine-related injuries number up to 100 per month, and an estimated 200,000 Afghans have been disabled by landmine/unexploded ordinances (UXO) accidents. As of March 2005 the United Nations Mine Action Program for Afghanistan had approximately 8,000 Afghan personnel, 700 demobilized soldiers, 22 international staff, and several NGOs deployed in Afghanistan. The goal of the program is to remove the impact of mines from all high-impact areas by 2007 and to make Afghanistan mine-free by 2012. Between January 2003 and March 2005 a total of 2,354,244 mines and pieces of UXOs were destroyed. Training programs are also being used to educate the public about the threat and dangers of land mines. The number of mine victims was reduced from approximately 150 a month in 2002 to less than 100 a month in 2004.

REFUGEES AND INTERNALLY DISPLACED PEOPLE

Afghanistan has had the largest refugee repatriation in the world in the last 30 years. The return of refugees is guided by the Ministry of Refugees and Repatriation (MORR) and supported by the United Nations High Commissioner for Refugees (UNHCR), International Organization of Migration (IOM), United Nations Children's Fund (UNICEF), the World Food Program (WFP), the World Health Organization (WHO) and a number of other national and international NGOs. Approximately 3.5 million Afghans remain in neighboring countries. The U.S. provided more than $350 million to support Afghan refugees, returnees, and other conflict victims between September 2001 and March 2006.

Health

In response to a strategy outlined by the Ministry of Health, the international community is supporting the government in rebuilding the primary health-care system. Tuberculosis remains a serious public health problem in Afghanistan. Since this strategy was outlined, the Afghan Government with support from the World Health Organization (WHO) has established 162 health facilities in 141 districts across the country. The treatment success rate in 2002 was 86%. WHO is also assisting the Ministry of Health and local health authorities to combat malaria where the disease is widespread. Through this project, 600,000 individuals are receiving full treatment for malaria every year. In addition 750,000 individuals are protected from malaria by sleeping under special nets provided under the project.

EDUCATION

There were 45,000 children enrolled in school in 1993, 19% were girls. The latest official statistics show there are now 64,000 children in school, one third are girls. In addition 29% of the teachers in the province are women, compared with 15% in 1993. Effort is being made to ensure that teachers receive salaries on time and increasing the attendance of girls in school. The total enrolment rate for Afghan children between 7 and 13 years of age has increased to 54% (67% for boys and 37% for girls). A number of factors such as distance to schools, poor facilities and lack of separate schooling for boys and girls continue to be challenges to higher enrollment.

FOREIGN RELATIONS

Before the Soviet invasion, Afghanistan pursued a policy of neutrality and nonalignment in its foreign relations. After the December 1979 invasion, Afghanistan's foreign policy mirrored that of the Soviet Union. Most Western countries, including the United States, maintained small diplomatic missions in Kabul during the Soviet occupation. Repeated Taliban efforts to occupy Afghanistan's seat at the UN and Organization of the Islamic Conference (OIC) were unsuccessful.

The fall of the Taliban in October 2001 opened a new chapter in Afghanistan's foreign relations. Afghanistan is now an active member of the international community, and has diplomatic relations with countries from around the world. In December 2002, the six nations that border Afghanistan signed a 'Good Neighbor' Declaration, in which they pledged to respect Afghanistan's independence and territorial integrity.

Pakistan
The 1978 Marxist coup strained relations between Pakistan and Afghanistan. Pakistan took the lead diplomatically in the United Nations, the Non-Aligned Movement, and the Organization of the Islamic Conference in opposing the Soviet occupation. During the war against the Soviet occupation, Pakistan served as the primary logistical conduit for the Afghan resistance. Pakistan initially developed close ties to the Taliban regime, and extended recognition in 1997. Pakistan dramatically altered its policy after September 11, 2001 by closing its border and downgrading its ties. Afghanistan and Pakistan are engaged in dialogue to resolve these bilateral issues.

Iran
Afghanistan's relations with Iran have fluctuated over the years, with periodic disputes over the water rights of the Helmand River as the main issue of contention. Following the Soviet invasion, which Iran opposed, relations deteriorated. Iran supported the cause of the Afghan resistance and provided financial and military assistance to rebel leaders who pledged loyalty to the Iranian vision of Islamic revolution. Iran still provides refuge to Afghan ex-patriots. Following the emergence of the Taliban and their harsh treatment of Afghanistan's Shi'a minority, Iran stepped up assistance to the Northern Alliance. Relations with the Taliban deteriorated further in 1998 after Taliban forces seized the Iranian consulate in Mazar-e-Sharif and executed Iranian diplomats. Since the fall of the Taliban, Afghanistan's relations with Iran have improved. Iran has been active in Afghan reconstruction efforts, particularly in the western portion of the country.

Russia
During the reign of the Taliban, Russia became increasingly disenchanted over Taliban support for Chechen rebels and for providing a sanctuary for terrorist groups active in Central Asia and in

Russia itself, and therefore provided military assistance to the Northern Alliance. Since the fall of the Taliban, the Karzai government has improved relations with Russia, but Afghanistan's outstanding foreign debt to Russia still continues to be a source of contention.

Tajikistan
Afghanistan's relations with Tajikistan have been complicated by political upheaval and civil war in Tajikistan, which spurred some 100,000 Tajiks to seek refuge in Afghanistan in late 1992 and early 1993. Also disenchanted by the Taliban's harsh treatment of Afghanistan's Tajik minority, Tajikistan facilitated assistance to the Northern Alliance. The Karzai government has sought to establish closer ties with its northern neighbor in order to capitalize on the potential economic benefits of increased trade.

UN Efforts
The United Nations was instrumental in obtaining a negotiated Soviet withdrawal under the terms of the 1988 Geneva Accords. In the aftermath of the Accords, the United Nations assisted in the repatriation of refugees and provided humanitarian aid such as food, health care, educational programs, and support for mine-clearing operations. From 1990-2001, the UN worked to promote a peaceful settlement between the Afghan factions as well as provide humanitarian aid. Since October 2001, the UN has played a key role in Afghanistan through the UN Assistance Mission to Afghanistan (UNAMA), including spearheading efforts to organize the Afghan presidential elections held in October 2004 and National Assembly elections held in 2005.

U.S.-AFGHAN RELATIONS

The first extensive American contact with Afghanistan was made by Josiah Harlan, an adventurer from Pennsylvania who was an adviser in Afghan politics in the 1830s and reputedly inspired Rudyard Kipling's story "The Man Who Would be King." After the establishment of diplomatic relations in 1934, the U.S. policy of helping developing nations raise their standard of living was an important factor in maintaining and improving U.S.-Afghan ties. From 1950 to 1979, U.S. foreign assistance provided Afghanistan with more than $500 million in loans, grants, and surplus agricultural commodities to develop transportation facilities, increase agricultural production, expand the educational system, stimulate industry, and improve government administration.

In the 1950s, the U.S. declined Afghanistan's request for defense cooperation but extended an economic assistance program focused on the development of Afghanistan's physical infrastructure--roads, dams, and power plants. Later, U.S. aid shifted from infrastructure projects to technical assistance programs to help develop the skills needed to build a modern economy. The Peace Corps was active in Afghanistan between 1962 and 1979.

After the April 1978 coup, relations deteriorated. In February 1979, U.S. Ambassador Adolph "Spike" Dubs was murdered in Kabul after Afghan security forces burst in on his kidnapers. The U.S. then reduced bilateral assistance and terminated a small military training program. All remaining assistance agreements were ended after the December 1979 Soviet invasion.

Following the Soviet invasion, the United States supported diplomatic efforts to achieve a Soviet withdrawal. U.S. contributions to the refugee program in Pakistan played a major part in efforts to assist Afghans in need. This cross-border humanitarian assistance program aimed to increase Afghan self-sufficiency and help Afghans resist Soviet attempts to drive civilians out of the rebel-dominated countryside. During the period of Soviet occupation of Afghanistan, the U.S. provided about $3 billion in military and economic assistance to Afghans and the resistance movement.

The U.S. supports the emergence of a broad-based government, representative of all Afghans and actively encourages a UN role in the national reconciliation process in Afghanistan. Today, the U.S. is assisting the Afghan people as they rebuild their country and establish a representative government that contributes to regional stability, is market friendly, and respects human rights. In May 2005, President Bush and President Karzai concluded a strategic partnership agreement committing both nations to a long-term relationship.

Principal U.S. Official

chief of mission: Ambassador W. Stuart SYMINGTON (since 1 December 2016)

The U.S. Embassy in Afghanistan is at the Great Masoud Road, Kabul (tel: +93-2-290002/5; fax: +93-2-290153).

The U.S. Embassy is located at Great Masood Road between Radio Afghanistan/Ministry of Transportation and the Ministry of Public Health in Kabul. Visitors to the Consular Section must enter the Embassy through the south entrance which is located next to the Ministry of Transportation/Radio Afghanistan.

Contact Information:

KabulACS@state.gov

ACS Help Desk: **+93 (0)700 108 499**
Sunday through Thursday: 8:00am-12:00pm and 1:00pm-4:00pm

To report an emergency involving a U.S. citizen: **+93 (0)700 10 8001**, during normal business hours and after hours. From the United States, please call 011-93-700-10-8001.

The ACS Help Desk and Emergency Line phone numbers are **NOT** to be used for visa questions. If you have a question regarding visas, you must use the email address below:

- Non-Immigrant / Tourist Visas: KabulNIV@state.gov
- Immigrant Visas: KabulIV@state.gov
- Special Immigrant Visas: KabulSIV@state.gov

TRAVEL AND BUSINESS INFORMATION

The U.S. Department of State's Consular Information Program provides Consular Information Sheets, Travel Warnings, and Public Announcements.

Consular Information Sheets exist for all countries and include information on entry requirements, currency regulations, health conditions, areas of instability, crime and security, political disturbances, and the addresses of the U.S. posts in the country.

Travel Warnings are issued when the State Department recommends that Americans avoid travel to a certain country. **Public Announcements** are issued as a means to disseminate information quickly about terrorist threats and other relatively short-term conditions overseas that pose significant risks to the security of American travelers. Free copies of this information are available by calling the Bureau of Consular Affairs at 202-647-5225 or via the fax-on-demand system: 202-647-3000. Consular Information Sheets and Travel Warnings also are available on the Consular Affairs Internet home page: http://travel.state.gov. Consular Affairs Tips for Travelers publication series, which contain information on obtaining passports and planning a safe trip abroad, are on the Internet and hard copies can be purchased from the Superintendent of Documents, U.S. Government Printing Office, telephone: 202-512-1800; fax 202-512-2250.

Emergency information concerning Americans traveling abroad may be obtained from the Office of Overseas Citizens Services at (202) 647-5225. For after-hours emergencies, Sundays and holidays, call 202-647-4000.

The National Passport Information Center (NPIC) is the U.S. Department of State's single, centralized public contact center for U.S. passport information. Telephone: 1-877-4USA-PPT (1-877-487-2778). Customer service representatives and operators for TDD/TTY are available Monday-Friday, 8:00 a.m. to 8:00 p.m., Eastern Time, excluding federal holidays.

Travelers can check the latest health information with the U.S. Centers for Disease Control and Prevention in Atlanta, Georgia. A hotline at 877-FYI-TRIP (877-394-8747) and a web site at http://www.cdc.gov/travel/index.htm give the most recent health advisories, immunization recommendations or requirements, and advice on food and drinking water safety for regions and countries. A booklet entitled Health Information for International Travel (HHS publication number CDC-95-8280) is available from the U.S. Government Printing Office, Washington, DC 20402, tel. (202) 512-1800.

Information on travel conditions, visa requirements, currency and customs regulations, legal holidays, and other items of interest to travelers also may be obtained before your departure from a country's embassy and/or consulates in the U.S. (for this country, see "Principal Government Officials" listing in this publication).

U.S. citizens who are long-term visitors or traveling in dangerous areas are encouraged to register their travel via the State Department's travel registration web site at https://travelregistration.state.gov or at the Consular section of the U.S. embassy upon arrival in a country by filling out a short form and sending in a copy of their passports. This may help family members contact you in case of an emergency.

CULTURE AND TRADITION

LANGUAGES

Pashtu and Dari (Afghan Persian/Farsi) are the official languages of Afghanistan. Pashtu (also written Pushtu) was declared the National Language of the country during the beginning of Zahir Shah's reign, however, Dari has always been used for business and government transactions. Both belong to the Indo-European group of languages. According to estimates, approximately 35% of the Afghan population speaks Pashtu, and about 50% speaks Dari. Turkic languages (Uzbek and Turkmen) are spoken by about 11% of the population. There are also numerous other languages spoken in the country (Baluchi, Pashai, Nuristani, etc.), and bilingualism is very common.

AFGHAN CULTURE & SOCIETY

Islam

Islam is practised by the majority of Afghanis and governs much of their personal, political, economic and legal lives.

Among certain obligations for Muslims are to pray five times a day - at dawn, noon, afternoon, sunset, and evening.

Friday is the Muslim holy day. Most shops and offices will be closed. Government offices and businesses may also close on Thursday, making the weekend Thursday and Friday.

During the holy month of Ramadan all Muslims must fast from dawn to dusk and are only permitted to work six hours per day. Fasting includes no eating, drinking, cigarette smoking, or gum chewing.

Foreigners are not required to fast; however, they must not eat, drink, smoke, or chew gum in public.

ETHNIC COMPOSITION AND TRIBES

Afghanistan is a vast country and as a result has a rich mix of ethnicities and tribes.

The Pashtun are Sunni Muslims who Pashtu. They constitute around 42% of the population and are concentrated in Nangrahar and Pakhtya provinces. A large population also live in neighbouring Pakistan.

Tajiks comprise roughly 27% of the population. They are Iranian in origin and speak a form of Persian found in Eastern Iran. Most are Sunni Muslim. Most reside in Kabul and Herat provinces,although some reside in the mountains north of Hindu Kush, and the Iranian border.

Hazaris make up about 9% of the population. They are descendants of the Mongols, and speak a dialect of Persian that contains many Turkish words. They are also Shiite Muslims which led to much of their persecution under Taliban rule. Most live in the Hazarajat region.

Uzbeks live in the northern parts of the country and also comprise only 9% of the population. They are Sunni Muslims and speak a dialect of Turkish.

The Turkomen are a small minority with making only 3% of the population.

Baluchis are pastoral nomads who speak Baluchi, an Iranian language. They comprise 2% of the population.

FAMILY

The family is the single most important unit in the Afghan culture.

Men and women's roles are much more defined along traditional lines.

Women are generally responsible for household duties, where as men will be the bread winners. In the cities professional women do exist.

Families commonly arrange marriages for their children. Factors such as tribe, status, network, and wealth are the major factors forming any choice.

Families traditionally live together in the same walled compound, known as the kala. When a son gets married he and his wife begin their married lives in a room under the same roof.

As with much of the Muslim world, the family is sacred and as such, is highly protected. As a result, probing about the family is not advised.

HONOUR AND SHAME

Honour in Afghan culture defines the reputation and worth of an individual, as well as those they are associated with.

The head male of a family is responsible for protecting the honour of the family. o The issue of honour drives much of the behaviour surrounding the protection of women, modes of dress, social interaction, education and economic activity.

If someone's honour has been compromised, they are shamed and will look for a way to exact revenge for themselves, their family or group.

The role of honour and tribalism has fuelled much of the disharmony in the country's recent history - with one group carrying out violent acts against another, the victims are forced to respond causing a circle of violence.

HOSPITALITY

Hospitality is an essential aspect of Afghan culture.

No matter who you are, if you visit a home you will be given the best the family has.

This relates back to the idea of gaining honour.

If you are invited for tea, which you inevitably will be, you will be offered snacks and your tea glass will be constantly filled. When you have had enough cover the glass with your hand and say "bus" (meaning 'enough').

CUSTOMS AND PROTOCOL

Meeting and Greeting

When meeting someone the handshake is the most common form on greeting. You will also see people place their hands over their hearts and nod slightly.

One should always enquire about things like a person's health, business, family, etc.

Women and men will never shake hands let alone speak directly to one another.

Eye contact should also be avoided between men and women. Between men eye contact is acceptable as long as it is not prolonged - it is best to only occasionally look someone in the eyes.

Genders

Free mixing between genders only takes places within families.

In professional situations such as at businesses or universities, males and females may be co-workers, but are nevertheless cautious to maintain each other's honour.

Foreign females must learn to read the rules and live by them.

If a man speaks to you directly in a social context, he is dishonouring you. If someone speaks to you on the street, that is equally inappropriate. You should avoid looking men in the eyes, and keep your eyes lowered when you walk down the street to maintain your reputation as a proper woman.

Women must always dress properly to avoid unwanted attention. Always wear loose fitting pants under your skirts and be sure the definition of your legs is undistinguishable. It is also strongly advisable to wear a headscarf in public.

On the other hand foreign men should note that it is inappropriate to initiate social conversation with a woman, and one should not ask a male about his wife or female relatives.

Men and women should never be alone in the same room. If this happens you should ensure a door is left open.

Men and women should never touch one another under any circumstances.

Gifts

First rule of gift giving is to never give alcohol. However, if you know from first hand experience that the receiver drinks you may do so but covertly to avoid shame.

The first time you go to someone's house for tea, it is appropriate to bring a small gift.

If you are invited to lunch or dinner, bring fruit, sweets or pastries. Make sure the box is wrapped nicely.

When bringing a gift be subtle in how it is given. Do not immediately give the present but rather discreetly place it near the door or where you sit down.

When it comes to wrapping gifts there is no special protocol. Green is good for weddings.

Dining

Dining in Afghanistan is a different experience and there are many differences in etiquette. o Always remove your shoes at the door if visiting a home.

If eating at someone's home, you will be seated on o the floor, usually on cushions.

Food is served on plastic or vinyl tablecloths spread on the floor.

Wait to be shown where to sit.

If you can, sit cross-legged. Otherwise sit as comfortably as you can. Do not site with legs outstretched and your feet facing people.

Food is generally served communally and everyone will share from the same dish.

Do not eat with the left hand.

Always pass and receive things using your right hand too. o Food is eaten with the hands. It will be a case of watch and learn. Food is usually scooped up into a ball at the tip of the fingers, then eaten.

Leave food on your plate otherwise it will keep getting filled up again.

BUSINESS ETIQUETTE

Business cards are not widely used in Afghanistan. They therefore carry a sense of importance and prestige.

If you are given a business card, take it respectfully and study it so that they see that you are spending time considering their credentials. Comment on it and any qualifications the giver may have.

Try not to keep cards in your pocket - slip it into a holder and somewhere else respectful.

There is no real protocol used for exchanging cards except to use your right hand.

It may be a good idea to have your card translated into Dari or Pashtu. Make sure you don't "translate" the address.

Men should wear conservative suits and shoes.

If working in the country in a non-commercial capacity then wearing the traditional Afghan dress (long shirt and trousers) is best.

Women must always dress modestly and conservatively. The general rule is to show as little flesh from the neck downwards.

If working in business, women should wear knee-length, loose fitting business skirts with loose fitting professional trousers underneath. Wearing headscarf is advisable.

Business is very much personal in Afghanistan. If you have not already invested some quality time in getting to know your counterparts, then you must use initial meetings to establish trust.

Once this has been accomplished you can move on to the nitty-gritty of business.

o Do not be surprised or offended if during meetings people walk in and out of a room or phone calls are taken.

If the meeting involves a group of people it will be led by the leader who will set the agenda, the content, and the pace of the activities.

Meetings are usually held to communicate information and decisions that have already been rather than a forum for discussion and brain storming.

Meeting schedules are not very structured. Start times, points of discussion, etc are all fluid and flexible. Be prepared for a lot of tangents in the discussions.

Afghani communication style is rather indirect. It is therefore sometimes necessary to read between the lines for an answer rather than expect it to be explicitly stated. For example, if someone is asked if they can complete a job on time, you will rarely get "no" as the answer. It is therefore also important to phrase questions intelligently.

Honour and shame should always be considered. Always express yourself in a way that is not direct or pins blame on someone. Never make accusations or speak down to anyone.

Negotiating can be a tricky, frustrating but often an enjoyable affair if approached correctly.

Always make sure you negotiate with the most senior person possible as they are the decision makers. If you negotiate with someone more junior they may be there to simply test the waters. o As a rule Afghans generally negotiate with a win-lose mentality. The goal is always to get the best for yourself at all costs.

This means that there is always a stronger/weaker party. This can however be used to your advantage if you play your cards right. Always start wildly high in negotiations and very slowly work your way down, always explaining why you are dropping in price but at the same time explaining the damage it is doing to you.

Always appeal to their sense of fairness and justice and use the fact you are looking to build a strong relationship.

If monetary matters do not work then try pushing the idea that a deal with you will bring prestige, honour and respect.

TRAVEL AND BUSINESS INFORMATION

The U.S. Department of State's Consular Information Program provides Consular Information Sheets, Travel Warnings, and Public Announcements.

Consular Information Sheets exist for all countries and include information on entry requirements, currency regulations, health conditions, areas of instability, crime and security, political disturbances, and the addresses of the U.S. posts in the country.

Travel Warnings are issued when the State Department recommends that Americans avoid travel to a certain country. **Public Announcements** are issued as a means to disseminate information quickly about terrorist threats and other relatively short-term conditions overseas that pose significant risks to the security of American travelers. Free copies of this information are available by calling the Bureau of Consular Affairs at 202-647-5225 or via the fax-on-demand system: 202-647-3000. Consular Information Sheets and Travel Warnings also are available on the Consular Affairs Internet home page: http://travel.state.gov. Consular Affairs Tips for Travelers publication series, which contain information on obtaining passports and planning a safe trip abroad, are on the Internet and hard copies can be purchased from the Superintendent of Documents, U.S. Government Printing Office, telephone: 202-512-1800; fax 202-512-2250.

Emergency information concerning Americans traveling abroad may be obtained from the Office of Overseas Citizens Services at (202) 647-5225. For after-hours emergencies, Sundays and holidays, call 202-647-4000.

The National Passport Information Center (NPIC) is the U.S. Department of State's single, centralized public contact center for U.S. passport information. Telephone: 1-877-4USA-PPT (1-877-487-2778). Customer service representatives and operators for TDD/TTY are available Monday-Friday, 8:00 a.m. to 8:00 p.m., Eastern Time, excluding federal holidays.

Travelers can check the latest health information with the U.S. Centers for Disease Control and Prevention in Atlanta, Georgia. A hotline at 877-FYI-TRIP (877-394-8747) and a web site at http://www.cdc.gov/travel/index.htm give the most recent health advisories, immunization recommendations or requirements, and advice on food and drinking water safety for regions and countries. A booklet entitled Health Information for International Travel (HHS publication number CDC-95-8280) is available from the U.S. Government Printing Office, Washington, DC 20402, tel. (202) 512-1800.

Information on travel conditions, visa requirements, currency and customs regulations, legal holidays, and other items of interest to travelers also may be obtained before your departure from a country's embassy and/or consulates in the U.S. (for this country, see "Principal Government Officials" listing in this publication).

U.S. citizens who are long-term visitors or traveling in dangerous areas are encouraged to register their travel via the State Department's travel registration web site at https://travelregistration.state.gov or at the Consular section of the U.S. embassy upon arrival in a country by filling out a short form and sending in a copy of their passports. This may help family members contact you in case of an emergency.

US ASSISTANCE - USAID/AFGHANISTAN STRATEGY

Twenty-five years of war have devastated the economy, institutions, and people of Afghanistan. The U.S. Government, NATO, and international partners have combined forces to support the Afghan Government in a civilian-military effort to secure and rebuild the country and combat terrorism.

United States Agency for International Development (USAID), as part of the U.S. Government effort, is supporting the Afghan Government to provide services and security for its citizens. President Barack Obama's Afghanistan-Pakistan strategy and the "Afghan First" initiative call to empower Afghan institutions to lead in development and reconstruction. Long-term development thrives best in stable conditions and USAID works as a partner to the joint Afghan-U.S. Government counterinsurgency strategy to implement programs that improve lives throughout the country.

PROGRAMS

INVESTING IN PEOPLE: HEALTH AND EDUCATION

Under the Taliban, 900,000 boys and no girls were enrolled in schools. Today, seven million children are in schools, two million of them supported by USAID and 37 percent of them are girls. USAID has trained 52,000 educators and printed 97 million textbooks. In areas with no government schools, USAID has set up 3,695 classes serving 52,504 students, 65 percent of them girls. To strengthen higher education institutions, USAID sponsored Afghan professors for master's degree and short-term study-abroad programs and raised the quality of university-level instruction by training professors in modern teaching. USAID's support to technical and vocational education is preparing Afghan youth and adults for an active role in a peaceful society.

USAID's Impact at a Glance

- Infant mortality rate has dropped by 33 percent
- Approximately 64 percent of the population now has access to some form of healthcare
- More than 60 percent of the judiciary has been trained through USAID-sponsored programs
- More than 70,000 loans have been extended to women-owned businesses
- Five mobile phone companies together have more than 13 million subscribers

Afghan health remains seriously at risk. One of every five Afghan children dies before age five. With USAID and other donors' support, most Afghans now live within two hours walking distance to a health facility. USAID support for midwife training has increased midwives' numbers from 468 to more than 2,700 in eight years. Finally, Afghanistan, as one of only four countries in the world where polio is endemic, has achieved a 90 percent vaccination rate for children less than age five since 2002.

ECONOMIC GROWTH, AGRICULTURE, AND INFRASTRUCTURE

Afghanistan's economy has been steadily growing at approximately 12 percent per year during the past six years. Direct assistance from the U.S. helps Afghanistan increase revenue collection, improve the legal and regulatory framework for private sector investment, and build the government's skills to manage the economy.

Reliable infrastructure and energy networks are critical for economic growth. Viable, secure roads are providing the way to bring farmers' crops to market, access to health and education, and regional trade. USAID's rehabilitation of more than 2,000 kilometers of roads – including regional and national highways - is increasing mobility and strengthening trade. As of 2010, international donors have rehabilitated more than 83 percent of Afghanistan's regional highways, including the majority of the Ring Road, linking national and regional population centers. Approximately 80 percent of Afghans live within 50 kilometers of the new Ring Road.

The U.S. and other donors increased power to two billion kilowatt hours through 2009, and aim to double power again by 2014. USAID built the Kabul Power Plant that provides backup power for 600,000 Afghans in Kabul, and is expanding energy infrastructure to provide reliable power to populations in the south and east. USAID also helped negotiate agreements with Uzbekistan, Tajikistan, and Turkmenistan to import affordable power.

USAID works with farmers to boost agricultural production and food security, provide market opportunities, and decrease the country's poppy production. In addition, better water management and watershed conservation has resulted in improved irrigation of scarce arable land. USAID also supports the private sector to expand access of Afghan farmers to improved technologies, higher quality seeds and fertilizers and financial services.

GOVERNING JUSTLY AND DEMOCRATICALLY

Key Afghan democracy and governance developments included the National peace jirga, the Kabul Conference, and the first Afghan-led parliamentary election.

USAID initiatives helped Afghans meet key governance objectives in 2010. These include training over 16,000 civil servants in core skills; strengthening independent electoral institutions to support the historic parliamentary elections in September 2010 and enhancing assistance to a more independent Parliament. Important civil society results included development of a national network of 10 Civil Society Support Centers for 247 Afghan civil society organizations, creation of three regional media training centers, and assistance in founding the Salaam Watandar, nationwide network of 43 community radio stations.

In the rule of law and anti-corruption arena, USAID piloted an innovative new program that strengthens linkages between the formal justice sector and community dispute resolution mechanisms. The program has established elder networks and helped communities resolve disputes in four kinetic districts. In concert, USAID also launched major new initiatives to strengthen the formal justice system and oversight institutions.

GEOGRAPHY, LOCATION, ADMINISTRATIVE STRUCTURE

Afghanistan is a landlocked and mountainous country that is usually designated as being located in South Asia. It is sometimes described as being the center or heart of Asia, connecting South and East Asia with Central and Western Asia. The country is the 41st largest in the world in size. Kabul is the capital and largest city of Afghanistan, located in the Kabul Province. Strategically located at the crossroads of major trade routes, Afghanistan has attracted a succession of invaders since the sixth century BCE.

The Hindu Kush mountains, running northeast to southwest across the country, divide it into three major regions: 1) the Central Highlands, which form part of the Himalayas and account for roughly two thirds of the country's area; 2) the Southwestern Plateau, which accounts for one-fourth of the land; and 3) the smaller Northern Plains area, which contains the country's most fertile soil.

Land elevations generally slope from northeast to southwest, following the general shape of the Hindu Kush massif, from its highest point in the Pamir Mountains near the Chinese border to the lower elevations near the border with Iran. To the north, west, and southwest there are no mountain barriers to neighboring countries. The northern plains pass almost imperceptibly into the plains of Turkmenistan. In the west and southwest, the plateaus and deserts merge into those of Iran. Afghanistan is located on the Eurasian Tectonic Plate. The Wakhan Corridor and the rest of northeastern Afghanistan, including Kabul, are situated in a geologically active area. Over a dozen earthquakes occurred there during the twentieth century.

The greater part of the northern border and a small section of the border with Pakistan are marked by rivers; the remaining boundary lines are political rather than natural. The northern frontier extends approximately 1,689 km (1,049 mi) southwestward, from the Pamir Mountains in the northeast to a region of hills and deserts in the west, at the border with Iran. The border with Iran runs generally southward from the Hari River across swamp and desert regions before reaching the northwestern tip of Pakistan. Its southern section crosses the Helmand River.

Afghanistan is bounded by six different countries. Its longest border is the poorly marked Durand Line, accounting for its entire southern and eastern boundary with Pakistan. The shortest one, bordering China's Xinjiang province, is a mere 76 km at the end of the Wakhan Corridor (the Afghan Panhandle), a narrow sliver of land 241 km (150 mi) long that extends eastward between Tajikistan and Pakistan. At its narrowest point it is only 11 km (7 mi) wide.

The border with Pakistan runs eastward from Iran through the Chagai Hills and the southern end of the Registan Desert, then northward through mountainous country. It then follows an irregular northeasterly course before reaching the Durand Line, established in 1893. This line continues on through mountainous regions to the Khyber Pass area. Beyond this point it rises to the crest of the Hindu Kush, which it follows eastward to the Pamir Mountains. The Durand Line divides the Pashtun tribes of the region between Afghanistan and Pakistan. Its creation has caused much dissatisfaction among Afghans and has given rise to political tensions between the two countries.

MOUNTAIN SYSTEMS

The Hindu Kush mountain range reaches a height of 7,492 m (24,580 ft) at Noshaq, Afghanistan's highest peak. Of the ranges extending southwestward from the Hindu Kush, the Foladi peak (Shah Foladi) of the Baba mountain range (Koh-i-Baba) reaches the greatest height:

5,142 m (16,870 ft). The Safed Koh range, which includes the Tora Bora area, dominates the border area southeast of Kabul.

Snow-covered Koh-i-Baba mountains in Bamyan Province of Afghanistan

Snow-covered Hindu Kush mountains in Afghanistan

Snow-covered mountains in the Paktia Province.

Important passes include the Unai Pass across the Safed Koh, the Kushan and Salang Passes through the Hindu Kush, and the Khyber Pass that connects Afghanistan with Pakistan. The summit of the Khyber Pass at 1,070 m (3,510 ft) at Landi Kotal, Pakistan is 5 km (3 mi) east of the border town of Torkham. Other key passages through the mountainous Pakistan border include two from Paktika Province into Pakistan's Waziristan region: one at Angoor Ada, a village that straddles both sides of the border east of Shkin, and, further south, the Gumal River crossing, plus the Charkai River passage south of Khost, Afghanistan, at Pakistan's Ghulam Khan village into North Waziristan. The busy Pak-Afghan border crossing at Wesh, Afghanistan is in a flat and dry area, though this route involves Pakistan's Khojak Pass at 2,707 m (8,881 ft) just 14 km (9 mi) from the border. The border connects Kandahar and Spin Boldak in Afghanistan with Quetta in Pakistan,

The Wakhan Corridor in the northeast lies between the Hindu Kush and the Pamir Mountains, which leads to the Wakhjir Pass into Xinjiang in China. Taking the highlands of the country as a whole, there is no great difference between the mean temperature of Afghanistan and that of the lower Himalaya. Each may be placed at a point between . However, the remarkable feature of Afghan climate is its extreme range of temperature within limited periods. The smallest daily range in the north is when the weather is cold; the greatest is when it is hot. For seven months of the year (from May to November) this range exceeds 17 °C (63 °F) daily. Waves of intense cold occur, lasting for several days, and one may have to endure a cold of −24 °C (−11 °F), rising to a maximum of −8 °C (18 °F). On the other hand, the summer temperature is exceedingly high, especially in the Oxus regions, where a shade maximum of 45–50 °C (113–122 °F) is not uncommon. At Kabul, and over all the northern part of the country to the descent at Gandamak, winter is rigorous, but especially so on the high Arachosian plateau. In Kabul the snow lies for two or three months; the people seldom leave their houses, and sleep close to stoves. At Ghazni the snow has been known to lie long beyond the vernal equinox; the thermometer sinks as low as −25 °C (−13 °F), and tradition relates the destruction of the entire population of Ghazni by snowstorms more than once.

Branches of the Kunar River meet with the Kabul River in Nangarhar Province

Arghandab district, between Kandahar and Lashkar Gah

The summer heat is great in the Sistan Basin, Jalalabad and Turkestan, especially Sistan. All over Kandahar province the summer heat is intense, and the simoom is not unknown. The hot season throughout this part of the country is rendered more trying by frequent dust storms and fiery winds; whilst the bare rocky ridges that traverse the country, absorbing heat by day and radiating it by night, render the summer nights most oppressive. At Kabul the summer sun has great power, though the heat is tempered occasionally by cool breezes from the Hindu Kush, and the nights are usually cool. At Kandahar snow seldom falls on the plains or lower hills; when it does, it melts at once.

Although Herat is approximately 240 m (787 ft) lower than Kandahar, the summer climate there is more temperate, and the climate throughout the year is far from disagreeable. From May to September, the wind blows from the northwest with great force, and this extends across the country to Kandahar. The winter is tolerably mild; snow melts as it falls, and even on the mountains does not lie long. Three years out of four at Herat it does not freeze hard enough for the people to store ice; yet it was not very far from Herat, and could not have been at a greatly higher level (at Rafir Kala, near Kassan) that, in 1750, Ahmad Shah's army, retreating from Persia, is said to have lost 18,000 men from cold in a single night. In the northern Herat districts, too, records of the coldest month (February) show the mean minimum as −8 °C (18 °F) and the maximum as 3 °C (37 °F). The eastern reaches of the Hari River, including the rapids, are frozen hard in the winter, and people travel on it as on a road.

The summer rains that accompany the southwest monsoon in India, beating along the southern slopes of the Himalaya, travel up the Kabul valley as far as Laghman, though they are more clearly felt in Bajour and Panjkora, under the high spurs of the Hindu Kush, and in the eastern branches of Safed Koh. Rain also falls at this season at the head of Kurram valley. South of this the Suliman mountains may be taken as the western limit of the monsoon's action. It is quite unfelt in the rest of Afghanistan, in which, as in all the west of Asia, the winter rains are the most considerable. The spring rain, though less copious, is more important to agriculture than the winter rain, unless where the latter falls in the form of snow. In the absence of monsoon influences there are steadier weather indications than in India. The north-west blizzards which occur in winter and spring are the most noticeable feature, and their influence is clearly felt on the Indian frontier. The cold is then intense and the force of the wind cyclonic. Speaking generally, the Afghanistan climate is a dry one. The sun shines with splendor for three-fourths of the year, and the nights are even more clear than the days. Marked characteristics are the great differences of summer and winter temperature and of day and night temperature, as well as the extent to which change of climate can be attained by slight change of place. The highest temperature ever recorded under standard conditions was 49.9 °C (121.8 °F) at Farah in August 2009 and the lowest was −52.2 °C (−62.0 °F) at Shahrak in January 1964. The emperor Babur observed:

Within a day's ride from Kabul it is possible to reach a place where snow never falls. But within two hours one can go where the snow never melts—except in the rare summer so severe that all snow disappears. Both tropical and cold-weather fruits are abundant in Kabul's dependencies, and they are nearby

RIVERS AND LAKES

Afghanistan usually does not face much water shortage because it receives snow during winter and once that melts the water runs into numerous rivers, lakes, and streams, but most of its national water flows into neighboring countries. It loses about two-thirds of its water to neighboring Pakistan, Iran, Tajikistan, Uzbekistan and Turkmenistan. The country needs several billion dollars to rehabilitate its irrigation systems so that the water is properly used. The Afghan government is requesting a $12 billion investment from the international community to construct a number of dams for the production of electricity and to help the irrigation of the country.

The nation's drainage system is essentially landlocked. Most of the rivers and streams end in shallow desert lakes or oases inside or outside the country's boundaries. Nearly half of the state's total area is drained by watercourses south of the Hindu Kush–Safid ridge line, and half of this area is drained by the Helmand and its tributaries alone. The Amu Darya on the northern border, the country's other major river, has the next largest drainage area.

The 2,661 km (1,653 mi) long Amu Darya originates in the glaciers of the Pamir Mountains in the northeast. Some 965 km of its upper course constitutes Afghanistan's border with Turkmenistan, Uzbekistan and Tajikistan. Flowing in rapid torrents in its upper course, the Amu Darya becomes calmer below the mouth of the Kokcha, 96 km (60 mi) west of Fayzabad. The Kunduz River is another major tributary. During its flood period the upper course of the Amu Darya, swollen by snow and melting ice, carries along much gravel and large boulders.

The Helmand River is the principal river in the southwest, bisecting the entire region. Starting some 80 km (50 mi) west of Kabul in the Baba mountain range, the Helmand is approximately 1,400 km (870 mi) long, making it the longest river situated entirely within Afghanistan. With its many tributaries, the most important of which is the Arghandab River, it drains more than 298 km2 (115 sq mi).

The Kabul River, 515 km (320 mi) long, is a vital source of water in the Baba Mountains and for Kabul itself, which it flows through. The Kabul and its tributaries are among the few in Afghanistan that eventually reach the sea, as it flows east into the Indus River in Pakistan.

In the west the sandy deserts along most of the Iranian frontier have no watercourses. However, in the northwest, the Hari and Morghab Rivers flow into Turkmenistan's Karakum Desert.

VEGETATION

The characteristic distribution of vegetation on the mountains of Afghanistan is worthy of attention. The great mass of it is confined to the main ranges and their immediate off-shoots, whilst on the more distant and terminal prolongations it is almost entirely absent; in fact, these are naked rock and stone. Take, for example, the Safed Koh. On the alpine range itself and its immediate branches, at a height of 1,800–3,000 m (5,900–9,800 ft) there is abundant growth of large forest trees, among which conifers are the most noble and prominent, such as Cedrus deodara, Abies excelsa, Pinus longifolia, Pinus pinaster, Stone pine (the edible pine, although this species is probably introduced, since it is original to Spain and Portugal) and the larch. There is also the yew, the hazel, juniper, walnut, wild peach and almond. Growing under the shade of these are several varieties of rose, honeysuckle, currant, gooseberry, hawthorn, rhododendron and a luxuriant herbage, among which the ranunculus family is important for frequency and number of genera. The lemon and wild vine are also here met with, but are more common on the northern mountains. The walnut and oak (evergreen, holly-leaved and kermes) descend to the secondary heights, where they become mixed with alder, ash, khinjak, Arbor-vitae, juniper, with species of Astragalus, &c. Here also are Indigoferae rind dwarf laburnum.

Nuristan Province

Takhar Province in northern Afghanistan

Down to 1,000 m (3,300 ft) there are wild olive, species of rock-rose, wild privet, acacias and mimosas, barberry and Zizyphus; and in the eastern ramifications of the chain, Chamaerops humilis (which is applied to a variety of useful purposes, and which it is also introduced since it is original to Western Mediterranean), Bignonia or trumpet flower, sissu, Salvadora persica, verbena, acanthus, varieties of Gesnerae.

The lowest terminal ridges, especially towards the west, are, as it has been said, naked in aspect. Their scanty vegetation is almost wholly herbal; shrubs are only occasional; trees almost non-existent. Labiate, composite and umbelliferous plants are most common. Ferns and mosses are almost confined to the higher ranges.

In the low brushwood scattered over portions of the dreary plains of the Kandahar tablelands, it is possible to find leguminous thorny plants of the papilionaceous suborder, such as camel-thorn (Hedysarum alhagi), Astragalus in several varieties, spiny rest-harrow (Ononis spinosa), the fibrous roots of which often serve as a tooth-brush; plants of the sub-order Mimosae, as the sensitive mimosa; a plant of the rue family, called by the natives lipad; the common wormwood; also certain orchids, and several species of Salsola. The rue and wormwood are in general use as domestic medicines—the former for rheumatism and neuralgia; the latter in fever, debility and dyspepsia, as well as for a vermifuge. The lipad, owing to its heavy nauseous odour, is believed to keep off evil spirits. In some places, occupying the sides and hollows of ravines, it is found the Rose Bay, called in Persian khar-zarah, or ass-bane, the wild laburnum and various Indigoferae.

In cultivated districts the chief trees seen are mulberry, willow, populus ash, and occasionally the plane; but these are because of man's planting.

It should be noted that in the last several decades, 90% of forests in Afghanistan have been destroyed and much of the timber has been exported to neighboring Pakistan. As a result, large percent of Afghanistan's land could be subject to soil erosion and desertification. On the positive note, the Karzai administration and international organizations are helping counter this problem by often planting millions of saplings. The city of Kabul began to see maple trees being planted in the last decade.

ADNINISTRATIVE STRUCTURE AND DEMOGRAPHICS

ADMINISTRATIVE STRUCTURE

Provinces (34), districts (361), cities and villages; majority of the estimated 24 million inhabitants resides in rural areas ("UNHCR's Eligibility Guidelines for Assessing the International Protection Needs of Afghan Asylum-Seekers") [ID 22023]

"The country is divided into 34 provinces – with two new provinces, Panjshir and Daikundi created in 2004 – comprising 361 districts,4 administered as follows:

• Provinces are the largest administrative units, each headed by a Governor (Waali), who is generally appointed by the President. Governors report to the Minister of Interior. At present, the only female Governor is the Governor of Bamyan, Mrs. Habiba Surabi.

• Cities (mainly provincial capitals and urban areas) are administrative units headed by mayors and each consisting of several municipal wards, which in turn are headed by the municipal ward mayor. Mayors of major cities are currently appointed by the President but will ultimately be elected in accordance with the electoral and municipal law.

• Districts (Woluswali) are decentralized administrative units within a province – mainly in the rural areas, headed by district administrators. District Governors are nominated by the Provincial Governors and appointed by the Minister of Interior. Pursuant to Presidential Decree No. 36, 34 provinces and 361 districts and municipal wards – including district centres without wards – are designated as electoral constituencies.

• Villages form the basic communities within rural districts, whilst guzars (neighbourhoods) are sub-divisions of nahiyas (municipal wards).

DEMOGRAPHICS

Population:	31,108,077 (est.)
Growth rate:	2.22% (est.)
Birth rate:	39.3 births/1,000 population
Death rate:	14.59 deaths/1,000 population
Life expectancy:	Upto 64 years
–male:	64 years
–female:	64 years
Fertility rate:	5.64 children born/woman
Infant mortality rate:	121.63 deaths/1,000 live births
	Age structure
0-14 years:	42.3% (male 6,464,070/female 6,149,468)
15-64 years:	55.3% (male 8,460,486/female 8,031,968)
65-over:	2.4% (male 349,349/female 380,051)
	Sex ratio
At birth:	1.05 male/female
Under 15:	1.03 male/female
15-64 years:	1.04 male/female
65-over:	0.87 male/female
	Nationality
Nationality:	noun: Afghan(s)
Major ethnic:	Pashtun, Tajik, Hazara, Uzbek, and others
	Language
Official:	Pashto and Dari
Spoken:	Pashto, Dari, Uzbeki, Turkmeni, and other

The population of Afghanistan is around 31 million as of the year 2013, which includes the 2.7 million Afghan refugees that are residing temporarily in Pakistan and Iran. The nation is composed of a multi-ethnic and multi-lingual society, reflecting its location astride historic trade and invasion routes between Central Asia, Southern Asia, and Western Asia. The majority of Afghanistan's population consist of the Iranian peoples, notably the Pashtuns and Tajiks. The Pashtun is the largest group followed by Tajik, Hazara, Uzbek, Aimak, Turkmen, Baloch and others.

Pashto and Dari are both the official languages of the country, Dari (Persian) is spoken by the Tajiks and Hazara people living in Afghanistan while Pashto is spoken widely all over the country as well as in neighboring northernwestern Pakistan. Uzbek language and Turkmen language are spoken in parts of the north. Smaller groups in various parts of the country speak about 30 other languages.

Islam is the religion of more than 99% of Afghanistan. An estimated 80-89% of the population practice Sunni Islam and belong to the Hanafi Islamic law school while 10-19% are Shi'a, majority of the Shia follow the Twelver branch with smaller numbers of Ismailis. The remaining 1% or less practice other religions such as Sikhism and Hinduism. Excluding urban populations in the principal cities, most Afghans are organized into tribal and other kinship-based groups, who follow their own traditional customs: for instance Pashtunwali. Majority of the Afghans live in rural areas and are involved in agricultural activities.

As of 2013, the total population of Afghanistan is around 31,108,077, which includes the 2.7 million Afghan refugees that are living in Pakistan and Iran. In 2009, a nationwide survey conducted by the Afghan Central Statistics Organization (CSO) estimated that the total number of Afghans living inside Afghanistan was about 24.5 million and by 2011 it reached 26 million. Of this, 5.7 million people were reported to be living in urban areas and the rest in rural or countryside.

A partial census conducted in 1979 showed roughly 15.5 million people living in the country. The Statistical Yearbook published in 1983 by the Babrak Karmal government claimed a total population of 15.96 million for 1981–82. Between 600,000 to 2 million Afghans were killed during the various 1979–2001 wars, majority of them during the Soviet war in the 1980s. At least 5 million more fled the country to neighboring countries. According to the Population Reference Bureau, the Afghan population is estimated to increase to 82 million by 2050.

Urban areas are experiencing rapid population growth since the Karzai administration began in late 2001, which is mainly due to the return of over 5 million expats. The only city in Afghanistan with over a million residents is its capital, Kabul. The other largest cities in the country are shown in the chart below.

Largest cities or towns of Afghanistan

Rank	City name	Province	Pop.
1	Kabul	Kabul Province	3,071,400
2	Kandahar	Kandahar Province	512,000
3	Herat	Herat Province	397,456
4	Mazar-i-Sharif	Balkh Province	375,000
5	Jalalabad	Nangarhar Province	205,423
6	Lashkar Gar	Helmand Province	201,546
7	Taloqan	Takhar Province	196,400
8	Khost	Khost Province	160,214
9	Sheberghan	Jowzjan Province	148,329
10	Ghazni	Ghazni Province	141,000

ENVIRONMENTAL ISSUES

Environmental issues in Afghanistan predate the political turmoil of the past few decades. Forests and wetlands have been depleted by centuries of grazing and farming, practices which have only increased with modern population growth. In Afghanistan, environmental conservation and economic concerns are not at odds; with 80% of the population dependent on herding or farming, the welfare of the environment is critical to the economic welfare of the people. In 2007, the World Health Organization released a report ranking Afghanistan as the lowest among non-African nations in deaths from environmental hazards

DEFORESTATION

Much of the population depends on forests for firewood and the revenue generated by export of pistachios and almonds, which grow in natural woodlands in the central and northern regions. The Badghis and Takhar provinces have lost more than 50% of pistachio woodland. During the conflicts of the past few decades, residents and the militias such as the Northern Alliance have used wood for fuel, and these militia forces have cleared trees which could have provided hiding places for ambushes from their opponents. Further, the use of the woodlands for grazing ground and the collection of nuts for export apparently prevent new pistachio trees from growing.

Denser forests in the eastern Nangarhar, Kunar, Nuristan, and other provinces are at risk from timber harvesting by timber mafia. Although the logging is illegal, profits from exporting the timber to neighboring Pakistan are very high. The reason for this is that Pakistani government has its forests tightly protected so the timber mafia are busy cutting down trees in Afghanistan instead. The timber makes its way not only to Peshawar but also to Islamabad, Rawalpindi, and Lahore, where most of it is used to make expensive furnitures.

As forest cover decreases, the land becomes less productive, threatening the livelihood of the rural population and the floods are washing the agricultural lands and destroying the houses. Loss of vegetation also creates a higher risk of floods, which not only endanger the people, but cause soil erosion and decrease the amount of land available for agriculture. To tackle this problem, the Afghan government and agencies from a number of NATO states have teamed up over the past several years to turn Afghanistan green again by planting new trees.

WILDLIFE

With very little government infrastructure to discourage hunting, and habitat disappearing because of conflict and drought, much of the country's wildlife is at risk. In 2006, Afghanistan and the Wildlife Conservation Society began a three-year project to protect wildlife and habitats along the Wakhan Corridor and Central Plateau regions.

- **Endangered species**
  - Snow leopard (Uncia uncia)
  - Wild goat (Capra aegagrus)
  - Markhor (Capra falconeri)
  - Marco Polo sheep (Ovis ammon polii)
  - Urial (Ovis orientalis)
  - Asiatic black bear (Ursus thibetanus)
  - Siberian crane (Grus leucogeranus)

- **Critically endangered species**
  - White-headed duck (Oxyura leucocephala)
  - Marbled teal (Marmaronetta angustirostris)
  - Pallas's sea eagle (Haliaeetus leucoryphus)
  - Greater spotted eagle (Aquilla clanga)
  - Imperial eagle (Aquilla heliaca)
  - Lesser kestrel (Falco naumanni)
  - Corncrake (Crex crex)
  - Sociable lapwing (Vanellus gregaria)
  - Pale-backed pigeon (Columba hodgsonii)

Little is known about the status of the salamander Batrachuperus mustersi, which is found only in the Hindu Kush.

WATER MANAGEMENT

The primary threat to Afghanistan's water supply is the droughts, which created food shortages for millions in the recent past. The resulting agricultural crises between 1995 to 2001 have driven major migrations from rural to urban areas. In response to drought, deep wells for irrigation have been drilled which decreased the under ground water level, further draining groundwater resources, which rely on rain for replenishment.

By 2003, about 99% of the Sistan wetlands were dry, another result of continued drought and lack of water management. The wetlands, an important habitat for breeding and migrant waterfowl including the dalmatian pelican and the marbled teal, have provided water for agricultural irrigation for at least 5,000 years. They are fed by the Helmand River, which ran at 98% below average in drought years 2001-2003. As in other areas of the country, the loss of natural vegetation resulted in soil erosion; here, sandstorms submerged as many as 100 villages by 2003.

Some of the major water reservoirs and dams include the following:

- Dahla Dam
- Naghlu Dam
- Darunta Dam
- Kajaki Dam
- Lake Qargha

POLLUTION

Urban populations have swelled in the past several years. Since 2002, over 5 million former refugees living in Pakistan and Iran have returned home to Afghanistan. Many of these settled in the capital Kabul, which also include migrants that have come from drought-ravaged rural areas.

NUCLEAR WASTE BY PAKISTAN

In 2008, the Afghan government alleged that Pakistan had dumped nuclear waste in southern Afghanistan during the Taliban rule (1994-2001). Farooq Wardak, Afghan Parliamentary affairs minster, said the government was setting up a commission to investigate the matter. Afghan President Hamid Karzai recently announced that his administration will investigate the matter.

DOMESTIC AND INDUSTRIAL WASTE

In 2002, the United Nations Environmental Program found that a lack of waste management systems was creating dangerous conditions in several urban areas. In Kabul's districts 5 and 6, household and medical waste was discarded on streets. Human waste was contained in open sewers, which flowed into the Kabul River and contaminated the city's drinking water.

Urban dumpsites are used in lieu of managed landfills in Kabul, Kandahar and Herat, often without protection of nearby rivers and groundwater supplies. Medical waste from hospitals is disposed in the dumpsites with the rest of the cities' waste, contaminating water and air with bacteria and viruses.

Lack of sewage management is not unique to Kabul. In urban areas, open sewers are common while wastewater treatment is not. Much of the urban water supply is contaminated by Escherichia coli and other bacteria.

Oil refineries are another source of water contamination. In Herat and Mazar-e-Sharif, crude oil spills and leaks are uncontained and unsafe levels of hydrocarbons reach residential water supplies.

AIR POLLUTION

Air pollution does not constitute a major problem in Afghanistan, but its reliance on inexpensive energy has created some issues. Most vehicles run on diesel fuel, and household energy often rely on burning wood and other materials. As a result, air pollution in urban areas is visible and may pose health issues

HEALTH

Health in Afghanistan is in need of improvement due to the country being in a state of civil war for the last three decades. According to the Human Development Index, Afghanistan is the 15th least developed country in the world. The Ministry of Public Health deals with matters concerning the health of Afghanistan's population.

After Operation Enduring Freedom in late 2001, when the United Nations began focusing on the situation in Afghanistan, improvement slowly began in the health care system of the country. According to USAID, infant mortality rate has decreased by 22% and child mortality has dropped by 26% since 2003. It was reported in 2006 that nearly 60% of the population lives within two hours walking distance of the nearest health facility, up from nine percent in 2002. The average life expectancy at birth is reported between 50 years to as high as 64 for both sexes

Beginning in 1979, military conflict destroyed the health system of Afghanistan. Most medical professionals left the country by 1992, and all medical training programs ceased. In 2003, there were 11 physicians and 18 nurses per 100,000 population, and the per capita health expenditure was $28 US dollars. The nation had one medical facility for every 27,000 people in 2004, and some centers were responsible for as many as 300,000 people. An estimated one-quarter of the population had no access to health care. The international organizations provided a large share of medical care. The drought of 1999–2002 exacerbated these conditions. An estimated 800,000 Afghans are disabled.

Afghan men inside a U.S.-run hospital at Bagram Air Base in the Parwan Province of Afghanistan.

Infant, child, and maternal mortality rates in Afghanistan reached the highest in the world, by some estimates as high as 275 per 1,000. In rural areas, one in six children die before reaching age five. This is because of poor sanitation and insufficient potable water supply, infectious and parasitic diseases such as malaria and diarrhea are very common. Malnutrition and poor nutrition also are pervasive.

User fees have been a major deterrent to accessing health care. Various interventions have been devised to improve uptake of health care services, including the distribution of waiver cards to very poor and female-headed households and the introduction of community-based health insurance.

Following the national user fee ban in 2008, a pilot study conducted by the Future Health Systems consortium found a 400% increase in utilization of services that had previously charged fees for services and medicine. The government's strategy to collaborate with non-governmental organisations has led to higher primary health outcomes among the poor, with relatively high levels of perceived health care quality reported by clients in a recent study of primary care services.

The physical and psychological effects of war have substantially increased the need for medical care. In the last decade a number of new hospitals were established, with the most advanced treatments being available in Kabul. The French Medical Institute for Children and Indira Gandhi Childrens Hospital in Kabul are the leading children's hospitals in the country. Some of the other main hospitals in Kabul include the 350-bed Jamhuriat Hospital, the Sardar Mohammad Daud Khan Hospital, and the Jinnah Hospital, which is still under construction. There are also a number of well-equipped military controlled hospitals in different regions of the country. 2011 surveys show that 57 percent of Afghans say they have good or very good access to clinics or hospitals, and Afghans themselves pay approximately 75% of health care costs directly.

According to a 2006 World Health Organization (WHO) estimate, 66% of the population has access to improved drinking water. About 75% of the population has improved access to sanitation.

DISEASES

Tuberculosis

Tuberculosis is endemic in Afghanistan, with over 76,000 cases reported per year. The United States Agency for International Development is engaged in promulgating DOTS (directly observed therapy, short course) treatments, as well as TB awareness and prevention.
BRAC is a development organisation that focuses on the alleviation of poverty through the empowerment of the poor so as to improve their own lives. BRAC Afghanistan is involved in assisting Ministry of Public Health (MoPH) of Islamic Republic of Afghanistan in the implementation of the Basic Package of Health Services (BPHS) in Kabul, Badghis, Balkh and Nimroz. This implementation is mainly funded by the World Bank and the USAID-REACH (United States Agency for International Development - Rural Expansion of Afghanistan Community-based Healthcare).
Tuberculosis is a serious public health problem in Afghanistan. In 2007, 8,200 people in the country died from Tuberculosis and in the WHO's Global Tuberculosis Control Report 2009, an annual estimated figure of 46,000 new cases of Tuberculosis occurs in Afghanistan. As such, Afghanistan is ranked 22nd in amongst highly-affected Tuberculosis countries.
To help control Tuberculosis, BRAC Afghanistan started the community based TB DOTS (Directly Observed Therapy – Short Course – a relatively cheap and highly effective treatment for TB; identified and recognized by the World Bank) under the Fund for Innovative DOTS Expansion through Local initiatives to Stop TB (FIDELIS) project in the year 2006. In the first phase of this programme, diagnostic facilities for Tuberculosis were expanded through the setting up of the fifty Tuberculosis Microscopy Centres. This phase lasted from January 2006 and up to March 2007. Over the next two years, facilities were further expanded and 92 more Tuberculosis Microscopy Centres were set up under the FIDELIS programme.
The Tuberculosis Control Assistance Programme (TB CAP) is another project taken up between BRAC Afghanistan, World Health Organization (WHO) and Management Sciences for Health (MSH) in a bid to fight against Tuberculosis in Afghanistan. In this project, BRAC Afghanistan supports the BPHS (Basic Package of Health Services) project by replicating the CB-DOTS model into health systems of four provinces, namely Baghlan, Jawzjan, Badakshan and Herat. Also, BRAC Afghanistan has been selected as Principal Recipient (PR) for both Malaria and Tuberculosis components of the Global Fund 8.

In 2009, 2,143,354 patients received treatment under the health programs mentioned. Furthermore, as of August 2010, BRAC Afghanistan has covered 388 districts and 25 million of the total population are under the BRAC Afghanistan Health Program. Health facilities also include six District Hospitals, 26 Comprehensive Health Centres, 53 Basic Health Centres, 18 Sub Health Centres as well as 533 Mobile Clinics every month.

HIV

According to Soraya Dalil, Minister of Public Health, "the fastest method of HIV and AIDS spread is the use and sharing of injections by drug addicts. A recent data shows a 7.1 percent HIV/AIDS prevalence rate in three urban centers, where 85 percent of drug users share needles." However, according to reliable scientific studies, the prevalence of HIV in Afghanistan is much lower, i.e. less than 1% (Todd CS, 2012 and 2008). <http://www.biomedcentral.com/1471-2334/8/119><http://www.biomedcentral.com/1471-2334/12/196>

In 2006 the United Nations Development Programme estimated that an HIV/acquired immune deficiency syndrome (AIDS) epidemic could occur in Afghanistan because of the high incidence of intravenous drug use, unsafe blood transfusion procedures, massive refugee repatriation, poor health facilities, and illiteracy. According to Afghanistan's National Aids Control Program (NACP), 504 cases of HIV/AIDS were documented in late 2008 but by 2011 the numbers reached to 1,250. Health officials estimate that between 2,000 to 3,000 people maybe living with the virus. About 11 people, most of them drugs addicts, have died in Afghanistan from AIDS.

Polio

Afghan Ministry of Public Health along with WHO and UNICEF are engaged in a campaign to eliminate polio in the country. Wild poliovirus is still present in Afghanistan, though in limited areas. Reported cases were on the decline, from 63 in 1999 to 17 in 2007, until increased violence in 2008 impeded vaccination efforts, causing cases to climb to 20 for the first nine months of 2009.

Leprosy

Despite anti-leprosy initiatives by Leprosy Control (LEPCO) dating back to 1984, leprosy is also present in Afghanistan, with 231 cases reported in the 2001-2007 period. Just over three-quarters of the cases were the MB-type, with the rest PB-type. Leprosy has been reported in the central Hindu Kush mountain area of the country. Mainly in the provinces of Bamyan, Ghazni, Balkh.

Typhoid Fever

Being the 15th least developed country in the world, Afghanistan faces difficulties in terms of sanitation. In urban areas 40% of the population have unimproved access to sanitation facilities. Because of this many Afghanistan natives are forced to combat Typhoid Fever. Typhoid fever is one of Afghanistan's major infectious diseases in terms of food/waterborne diseases. This infectious disease occurs when fecal material comes into contact with food or water. Symptoms vary from case to case but often mild fever is present and if left untreated death may occur.

Hepatitis A

Fighting sanitation issues additionally places the Afghanistan population at risk of contracting Hepatitis A through the consumption of food and water that has been contaminated by fecal material. Hepatitis A works by inhibiting the liver from functioning properly. Symptoms generally include: jaundice, fatigue, loss of appetite, while some victims may experience diarrhea. Furthermore, symptoms will appear 2–6 weeks after an individual has come into contact with the Hepatitis A virus.

Leishmaniasis

Visceral leishmaniasis infections are often recognised by fever, swelling of the liver and spleen, and anemia. They are known by many local names, of which the most common is probably *Kala azar*,. A total of 21 cases of VL acquired in Afghanistan, all in the 1980s according to CDC reporting.

MATERNAL AND CHILD HEALTH CARE

An improvement in child health services in 500 - 600 health facilities was noted in 2006; the improvement correlates with the presence of clinical guidelines and the frequency of supervision of health care providers. A 2008 study by Future Health Systems and the Johns Hopkins Bloomberg School of Public Health indicated that only 13% of respondents had used skilled birth attendants. By 2010, the maternal mortality rate per 100,000 births for Afghanistan was 1,400. The under 5 mortality rate, per 1,000 births was 201 and the neonatal mortality as a percentage of under 5's mortality was 27. The aim of this report was to highlight ways in which the Millennium Development Goals can be achieved, particularly Goal 4 – Reduce child mortality and Goal 5 – improve maternal death.

In June 2011, the United Nations Population Fund released a report, which contained new data on the midwifery workforce and policies relating to newborn and maternal mortality for 58 countries. Afghanistan has more than 3,000 midwives with an additional 300 to 400 being trained each year. According to Afghanistan's Ministry of Health about 1 in 50 women die while giving birth and the number of children who died before the age of 5 is about 1 in 10. According to Sima Ayubi, a maternity doctor in Kabul who advocates hospital births, explains: "Now pregnant women have more information about health. This mortality rate is still a problem. There's just a decrease. The problem is not completely eliminated or under control."

According to a 2012 report by Save the Children, improved healthcare and the rise of females attending school have made Afghanistan climb up from its position as the worst place on earth to be a mother."More mothers are surviving and fewer children are dying and this is something we need to be celebrating," said Rachel Maranto, Advocacy and Mobilisation senior Manager at Save the Children in Kabul. Despite the better healthcare, about 275 children die every day in the country of 30 million

HISTORY AND POLITICAL DEVELOPMENTS

CONTEMPORARY ERA (1973–PRESENT)

REPUBLIC OF AFGHANISTAN AND THE END OF MONARCHY

Amid charges of corruption and malfeasance against the royal family and poor economic conditions created by the severe 1971–72 drought, former Prime Minister Mohammad Sardar Daoud Khan seized power in a non-violent coup on July 17, 1973, while Zahir Shah was receiving treatment for eye problems and therapy for lumbago in Italy. Daoud abolished the monarchy, abrogated the 1964 constitution, and declared Afghanistan a republic with himself as its first President and Prime Minister. His attempts to carry out badly needed economic and social reforms met with little success, and the new constitution promulgated in February 1977 failed to quell chronic political instability.

As disillusionment set in, in 1978 a prominent member of the People's Democratic Party of Afghanistan (PDPA), Mir Akbar Khyber (or "Kaibar"), was killed by the government. The leaders of PDPA apparently feared that Daoud was planning to exterminate them all, especially since most of them were arrested by the government shortly after. Nonetheless, Hafizullah Amin and a number of military wing officers of the PDPA's Khalq faction managed to remain at large and organize a military coup.

DEMOCRATIC REPUBLIC AND SOVIET WAR

On 27 April 1978, the PDPA, led by Nur Mohammad Taraki, Babrak Karmal and Amin Taha overthrew the government of Mohammad Daoud, who was assassinated along with all his family members in a bloody military coup. The coup became known as the Saur Revolution. On 1 May, Taraki became President, Prime Minister and General Secretary of the PDPA. The country was then renamed the Democratic Republic of Afghanistan (DRA), and the PDPA regime lasted, in some form or another, until April 1992.

In March 1979, Hafizullah Amin took over as prime minister, retaining the position of field marshal and becoming vice-president of the Supreme Defence Council. Taraki remained President and in control of the Army. On 14 September, Amin overthrew Taraki, who was killed. Amin stated that "the Afghans recognize only crude force." Afghanistan expert Amin Saikal writes: "As his powers grew, so apparently did his craving for personal dictatorship ... and his vision of the revolutionary process based on terror."

Once in power, the PDPA implemented a liberal and Marxist-Leninist agenda. It moved to replace religious and traditional laws with secular and Marxist-Leninist ones. Men were obliged to cut their beards, women could not wear a chador, and mosques were placed off limits. The PDPA made a number of reforms on women's rights, banning forced marriages, giving state recognition of women's right to vote, and introducing women to political life. A prominent example was Anahita Ratebzad, who was a major Marxist leader and a member of the Revolutionary Council. Ratebzad wrote the famous *New Kabul Times* editorial (May 28, 1978) which declared: "Privileges which women, by right, must have are equal education, job security, health services, and free time to rear a healthy generation for building the future of the country ... Educating and enlightening women is now the subject of close government attention." The PDPA also carried out socialist land reforms and moved to promote state atheism.

They also prohibited usury and took a number of measures in favor of women's rights, by declaring equality of the sexes and introducing women to political life. The PDPA invited the Soviet Union to assist in modernizing its economic infrastructure (predominantly its exploration and mining of rare minerals and natural gas). The USSR also sent contractors to build roads, hospitals and schools and to drill water wells; they also trained and equipped the Afghan army. Upon the PDPA's ascension to power, and the establishment of the DRA, the Soviet Union promised monetary aid amounting to at least $1.262 billion.

At the same time, the PDPA imprisoned, tortured or murdered thousands of members of the traditional elite, the religious establishment, and the intelligentsia. The government launched a campaign of violent repression, killing some 10,000 to 27,000 people and imprisoning 14,000 to 20,000 more, mostly at Pul-e-Charkhi prison. In December 1978 the PDPA leadership signed an agreement with the Soviet Union which would allow military support for the PDPA in Afghanistan if needed. The majority of people in the cities including Kabul either welcomed or were ambivalent to these policies.

However, the Marxist-Leninist and secular nature of the government as well as its heavy dependence on the Soviet Union made it unpopular with a majority of the Afghan population. Repressions plunged large parts of the country, especially the rural areas, into open revolt against the new Marxist-Leninist government. By spring 1979 unrests had reached 24 out of 28 Afghan provinces including major urban areas. Over half of the Afghan army would either desert or join the insurrection. Most of the government's new policies clashed directly with the traditional Afghan understanding of Islam, making religion one of the only forces capable of unifying the tribally and ethnically divided population against the unpopular new government, and ushering in the advent of Islamist participation in Afghan politics.

In the wake of the Iranian Revolution, the US sought rapprochement with the Afghan government—a prospect that the USSR found unacceptable due to weakening Soviet leverage over the regime. In February 1979, U.S. Ambassador Adolph "Spike" Dubs was murdered in Kabul after Afghan security forces burst in on his kidnappers. The U.S. then reduced bilateral assistance and terminated a small military training program. All remaining assistance agreements were ended after the Soviet invasion of Afghanistan. Following the Soviet invasion, the United States supported diplomatic efforts to achieve a Soviet withdrawal. In addition, generous U.S. contributions to the refugee program in Pakistan played a major part in efforts to assist Afghan refugees.

To bolster the Parcham faction, the Soviet Union decided to intervene on December 24, 1979, when the Red Army invaded its southern neighbor. Over 100,000 Soviet troops took part in the invasion, which was backed by another one hundred thousand Afghan military men and supporters of the Parcham faction. In the meantime, Hafizullah Amin was killed and replaced by Babrak Karmal.

In response to the Soviet occupation of Afghanistan, the Carter administration and Reagan administration in the U.S. began arming the Mujahideen, thanks in large part to the efforts of Charlie Wilson and CIA officer Gust Avrakotos. Early reports estimated that $6–20 billion had been spent by the U.S. and Saudi Arabia but more recent reports state that the U.S. and Saudi Arabia provided as much as up to $40 billionin cash and weapons, which included over two thousand FIM-92 Stinger surface-to-air missiles, for building up Islamic groups against the Soviet Union. The U.S. handled most of its support through Pakistan's ISI. Saudi Arabia was also providing financial support.

The 10-year Soviet occupation resulted in the deaths of between 850,000 and 1,500,000 Afghan civilians.

About 6 million fled as Afghan refugees to Pakistan and Iran, and from there over 38,000 made it to the United States and many more to the European Union. Faced with mounting international pressure and great number of casualties on both sides, the Soviets withdrew in 1989. Their withdrawal from Afghanistan was seen as an ideological victory in the United States, which had backed some Mujahideen factions through three U.S. presidential administrations to counter Soviet influence in the vicinity of the oil-rich Persian Gulf. The USSR continued to support President Mohammad Najibullah (former head of the Afghan secret service, *KHAD*) until 1992.

FOREIGN INTERFERENCE AND CIVIL WAR

1992-1996

After the fall of the communist Najibullah-regime in 1992, the Afghan political parties agreed on a peace and power-sharing agreement (the Peshawar Accords). The Peshawar Accords created the Islamic State of Afghanistan and appointed an interim government for a transitional period. According to Human Rights Watch:

> The sovereignty of Afghanistan was vested formally in the *Islamic State of Afghanistan*, an entity created in April 1992, after the fall of the Soviet-backed Najibullah government. [...] With the exception of Gulbuddin Hekmatyar's Hezb-e Islami, all of the parties [...] were ostensibly unified under this government in April 1992. [...] Hekmatyar's Hezb-e Islami, for its part, refused to recognize the government for most of the period discussed in this report and launched attacks against government forces and Kabul generally. [...] Shells and rockets fell everywhere.

Gulbuddin Hekmatyar was directed, funded and supplied by the Pakistani army. Afghanistan analyst Amin Saikal concludes in his book *Modern Afghanistan: A History of Struggle and Survival*:

> Pakistan was keen to gear up for a breakthrough in Central Asia. [...] Islamabad could not possibly expect the new Islamic government leaders [...] to subordinate their own nationalist objectives in order to help Pakistan realize its regional ambitions. [...] Had it not been for the ISI's logistic support and supply of a large number of rockets, Hekmatyar's forces would not have been able to target and destroy half of Kabul.

There was no time for the interim government to create working government departments, police units or a system of justice and accountability. Saudi Arabia and Iran also armed and directed Afghan militias. A publication by the George Washington University describes:

> [O]utside forces saw instability in Afghanistan as an opportunity to press their own security and political agendas.

According to Human Rights Watch, numerous Iranian agents were assisting the Shia Hezb-i Wahdat forces of Abdul Ali Mazari, as Iran was attempting to maximize Wahdat's military power and influence. Saudi Arabia was trying to strengthen the Wahhabite Abdul Rasul Sayyaf and his Ittihad-i Islami faction. Atrocities were committed by individuals of the different factions while Kabul descended into lawlessness and chaos as described in reports by Human Rights Watch and the Afghanistan Justice Project. Again, Human Rights Watch writes:

> Rare ceasefires, usually negotiated by representatives of Ahmad Shah Massoud, Sibghatullah Mojaddedi or Burhanuddin Rabbani (the interim government), or officials from the International Committee of the Red Cross (ICRC), commonly collapsed within days.

The main forces involved during that period in Kabul, northern, central and eastern Afghanistan were the Hezb-i Islami of Gulbuddin Hekmatyar directed by Pakistan, the Hezb-i Wahdat of Abdul Ali Mazari directed by Iran, the Ittehad-i Islami of Abdul Rasul Sayyaf supported by Saudi Arabia, the Junbish-i Milli of Abdul Rashid Dostum backed by Uzbekisten, the Harakat-i Islami of Hussain Anwari and the Shura-i Nazar operating as the regular Islamic State forces (as agreed upon in the Peshawar Accords) under the defense ministry of Ahmad Shah Massoud.

Meanwhile southern Afghanistan was neither under the control of foreign-backed militias nor the interim government in Kabul, which had no hands in the affairs of southern Afghanistan during that time. Southern Afghanistan was ruled by Gul Agha Sherzai. The southern city of Kandahar was a centre of lawlessness, crime and atrocities fuelled by complex Pashtun tribal rivalries.

In 1994, the Taliban (a movement originating from Jamiat Ulema-e-Islam-run religious schools for Afghan refugees in Pakistan) also developed in Afghanistan as a politico-religious force, reportedly in opposition to the tyranny of the local governor. Mullah Omar started his movement with fewer than 50 armed madrassah students in his hometown of Kandahar. As Gulbuddin Hekmatyar remained unsuccessful in conquering Kabul, Pakistan started its support to the Taliban. Many analysts like Amin Saikal describe the Taliban as developing into a proxy force for Pakistan's regional interests which the Taliban decline. In 1994 the Taliban took power in several provinces in southern and central Afghanistan.

In 1995 the Hezb-i Islami of Gulbuddin Hekmatyar, the Iranian-backed Hezb-i Wahdat as well as Rashid Dostum's Junbish forces were defeated militarily in the capital Kabul by forces of the interim government under Massoud who subsequently tried to initiate a nationwide political process with the goal of national consolidation and democratic elections, also inviting the Taliban to join the process. The Taliban declined.

TALIBAN AND THE UNITED FRONT

The Taliban started shelling Kabul in early 1995 but were defeated by forces of the Islamic State government under Ahmad Shah Massoud. Amnesty International, referring to the Taliban offensive, wrote in a 1995 report:

> This is the first time in several months that Kabul civilians have become the targets of rocket attacks and shelling aimed at residential areas in the city.

On September 26, 1996, as the Taliban with military support by Pakistan and financial support by Saudi Arabia prepared for another major offensive Massoud ordered a full retreat from Kabul.

The Taliban seized Kabul on September 27, 1996, and established the Islamic Emirate of Afghanistan. They imposed on the parts of Afghanistan under their control their political and judicial interpretation of Islam issuing edicts forbidding women to work outside the home, attend school, or to leave their homes unless accompanied by a male relative The Physicians for Human Rights (PHR) analyze:

> To PHR's knowledge, no other regime in the world has methodically and violently forced half of its population into virtual house arrest, prohibiting them on pain of physical punishment.

After the fall of Kabul to the Taliban on September 27, 1996,

Ahmad Shah Massoud and Abdul Rashid Dostum, two former archnemesis, created the United Front (Northern Alliance) against the Taliban that were preparing offensives against the remaining areas under the control of Massoud and those under the control of Dostum. see video The United Front included beside the dominantly Tajik forces of Massoud and the Uzbek forces of Dostum, Hazara factions and Pashtun forces under the leadership of commanders such as Abdul Haq, Haji Abdul Qadir, Qari Baba or diplomat Abdul Rahim Ghafoorzai. From the Taliban conquest in 1996 until November 2001 the United Front controlled roughly 30% of Afghanistan's population in provinces such as Badakhshan, Kapisa, Takhar and parts of Parwan, Kunar, Nuristan, Laghman, Samangan, Kunduz, Ghōr and Bamyan.

According to a 55-page report by the United Nations, the Taliban, while trying to consolidate control over northern and western Afghanistan, committed systematic massacres against civilians. UN officials stated that there had been "15 massacres" between 1996 and 2001. They also said, that "[t]hese have been highly systematic and they all lead back to the [Taliban] Ministry of Defense or to Mullah Omar himself." The Taliban especially targeted people of Shia religious or Hazara ethnic background.

Upon taking Mazar-i-Sharif in 1998, about 4,000 civilians were executed by the Taliban and many more reported tortured. Among those killed in Mazari Sharif were several Iranian diplomats. Others were kidnapped by the Taliban, touching off a hostage crisis that nearly escalated to a full scale war, with 150,000 Iranian soldiers massed on the Afghan border at one time. It was later admitted that the diplomats were killed by the Taliban, and their bodies were returned to Iran.

The documents also reveal the role of Arab and Pakistani support troops in these killings. Bin Laden's so-called 055 Brigade was responsible for mass-killings of Afghan civilians. The report by the United Nations quotes eyewitnesses in many villages describing Arab fighters carrying long knives used for slitting throats and skinning people.

Pakistani President Pervez Musharraf - then as Chief of Army Staff - was responsible for sending thousands of Pakistanis to fight alongside the Taliban and Bin Laden against the forces of Massoud. In total there were believed to be 28,000 Pakistani nationals fighting inside Afghanistan. 20,000 were regular Pakistani soldiers either from the Frontier Corps or army and an estimated 8,000 were militants recruited in madrassas filling regular Taliban ranks. The estimated 25,000 Taliban regular force thus comprised more than 8,000 Pakistani nationals. A 1998 document by the U.S. State Department confirms that "20-40 percent of [regular] Taliban soldiers are Pakistani."

The document further states that the parents of those Pakistani nationals "know nothing regarding their child's military involvement with the Taliban until their bodies are brought back to Pakistan." A further 3,000 fighter of the regular Taliban army were Arab and Central Asian militants. From 1996 to 2001 the Al Qaeda of Osama Bin Laden and Ayman al-Zawahiri became a state within the Taliban state. Bin Laden sent Arab recruits to join the fight against the United Front. Of roughly 45,000 Pakistani, Taliban and Al Qaeda soldiers fighting against the forces of Massoud only 14,000 were Afghan.

According to Human Rights Watch in 1997 Taliban soldiers were summarily executed in and around Mazar-i Sharif by Dostum's Junbish forces. Dostum was defeated by the Taliban in 1998 with the fall of Mazar-i-Sharif. Massoud remained the only leader of the United Front in Afghanistan.

In the areas under his control Ahmad Shah Massoud set up democratic institutions and signed the Women's Rights Charter. Human Rights Watch cites no human rights crimes for the forces under direct control of Massoud for the period from October 1996 until the assassination of Massoud in September 2001. As a consequence many civilians fled to the area of Ahmad Shah Massoud. National Geographic concluded in its documentary *"Inside the Taliban"*:

> The only thing standing in the way of future Taliban massacres is Ahmad Shah Massoud."

The Taliban repeatedly offered Massoud a position of power to make him stop his resistance. Massoud declined for he did not fight to obtain a position of power. He explained in one interview:

> "The Taliban say: "Come and accept the post of prime minister and be with us", and they would keep the highest office in the country, the presidentship. But for what price?! The difference between us concerns mainly our way of thinking about the very principles of the society and the state. We can not accept their conditions of compromise, or else we would have to give up the principles of modern democracy. We are fundamentally against the system called "the Emirate of Afghanistan"."
>
> "There should be an Afghanistan where every Afghan finds himself or herself happy. And I think that can only be assured by democracy based on consensus."

Massoud wanted to convince the Taliban to join a political process leading towards democratic elections in a foreseeable future. His proposals for peace can be seen here: Proposal for Peace, promoted by Commander Massoud. Massoud also stated:

> "The Taliban are not a force to be considered invincible. They are distanced from the people now. They are weaker than in the past. There is only the assistance given by Pakistan, Osama bin Laden and other extremist groups that keep the Taliban on their feet. With a halt to that assistance, it is extremely difficult to survive." In early 2001 Massoud employed a new strategy of local military pressure and global political appeals. Resentment was increasingly gathering against Taliban rule from the bottom of Afghan society including the Pashtun areas. Massoud publicized their cause "popular consensus, general elections and democracy" worldwide. At the same time he was very wary not to revive the failed Kabul government of the early 1990s. Already in 1999 he started the training of police forces which he trained specifically to keep order and protect the civilian population in case the United Front would be successful.

In early 2001 Massoud addressed the European Parliament in Brussels asking the international community to provide humanitarian help to the people of Afghanistan.

He stated that the Taliban and Al Qaeda had introduced "a very wrong perception of Islam" and that without the support of Pakistan the Taliban would not be able to sustain their military campaign for up to a year. On this visit to Europe he also warned that his intelligence had gathered information about a large-scale attack on U.S. soil being imminent.

NATO PRESENCE AND THE KARZAI ADMINISTRATION

On 9 September 2001, Ahmad Shah Massoud was assassinated by two Arab suicide attackers inside Afghanistan and two days later about 3,000 people became victims of the September 11, 2001 attacks in the United States. Then US President George W. Bush accused Osama bin Laden and Khalid Sheikh Mohammed as the faces behind the attacks.

When the Taliban refused to hand over bin Laden to US authorities and to disband al-Qaeda bases in Afghanistan, Operation Enduring Freedom was launched in which teams of American and British special forces worked with commanders of the United Front (Northern Alliance) against the Taliban. At the same time the US-led forces were bombing Taliban and al-Qaeda targets everywhere inside Afghanistan with cruise missiles.

These actions led to the fall of Mazar-i-Sharif in the north followed by all the other cities, as the Taliban and al-Qaeda crossed over the porous Durand Line border into Pakistan. In December 2001, after the Taliban government was toppled and the new Afghan government under Hamid Karzai was formed, the International Security Assistance Force (ISAF) was established by the UN Security Council to help assist the Karzai administration and provide basic security to the Afghan people.

While the Taliban began regrouping inside Pakistan, more coalition troops entered the escalating US-led war. Meanwhile, the rebuilding of war-torn Afghanistan kicked off in 2002. The Afghan nation was able to build democratic structures over the years, and some progress was made in key areas such as governance, economy, health, education, transport, and agriculture. NATO is training the Afghan armed forces as well its national police.

ISAF and Afghan troops led many offensives against the Taliban but failed to fully defeat them. By 2009, a Taliban-led shadow government began to form in many parts of the country complete with their own version of mediation court. After U.S. President Barack Obama announced the deployment of another 30,000 soldiers in 2010 for a period of two years, Der Spiegel published images of the US soldiers who killed unarmed Afghan civilians.

In FY 2009, the United States resettled just 328 refugees from Afghanistan. By contrast, the U.S. admitted more than 100,000 Vietnamese refugees for resettlement during the Vietnam War. On the other hand, over five million Afghan refugees were repatriated in the last decade, including many who were forcefully deported from NATO countries.

This large return of Afghans may have helped the nation's economy but the country still remains one of the poorest in the world due to the decades of war, lack of foreign investment, ongoing government corruption and the Pakistani-backed Taliban insurgency.

The United States also accuses neighboring Iran of providing small level of support to the Taliban insurgents. According to a report by the United Nations, the Taliban and other militants were responsible for 76% of civilian casualties in 2009, 75% in 2010 and 80% in 2011.

In October 2008 U.S. Defense Secretary Gates had asserted that a political settlement with the Taliban was the endgame for the Afghanistan war. "There has to be ultimately – and I'll underscore ultimately – reconciliation as part of a political outcome to this," Gates stated.

By 2010 peace efforts began. In early January, Taliban commanders held secret exploratory talks with a United Nations special envoy to discuss peace terms. Regional commanders on the Taliban's leadership council, the Quetta Shura, sought a meeting with the UN special representative in Afghanistan, Kai Eide, and it took place in Dubai on January 8. It was the first such meeting between the UN and senior members of the Taliban.

On 26 January 2010, at a major conference in London which brought together some 70 countries and organizations, Afghan President Hamid Karzai said he intends to reach out to the Taliban leadership (including Mullah Omar, Sirajuddin Haqqani and Gulbuddin Hekmatyar). Supported by NATO, Karzai called on the group's leadership to take part in a loya jirga meeting to initiate peace talks. These steps have resulted in an intensification of bombings, assassinations and ambushes. Some Afghan groups (including the former intelligence chief Amrullah Saleh and opposition leader Dr. Abdullah Abdullah) believe that Karzai plans to appease the insurgents' senior leadership at the cost of the democratic constitution, the democratic process and progress in the field of human rights especially women's rights. Dr. Abdullah stated:

> "I should say that Taliban are not fighting in order to be accommodated. They are fighting in order to bring the state down. So it's a futile exercise, and it's just misleading. ... There are groups that will fight to the death. Whether we like to talk to them or we don't like to talk to them, they will continue to fight. So, for them, I don't think that we have a way forward with talks or negotiations or contacts or anything as such. Then we have to be prepared to tackle and deal with them militarily. In terms of the Taliban on the ground, there are lots of possibilities and opportunities that with the help of the people in different parts of the country, we can attract them to the peace process; provided, we create a favorable environment on this side of the line. At the moment, the people are leaving support for the government because of corruption. So that expectation is also not realistic at this stage."

Afghan President Hamid Karzai told world leaders during the London conference that he intends to reach out to the top echelons of the Taliban within a few weeks with a peace initiative.

Karzai set the framework for dialogue with Taliban leaders when he called on the group's leadership to take part in a "loya jirga" – or large assembly of elders – to initiate peace talks. Karzai also asked for creation of a new peacemaking organization, to be called the National Council for Peace, Reconciliation and Reintegration. Karzai's top adviser on the reconciliation process with the insurgents said that the country must learn to forgive the Taliban.

In March 2010, the Karzai government held preliminary talks with Hezb-i-Islami, who presented a plan which included the withdrawal of all foreign troops by the end of 2010. The Taliban declined to participate, saying "The Islamic Emirate has a clear position. We have said this many, many times. There will be no talks when there are foreign troops on Afghanistan's soil killing innocent Afghans on daily basis." In June 2010 the Afghan Peace Jirga 2010 took place. In September 2010 General David Petraeus commented on the progress of peace talks to date, stating, "The prospect for reconciliation with senior Taliban leaders certainly looms out there...and there have been approaches at (a) very senior level that hold some promise."

After the May 2011 death of Osama bin Laden in Pakistan, many prominent Afghan figures began being assassinated, including Mohammed Daud Daud, Ahmad Wali Karzai, Jan Mohammad Khan, Ghulam Haider Hamidi, Burhanuddin Rabbani and others. Also in the same year, the Pakistani-Afghan border skirmishes intensified and many large scale attacks by the Pakistani-based Haqqani network took place across Afghanistan.

This led to the United States warning Pakistan of a possible military action against the Haqqanis in the Federally Administered Tribal Areas. The U.S. blamed Pakistan's government, mainly Pakistani Army and its ISI spy network as the masterminds behind all of this.

> "In choosing to use violent extremism as an instrument of policy, the government of Pakistan, and most especially the Pakistani army and ISI, jeopardizes not only the prospect of our strategic partnership but Pakistan's opportunity to be a

respected nation with legitimate regional influence. They may believe that by using these proxies, they are hedging their bets or redressing what they feel is an imbalance in regional power. But in reality, they have already lost that bet."

—Admiral Mike Mullen, *Chairman of the Joint Chiefs of Staff*

U.S. Ambassador to Pakistan, Cameron Munter, told Radio Pakistan that "The attack that took place in Kabul a few days ago, that was the work of the Haqqani network. There is evidence linking the Haqqani Network to the Pakistan government. This is something that must stop."

Other top U.S. officials such as Hillary Clinton and Leon Panetta made similar statements. On October 16, 2011, "Operation Knife Edge" was launched by NATO and Afghan forces against the Haqqani network in south-eastern Afghanistan. Afghan Defense Minister, Abdul Rahim Wardak, explained that the operation will "help eliminate the insurgents before they struck in areas along the troubled frontier".In November 2011, NATO forces killed 24 Pakistani Army soldiers around the border region with Pakistan.

POLITICAL AND GOVERNMENT SYSTEM

AFGHANISTAN GOVERNMENTSL, JUDICIAL AND LEGAL SYSTEMS

GOVERNMENT – THE EXECUTIVE BRANCH

The Executive Branch of the Afghan government consists of a powerful and popularly elected President and two Vice Presidents.

The constitution involves a strong presidential system. The President of Afghanistan is elected directly by the Afghan people to a five-year term, and can be elected no more than twice.

The president must be Muslim, an Afghan citizen born of Afghan parents, and should not be guilty of war crimes. The president is the commander-in-chief of the armed forces.

Presidential responsibilities include:

- Determining policies with the approval of the National Assembly.
- Appointing the nation's ministers, the attorney general, the director of the central bank, and the justices of the Supreme Court with the approval of the main legislative body, the Wolesi Jirga.
- Appointing the nation's first and second vice presidents.

GOVERNMENT – THE LEGISLATIVE BRANCH

A National Assembly consisting of two Houses, the House of People (Wolesi Jirga) with 249 seats, and the House of Elders (Meshrano Jirga) with 102 seats, forms the Legislative Branch.

There is an independent Judiciary branch consisting of the Supreme Court (Stera Mahkama), High Courts and Appeal Courts. The President appoints the nine members of the Supreme Court with the approval of the Wolesi Jirga.

COMPOSITION OF THE NATIONAL ASSEMBLY

"The National Assembly of the Islamic Republic of Afghanistan as the highest legislative organ is the manifestation of the will of its people and represents the whole nation. Every member of the National Assembly takes into judgment the general welfare and supreme interests of all people of Afghanistan at the time of casting their vote." *Constitution of the Islamic Republic of Afghanistan (Article Eighty-One)*

The National Assembly, as envisaged in the Constitution, consists of two houses: the Wolesi Jirga (the House of the People) and theMeshrano Jirga (the House of Elders).

Article Ninety of the Afghan Constitution stipulates that the National Assembly shall have the following duties:

- Ratification, modification or abrogation of laws or legislative decrees;

- Approval of social, cultural, economic as well as technological development programs;
- Approval of the state budget as well as permission to obtain or grant loans;
- Creation, modification and or abrogation of administrative units;
- Ratification of international treaties and agreements, or abrogation of membership of Afghanistan in them;
- Other authorities enshrined in this Constitution.

THE WOLESI JIRGA (HOUSE OF PEOPLE)

The Wolesi Jirga has 249 seats with members directly elected by the people.

Sixty-eight women were elected to the seats reserved under the Constitution, while 17 of them have been elected in their own rights.

Each province was given proportionate representation in the Wolesi Jirga according to its population. Each member of the Wolesi Jirga will enjoy a five year term expiring on the twenty-first of June of the fifth year (June 21, 2010).

An aspiring candidate for the Wolesi Jirga must fulfil the following criteria:

- Be at least 25 years of age
- Be a citizen of Afghanistan
- Be registered as a voter
- Be running as a representative in only one province
- Pay a registration fee of 15,000 Afghanis (approximately US$300) which will be refunded provided the candidate wins at least three percent (3%) of the vote
- Submit a nomination form along with photocopies of 500 voter ID cards supporting the candidacy

In addition, no candidate can have been charged with crimes against humanity.

THE MESHRANO JIRGA (HOUSE OF ELDERS)

The Meshrano Jirga consists of a mixture of appointed and elected members (total 102 members). Sixty-eight members were selected by 34 directly elected Provincial Councils, and 34 were appointed by the President.

President Karzai's appointments were vetted by an independent UN sponsored election board and included 17 women (50 %), as required by the Constitution.

Each provincial council has elected one council member to serve in the Jirga (34 members), also each district council (34 members). Representatives of provincial councils will serve a term of four years, while representatives of district councils will serve a term of three years. Sebghatulla Mojadeddi was appointed President of Meshrano Jirga.

An aspiring candidate for the Meshrano Jirga must fulfil the following criteria:

- Be at least 35 years of age
- Be a citizen of Afghanistan

In addition, no potential member of the Meshrano Jirga can have been charged with crimes against humanity

SESSIONS OF THE NATIONAL ASSEMBLY

Both Houses of the National Assembly will convene two regular sessions for the term of nine months annually. The sessions are held concurrently, but separately, unless:

- The legislative term or annual sessions are inaugurated by the President;
- It is deemed necessary by the President.

The speaker of the Lower House shall preside over the joint sessions of the National Assembly. The sessions are open, except when the Speaker of the National Assembly or ten members of the House request its secrecy and it is granted by the National Assembly.

The President can order extraordinary sessions of the National Assembly during recess.

THE SECRETARIAT OF THE NATIONAL ASSEMBLY

Upon commencement of their work period, each of the two houses of the National Assembly elects one member as the Speaker for the term of the legislature, and two members as, first and second deputies, and two members as secretary and assistant secretary for a period of one year.

These individuals shall form the administrative teams of the Lower House as well as the Upper House.

The Lower House has the authority to establish a special commission on the proposal of one third of its members to review, as well as, investigate the actions of Government.

THE LEGISLATIVE PROCESS

Any law has to be approved by both Houses of the National Assembly (NA) and endorsed by the President.

Proposal for drafting a law is made by the Government or members of the NA, or if related to regulating judiciary, by the Supreme Court through the Government. It is first submitted to the Wolesi Jirga (the Lower House), which has one month to either approve or reject it by two-third.

The proposal is then submitted to the Meshrano Jirga (the Upper House), which will decide its approval or rejection in fifteen days.

In case the President rejects what the National Assembly has approved, he/she shall send it back, within fifteen days from the date it was presented to the Lower House outlining the reasons for rejection and, expiration of the period. If the House of People re-approves it with two thirds of all the votes, the draft will be considered endorsed and enforceable.

Proposals for drafting the budget and financial affairs law shall be made only by the Government.

While deciding about the proposed laws, the National Assembly shall give priority to treaties and development programs if the government considers them to be urgent.

The state budget and development program of the government shall be submitted, through the Upper House to the Lower House. If it is approved by the Lower House, it will be implemented without being submitting to the Upper House, after endorsement by the President.

In case of discussing urgent matters such as the annual budget, or development program, or issues related to the national security, territorial integrity and independence of the country, the sessions of the Assembly shall not end until a decision is made.

If one House rejects decisions of the other, a joint commission comprised of an equal number of members from each House will be formed to solve the difference. The decision of the commission shall be enforced, after endorsement by the President. In case the joint commission can not solve the difference, the decision will be considered rejected. In such cases, the Lower House will pass it with two-thirds majority in its next session, and will have it endorsed by the President.

THE CONSTITUTION

The present Constitution of the Islamic Republic of Afghanistan was agreed upon by more than 500 delegates representing Afghan men and women from across the country at the Constitutional Loya Jirga (December 13, 2003 - January 4, 2004). The Constitution was formally ratified by President Hamid Karzai at a ceremony in Kabul on January 26, 2004.

The key points of the Constitution are as follows:

- Afghanistan is an Islamic republic with Islam as its "sacred religion";
- Followers of other religions are free to perform religious ceremonies in accordance with the provisions of the law;
- No law shall be contrary to the beliefs and practices of Islam;
- Men and women have equal rights and duties before the law;
- Afghanistan will have a presidential system of government;
- The president is responsible to the nation and the lower house, or Wolesi Jirga;
- The president will be directly elected by the Afghan people with two vice-presidents, who are nominated by presidential candidates when standing for election;
- A national assembly will consist of two houses: a Wolesi Jirga or "house of people" and a Meshrano Jirga or "house of elders";
- The Wolesi Jirga will be directly elected by the Afghan people;
- The Wolesi Jirga has the authority to impeach ministers;
- The president will appoint ministers, the attorney general and central bank governor with the approval of the Wolesi Jirga;
- Ministers should not hold foreign passports but the Wolesi Jirga should vote whether to approve appointments of ministers holding dual nationality;
- Former king Mohammad Zahir Shah is to be accorded the title "Father of the Nation" for his lifetime ;
- Pashto and Dari are the official languages with other minority languages to be considered official languages in the areas in which they are spoken.

THE JUDICIARY

The Judiciary in Afghanistan is composed of the Supreme Court, Courts of Appeal and Primary Courts. Travelling courts may be established when needed, on recommendation by the Supreme Court and approval of the President.

The Judiciary is empowered to resolve disputes between and among individuals, legal entities including the state in accordance with law.

Cases are resolved in courts taking into consideration the quality and nature of the case in two stages, primary and appeal. The Supreme Court deals with the referred cases of Courts of Appeal only in terms of accurate application of law(to see if any provision of law is breached or accurately applied), unless it has been authorized by law to resolve a case taking into consideration the quality and nature of the case.

Cases in court are handled as follows:

- At the primary stage, with participation of three judges. Except less than three judges may decide a case when they are not available.
- At the appeal stage, three judges shall decide any case.
- At the cessation stage, shall take place by two or more persons

The courts are required to resolve cases in accordance with the constitution and other laws of the Islamic Republic of Afghanistan. If there is no clear legal provision for the case, the case shall be handled in accordance with articles 130 and 131 of the constitution.

Trials in the Afghanistan courts happen in open procedure in which everybody may attend, subject to law. The court may convene the trials in a close procedure only if they are legally required or that it is deemed necessary. Making notice of the final decision shall always be open to public.

The courts shall be duty bound to rely on the reasons, grounds and legal provisions for a decision to issue.

THE SUPREME COURT

The Supreme Court constitutes the highest authority of the judiciary of the Islamic Republic of Afghanistan.

The Supreme Court is composed of nine persons appointed by the president in an agreement with Wolusi Jirga (house of people) in accordance with article one hundred seventeen and one hundred eighteen of the Constitution. The president shall appoint one of the members as the chief of the Supreme Court.

Supreme Court Dewans

The Supreme Court consists of the following Dewans:

- General Criminal Dewan
- Public Security Dewan
- Civil and Public Rights Dewan
- Commercial Dewan

Each Dewan is headed by a member of the Supreme Court as selected on rotation basis by the chief justice for the period of one year.

Powers of heads of Dewans

Each head of the Supreme Court Dewans has the following powers and duties:

- Leading relevant Dewan's activities.
- Holding and presiding over relevant Dewan's sessions.
- Arranging affairs, coordinating judicial experiences of the Dewans and submission of report to the Supreme Court.

Judicial advisors

The Supreme Court has judicial advisors and their total number is not to be more than thirty six persons. Their duties consist of analyzing and studying the cases filed and provide a report to the judicial meeting for decision to be made.

Judicial powers and duties of the Supreme Court

The Supreme Court has the following jurisdictions and duties within the scope of interpretation of laws and judicial issues:

- Assessment on conformity of laws, decrees, legal documents, international contracts and conventions with the Constitution and their interpretation based on the government or courts demand in accordance with law.
- Propose for draft law on regulating the judicial affairs to the national assembly through government.
- Revising the rulings of courts due to presence of new reasons based on complaint by the AGO or by party to the claim according to the mentioned provisions and arrangement in the law.
- Resolving Courts' Conflict of Jurisdiction and submitting jurisdiction of resolving a case from one court to the other based on proposal by the AGO or party to the claim when reasonable grounds arise.
- Studying reasons and making decision on extraditing criminals to foreign states in accordance with law.
- Studying reasons of a charge made and making decision on submitting the Afghan citizen to the foreign state in the light of article 28 of the Constitution.
- Ensuring uniformity in judicial treatment.
- Taking measures on criminal and disciplinary offences by judges.
- Evaluating the courts inquiries on judicial issues and providing responses accordingly.

Powers of the head of Supreme Court (chief justice)

The Chief Justice represents the Judicial Authority of Islamic Republic of Afghanistan and has the following jurisdiction and duties:

- lead the judicial and administrative activities of the Supreme Court;
- preside over the meetings of the Supreme Court;
- chair the judicial sessions of the relevant Dewans of the Supreme Court as needed;
- issue orders on the inspection of courts' activities;

- issue orders on resolving cases resulting from crimes and judicial and administrative
- violation by judges;
- monitor the implementation of courts final decisions;
- monitor and control appropriate expenditure of the judicial budget;
- delegate all or some of his/her powers to one of the members of the Supreme Court when sick, on leave, absence and other reasons;
- monitor activities the General Administration Office of the judiciary;
- provide reports on judicial and administrative activities of the judiciary to the president;
- propose on pardoning, mitigation of imprisonment and other punishments of judges to the president's office;
- other assigned powers in accordance with the provisions of this and other laws.

THE COURT OF APPEALS

The Court of Appeals is established in all the provinces in accordance with this law. The Court of Appeals is composed of chief of the court, heads of Dewans and other judicial members. Head of the Court of Appeals shall be selected from among the judges who have enough qualification, experience and competency. Head of the General Criminal Dewan is the deputy head of court of appeals.

Structure of Dewans of Courts of Appeal

The Courts of Appeal contains the following Dewans:

- General Criminal Dewan
- Public Security Dewan
- Civil and Family Dewan
- Public Rights Dewan
- Commercial Dewan
- Juveniles Dewan

There can not be more than six judicial members within each Dewan of the Court of Appeals.

The Supreme Court may as needed establish other Dewans within the structure of the Court of Appeals with the approval of the President.

Powers of the Court of Appeals

- The Court of Appeals oversees the rulings and decisions of the lower courts, in situations according to the provisions of the related laws.
- The Court of Appeals while resolving cases reconsiders the whole legal process. It may correct, overturn, amend, confirm or repeal the rulings and decisions of the lower courts.

Duties and Powers of head of the Court of Appeals

The head of the Court of Appeals has the following responsibilities and powers:

- lead and organize activities of the respective Dewans
- preside over the judicial meetings of the Dewans, when necessary
- assign member of one Dewan to another on temporary basis.
- assign one of the judges of the court of appeals to the primary courts when necessary.

- delegate the authority of resolving a certain case from one Dewan to another, when necessary.
- coordinate judicial experiences of respective Dewans.
- preparation of activity reports of Dewans and courts and delivery of the reports to the Supreme Court.

THE PRIMARY COURTS

In the jurisdictional area of each Court of Appeals, there are these primary courts:

- Central provincial primary court
- Juveniles Court
- Commercial Primary Court
- District Primary Court
- Family Issues primary court

The Supreme Court may establish more courts in the centres of provinces when required after approval of the president.

Primary Court Structure

A Central Primary Court comprises of the following Dewans:

- General Criminal Dewan
- Civil Dewan
- Public Rights Dewan
- Public Security Dewan
- Traffic Criminal Dewan

The Dewans of Central Primary Court shall have one head and no more than four members.

Resolving cases by Dewans of primary courts

Central provincial primary courts have the relevant Dewans to resolve cases in primary level in accordance with law:

- Resolving general criminal cases by General Criminal Dewan.
- Resolving civil disputes between natural persons by Civil Dewan.
- Resolving civil disputes between natural and legal individuals/entities or among legal entities by Public Rights Dewan.
- Resolving criminal cases of public security and interest, drug trafficking and other crimes by Public Security Dewan in accordance with law.
- Resolving traffic criminal cases by Traffic related Crimes Dewan.

Leading Court and Dewans

There is a head for the central provincial primary court to lead and manage the judicial and administrative activities of the Dewans and to attend their meetings when required.

JUVENILE COURT

There is a juvenile primary court in the centre of every province. The juvenile primary court is made up of a head and four members. In case the head is absent due to any reason, his/her powers and duties shall be transferred to one of the judicially experienced judges. The method to resolve juveniles' offences is to be determined by a special regulation.

THE COMMERCIAL COURT

A commercial court is to be established in centre of every province. This court shall have a chief and four other members. In provinces where commercial court is not available, dealing with commercial cases is the jurisdiction of the civil Dewan of the provincial central primary court.

Resolving special cases

Based on the case, the commercial, public rights and public security cases within the judicial jurisdiction of a Court of Appeals shall be initiated in the commercial court and in the relevant Dewans of the provincial central primary court.

DISTRICT PRIMARY COURT STRUCTURE

The District primary court shall consist of a chief and two members. In the areas where there are no members available, the cases shall be decided by fewer than three. The chief of the district primary court shall lead the court. In his/her absence, the responsibilities and powers shall be transferred to the most judicially experienced judge on the court.

District Primary Court Jurisdiction

District Primary courts shall deal in primary stage with all ordinary criminal, civil and family cases which are legally presented to them.

Responsibility

The chief of each Primary Court, heads of Dewans and their judicial members shall be responsible for deciding cases in a timely manner according to the law, correct application of the law, and for explaining the ground for their decision.

Finality of Decision

The decisions of the primary courts are absolute and final in the following situations:

- When both parties agree upon the issued decision of the court.
- When the time for appealing has expired.
- When the disputed property is worth up to 100,000 Afgs.
- When the order for a cash fine of 50,000 Afgs is issued
- Other situations set forth in law.

REGISTRATION OF DOCUMENTS AND DEEDS BRANCHES

In the structure of every Court of Appeals, there is a Directorate of Documents and Deeds Registration (DDDR). There shall be a head in charge of a directorate and shall lead and manage the activities of the directorate. In the districts where there is no such directorate for legal documents registration, the district courts shall have the authority to perform these duties. Duties and powers of the DDDR's are regulated through special legislation.

REGISTRATION OF DOCUMENTS AND TRADEMARKS

Registration of commercial documents and trade marks shall be the jurisdiction of the commercial court.

CONDITIONS OF BEING A JUDGE

On the recommendation of the Supreme Court and with approval of the president, any qualified person meeting following requirements shall be appointed as a judge:

- Upon appointment as judge, hold the citizenship of Islamic Republic of Afghanistan for at least ten yeas.
- Not be convicted of any crime or intentional misdemeanour by absolute and final decision of an authorized court.
- Hold the BA degree from any faculties of law or Shari a or above it or holds diploma on Religious Studies from an officially recognized centre or equivalent.
- Not have any illness or disability which impedes a judge performance of duties.
- Has completed the age of 25 upon appointment.
- Have passed the practical stage of judicial training course successfully.

OATH TAKING

Before occupying the position as judge, a person must swear in front of chief and members of Supreme Court as follow:

"I swear by the name of the Almighty Allah that I perform my duty with full trust and dignity and impartiality, respect and implement provision of Islamic shariah, constitution of Afghanistan and other laws of the country , respect confidentiality of my duty ,will not commit any crime , violation of other rights, injustice and bribery directly and in directly."

The **politics of Afghanistan** consists of the Council of Ministers and the National Assembly, with a president serving as the head of state and commander-in-chief of the military. The nation is currently led by the Karzai administration under President Hamid Karzai who is backed by two vice presidents, Mohammed Qasem Fahim and Mohammad Karim Khalili. In the last decade the politics of Afghanistan have been heavily influenced by NATO countries, especially by the United States, in an effort to stabilise and democratise the country. In 2004, the nation's new constitution was adopted and an executive president was elected. The following year a general election to choose parliamentarians took place.

The current president Hamid Karzai was declared the first ever democratically elected head of state in Afghanistan in 2004, winning a second five-year term in 2009. The National Assembly is Afghanistan's national legislature. It is a bicameral body, composed of the House of the People and the House of Elders. The first legislature was elected in 2005 and the current one in 2010. Members of the Supreme Court were appointed by the president to form the judiciary. Together, this new system is to provide a new set of checks and balances that was unheard of in the country

Government operation in Afghanistan historically has consisted of power struggles, bloody coups and unstable transfers of power. The country has been governed by many systems of government, including a monarchy, republic, theocracy, dictatorship, and a pro-communist state.

- 1709 - Mirwais Hotak declares Afghanistan (*land of the Afghans*) an independent state and establishes the Hotaki dynasty at Kandahar.
- 1747 - Ahmad Shah Durrani expands Afghanistan and establishes the Durrani Empire.
- 1838 - British India invades the land during the First Anglo-Afghan War and begins to influence the politics of Afghanistan.
- 1919 - King Amanullah Khan takes the throne after the Third Anglo-Afghan War, British influence ends.
- 1973 - Mohammed Daoud Khan, Prime Minister and a member of the royal family, seizes power while King Mohammad Zahir Shah is in Italy.
- 1978 – The leftist People's Democratic Party of Afghanistan (PDPA) seizes power during the Saur Revolution. Daoud Khan is assassinated along with his family and supporters.
- 1979 – President Nur Muhammad Taraki, leader of PDPA, is assassinated and replaced by Hafizullah Amin. Amin is then assassinated and the Soviet Union invades. Babrak Karmal is installed as president.
- 1987 - Mohammad Najibullah replaces Babrak Karmal as president.
- 1989 – Soviet army withdraws all troops from the country, and the United States also abandons Afghanistan.
- 1992 – Kabul falls to mujahideen factions. Burhanuddin Rabbani becomes president of the new Islamic State of Afghanistan and a civil war starts.
- 1996 – Kabul along with most part of the country falls to the Taliban.
- 2001 – United States and coalition forces invade Afghanistan. Hamid Karzai is appointed leader of the nation at the International Conference on Afghanistan in Berlin the capital of Germany.
- 2003 - Loya Jirga adopts new constitution, restructuring the government as an Islamic republic.
- 2004 - Hamid Karzai is elected President of Afghanistan.

RECENT POLITICAL DEVELOPMENTS

Afghanistan is an Islamic republic consisting of three branches of power (executive, legislative, and judiciary) overseen by checks and balances. It is currently led by the Karzai administration under President Hamid Karzai, who was elected in 2004 and re-elected in 2009. Before the election of 2004, Karzai led the country after being chosen by delegates of the Bonn Conference in December 2001 to head an interim government after the removal of the Taliban Emirate. While supporters have praised Karzai's efforts to promote national reconciliation and a growing economy, critics charge him with failing to stem corruption and the drug trade, and the slow pace of reconstruction.

The current parliament was elected in 2005 and then in 2010. Among the elected officials are former mujahideen, Islamic fundamentalists, reformists, communists, and several Taliban members. About 28% of the delegates elected were women, 3% more than the 25% minimum guaranteed under the constitution. This made Afghanistan, long known under the Taliban for its oppression of women, one of the leading countries in terms of female representation.

The Supreme Court of Afghanistan is led by Chief Justice Abdul Salam Azimi. Dominated by fundamentalist religious figures, it has tried to ban a candidate in the 2004 presidential election for questioning polygamy laws, and limited the rights of women, as well as overstepped its constitutional authority by issuing rulings on subjects not yet brought before the court.

NORTHERN ALLIANCE AND TALIBAN GOVERNMENT

In September 1996, government officials of the Islamic State of Afghanistan under Burhanuddin Rabbani were displaced by forces of the Taliban.while The United Nations refused to recognize the Taliban government, instead it recognized the Islamic State as the official government in exile the Pakistan and two other countries has recognized the Taliban government. The Organisation of the Islamic Conference left the Afghan seat vacant until the question of legitimacy could be resolved through negotiations among the warring factions.

The Taliban controlled 95% of the territory by 2001 and only Pakistan, Saudi Arabia, and the United Arab Emirates recognized them as the government of Afghanistan. The remaining 5% belonged to rebel forces that became known as the Northern Alliance.

MILITARY ACTION BY THE UNITED STATES AND ALLIES

After the Taliban's refusal to hand over Osama bin Laden to U.S. authorities for his suspected involvement in the 11 September 2001 attacks in New York City and Washington, D.C., a US-led international coalition was formed; after several weeks of aerial bombardment by coalition forces and military action on the ground, including Afghan opposition forces, the Taliban was officially ousted from power on November 17, 2001.

BONN AGREEMENT

In December 2001, a number of prominent Afghans met under the United Nations auspices in Germany to decide on a plan for governing the country. As a result, the Afghan Interim Administration (AIA) - made up of 30 members, headed by a chairman - was inaugurated on December 22, 2001, with a six-month mandate to be followed by a two-year Afghan Transitional Administration (ATA), after which elections are to be held. Some provisions in the agreement have expired, due to the creation of the constitution. Still, the agreement paved the way for the creation of a democratic Afghanistan.

ISAF AND AFGHAN SECURITY FORCES

The United Nations Security Council authorized the creation of the International Security Assistance Force (ISAF) to help provide basic security for Afghanistan. Members of the United States armed forces and NATO countries began sending troops to Afghanistan since late 2001 to early 2011, at a time when the total number of foreign soldiers reached about 150,000. In the meantime the newly-trained Afghan National Army and Afghan National Police reached over 200,000 by 2011.

NEW CONSTITUTION AND NATIONAL ELECTIONS

The structure of the Transitional Authority was announced on June 10, 2002, when an emergency loya jirga (grand assembly) convened establishing the Transitional Islamic State of Afghanistan (TISA), which had 18 months to hold a constitutional loya jirga to adopt a constitution and 24 months to hold nationwide elections. The loya jirga was replaced by the National Assembly.

Under the Bonn Agreement the Afghan Constitution Commission was established to consult with the public and formulate a draft constitution. The meeting of a constitutional *loya jirga* was held in December 2003, when a new constitution was adopted creating a presidential form of government with a bicameral legislature: the House of Elders (Meshrano Jirga) and the House of the People (Wolesi Jirga).

The 2004 presidential election was held on October 9, with over 10 million Afghans being registered to vote. Many of the candidates running against Hamid Karzai tried to boycott the election because they feared irregularities. However, Karzai made this statement to the media:

> *"It is too late to call for a boycott now that millions of Afghans have come from their homes despite rain and snow and they have voted... We should respect the people's will. I'm very delighted that all over Afghanistan, with the help of God, people with a lot of happiness and enthusiasm went to ballot boxes and voted. This shows the political understanding of Afghans and their will for a peaceful future."*
>
> —Hamid Karzai, *October 9, 2004*

An independent commission found evidence of fraud, but ruled that it did not affect the outcome of the poll and Karzai won with 55.4% of the vote. He was inaugurated as President on December 7 of that year. It was the country's first national election since 1969, when parliamentary elections were last held.

On September 18, 2005, parliamentary elections were held; the parliament opened after the results were announced. On December 20 Karzai's close ally and president of the first mujahideen government, Sibghatullah Mojadeddi, was picked to head the 102-seat upper house. On December 21, Yunus Qanuni, Afghan opposition leader and Karzai's main opponent was chosen to lead the 249-seat lower house of parliament with 122 votes against 117 for his closest challenge.

EXECUTIVE BRANCH

The Constitution of Afghanistan creates a strong presidency, serving as the head of state and Commander-in-Chief of the armed forces. A president is elected with two vice-presidents. The president appoints cabinet ministers and governors, which are to be approved by the National Assembly.

ELECTORAL SYSTEM

The President is elected by absolute majority vote through a two-round system to serve a 5-year term.

In the House of Elders (*Meshrano Jirga*), 34 members are elected by regional legislatures to serve 4-year terms, 34 members are elected by regional legislatures to serve 3-year terms and 34 members are appointed by the President to serve 5-year terms*. In the House of People (*Wolesi Jirga*) 249 members are elected by single non-transferable vote to serve 5-year terms.**

* Each Provincial Council elects one of its members to the House of Elders under a two-round system. (4-year term.) Each District Council elects one of its members to the House of Elders under a two-round system. (3-year term.) Due to the fact that district boundaries had not yet been

established, District Councils did not elect members to the House of Elders in 2005. To compensate, provincial councils each elected two members. Half of the Presidential appointments must be women, two must be representatives from the Kuchi community, and two must represent the disabled community.

** There are 34 multi-member districts corresponding to the 34 provinces. Seats are allocated in proportion to provincial population. District magnitudes range from 2 to 33. The constitution reserves 68 seats to women. However, even if a female candidate receives enough votes to win a seat without the quota system, she is still awarded a reserve seat.

POPULATION:

- Population: 31,108,077 (July 2013 est.)

AFGHANISTAN CONSTITUTION

Adopted by Grand Council on: 4 Jan 2004
In Force Since: 4 Jan 2004 (cf. Article 162)
Official Title: Constitution of the Islamic Republic of Afghanistan
ICL Document Status: 26 Jan 2004

In the name of God, the Merciful, the Compassionate

PREAMBLE

We the people of Afghanistan:
1. With firm faith in God Almighty and relying on His lawful mercy, and Believing in the Sacred religion of Islam,
2. Realizing the injustice and shortcoming of the past, and the numerous troubles imposed on our country,
3. While acknowledging the sacrifices and the historic struggles, rightful Jehad and just resistance of all people of Afghanistan, and respecting the high position of the martyrs for the freedom of Afghanistan,
4. Understanding the fact that Afghanistan is a single and united country and belongs to all ethnicities residing in this country,
5. Observing the United Nations Charter and respecting the Universal Declaration of Human Rights,
6. For consolidating national unity, safeguarding independence, national sovereignty, and territorial integrity of the country,
7. For establishing a government based on people's will and democracy,
8. For creation of a civil society free of oppression, atrocity, discrimination, and violence and based on the rule of law, social justice, protection of human rights, and dignity, and ensuring the fundamental rights and freedoms of the people,
9. For strengthening of political, social, economic, and defensive institutions of the country,
10. For ensuring a prosperous life, and sound environment for all those residing in this land,
11. And finally for regaining Afghanistan's deserving place in the international community,
Have adopted this constitution in compliance with historical, cultural, and social requirements of the era, through our elected representatives in the Grand Council [*Loya Jirga*] dated 14 Jaddi 1382 in the city of Kabul.

CHAPTER I THE STATE

Article 1 [Islamic Republic]
Afghanistan is an Islamic Republic, independent, unitary and indivisible state.

Article 2 [Religions]
(1) The religion of the state of the Islamic Republic of Afghanistan is the sacred Religion of Isman
(2) Followers of other religions are free to exercise their faith and perform their religious rites within the limits of the provisions of law.

Article 3 [Law and Religion]
In Afghanistan, no law can be contrary to the beliefs and provisions of the sacred religion of Islam.

Article 4 [Sovereignty, Ethnic Groups, Citizenship]

(1) National sovereignty in Afghanistan belongs to the nation that exercises it directly or through its representatives.
(2) The nation of Afghanistan consists of all individuals who are the citizen of Afghanistan.
(3) The nation of Afghanistan is comprised of the following ethnic groups: Pashtun, Tajik, Hazara, Uzbak, Turkman, Baluch, Pashai, Nuristani, Aymaq, Arab, Qirghiz, Qizilbash, Gujur, Brahwui and others.
(4) The word Afghan applies to every citizen of Afghanistan.
(5) No member of the nation can be deprived of his citizenship of Afghanistan.
(6) Affairs related to the citizenship and asylum are regulated by law.

Article 5 [Territorial Integrity]
Implementation of the provisions of this constitution and other laws, defending independence, national sovereignty, territorial integrity, and ensuring the security and defense capability of the country, are the basic duties of the state.

Article 6 [Purposes]
The state is obliged to create a prosperous and progressive society based on social justice, protection of human dignity, protection of human rights, realization of democracy, and to ensure national unity and equality among all ethnic groups and tribes and to provide for balanced development in all areas of the country.

Article 7 [International Law]
(1) The state shall abide by the UN charter, international treaties, international conventions that Afghanistan has signed, and the Universal Declaration of Human Rights.
(2) The state prevents all types of terrorist activities, production and consumption of intoxicants (muskirat), production and smuggling of narcotics.

Article 8 [State Policy]
The state regulates the policy of the country on the basis of preserving the independence, national interests, territorial integrity, non-aggression, good neighborliness, mutual respect, and equal rights.

Article 9 [Natural Resources]
(1) Mines, underground resources are properties of the state.
(2) Protection, use, management, and mode of utilization of the public properties shall be regulated by law.

Article 10 [Private Investments]
The State encourages and protects private capital investments and enterprises based on the market economy and guarantees their protection in accordance with the provisions of law.

Article 11 [Trade]
Affairs related to the domestic and external trade shall be regulated by law in accordance with the needs of the national economy and public interests.

Article 12 [Bank]
(1) Da Afghanistan Bank is the central and independent bank of the state.
(2) Issuance of currency, and formulation and implementation of monetary policy of the country are the mandates of the central bank in accordance with law.
(3) The central bank shall consult with the economic committee of the House of Representatives [*Wolesi Jirga*] in matters related to the printing of money.
(4) Structure and operation of this bank shall be regulated by law.

Article 13 [Economy]

The state shall formulate and implement effective programs for development of industries, growth of production, increasing of public living standards, and support to craftsmanship.

Article 14 [Farming, Housing]
(1) The state shall design and implement within its financial resources effective programs for development of agriculture and animal husbandry, improving the economic, social and living conditions of farmers, herders, settlement and living conditions of nomads.
(2) The state adopts necessary measures for housing and distribution of public estates to deserving citizens in accordance within its financial resources and the law.

Article 15 [Environment]
The state is obliged to adopt necessary measures for safeguarding forests and the environment.

Article 16 [Languages]
(1) From among the languages of Pashtu, Dari, Uzbeki, Turkmani, Baluchi, Pashai, Nuristani, Pamiri (alsana), Arab and other languages spoken in the country, Pashtu and Dari are the official languages of the state.
(2) The Turkic languages (Uzbaki and Turkmen), Baluchi, Pashai, Nuristani and Pamiri (alsana) are -- in addition to Pashto and Dari -- the third official language in areas where the majority speaks them. The practical modalities for implementation of this provision shall be specified by law.
(3) The state adopts and implements effective plans for strengthening, and developing all languages of Afghanistan.
(4) Publications and radio and television broadcasting are allowed in all languages spoken in the country.

Article 17 [Education]
The state shall adopt necessary measures for promotion of education in all levels, development of religious education, organizing and improving the conditions of mosques, madrasas and religious centers.

Article 18 [Calendar]
(1) The calendar of the country shall be based on the flight of the Prophet (PBUH).
(2) The basis of work for state offices is the solar calendar.
(3) Fridays and the 28 Asad and the 8 Sawr are public holidays. Other holidays shall be regulated by law.

Article 19 [Flag, Insignia, Emblem]
(1) The Afghan flag is made up of three equal parts, with black, red and green colors juxtaposed from left to right perpendicularly.
(2) The width of every colored piece is equal to half of its length. The national insignia is located in the center of the flag.
(3) The national insignia of the state of Afghanistan is composed of Mehrab and pulpit in white color.
(4) Two flags are located on its two sides. In the upper-middle part of the insignia the sacred phrase of "There is no God but Allah and Mohammad is his prophet, and Allah is Great" is placed, along with a rising sun. The word "Afghanistan" and year 1298 (solar calendar) is located in the lower part of the insignia. The insignia is encircled with two branches of wheat.
(5) The law shall regulate the use of national flag and emblem.

Article 20 [Anthem]
The National Anthem of Afghanistan shall be in Pashtu and mention "Allahu Akbar" and the names of the ethnic groups of Afghanistan.

Article 21 [Capital]
The capital of Afghanistan is the city of Kabul.

CHAPTER II FUNDAMENTAL RIGHTS AND DUTIES OF CITIZENS

Article 22 [Equality]
(1) Any kind of discrimination and privilege between the citizens of Afghanistan are prohibited.
(2) The citizens of Afghanistan -- whether man or woman -- have equal rights and duties before the law.

Article 23 [Life]
Life is a gift of God and a natural right of human beings. No one shall be deprived of this right except by the provision of law.

Article 24 [Liberty, Human Dignity]
(1) Liberty is the natural right of human beings. This right has no limits unless affecting the rights of others or public interests, which are regulated by law.
(2) Liberty and dignity of human beings are inviolable.
(3) The state has the duty to respect and protect the liberty and dignity of human beings.

Article 25 [Presumption of Innocence]
(1) Innocence is the original state.
(2) An accused is considered innocent until convicted by a final decision of an authorized court.

Article 26 [Criminal Responsibility]
(1) Crime is a personal action.
(2) The prosecution, arrest, and detention of an accused and the execution of penalty can not affect another person.

Article 27 [Punishment]
(1) No act is considered a crime, unless determined by a law adopted prior to the date the offense is committed.
(2) No person can be pursued, arrested or detained but in accordance with provisions of law.
(3) No person can be punished but in accordance with the decision of an authorized court and in conformity with the law adopted before the date of offense.

Article 28 [Extradition]
(1) No citizen of Afghanistan accused of a crime can be extradited to a foreign state unless according mutual agreement and international conventions that Afghanistan has joined.
(2) No Afghan would be sentenced to deprivation of citizenship or to exile inside the country or abroad.

Article 29 [Torture]
(1) Torture of human beings is prohibited.
(2) No person, even with the intention of discovering the truth, can resort to torture or order the torture of another person who may be under prosecution, arrest, or imprisoned, or convicted to punishment.
(3) Punishment contrary to human integrity is prohibited.

Article 30 [Compulsion, Confession]
(1) Any statement, testimony, or confession obtained from an accused or of another person by means of compulsion, are invalid.

(2) Confession to a crime is: a voluntary confession before an authorized court by an accused in a sound state of mind.

Article 31 [Defence]
(1) Every person upon arrest can seek an advocate to defend his rights or to defend his case for which he is accused under the law.
(2) The accused upon arrest has the right to be informed of the attributed accusation and to be summoned to the court within the limits determined by law.
(3) In criminal cases, the state shall appoint an advocate for a destitute.
(4) The confidentiality of oral, written or telephonic communications between an advocate and his accused client are immune from invasion.
(5) The duties and authorities of advocates shall be regulated by law.

Article 32 [Debt Relief]
(1) Being in debt does not limit a person's freedom or deprive him of his liberties.
(2) The mode and means of recovering a debt shall be regulated by law.

Article 33 [Electoral Rights]
(1) The citizens of Afghanistan have the right to elect and be elected.
(2) Law regulates the conditions and means to exercise this right.

Article 34 [Expression, Press, Media]
(1) Freedom of expression is inviolable.
(2) Every Afghan has the right to express his thought through speech, writing, or illustration or other means, by observing the provisions stated in this Constitution.
(3) Every Afghan has the right to print or publish topics without prior submission to the state authorities in accordance with the law.
(4) Directives related to printing house, radio, television, press, and other mass media, will be regulated by the law.

Article 35 [Organizations, Parties]
(1) The citizens of Afghanistan have the right to form social organizations for the purpose of securing material or spiritual aims in accordance with the provisions of the law.
(2) The citizens of Afghanistan have the right to form political parties in accordance with the provisions of the law, provided that:
-- The program and charter of the party are not contrary to the principles of sacred religion of Islam, and the provisions and values of this Constitution.
-- The organizational structure, and financial sources of the party are made public.
-- The party does not have military or paramilitary aims and structures.
-- The party should have no affiliation to a foreign political party or sources.
(3 Formation and functioning of a party based on ethnicity, language, Islamic school of thought (mazhab-i fiqhi) and region is not permissible.
(4 A party set up in accordance with provisions of the law shall not be dissolved without lawful reasons and the decision of an authorized court.

Article 36 [Demonstration]
The citizens of Afghanistan have the right to un-armed demonstrations, for legitimate peaceful purposes.

Article 37 [Confidentiality of Communication]
(1) Confidentiality and freedom of correspondence and communication whether in the form of letters or through telephone, telegraph and other means, are immune from invasion.
(2) The state does not have the right to inspect personal correspondence and communication unless authorized by the provisions of law.

Article 38 [Residence, Home, Search]
(1) A person's residence is immune from invasion.
(2) Other than the situations and methods indicated in the law, no one, including the state, are allowed to enter or inspect a private residence without prior permission of the resident or holding a court order.
(3) In case of an evident crime, an official in-charge of the situation can enter or conduct a house search prior to the permission of the court.
(4) The official involved in the situation is required to obtain a subsequent court order for the house search within the period indicated by law.

Article 39 [Movement, Settlement, Travel]
(1) Every Afghan has the right to travel or settle in any part of the country except in the regions forbidden by law.
(2) Every Afghan has the right to travel abroad and return home in accordance with the provisions of law.
(3) The state shall protect the rights of the citizens of Afghanistan abroad.

Article 40 [Private Property]
(1) Property is immune from invasion.
(2) No person shall be forbidden from acquiring and making use of a property except within the limits of law.
(3) Nobody's property shall be confiscated without the provisions of law and the order of an authorized court.
(4) Acquisition of a person's property, in return for a prior and just compensation within the bounds of law, is permitted only for securing public interests in accordance with the provisions of law.
(5) Inspection and disclosure of a private property are carried out only in accordance with the provisions of law.

Article 41 [Property of Foreigners]
(1) Foreign individuals do not have the right to own immovable property in Afghanistan.
(2) Lease of immovable property for the purpose of investment is permissible in accord with law.
(3) The sale of estates to diplomatic missions of foreign countries and to those international agencies, of which Afghanistan is a member, is permissible in accordance with the provisions of law.

Article 42 [Taxes, Duties]
(1) Every Afghan is obligated to pay taxes and duties to the government in accordance with the provisions of law.
(2) No taxes and duties are enforced without provisions of law.
(3) The rate of taxes and duties and the method of payment are determined by law on the basis of observing social justice.
(4) This provision is also applied to foreign individuals and agencies.
(5) Every kind of tax, duties, and incomes collected, shall be delivered to the State account.

Article 43 [Education]
(1) Education is the right of all citizens of Afghanistan, which shall be provided up to the level of the B.A. (lisâns), free of charge by the state.
(2) The state is obliged to devise and implement effective programs for a balanced expansion of education all over Afghanistan, and to provide compulsory intermediate level education.
(3) The state is also required to provide the opportunity to teach native languages in the areas where they are spoken.

Article 44 [Education for Women and Nomads, Illiteracy]
The state shall devise and implement effective programs for balancing and promoting of education for women, improving of education of nomads and elimination of illiteracy in the country.

Article 45 [Unified Educational Curriculum]
The state shall devise and implement a unified educational curriculum based on the provisions of the sacred religion of Islam, national culture, and in accordance with academic principles, and develops the curriculum of religious subjects on the basis of the Islamic sects existing in Afghanistan.

Article 46 [Higher Education, Schools]
(1) Establishing and operating of higher, general and vocational education are the duties of the state.
(2) The citizens of Afghanistan also can establish higher, general, and vocational private educational institutions and literacy courses with the permission of the state.
(3) The state can also permit foreign persons to set up higher, general and vocational educational private institutes in accordance with the law.
(4) The conditions for admission to state higher education institutions and other related matters to be regulated by the law.

Article 47 [Science, Culture, Literature, Arts]
(1) The state shall devise effective programs for the promotion of science, culture, literature and the arts.
(2) The state guarantees the rights of authors, inventors, and discoverers, and encourages and supports scientific researches in all areas, and publicizes the effective use of their results in accordance with the law.

Article 48 [Work]
(1) Work is the right of every Afghan.
(2) Working hours, paid holidays, right of employment and employee, and other related affairs are regulated by law.
(3) Choice of occupation and craft is free within the limits of law.

Article 49 [Forced Labor]
(1) Forced labor is forbidden.
(2) Active participation, in times of war, calamity, and other situations threatening lives and public welfare is one of the primary duties of every Afghan.
(3) Children shall not be subjected to forced labor.

Article 50 [Public Administration, Offices, Information]
(1) The state is obliged to adopt necessary measures for creation of a strong and sound administration and realization of reforms in the administration system of the country after authorisation by the National Assembly.
(2) Government offices are bound to carry their work with full neutrality and incompliance with the provisions of law.
(3) The citizens of Afghanistan have the right of access to the information from the government offices in accordance with the provisions of law.
(4) This right has no limits, unless violation of the rights of the others.
(5) The citizens of Afghanistan are employed for state services on the basis of qualification without any kind of discrimination and in accordance with law.

Article 51 [Compensation]
(1) Any person suffering undue harm by government action is entitled to compensation, which he

can claim by appealing to court.
(2) With the exception of situation stated in the law, the state cannot claim its right without the order of an authorized court.

Article 52 [Health Care, Hospitals, Physical Education, Sports]
(1) The state is obliged to provide free means of preventive health care and medical treatment, and proper health facilities to all citizens of Afghanistan in accordance with the law.
(2) The state encourages and protects the establishment and expansion of private medical services and health centers in accordance with law.
(3) The state in order to promote physical education and improve national and local sports adopts necessary measures.

Article 53 [Handicapped]
(1) The state takes necessary measures for regulating medical services and financial support to descendants of those who were martyred or are missing, to disabled or handicapped, and their active participation and re-integration into society in accordance with the law.
(2) The state guarantees the rights and privileges of pensioners and disabled and handicapped individuals and as well renders necessary assistance to needy elders, women without caretakers, and needy orphans in accordance with the law.

Article 54 [Family]
(1) Family is a fundamental unit of society and is supported by the state.
(2) The state adopts necessary measures to ensure physical and psychological well being of family, especially of child and mother, upbringing of children and the elimination of traditions contrary to the principles of sacred religion of Islam.

Article 55 [Defense, Military Service]
(1) The defense of the country is the responsibility of all citizens of Afghanistan.
(2) The conditions for military services are regulated by law.

Article 56 [Obeying the Law]
(1) Observing the provisions of the Constitution, obeying the laws, adhering to public law and order are the duties of all people of Afghanistan.
(2) Ignorance about the provisions of law is not considered an excuse.

Article 57 [Rights of Foreigners]
(1) The state guarantees the rights and liberties of the foreign citizens residing in Afghanistan in accordance with the law.
(2) These people are obliged to observe the laws of the state of Afghanistan in accordance with the International Law.

Article 58 [Human Rights Commission]
(1) The State, for the purpose of monitoring the observation of human rights in Afghanistan, to promote their advancement (behbud) and protection, shall establish the Independent Human Rights Commission of Afghanistan.
(2) Any person, whose fundamental rights have been violated can file complaint to the Commission.
(3) The Commission can refer cases of violation of human rights to the legal authorities, and assist in defending the rights of the complainant.
(4) The structure, and functions of this Commission shall be regulated by law.

Article 59 [Misuse of Rights]
No one can misuse the rights and freedoms under this Constitution against the independence, territorial integrity, sovereignty and national unity.

CHAPTER III THE PRESIDENT

Article 60 [Head of State, Vice Presidents]
(1) The President is the head of state of the Islamic Republic of Afghanistan, and conducts his authorities in executive, legislative, and judiciary branches in accordance with the provisions of this Constitution.
(2) The President shall have two Vice Presidents, one first and one second.
(3) The candidate to the Presidency on his or her candidacy shall declare the name of the Vice Presidents to the nation.
(4) The Vice President in the absence, resignation, and or death of the President, acts in accordance with the provisions of this constitution.

Article 61 [Direct Election]
(1) The President is elected by receiving more than 50% of the votes cast through free, general, secret, and direct voting.
(2) The presidential term is expired at the first of Jawza of the fifth years after the elections.
(3) Elections for the new president are held within thirty, to sixty days before the end of the presidential term.
(4) If none of the candidates succeeds to receive more than 50% of the votes in the first round, a run-off election shall be held within two weeks.
(5) In this round, only two candidates with the highest number of votes will participate.
(6) In the run-off, the candidate who gets the majority of the votes shall be elected as the President.
(7) In case of death of one of the candidates during the first or second round, after the elections or prior to the announcement of the results of elections, new elections shall be held in accordance with the provisions of law.
(8) The elections for the post of president shall be held under the supervision of the Independent Commission supervising of the Elections.
(9) This Commission shall be established to supervise all elections and referendums in the country, in accordance with the provisions of law.

Article 62 [Qualifications]
(1) Presidential candidates should posses the following qualification:
-- Should be citizen of Afghanistan, Muslim and born of Afghan parents, and should not have citizenship of another country.
-- On the day of becoming a candidate, his age should not be less than forty years.
-- Should not have been convicted of crimes against humanity, criminal act, or deprivation of the civil rights by a court.
(2) No one can be elected as president for more than two terms.
(3) The provision of this article is applied to the Vice Presidents as well.

Article 63 [Oath of Allegiance]
The President-elect, prior to resumption of his/her duties, performs the following oath of allegiance in the presence of members of the National Assembly and the chief justice:
"In the name Allah, the Merciful, the Compassionate
In the name God Almighty, in the presence of you representatives of the nation of Afghanistan, I swear to obey and safeguard the provisions of the sacred religion of Islam, to observe the Constitution and other laws of Afghanistan and supervise their implementation; to safeguard the independence, national sovereignty, and the territorial integrity of Afghanistan and the fundamental rights and interests of the people of Afghanistan, and with the assistance of God and the support of the nation, to make great and sincere efforts for the happiness and progress of the people of Afghanistan."

Article 64 [Powers and Duties]
The powers and duties of the President are as follows:
-- Supervising the implementation of the Constitution.
-- Determining the fundamental policies of the state with the approval of the National Assembly.
-- Being the Command-in-Chief of the armed forces of Afghanistan.
-- Declaration of war and ceasefire with the approval of the National Assembly.
-- Taking the required decision during defending of territorial integrity and protecting of the independence.
-- Sending contingents of the armed forces to foreign countries with the approval of the National Assembly.
-- Convening Grand Council [*Loya Jirga*] except in a situation stated in Article 68 of this Constitution.
-- Declaring the state of emergency and ending it with the approval of the National Assembly.
-- Inaugurating the National Assembly and the Grand Council [*Loya Jirga*].
-- Accepting resignation of the Vice President.
-- Appointing of Ministers, the Attorney General, the Director of the Central Bank, Head of the National Security Directorate and the President of the Afghan Red Crescent Society with the approval of the House of Representatives [*Wolesi Jirga*], and acceptance of their dismissal and resignation.
-- Appointing the head and members of the Supreme Court with the approval of the House of Representatives [*Wolesi Jirga*].
-- Appointment, retirement and acceptance of resignation and dismissal of judges, officers of the armed forces, police, national security, and high-ranking officials in accordance with the law.
-- Appointment of heads of diplomatic missions of Afghanistan in foreign countries and international organizations.
-- Accepting the credentials of diplomatic missions in Afghanistan.
-- Signing of laws and legislative decrees.
-- Issuing credential letter for the conclusion of bi-lateral and international treaties in accordance with the provisions of law.
-- Reducing and pardoning penalties in accordance with law.
-- Issuing medals, and honorary titles in accordance with the provision of law.
-- The establishment of commissions for the improvement of the administrative condition of the country, in accordance with law.
-- Exercising other authorities in accordance with the provisions of this Constitution.

Article 65 [Call for Referendum]
(1) The President can call for a referendum on important national, political, social or economic issues.
(2) Call for referendum shall not be contrary to the provisions of this constitution or for the amendment of it.

Article 66 [Restrictions]
(1) The President takes into consideration the supreme interests of the people of Afghanistan while enforcing the powers stated in this Constitution.
(2) The President cannot sell or bestow state properties without the provisions of the law.
(3) The President cannot act based on linguistic, ethnic, religious, political, and regional considerations during his term in office.

Article 67 [Resignation]
(1) In case of resignation, impeachment, or death of the President, or of a serious illness that could hinder the performance of duties, the First Vice President undertakes his duties and authorities.
(2) The President declares his resignation personally to the National Assembly.
(3) The serious illness shall be proved by an authorized medical committee appointed by the

Supreme Court.
(4) In this case, election for the new President shall be held within the period of three months in accordance with the Article 61 of this constitution.
(5) During the time when the First Vice President fills in as the interim President, he cannot perform the following:
-- Amendment of the constitution
-- Dismissal of ministers.
-- Call for a referendum.
(6) During this period the Vice Presidents can nominate themselves as candidates for the post of President in accordance with the provisions of this constitution.
(7) In the absence of the President, the duties of the First Vice President shall be determined by the President.

Article 68 [Replacement]
(1) In case of resignation and or death of one of the Vice President, another person shall replace him by the proposal of the President and approval of the House of Representatives [*Wolesi Jirga*].
(2) In case of simultaneously death of the President and First Vice President, his duties shall be implemented in turn by the Second Vice President, by the Chair of the Senate [*Meshrano Jirga*] and in the absence of the chair of the Senate [*Meshrano Jirga*], Chair of the House of Representatives [*Wolesi Jirga*], and in the absence of the Chair of the House of Representatives [*Wolesi Jirga*], the Foreign Minister shall take the duties of the President in accordance with the Article 67 of this constitution.

Article 69 [Impeachment]
(1) The President is responsible to the nation and the House of Representatives [*Wolesi Jirga*] in accordance with this article.
(2) Accusations of crime against humanity, national treason or crime can be leveled against the President by one third of the members of the House of Representatives [*Wolesi Jirga*].
(3) If two third of the House of Representatives [*Wolesi Jirga*] votes for charges to be brought forth, the House of Representatives [*Wolesi Jirga*] shall convene a Grand Council [*Loya Jirga*] within one month.
(4) If the Grand Council [*Loya Jirga*] approve the accusation by a two-thirds majority of votes the President is then dismissed, and the case is referred to a special court.
(5) The special court is composed of three members of the House of Representatives [*Wolesi Jirga*], and three members of the Supreme Court appointed by the Grand Council [*Loya Jirga*] and the Chair of the Senate [*Meshrano Jirga*].
(6) The lawsuit is conducted by a person appointed by the Grand Council [*Loya Jirga*].
(7) In this situation, the provisions of Article 67 of this Constitution are applied.

Article 70 [Salary]
(1) The salary and expenditures of the President are regulated by law.
(2) After expiration of his term, the President is entitled to financial benefits of the presidency for the rest of his life in accordance with the law except in the case of dismissal.

CHAPTER IV THE GOVERNMENT

Article 71 [Ministers]
(1) The government consists of the ministers who work under the Chairmanship of the President.
(2) Ministers are appointed by the President and shall be introduced for approval to the National Assembly.

Article 72 [Qualifications]
The person who is appointed as the Minister, should have the following qualifications:

-- Must have only the citizenship of Afghanistan. Should a nominee for a ministerial post also hold the citizenship of another country, the House of Representatives [*Wolesi Jirga*] shall have the right to confirm or reject his or her nomination.
-- Should have higher education, work experience and, good reputation.
-- His age should not be less than thirty-five.
-- Should not have been convicted of crimes against humanity, criminal act, or deprivation of civil rights by a court.

Article 73 [Incompatibility]
(1) The Ministers can be appointed from within and without the National Assembly.
(2) If a member of the National Assembly is appointed as a minister, he loses his membership in the National Assembly, and is replaced by another person in accordance with the provisions of law.

Article 74 [Oath of Office]
Prior to taking office, the minister perform the following oath in the presence of the President:
"In the name of Allah, the merciful and compassionate:
I swear in the name of God Almighty to support the provisions of the sacred religion of Islam, follow the Constitution and other laws of Afghanistan, protect the rights of citizens, and safeguard the independence, territorial integrity and national unity of Afghanistan, and consider God Almighty present in performing all my responsibilities, and honestly perform the duties assigned to me."

Article 75 [Duties of the Government]
The government has the following duties.
-- Execute the provision of this Constitution, other laws, and final orders of the courts.
-- Protect the independence, defend the territorial integrity, and safeguard the interests and dignity of Afghanistan in the international community.
-- Maintenance of public law and order and elimination of administrative corruption.
-- Prepare the budget, regulate financial affairs, and protect public wealth.
-- Devise and implement programs for social, cultural, economic, and technological progress.
-- Report to the National Assembly at the end of the fiscal year about the tasks accomplished and about the main plans for the new fiscal year.
-- Perform other duties as recognized by this Constitution and other laws to be duties of the government.

Article 76 [Regulations]
(1) In order to implement the main policies of the country, and regulation of its duties, the government shall devise and approve regulations.
(2) These regulations should not be contradictory to the text and spirit of any law.

Article 77 [Heads of Administrative Units]
(1) As heads of administrative units and members of the government, the ministers perform their duties within the limits determined by this Constitution and other laws.
(2) The Ministers are responsible to the President and the House of Representatives [*Wolesi Jirga*] for their particular duties.

Article 78 [Impeachment]
If a Minister is accused of crime against humanity, national treason or criminal act of a crime, the case shall be referred to a special court in accordance with the Article 134 of this constitution.

Article 79 [Emergency Legislation by Decree]
(1) In cases of recess of the House of Representatives [*Wolesi Jirga*], the government can adopt legislation in an emergency situation on matters other than those related to budget and financial

affairs.
(2) The legislative decrees become laws after they are signed by the President.
(3) The legislative decrees should be submitted to the National Assembly in the course of thirty days beginning from the first session of the National Assembly.
(4) In case of rejection by the National Assembly, the legislations become void.

Article 80 [Restrictions]
The Minister during the course of their work cannot use their posts for linguistic, regional, ethnic, religion and partisan purposes.

CHAPTER V THE NATIONAL ASSEMBLY

Article 81 [National Assembly]
(1) The National Assembly of the Islamic Republic of Afghanistan as the highest legislative organ is the manifestation of the will of its people and represents the whole nation.
(2) Every member of the National Assembly takes into judgment the general welfare and supreme interests of all people of Afghanistan at the time of casting their vote.

Article 82 [Two Houses]
(1) The National Assembly consists of two houses: House of Representatives [*Wolesi Jirga*] (the House of People) and Senate [*Meshrano Jirga*]. (House of Elders).
(2) No one can become member of both houses simultaneously.

Article 83 [House of Representatives]
(1) Members of the House of Representatives [*Wolesi Jirga*] are elected by the people through free, general, secret, and direct elections.
(2) Their mandate ends on the 1st of Saratan of the fifth year after the elections, and the new assembly starts its work.
(3) The election of the members of the House of Representatives [*Wolesi Jirga*] shall be held within 30 to 60 days before the expiry of the term of the House of Representatives [*Wolesi Jirga*].
(4) The number of members of the House of Representatives [*Wolesi Jirga*], proportionate to the population of each region, shall be not more than two hundred and fifty.
(5) Electoral constituency and other related issues shall be determined by election laws.
(6) In the election law measures should be adopted for so the election system shall provide general and just representation for all the people of the country, and at least two female delegate should be elected from each province.

Article 84 [Senate]
(1) Members of the Senate [*Meshrano Jirga*] are elected and appointed as follows:
(2) From among the members of each provincial council, the respective council elects one person for a period of four years.
(3) From among the district councils of each province, the respective councils elect one person for a period of three years.
(4) The President from among experts and experienced personalities -- including two representatives from the disabled and impaired and two representatives from the Kochis -- appoints the remaining one-third of the members for a period of five years.
(5) The president appoints 50% of these people from among women.
(6) A person, who is appointed as a member of the Senate [*Meshrano Jirga*], shall relinquish his membership in the respective council, and another person replaces him in accordance with the law.

Article 85 [Qualifications]
(1) A person who is nominated or appointed as a member of the National Assembly should have

the following qualifications in addition to those considered by voters.
(2) Should be the citizen of Afghanistan, or has obtained the citizenship of the state of Afghanistan at least ten years before becoming a candidate.
(3) Should not have been convicted by a court for committing a crime against humanity, a crime, or sentenced of deprivation of his civil rights .
(4) Members of House of Representatives [*Wolesi Jirga*] should be Twenty Five years old at the date of candidacy, and members of the Senate [*Meshrano Jirga*] should be Thirty Five years old at the date of candidacy or appointment.

Article 86 [Independent Electoral Commission]
Credentials of members of the National Assembly are reviewed by the Independent Electoral Commission in accordance with law.

Article 87 [Chairperson]
(1) In the beginning of the legislative period, each one of the two houses elects one of its members as the Chairperson, and two people as the first and second Vice Chairperson, and two people as the secretary and assistant secretary for a period of one year.
(2) These individuals constitute the administrative board in their respective houses.
(3) The duties of the administrative boards are determined in the regulations pertaining to the internal duties of each house.

Article 88 [Commissions]
Each house of the National Assembly sets up commissions to study the topics under discussion in accordance with its internal regulations.

Article 89 [Special Commission for Inquiry]
(1) The House of Representatives [*Wolesi Jirga*] has the authority to set up a special commission if one-third of its members put forward a proposal to inquire about and study government actions.
(2) The composition and procedure of this commission shall be specified by the internal regulations of the House of Representatives [*Wolesi Jirga*].

Article 90 [Powers of then National Assembly]
The National Assembly has the following powers:
-- Ratification, modification, or abrogation of laws and or legislative decrees.
-- Approval of plans for economic, social, cultural, and technological development.
-- Approval of state budget, permission for obtaining, and granting loans.
-- Creation, modification of administrative units.
-- Ratification of international treaties and agreements, or abrogation of the membership of Afghanistan to them.
-- Other authorities specified in this Constitution.

Article 91 [Powers of the House of Representatives]
House of Representatives [*Wolesi Jirga*] has the following special powers:
-- Deciding on interpellation of each of the ministers in accordance with the provisions of Article 92 of this constitution.
-- Taking the final decision about the state's development programs and state budget, in case of a disagreement between the House of Representatives [*Wolesi Jirga*] and the Senate [*Meshrano Jirga*].
-- Approval of the appointments according to the provisions of this constitution.

Article 92 [Interpellation, Vote of No Confidence]
(1) House of Representatives [*Wolesi Jirga*], based on a proposal by one-tenth of all members, can interpellate each of the Ministers.
(2) If the responses given are not satisfactory, House of Representatives [*Wolesi Jirga*] shall

consider the issue of vote of no confidence.
(3) Vote of no confidence on a Minister should be explicit, direct, and on the basis of well founded reasons.
(4) This vote should be approved by a majority of all members of the House of Representatives [*Wolesi Jirga*].

Article 93 [Questioning]
(1) Any commission of both Houses of the National Assembly can question each of the Ministers about specific topics.
(2) The person questioned can provide verbal or written response.

Article 94 [Legislation, Veto, Qualified Vote]
(1) Law is what both Houses of the National Assembly approve and the President endorses unless this Constitution states otherwise.
(2) In case the President does not agree to what the National Assembly approves, he or she can send the document back with justifiable reasons to the House of Representatives [*Wolesi Jirga*] within fifteen days of its submission.
(3) With the passage of this period or in case the House of Representatives [*Wolesi Jirga*] approves a particular case again with a majority of two-thirds votes, the bill is considered endorsed and enforced.

Article 95 [Initiatives]
Proposal for the promulgation of a law can be initiated by the government, or members of the National Assembly, and in the domain of regulating the judicial affairs through the Supreme Court by the government.

Article 96 [Financial Affairs]
Proposal for budget and financial affairs are initiated only by the government.

Article 97 [Form and Procedure]
(1) Proposals for promulgation of law initiated by the government are submitted first to the House of Representatives [*Wolesi Jirga*].
(2) If a proposal for the promulgation of law includes imposition of new taxes or reduction in state incomes, it is included in the working agenda on condition that an alternative source is also envisioned.
(3) The House of Representatives [*Wolesi Jirga*] approves or rejects the proposal of the promulgation of law including budget and financial affairs and the proposal of taking or giving loan after discussion as a whole.
(4) The House of Representatives [*Wolesi Jirga*] cannot delay the proposal more than one month.
(5) The proposed draft of law is submitted to the Senate [*Meshrano Jirga*], after its approval by the House of Representatives [*Wolesi Jirga*].
(6) The Senate [*Meshrano Jirga*] decides on the draft within a period of fifteen days
(7) The National Assembly shall give priority to the promulgation of laws, treaties, and development plans of the government that require argent consideration and decision as per the request of the government.
(8) If a proposal for promulgation of law is initiated by ten members of one of the two Houses and then approved by one fifth members of the respective houses, it can be admitted to the agenda of the respective houses.

Article 98 [Budget]
(1) The state budget and development plan of the government is submitted through the Senate [*Meshrano Jirga*] along with an advisory comments to the House of Representatives [*Wolesi Jirga*].
(2) The decision of the House of Representatives [*Wolesi Jirga*], irrespective of the consent of the

Senate [*Meshrano Jirga*], is enforceable after it is signed by the President.
(3) If for some reasons the budget is not approved before the beginning of the new fiscal year, the budget of the year before is applied until the approval of the new budget.
(4) The government is obligated to give to the House of Representatives [*Wolesi Jirga*] the budget of the new fiscal year and a brief account of the current year's budget within the forth quarter of the fiscal year.
(5) The definite account of the previous fiscal year shall be submitted by the government to the House of Representatives [*Wolesi Jirga*] within six months of the new year, in accordance with the provisions of law
(6) House of Representatives [*Wolesi Jirga*] cannot delay the approval of the budget for more than one month or permission to give or take loan for more than a 15 days.
(7) If during this period House of Representatives [*Wolesi Jirga*] does not take any decision with regards to taking or giving loan, the proposal will be considered as approved.

Article 99 [Budget Debate]
If, during a session of the National Assembly, the annual budget or a developmental plan or an issue related to public security, territorial integrity, and the country's independence is under discussion, the session of the assembly cannot end before the approval of the matter.

Article 100 [Combined Committee]
(1) In case the decision of one house is rejected by another house, a combined committee composed of equal members of each house is formed to resolve the disagreement.
(2) The decision of the committee is enforced after its approval by the President.
(3) In case the combined committee cannot solve the disagreement, the defeated resolution is considered void. And, if the resolution is approved by the House of Representatives [*Wolesi Jirga*], it can be approved in the next session of the House of Representatives [*Wolesi Jirga*] by the majority of its members.
(4) This approval is assumed as enforceable, after it is signed by the President, without submission to the Senate [*Meshrano Jirga*].
(5) In case the disagreement between the two houses is over legislations involving financial affairs, and the combined committee is not able to resolve it, the House of Representatives [*Wolesi Jirga*] can approve the draft by the majority vote of its members.
(6) This draft is assumed as enforceable without submission to the Senate [*Meshrano Jirga*] after it is signed by the President.

Article 101 [Indemnity]
No member of the National Assembly is legally prosecuted due to expressing his views while performing his duty.

Article 102 [Immunity]
(1) When a member of the National Assembly is accused of a crime, the law enforcement authority informs the house, of which the accused is member, about the case, and the accused member can be prosecuted.
(2) In case of an evident crime, the law enforcement authority can legally pursue and arrest the accused without the permission of the house, which the accused is a member of.
(3) In both cases, when legal prosecution requires detention of the accused, law enforcement authorities are obligated to inform the respective house, about the case immediately.
(4) If the accusation takes place when the assembly is in recess, the permission of arrest is obtained from the administrative board of the respective house and the decision of this board is presented to the first session of the aforementioned house for a decision.

Article 103 [Ministerial Participation]
(1) The ministers can participate in the sessions of each one of the two houses of the National Assembly.

(2) Each house of the National Assembly can demand the participation of Ministers to take part in its session.

Article 104 [Sessions]
(1) Both houses of the National Assembly hold their sessions separately at the same time.
(2) Under the following circumstances, both houses can hold joint sessions:
-- When the legislative session, or the annual session is inaugurated by the President.
-- When it is deemed necessary by the President.
(3) In this case the head of the House of Representatives [*Wolesi Jirga*], chairs the joint session of the National Assembly.

Article 105 [Publicity]
(1) The sessions of the National Assembly are open unless the Chairman of the assembly, or at least ten members of the National Assembly request their secrecy and the assembly accepts this request.
(2) No one shall enter the building of the National Assembly by force.

Article 106 [Quorum]
The quorum for sessions of each house of the National Assembly is a majority of its members, and its decisions are taken by majority of the members present, unless this Constitution states otherwise.

Article 107 [Ordinary and Extraordinary Sessions]
(1) The National Assembly convenes two ordinary sessions each year.
(2) The term of the National Assembly in each year is nine months.
(3) When necessary, the assembly can extend this period.
(4) Extraordinary sessions of the assembly during recess can take place by the order of the President.

Article 108 [Death, Resignation, Dismissal]
(1) In cases of death, resignation or dismissal of a member of the House of Representatives [*Wolesi Jirga*], and/or disability or handicap, which prevents performance of duties permanently, election in the related constituency is held for a new representative for the rest of the legislative period, in accordance with the law.
(2) In the above-mentioned situations, a new member of the Senate [*Meshrano Jirga*] shall be appointed in accordance with Article 87 of this Constitution.
(3) Matters involving the presence or absence of members of the National Assembly are regulated according to internal rules.

Article 109 [Amendments of the Electoral Law]
Proposals for amendments of the electoral law cannot be included in the working agenda of the assembly during the last year of the legislative period.

CHAPTER VI GRAND COUNCIL [*LOYA JIRGA*]

Article 110 [Composition, Participation]
(1) Grand Council [*Loya Jirga*] is the highest manifestation of the people of Afghanistan.
(2) Grand Council [*Loya Jirga*] consists of the following:
-- Members of the National Assembly.
-- Chairpersons of the provincial, and district councils.
(3) The ministers, Chief Justice and members of the Supreme Court, can participate in the sessions of the Grand Council [*Loya Jirga*] without the right to vote.

Article 111 [Powers]
Grand Council [*Loya Jirga*] is convened in the following situations:
-- To take decision on the issues related to independence, national sovereignty, territorial integrity, and supreme interests of the country.
-- To amend the provisions of this Constitution.
-- To prosecute the President in accordance with the provisions of Article 69 of this Constitution.

Article 112 [Chairperson]
The Grand Council [*Loya Jirga*] in its first session elects from among its members a chairperson, a deputy-chair, and a secretary and an assistant secretary.

Article 113 [Quorum]
(1) The quorum of the Grand Council [*Loya Jirga*] for voting is completed by the majority of members.
(2) The decisions of the Grand Council [*Loya Jirga*] are taken by a majority of the present members except in cases as explicitly stated in this Constitution.

Article 114 [Publicity]
Discussions of the Grand Council [*Loya Jirga*] are open except when one--fourth of its members demand their secrecy, and the Grand Council [*Loya Jirga*] accepts this demand.

Article 115 [Indemnity and Immunity]
During the session of a Grand Council [*Loya Jirga*], the provision of Articles 101 and 102 of this Constitution are applied on its members.

CHAPTER VII THE JUDICIARY

Article 116 [Indpendence]
(1) The judicial branch is an independent organ of the state of the Islamic Republic of Afghanistan.
(2) The judicial branch consists of the Supreme Court (*Stera Mahkama*), High Courts, Appeal Courts. Structure of authorities of which are determined by law.
(3) The Supreme Court as the highest judicial organ, heads the judiciary organ of the Islamic Republic of Afghanistan.

Article 117 [Supreme Court]
(1) The Supreme Court is composed of nine members who are appointed by the President for a period of ten years with the approval of the House of Representatives [*Wolesi Jirga*] with observance of the provisions of last paragraph of the Article 50 and Article 118 of this Constitution. In the beginning the appointment will be as such:
(2) Three members are appointed for a period of four years, three members for seven years and three members for ten years. Later appointments will be for a period of ten years.
(3) The appointment of the members for the second term is not permissible.
(4) The President appoints one of its members as the Head of the Supreme Court.
(5) Members in no way can be dismissed from their service until the end of their term, except circumstances stated in Article 127 of this Constitution.

Article 118 [Qualifications for the Supreme Court]
A member of the Supreme Court shall have the following qualifications:
-- The age of the Head of the Supreme Court and its members should not be lower than forty at the time of appointment
-- Shall be a citizen of Afghanistan.

-- Shall have a higher education in law or in Islamic jurisprudence, and shall have sufficient expertise and experience in the judicial system of Afghanistan.
-- Shall have high ethical standards and a reputation of good deeds.
-- Shall not have been convicted of crimes against humanity, crimes, and sentenced of deprivation of his civil rights by a court.
-- Shall not be a member of any political party during the term of official duty.

Article 119 [Oath of Office for the Supreme Court]
Members of the Supreme Court take the following oath in the presence of the President before occupying the post:
"In the name Allah, the Merciful and the Compassionate
I swear in the name of God Almighty to support justice and righteousness in accord with the provisions of the sacred religion of Islam and the provisions of this Constitution and other laws of Afghanistan, and to execute the duty of being a judge with utmost honesty, righteousness and nonpartisanship."

Article 120 [Duty to Decide]
The authority of the judicial organ is to attend to all lawsuits in which real individuals or incorporeal including the state stand before it as plaintiff or defendant and in its presence is expressed in accord with provisions of the law.

Article 121 [Judicial Review]
The Supreme Court upon request of the Government or the Courts can review compliance with the Constitution of laws, legislative decrees, international treaties, and international conventions, and interpret them, in accordance with the law.

Article 122 [Guaranteed Jurisdiction]
(1) No law, under any circumstance, can transfer a case from the jurisdiction of the judicial branch to another organ as has been determined in this Constitution.
(2) This provision does not apply to establishing special Courts stated in Articles 69, 78 and 127 of this Constitution and military courts in matters relating to them.
(3) The structure and authority of these courts are regulated by law.

Article 123 [Judiciary]
With observance of the provisions of this Constitution, the rules related to the structure, authority, and performances of the courts, and the duties of judges are regulated by law.

Article 124 [Judicial Administration]
Other officials and administrative personnel of the judicial branch are subject to the provisions of the laws related to the officials and other administrative personnel of the state, but their appointment, dismissal, promotion, pension, rewards and punishments are regulated by the Supreme Court in accordance with the law.

Article 125 [Judicial Budget]
(1) The budget of the judicial branch is arranged in consultation with the government by the Supreme Court and presented to the National Assembly by the government as part of the state budget.
(2) Implementation of the budget of the judicial branch is the authority of the Supreme Court.

Article 126 [Remuneration of the Supreme Court]
Members of the Supreme Court enjoy official financial benefits for the rest of their lives provided they do not occupy state and political positions.

Article 127 [Judicial Impeachment]

(1) When more than one-third of the members of the House of Representatives [*Wolesi Jirga*] demand the trial of the Chief Justice, or a member of the Supreme Court due to a crime committed during the performance of duty, and the House of Representatives [*Wolesi Jirga*] approves of this demand by a majority of two-thirds votes, the accused is dismissed from his post and the case is referred to a special court.
(2) The setting up of the court and the procedures of trial are regulated by law.

Article 128 [Publicity of Courts]
(1) In the courts of Afghanistan, trials are open and everyone is entitled to attend trials within the bounds of law.
(2) The court, in situations which are stated in the law or in situations in which the secrecy of the trial is deemed necessary, can conduct the trial behind closed doors, but the announcement of the court decision should be open in all instances.

Article 129 [Legal Reasoning, Capital Punishment]
(1) The court is obliged to state the reasons for the decision it issues.
(2) All specific decisions of the courts are enforceable, except for capital punishment, which is conditional upon approval of the President.

Article 130 [Judicial Discretion]
(1) While processing the cases, the courts apply the provisions of this Constitution and other laws.
(2) When there is no provision in the Constitution or other laws regarding ruling on an issue, the courts' decisions shall be within the limits of this Constitution in accord with the *Hanafi* jurisprudence and in a way to serve justice in the best possible manner.

Article 131 [*Shia* Law for *Shia* Followers]
(1) Courts shall apply *Shia* school of law in cases dealing with personal matters involving the followers of *Shia* Sect in accordance with the provisions of law.
(2) In other cases if no clarification by this constitution and other laws exist and both sides of the case are followers of the *Shia* Sect, courts will resolve the matter according to laws of this Sect.

Article 132 [Appointment of Judges]
(1) Judges are appointed with the recommendation of the Supreme Court and approval of the President.
(2) The appointment, transfer, promotion, punishment, and proposals to retire judges are within the authority of the Supreme Court in accordance with the law.
(3) The Supreme Court shall establish the General Administration Office of the Judicial Power for the purpose of better arrangement of the administration and judicial affairs and insuring the required improvements.

Article 133 [Prosecution of Judges]
(1) When a judge is accused of having committed a crime, the Supreme Court shall inquire about the case involving the judge in accordance with the law.
(2) After listening to his defense, when the Supreme Court regards the accusation to be valid, it shall present a proposal about the judge's dismissal to the President.
(3) After the Presidential approval, the accused judge is dismissed from duty, and punished in accordance with the provisions of the law.

Article 134 [Attorney's Office]
(1) Discovery of crimes is the duty of the police and investigation and prosecution are conducted by the Attorney's Office in accordance with the provisions of the law.
(2) The Attorney's Office is part the Executive branch, and is independent in its performances.
(3) The structure, authority, and activities of the Attorney's Office are regulated by law.

(4) Discovery and investigation of crimes related to the armed forces are regulated by a special law.

Article 135 [Trial Language]
If parties involved in a case do not know the language in which the trial is conducted, they have the right to understand the material and documents related to the case through an interpreter and the right to speak in their mother language in the court.

CHAPTER VIII THE ADMINISTRATION

Article 136 [Principles]
(1) The Administration of Islamic Republic of Afghanistan shall be based on central and local administrative units in accordance with the law.
(2) The central administration is divided into a number of administrative units, each of which shall be headed by a minister.
(3) The local administrative unit is a province.
(4) The number, area, parts, and structures of the provinces and the related administrations are regulated by law on the basis of population, social and economic conditions, and geographic location.

Article 137 [Decentralization]
The government, while preserving the principle of centralism, shall -- in accordance with the law -- delegate certain authorities to local administration units for the purpose of expediting and promoting economic, social, and cultural affairs, and increasing the participation of people in the development of the nation.

Article 138 [Provincial Council]
(1) In every province a provincial council is to be formed.
(2) Members of the provincial council are elected in proportion to the population by free, direct, secret ballot, and general elections by the residents of the province for a period of four years in accordance with the law.
(3) The provincial council elects one of its members as Chairman.

Article 139 [Development Targets]
(1) The provincial council takes part in securing the developmental targets of the state and improving its affairs in a way stated in the law, and gives advice on important issues falling within the domain of the province.
(2) Provincial councils perform their duties in cooperation with the provincial administration.

Article 140 [District and Village Councils]
(1) In order to organize activities involving people and provide them with the opportunity to actively participate in the local administration, councils are set up in districts and villages in accordance with the provisions of the law.
(2) Members of these councils are elected by the local people through, free, general, secret and direct elections for a period of three years.
(3) The participation of nomads in these councils is regulated by law.

Article 141 [Municipalities]
(1) Municipalities shall be set up in order to administer city affairs.
(2) The mayor and members of the municipal councils are elected by free, general, secret, and direct elections.
(3) The affairs related to municipalities are regulated by law.

Article 142 [Administrative Departments]
For the purpose of the implementation of the provisions, and ensuring the values of this constitution, the state shall establish the required departments.

CHAPTER IX THE STATE OF EMERGENCY

Article 143 [Declaration]
(1) If due to war, threat of war, serious rebellion, natural disasters, or situations similar to these protecting the independence or nation's survival becomes impossible by following the provision of this Constitution, the President in confirmation of National Assembly shall declare a state of emergency in some or all parts of the country.
(2) If the state of emergency continues for more than two months, the agreement of National Assembly is required for its extension.

Article 144 [Government Authority]
During the state of emergency, the President, with the consultations of heads of the National Assembly, and Chief Justice can transfer some authorities of the National Assembly to the government.

Article 145 [Suspended Provisions]
During the state of emergency, the President with the consent of the heads of the National Assembly and the Supreme Court, can suspend the validity of the following Articles or can place restrictions on them:
1. Paragraph two of Article 27.
2. Article 36.
3. Paragraph two of Article 37.
4. Paragraph two of Article 38.

Article 146 [Prohibition of Constitutional Amendments]
During the state of emergency, the Constitution cannot be amended.

Article 147 [Extended Terms of Office]
(1) If the Presidential term of office, and or the legislative period expire during a state of emergency, the new elections shall be postponed, and the presidency, and the legislative period shall be extended for up to four months.
(2) If the state of emergency continues for more than four months, a Grand Council [*Loya Jirga*] shall be called by the President for further decisions.
(3) Following the termination of state of emergency, election would be held within two months

Article 148 [Invalidation of Emergency Measures]
After the end of the state of emergency, the measures adopted on the basis of Articles 144 and 145 of this Constitution shall be considered invalid immediately.

CHAPTER X AMENDMENTS

Article 149 [Islam, Fundamental Rights]
(1) The provisions of adherence to the fundamentals of the sacred religion of Islam and the regime of the Islamic Republic cannot be amended.
(2) The amendment of the fundamental rights of the people are permitted only in order to make them more effective.

(3) Considering new experiences and requirements of the time, other contents of this Constitution can be amended by the proposal of the President or by the majority of the National Assembly in accordance with the provisions of Article 67 and 146 of this constitution.

Article 150 [Drafting Commission, Grand Council]
(1) In order to implement proposals regarding the amendment of the Constitution, a Commission composed of members of the Government, National Assembly, and the Supreme Court, shall be established by a Presidential decree, and the commission shall prepare a draft of the amendments.
(2) For approval of the amendments, a Grand Council [*Loya Jirga*] shall be convened by the decree of the President in accordance with the provisions of the Chapter on the Loy Jirga.
(3) When the Grand Council [*Loya Jirga*] approves an amendment by a majority of two-thirds of its members, it shall be enforced after endorsement by the President.

CHAPTER XI MISCELLANEOUS PROVISIONS

Article 151 [Economic Incompatibility]
(1) The President, Vice Presidents, Ministers, Head and members of the Supreme Court, Head of the Central Bank, National Security Directorate, Governors and Mayors cannot engage in any profitable business contracts with the government or individuals during their term of office.
(2) Contracts for the purpose of fulfilling personal needs are exception to this provision.

Article 152 [Official Incompatibility]
The President, Vice President, ministers, heads and members of the National Assembly, the Supreme Court, and judges, cannot undertake other jobs during their terms of office.

Article 153 [Party Incompatibility]
Judges, Attorneys, and Officers of the Armed Forces and Police, and members of the National Security, cannot be members of political parties during their terms of office.

Article 154 [Economic Transparency]
Property of the President, Vice Presidents, ministers, members of the Supreme Court and the Attorney General before and after their term of office would be registered and monitored by an organ to be set by law.

Article 155 [Salaries and Remuneration]
For the ministers, members of the National Assembly, the Supreme Court, Attorney General and judges, appropriate salaries shall be paid in accordance with the provisions of law.

Article 156 [Election and Referendum]
The Independent Electoral Commission will be established to organise and supervise any election and to hold a referendum within the country based on the provisions of the law.

Article 157 [Implementation of the Constitution]
The Independent Commission for the Supervision of the Implementation of the Constitution will be established by law. Members of this Commission will be appointed by the President.

CHAPTER XII TRANSITIONAL PROVISIONS

Article 158 [Father of the Nation]
The Title of the Father of the Nation and the privileges granted by the Emergency Grand Council

[*Loya Jirga*] of 1381 (2002) to His Majesty *Mohammad Zahir* Former King of Afghanistan are preserved for him during his lifetime, in accordance with the provisions of this constitution.

Article 159 [Transitional Period]
(1) The period, following the adoption of this Constitution, until the date of inauguration of the National Assembly, is deemed as a transitional period.
(2) During the transitional period, the Islamic Transitional State of Afghanistan shall carry out the following tasks:
-- Issue decrees related to the election of the President, National Assembly and local councils within six months.
-- Issue decrees regarding the structure and authorities of the courts and basic administration structures within one year.
-- Establish an Independent Electoral Commission.
-- Implement the reform of the executive and judiciary.
-- Adopt necessary measures for preparing the ground for enforcement of the provisions of this Constitution.

Article 160 [Presidential Election]
(1) The first elected President takes up his or her duties within thirty days after the result of the election has been proclaimed, in accordance with this constitution.
(2) Every effort shall be made to hold the first presidential election and the parliamentary election at the same time.
(3) Until the establishment of the National Assembly, the powers of the National Assemby outlined in this constitution shall be held by the Government. The interim Supreme Court shall be established by Presidential Decree.

Article 161 [Establishing Institutions]
(1) The National Assembly shall exercise its powers immediately after its establishment in accordance with this constitution.
(2) The Government, and the Supreme Court shall be established within thirty days after the first session of the House of Representatives [*Wolesi Jirga*] is taken place.
(3) The President of the Transitional Islamic State of Afghanistan shall continue his duties until the elected President has taken up office.
(4) The executive and judicial organs of the State in accordance with provisions of paragraph 3 of Article 157 of this constitution shall continue their duties, until the formation of the Government and the Supreme Court.
(5) The decrees enforced from the beginning of the interim period, shall be submitted to the first session of the National Assembly. These decrees are enforceable until annulment by the National Assembly.

Article 162 [Entry Into Force]
(1) This constitution enters into force upon its approval by the Grand Council [*Loya Jirga*], and will be signed and proclaimed by the President of the Transitional Islamic State of Afghanistan.
(2) Upon its enforcement, laws and decrees contrary to the provisions of this constitution are void.

AFGHANISTAN NATIONAL DEVELOPMENT STRATEGY[1]

BASIC INFORMATION

Contacts: Mohammad Sediq Orya, Programme officer (mohammad.sediq.orya@undp.org)

The Afghanistan Compact and the Interim Afghanistan National Development Strategy (IANDS) were both approved at the London Conference in January 2006. The Compact was subsequently endorsed by the UN Security Council.

The preparation phase of the ANDS started in June 2006 and ended in January 2007. This phase was developed between UNDP and the Government of Afghanistan with the financial support from DfID and UNDP core resources. The preparatory phase provided the basis to develop the ANDS work plan, recruiting the national staff and international support teams and consulting and agreeing upon the support and engagement required from the donors for the full programme document.

During this phase, a number of key issues were identified, consulted and addressed during the consultation with the donors. These included the institutional relationship between the ANDS Directorate and the line ministries, overall costed sustainability, national ownership, operating costs, and the ratio of international consultants employed either directly through the project or via parallel mechanisms. In 2007, the original project document has been refined and adjusted in the preparatory phase to incorporate these concerns and signed by the Government of Afghanistan and UNDP management in February 2007. This project focus on support deemed essential for the production of the ANDS and operation of the JCMB Secretariat. Capacity development support to line ministries and other Government agencies – originally a part of the project – will now be undertaken as a separate and complementary initiative.

The main objective of the process is to develop and implement a pro-poor strategy that will be costed, prioritized, sequenced and budgeted and that reflects a broad consensus on national and provincial priorities in order to fight poverty.

During the project period, the Afghan Government will formulate and commence implementation of its National Development Strategy to meet the requirements of a Poverty Reduction Strategy Paper (PRSP). To prepare the ANDS it will develop and implement ministry-based sector strategies to reach the Compact benchmarks. Collectively these strategies will combine to create the full Afghanistan National Development Strategy (ANDS).

Major Achievements

UNDP strongly supported the ANDS/JCMB team in recruitment for provincial consultation officers, sector coordinators, pillar coordinators, communication office and other support staff that strongly contribute to the process of I -ANDS preparation. Regular consultative Group and Working Group meetings are taking place. During the past months, a wide-ranging awareness campaign was initiated on June 24 in parallel to the launch of the sub-national consultations throughout the country in which the sub-national consultations were conducted.

During this consultation process, media packages were disseminated to the local media where the consultations were taking place in different provinces. These packages were also shared with

[1] Afghanistan National Development Strategy 2008-1013

the participants of the sub-national consultations one week prior to the initiation of the consultation.
Support materials for this campaign were being developed. Big billboards advertising the overall development process in Afghanistan were put up in all main cities throughout the country.

During the consultation process, the Ministry of Rural Rehabilitation and Development (MRRD) played the role of facilitator and coordinated the sub-national consultations through UNDP's National Area Based Development (NABDP) project. These series consultations were divided into two sets of workshops. During the first phase of these workshops were dedicated to presenting ministry strategies to the consultation participants for their advice and validation. The second set of workshops focused to develop all essential inputs for provincial development plans (PDPs).

All ministries provided the opportunity to comment on their won strategies received during the sub-national consultations, and ANDS has discussed with all concerned on how to integrate these comments into their ministry strategies.

These consultations were attended by 8,000 participants from all 34 participants, donors, NGOs and Civil Society organizations. On average, approximately 40% of the participants were female.

The first draft of 17 sector strategies had been prepared by line ministries. ANDS sector strategies have been drafted for the following sectors: 1) Agriculture and Rural Development, 2) Information and Communication Technology, 3) Education, 4) Energy, 5) Health, 6) Justice and the Rule of Law, 7) Governance, 8) Media and Culture, 9) Mines and Natural Resources, 10) Private Sector Development, 11) Refugees, Returnees, and IDPs, 12) Religious Affairs, 13) Social Protection, 14) Transport, 15) Water Resource Management, 16) Urban Development, and the 17) Macroeconomic Framework. Strategies have also been written for five cross cutting issues: 1) Gender, 2) Counter-Narcotics, 3) Anti-Corruption, 4) Environment and 5) Regional Cooperation. The preparation of three of the sector strategies – Education, Health, and Transport – has been sped up so that they can be costed and integrated into the 1387 budget.
Based on the request of the ANDS Secretariat UNDP has commenced facilitating a dialogue process with donors and representatives of international organizations on every sector strategy of the ANDS. ANDS secretariat was provided by the outcome of the donor dialogue and a package of consolidated and specific comments from participants.

Future Priorities

• Identifying the costing for the MDG
• Finalizing the sector strategies in consideration of comments received during the donor dialogue.
• Number of donors are engaged in dialogue on the ANDS
• ANDS translated and disseminated nationally and sub-national
• Costing of the prioritized sectoral strategies;
• Recruitment of consultants to work on conflict management and poverty related issues;
• Provide training to CSO and ANDS staff on poverty line, Poverty Gap and measurement;
• ANDS/PRSP production, publication and dissemination at provincial level;
• Development of materials in Pastho/ Dari for the awareness-raising campaigns - including dramas, radio programmes, short movies, media packages, briefing packages for MPs and Civil servants, and Afghan Embassies;
• Organize the training of local media on the MDGs, and the ANDS (newspapers, radios, TV);
• Support to JCMB secretariat establishment;

Partnerships and Resources

Target Budget: USD 8,773,141
Received budget: all donor contributions listed here have been pledged in writing and formalized through signed agreements. So far we received USD 4,580,789 from the following donors. Donors: CIDA USD 1,909, 189, DFID USD 2,337,861 Italy USD 249,688, UN RC 55,000, Norway USD 269,841 (139,417 USD received), Netherlands USD 239,141 and UNDP Core USD 309,000.

IMPORTANT ACHIEVEMENTS

In 2001 Afghanistan was certainly a thoroughly devastated country in virtually every respect. The political, social and economic structures of the country had been severely damaged or completely destroyed. Massive numbers of Afghans had left as refugees, had died during the conflict or were severely disabled. Every family had paid a price – many had to cope with the loss of main breadwinner. For the young people that remained, their education had been disrupted and in many cases, including for all girls and women, ended. Today Afghanistan has among the highest rates of illiteracy in the world. Yet despite these desperate conditions, since 2001 the country has had some remarkable achievements. The progress that has been made should be measured against the desperate conditions that prevailed at the time of the fall of the Taliban. While Afghanistan still faces many enormous challenges, the progress that has been made gives cause for some optimism that with the determination of the Afghan people to rebuild their lives and their country, the transformation to a peaceful and prosperous can be achieved.

The goals of the ANDS for the next five years ought to be viewed against what has been accomplished during the last six years. Only some of the most significant achievements can be mentioned here.

POLITICAL ACHIEVEMENTS:

In 1380 (2001) the Bonn Agreement established a roadmap for the political transformation of Afghanistan to a legitimate democratic state. The targets set in the Bonn Agreement were fully met on time and included:

The Transitional Administration was established to guide the process. It derived its authority through an Emergency Loya Jirga, the first genuinely representative Afghan national meeting in decades.

In 1383 (2004) Afghanistan adopted its first constitution in 30 years, which laid the political and development foundation for the country and established legal protections for private property and a market economy.

Free and fair democratic elections for President, the National Assembly and Provincial Councils were conducted. 76 percent of eligible voters participated in the presidential election. Women were elected to 27

Introduction

1

percent of the seats in the National Assembly.

After the successful completion of the Bonn Agreement, Afghanistan and the international community entered into a new partnership, based upon the Afghanistan Compact, which was agreed at the London Conference of 1384 (2005). The Compact set ambitious goals for comprehensive state building, setting benchmarks in all sectors of security, governance, and development, including the cross-cutting goals of counter-narcotics and regional cooperation.

In 1385 (2006) the new National Assembly began its work, including the approval of a new cabinet; a new Chief Justice and other judges for the Supreme Court; and the National Budget. A new Attorney General with a new mission to fight corruption was appointed. New Provincial Governors were named.

The disarmament, demobilization and reintegration of ex-combatants has been completed. Today the national army and police forces are close to full strength. Afghanistan is no longer a safe haven for terrorists.

SOCIAL AND HUMANITARIAN ACHIEVEMENTS:

Since 1381 (2002), more than five million Afghan refugees have returned home. In 1385 (2006) 342,925 Afghan refugees returned from Pakistan and Iran and 1,004 from other countries. More than 150,000 benefited from the assistance package provided by UNHCR.

The Government has so far distributed 30,000 residential plots of land to needy returning refugee families.

From under one million in 2001 the school population has grown to 5.7 million in 2007 and new enrolments into Grade 1 have ranged between 12-14 percent per annum in the last 5 years. Two million of the children (or 35 percent) enrolled are girls – a 35 percent increase in five years. The number of schools has trebled to 9,062 in 2007 including 1,337 all girls' and 4,325 coeducational schools. Similarly, the number of teachers has increased seven-fold to

142,500 of who nearly 40,000 are female. Fifty thousand of these teachers have received in-service teacher training.

Major advances have been made in extending health care services throughout the country and rebuilding a decimated educational system. The percentage of the population living in districts where the Basic Package of Health Services is being implemented has increased from 9 percent in 2003 to 82 percent in 2006.

Over 2.5 million people have benefited from social protection arrangements covering (i) martyr's families; (ii) disabled with war-related disabilities; (iii) orphans and children enrolled in kindergartens; (iv) victims of natural disasters; (v) pensioners; and (vi) unemployed.

Measurable progress has been achieved since 2003 in improving rural livelihoods. Almost 20,000 km of rural access roads (i.e., all weather, village-to-village and villageto-district centre roads) have been constructed or repaired, increasing access to markets, employment and social services. More than 500,000 households (36 percent of villages) have benefited from small-scale irrigation projects. Currently, 32.5 percent of the rural population has access to safe drinking water and 4,285 improved sanitation facilities have been provided. More than 336,000 households have benefited from improved access to financial services. Some 18,000 CDCs have been established and are implementing community-led development projects. Efforts have made to assist the poorest and most vulnerable.

ECONOMIC ACHIEVEMENTS:

Macroeconomic stability has been maintained, based upon disciplined fiscal and monetary policies. A new unified currency was successfully introduced; inflation has remained low while the exchange rate has been stable.

Sixteen private commercial banks have been licensed; a leasing and financing company is operating; an equity fund is underway to invest in local businesses. There are also thirteen microfinance insti-

tutions providing services to almost 200,000 active clients in 27 provinces.

State owned enterprises are being privatized, corporatized or liquidated.

A lively free and privately owned media have developed and over which people are able to express political views freely – which they do daily.

The legal and commercial infrastructure is being put in place for a market oriented economy.

Electricity capacity has almost doubled compared to 2002.

Over 12,000 kilometers of roads have been rehabilitated, improved, or built. This includes the ring road system, national highways, provincial roads and rural roads.

Kabul International Airport has been expanded and extensively rehabilitated.

Private airlines have entered the aviation sector and established air links throughout the region.

A key bridge investment has opened up direct road links to Tajikistan and greatly reduced transportation times through to Urumqi in China, one of the fastest growing trade hubs in the world.

Two million urban residents have benefited from investments in water supply and 12 percent from investment in sanitation in major cities between 2002 and 2007.

About 35,000 water points 59 networks and 1,713 water reservoirs and 23,884 demonstration latrines have been constructed.

More than three million people have benefited directly from the rural water supply and sanitation activities in the country.

Around a third of the provinces reported some improvement in access to clean drinking water during the consultative process under the ANDS.

Irrigation Rehabilitation has been given high priority over the past four or five years. Of some 2,100 rehabilitation projects, approximately 1,200 have been completed and have been placed back into commercial service.

Major advances have been made in opening up the telecommunications sector to private sector investment under a 'investment friendly' regulatory framework aimed at maintaining a competitive market for services, and phone subscribers have increased from less than 20 thousand to more than 5 million in less than 6 years.

A rapid urbanization process has seen the urban population increase to almost a quarter of the total population. Despite the pressures implied by rapid urbanization, two million urban residents (31 percent of the total urban population) have benefited from investments in water supply and 12 percent from investment in sanitation in major cities between 2002 and 2007.

Afghanistan has world class mineral deposits that are being opened up for exploration and development. The first major investment has recently been announced for developing the Aynak copper deposits in central Logar province, an almost $3 billion investment after an extensive evaluation of tenders from nine major international mining companies.

When seen against the desperate conditions that prevailed in the country in 2001, these achievements constitute an impressive record. The ANDS sets goals for the next five years that will require even greater achievements.

CHALLENGES

Few countries have simultaneously faced the range and extent of challenges with which the people and Government of Afghanistan must now contend. After nearly three decades of continuous conflict the country emerged in late 2001 as a truly devastated state with its human, physical and institutional infrastructure destroyed or severely damaged. At that time the UN Human Development Report ranked Afghanistan as the second poorest country in the World. In addition to the widespread poverty, the Government must deal with continuing threats to security from extremists and terrorists, weak capacity of governance and corruption; a poor environment for private sector investment, the corrosive effects of a large and growing narcotics industry; and major human capacity limitations throughout the public and private sectors. Meeting these challenges and rebuilding the country will take many years and require consistent international support.

The successful transformation of Afghanistan into a secure, economically viable state that can meet the aspirations of the Afghan people, live at peace with itself and its neighbors and contribute to regional and international stability will depend upon the effective utilization of all available human, natural and financial resources. In this partnership a critical role must be played by the private sector. Significantly reducing poverty will require substantially increasing employment which depends on maintaining high rates of economic growth in the years ahead. It is not sufficient to rely on the Government and the international community to sustain the high rates of investment needed to generate the levels of employment to have a major impact on reducing poverty. As the macroeconomic projections presented in Chapter 4 indicate, a substantial increase in private investment will be essential if significant progress is to be realized in meeting the social and economic objectives of the country.

Afghanistan is a country with significant potential for economic development. It has substantial water, agricultural and mineral resources and is well positioned to become a trade and business hub linking the markets of Central Asia, the Middle East, South Asia and China. The potential exists or sustainable economic growth in the future. However, there are a number of fundamental limitations in the economic environment that must be addressed if these efforts are to succeed:

The country's 'hard infrastructure', including roads and reliable supplies of water and power, is inadequate to support rapid and sustained economic growth.

The corresponding 'soft infrastructure', which includes the human and institutional capacity necessary for an economy to function, is also extremely limited. Considerable emphasis is being given to developing capacity in both the public and private sectors and to institutional development, but these efforts will take time.

Economic governance is weak. The Government is pursuing comprehensive economic reform, including the introduction of new commercial laws and regulations, but the establishment of institutions needed for effective implementation and enforcement are largely lacking and will take years to develop.1

Afghanistan's commercial connections to regional and global economies were severely disrupted and must be redeveloped. The development of a competitive private sector will depend on establishing access to foreign markets and developing viable export activities.

Critical markets for land and finance are largely undeveloped, limiting the ability of private investors to establish and operate businesses. Property rights are often contested or difficult to defend.

Afghanistan is experiencing high population. Continued rapid population growth will substantially increase the levels of investment that will be required to substantially reduce poverty.

Both the Government and the international community recognize that prolonged aid dependency will undermine the chances of achieving sustained economic growth and poverty reduction. However, given the major limitations in the economic environment that must be addressed, the successful transition to a competitive market economy will require sustained commitment by the Government, with the support of the international community. Simply creating conditions in which the private sector can operate alone will not be sufficient. Increased efforts by both the Government and the donor community to attract Afghan and foreign investors are needed if the goals of the ANDS are to be realized.

Social and economic development will also be severely curtailed if the insecurity that prevails is not resolved. Despite the considerable efforts by the Government and the international community, security has steadily deteriorated since 2004 in some parts of the country. Ongoing cross-border activities, particularly in the southern and southeastern provinces, have resulted in several areas being effectively off limits to meaningful development assistance.

The lack of stability reduces the ability of aid agencies and the Government to operate in many areas and to effectively implement projects and programs. The impacts of these limitations typically fall most heavily on the poor. Insecurity also increases the cost of doing business and undermines private sector growth and development.[2] The difficulties in maintaining security contribute significantly to two closely related issues: increasing corruption in the public sector and the rapid growth of the narcotics industry. There is a consensus that corruption in Afghanistan is widespread and has been getting worse.[3] Public corruption represents a major disincentive for private investment, substantially increasing the costs and risks of doing business. A lack of security in some parts of the country has created conditions in which poppy cultivation has flourished, feeding a growing narcotics industry that both funds terrorist activity and feeds public corruption. Although poppy cultivation has been greatly reduced in 29 of the 34 provinces, in the remaining five it has seen explosive growth to where Afghanistan accounts for around 90 percent of the world's opium production.

INTERNATIONAL SUPPORT

After the fall of the Taliban, the international community's response was not only military but also began to provide Afghanistan with the institutional and financial resources to start the state building process. In 2006, the Afghanistan Compact agreed between the Government and international community established goals for state building, setting benchmarks in core sectors of security, governance, and development, including the cross-cutting goals of counter-narcotics. To implement its obligations under the Afghanistan Compact, the Government developed the Afghanistan National Development Strategy (ANDS) to clarify existing conditions, establish objectives and define the policies, programs and projects needed to achieve those objections. The international community made new pledges of financial and security assistance and set out to improve its coordination by renewing and upgrading the UN Assistance Mission for Afghanistan (UNAMA), headed by a Special Representative of the Secretary General with enhanced powers for coordination.[4]

The ANDS represents an important milestone in the efforts to rebuilding of Afghanistan which has been underway since late 1380 (2001). During this time there have been a number of reports, conferences and strategies developed to address Afghanistan's challenges.[5] In addition, the Government and the international community have entered into a series of agreements concerning the direction and support for the country's development efforts, including notably the Bonn Agreement, the commitment to the Millennium Development Goals (MDGs) and the Afghanistan Compact. The ANDS builds on all of these and provides a comprehensive and integrated strategy that reflects recent experience and current conditions.

THE AFGHANISTAN NATIONAL DEVELOPMENT STRATEGY

The Afghanistan National Development Strategy (ANDS) represents the combined efforts of the Afghan people and the Afghan Government with the support of the international community to address the major challenges facing the country. To comprehensively address the security, governance, and development needs of Afghanistan, the government has developed the ANDS. The ANDS reflects the government's vision, principles and goals for Afghanistan which builds on its commitment to achieve the Millennium Development Goals by 2020 and the implementation of the Afghanistan Compact benchmarks.

The strategy is based upon an assessment of current social and economic conditions; offers clear intermediate objectives; and identifies the actions that must be taken to achieve these national goals. The ANDS largely focuses on the next five years, but reflects Afghanistan's long-term goals which include the elimination of poverty through the emergence of a vibrant middle class, an efficient and stable democratic political environment and security throughout the country.

Despite the full commitment of the Government and the considerable assistance being provided by the international community, it will not be possible to fully achieve all of these objectives during the next five years. Therefore it is essential that well defined priorities be established that reflect the relative contributions of potential policies, programs and projects towards reaching these goals. This is a difficult process. The contribution of any project to increasing economic growth is uncertain and is inevitably contingent on progress in other areas. It also requires a careful analysis of benefits versus costs with alternative allocations of resources. As a result, the prioritization of activities should be seen as an ongoing process that adapts to changing circumstances and the results of program and project appraisal work on alternative use of resources. In meeting this challenge, the ANDS aims to establish institutional mechanisms that will include the Afghan people, the Government, civil society and the international community in identifying priorities in an evolving environment.

A comprehensive 'bottom-up' approach was used in the development of the ANDS that has taken into account all aspects of social and economic life as well as fully reflecting the diversity of people in all parts of the country. Considerable efforts were made to ensure that sub-national consultations (i.e., outside of the central government in the capital Kabul) identified each of the 34 provinces. In addition, a comprehensive series of sector and ministry strategies were developed that address all aspects of social and economic development. The result of this inclusive process is a national strategy that is fully reflective of the aspirations of the Afghan people. The ANDS is the product of extensive consultations at the national, provincial and local levels. The Government is committed to programs and projects that directly target the poorest and most vulnerable groups for assistance. Well targeted poverty reductions programs are emphasized both in the strategy for social protection and integrated into the design of strategies across the other sectors of the economy.

The overriding objective of the ANDS is to substantially reduce poverty, improve the lives of the Afghan people, and create the foundation for a secure and stable country. This requires building a strong, rapidly expanding economy able to generate the employment opportunities and increasing incomes essential for poverty reduction. The ANDS establishes the Government's strategy and defines the policies, programs and projects that will be implemented over the next five years and the means for effectively implementing, monitoring and evaluating these actions. The goals included in the ANDS are fully consistent with the commitments entered into in previous strategies and agreements and build on the considerable progress that has been achieved since 1380 (2001). While focus of the ANDS is on the next five years, it will continue to adjust to changing circumstances – it is intended to be a 'living document'.

The ANDS serves as the country's Poverty Reduction Strategy Paper (PRSP). As such, it establishes the joint Government/international community commitment to reducing poverty; describes the extent and patterns of poverty that exist; presents the main elements of its poverty reduction strategy; summarizes the projects and programs that will assist the poor; and provide a three-year macroeconomic framework and three-year policy matrix relevant to the poverty reduction efforts. The PRSP has been prepared based on an inclusive consultative process to ensure broad participation and support, while also ensuring policies are based on evidence. A public policy dialogue with all key stakeholders was carried out across all provinces, allowing government officials, private sector representatives, NGOs, the media and ordinary citizens an opportunity to discuss local conditions and concerns. This allowed these communities to participate effectively in defining the poverty problem as they experience it. In so doing, a broader choice of poverty actions based on the specific concerns of the poor have been established for each province, as well as each district.

Key issues identified by stakeholders included:

(i) the lack of access to clean drinking water in all provinces; (ii) the needed improvement in provincial roads; (iii) the poor quality of public services; (iv) poorly trained teachers and doctors; (v) the lack of alternatives to poppy cultivation; (vi) the lack of vocational training for returnees and disabled people; (vii) poor access to electricity; (viii) corruption within the public administration particularly respect to the security services. The Government has examined a range of poverty actions based on the specific concerns of the poor including vulnerability, conflict sensitivity, insecurity and governance.

The ANDS lays out the strategic priorities and the policies, programs and projects for achieving the Government's development objectives. These are organized under three pillars: (i) Security; (ii) Governance, Rule of Law and Human Rights; and (iii) Economic and Social Development.

SECURITY

Security and stability in all parts of the country is essential for economic growth and poverty reduction. Afghanistan still faces a number of serious challenges before it can assume full responsibility for this. International terrorists and domestic extremists prevent the Government from establishing effective control in some areas, particularly in the south and southeast. The large-scale production of narcotics continues to provide funds to these groups. Unexploded ordinance remains a significant threat to Afghans, with some five thousand citizens either killed or wounded in mine explosions since 1380 (2001). Currently only two

The ANDS: An Overview

5

of the country's 34 provinces are completely clear of land mines. A long standing presence of illegal armed groups in different parts of the country is hindering the process of empowerment of local democratic institutions. Some of these groups have close links with police or even belong to local governments. This situation enhances corruption and is considered a key obstacle in cracking down the narcotics industry.

The Government is fully committed to, and is giving the highest priority, to successfully: (i) implementing an integrated and comprehensive national security policy and strategy; (ii) building a robust security sector reform program; (iii) strengthening civil and military operations and coordination; (iv) increasing the role of security forces in counter-narcotics activities; and (v) strengthening the civilian components of security entities. Detailed Compact benchmarks have been established to measure progress in improving capacity within the security organizations and improving security.

Significant progress has been made since 2001 in strengthening the ANA and ANP. For example, militias have been integrated into the Ministry of Defense (MoD), with the majority demobilized. A multi-sector donor support scheme has been established where individual donors are allocated responsibility for overseeing support for each of the key elements of the reform, including: disarmament, demobilization, and reintegration of ex-combatants; military reform; police reform; judicial reform; and counter-narcotics. The ANP has been receiving extensive training and equipment from the international community.

GOVERNANCE, RULE OF LAW, JUSTICE AND HUMAN RIGHTS

In 2000 the World Bank assessed the 'quality' of Afghanistan's governance institutions as falling in the bottom one percent of all countries. Progress since 2001 includes the adoption of the constitution; successful parliamentary and presidential elections, and progress in improving the livelihood and welfare of women and other disenfranchised groups. Despite some progress, a number of significant issues must be addressed, including: (i) the existence of multiple and often parallel structures of state and non-state governance entities; (ii) the confusion over core centre-periphery administration and fiscal relations; (iii) weak public sector institutions and underdeveloped governance and administrative capabilities; (iv) high levels of corruption; (v) fiscal uncertainty; (vi) weak legislative development and enforcement; (vii) weak political and parliamentary oversight capacities; (viii) weak community and civil society institutions; (ix) limited capacity in a justice system; (x) gender inequality; and (xi) underdeveloped human rights enforcement capacities.

If significantly improved governance is not rapidly achieved it will be difficult to make substantial progress with respect to security and economic development. An emerging political and administrative vacuum will be filled by non-state structures driven by illegal and narcotic interests, not by the Government.

RELIGIOUS AFFAIRS

The Government will focus on the following priorities: (i) to improve infrastructure for religious affairs, such as mosques, shrines, holy places, and religious schools; (ii) improve the training and capacity of Imams, preachers, religious teachers and other scholars to raise public awareness and to teach; (iii) finalize a comprehensive culture curriculum for primary and higher education; (iv) strengthen Hajj arrangement systems for Afghan pilgrims; (iv) support efforts by religious organizations to help alleviate poverty and protect vulnerable groups; (v) support efforts of the other government agencies to improve literacy, dispute resolution and to contribute to strengthening of the national solidarity. The expected results include: (i) reforms implemented in line with Islamic values;

(b) improved infrastructure and financial sustainability of religious affairs, particularly of the religious education system; (iii) greater participation of Islamic scholars in raising awareness about importance of implementation of key reforms; (iv) a greatly strengthened role of the religious institutions in programs for poverty reduction.

ECONOMIC AND SOCIAL DEVELOPMENT

The economic and social development strategy, vision, objectives and expected outcomes have

been prioritized within the overall macro-fiscal framework to allow a logical progression of investments that systematically overcome the core binding constraints to growth and social development. An integrated approach focuses investments through the sector strategies summarized below. The sector strategies were developed based on strategies first put forward by individual ministries and groups of ministries. Although Ministry strategies were the starting point, the sector strategies are broader than those of the ministries for several very important reasons. First, the sector strategies in many cases involve actions and programs that need to be undertaken by several ministries. Considerable attention has therefore been given to developing better coordination between ministries through Inter-Ministerial Committees. The sector strategies have also taken account of donor activities being implemented outside of ministries and informed by the Provincial Development Plans (PDPs). The success of the sector strategies will be heavily dependent on resource effectiveness, revenue enhancement and fiscal sustainability, human and natural resource development and investments in productive and trade-based infrastructure and private sector driven development.

PRIVATE SECTOR DEVELOPMENT

The ANDS strategic objective is to enable the private sector to lead Afghanistan's development within a competitive market-based economy in which the Government is the policy maker and regulator of the economy, not its competitor. The establishment of a strong enabling environment for a competitive private sector is an on-going effort by both the Government and donors. Almost all sector strategies involve the development of new legislation. The Government will enact and implement key laws and amendments to establish the basic legal and regulatory framework that will encourage private sector involvement in social and economic development. Almost all sector strategies involve institutional strengthening that is designed to improve the ability of ministries and other agencies to administer legislation in an unbiased and predictable manner.

Privatization and corporatization of state owned enterprises is an on-going program that is on schedule. It represents an important step in expanding the scope for private sector growth and development. These steps will: (i) improve general levels of efficiency in the economy; (ii) assist in eliminating corruption;

(iii) encourage better resource allocation, and

(iv) generate increased government revenues.

An open trade policy will facilitate a competitive environment for private sector development, avoid the high costs incurred with protectionist policies and facilitate Afghanistan becoming better integrated as a 'trading hub' in the region. Any proposals to provide protection to particular industries will be evaluated with a proper 'economy wide' perspective that fully accounts for the costs and benefits from such actions, including the negative impacts on other firms and on the consumers who must pay higher prices. Increased priority will be given to regional economic cooperation initiatives aimed at developing regional transportation and transit infrastructure, facilitating regional trade and investment flows and developing Afghanistan as a regional business hub linking Central and East Asia with the Middle East and South Asia.

A second major component of the private sector development strategy attempts to encourage increased private sector investment by creating investor friendly regulatory frameworks for private sector operations in the development of natural resources and infrastructure. This approach has been very successful in the telecommunications sector, where phone usage went from less than 15,000 under a state monopoly to over five million subscribers as private investments in cellular communication were encouraged. Significant initiatives are included in the sector strategies for energy, mining and agriculture based on leased access to state lands to strengthen these investor friendly regulatory frameworks, and pilot projects and innovative initiatives are being investigated to allow public funding to support private sector activities in the provision of education services, vocational training and public health services.

A third and closely related component of the strategy is based on a concerted effort by the Government and the donor community to more vigorously promote private sector investment. Given the limited capacities in the public sector and in the nascent domestic private sector, much of this effort will focus on trying to encourage foreign firms with the ex-

pertise, ability to manage risk and access to financial resources to take advantage of the many opportunities that exist for investment in Afghanistan. Efforts at investment promotion will be designed to convince these investors that they are both needed in Afghanistan and that they will be able to operate profitably with full government support consistent with maintaining a competitive environment.

ENERGY

The ANDS strategic objective for the energy sector strategy is an energy sector that provides reliable, affordable energy increasingly based on market-based private sector investment and public sector oversight. The immediate task of the ANDS strategy, with assistance from the donor community, is to expand energy availability at a price that covers cost (for all but the poorest members of society) and to do so in the most cost effective manner. The Government will also take steps to provide the basis for the transition of the sector from public provision to private provision of electricity. As the Afghan energy sector moves from primarily state owned operations to a more private market orientation, new institutional arrangements will be established.

Until recently a focus in the energy sector has been on using donor funds and contractors to rehabilitate and expand the infrastructure of the government-owned electric company DABM, with virtually no attention being given to establishing an enabling environment that would promote increased private investment in the sector. This will change with a major effort to set up a transparent regulatory framework and a pricing system that is designed to encourage private sector investment in the sector. A new market oriented paradigm, significant institutional changes and considerable capacity development will be established under guidance from the Inter-Ministerial Commission for Energy (ICE). Streamlined government oversight and greater reliance on private sector investment is essential. As the energy line ministries shift from operating as production-based institutions to becoming policy making regulatory agencies, staff capacity and in-house functions will be reoriented to market practices. The Government will assess its sector assets and establish a plan for liquidation, restructuring and commercialization or sale. In particular the Government will provide more support for the corporatization and commercialization of national power operations. All these efforts will occur even while donor funded projects continue to work to relax the severe constraints in the energy and power sectors, but will lay the framework for a shift to a more commercial energy system in the coming years..

Mining

While geological studies of Afghanistan have been conducted over the last 50 years, due to political, social and economic factors, 90 percent of the territory of Afghanistan has not been systematically studied. However the limited results have been highly promising with over 400 mineral occurrences having been identified, including Aynak copper, coal and a number of small and medium mines such as gold, silver, platinum, zinc, nickel, emerald, lapis, ruby, canset, tourmaline, fluorite, chromate, salt, radioactive elements and numerous deposits suitable for construction materials. The availability of significant oil and gas fields in Afghanistan has been well known for almost 50 years.

The ANDS strategic objective in the mining sector is to encourage legitimate private investment in the sector so as to substantially increase government revenues, improve employment opportunities and foster ancillary development. Implementation of the strategy will help to develop effective market-based economy sector policies, promote and regulate sustainable development of minerals and ensure that the nation's geological resources are progressively investigated and developed. The Ministry of Mines is making the transition from being primarily a producer of minerals and other commodities to a policy making and regulatory institution. For mining and minerals, the emphasis is on the exploration, extraction and delivery to market; for hydrocarbons the emphasis is exploration and development. There is a great potential for the mining sector. The test will be in moving quickly from the success in attracting investment in the Aynak copper deposits to the development and exploration of the many other mineral resources of the country.

Afghanistan National Development Strategy (ANDS)

Water Resources

Agriculture accounts for 95 percent of water consumption. In the 1970s, some 3.3 million hectares were cultivated using various irrigation methods. However, because of civil conflict and drought, at present only about 1.8 million hectares of land are being irrigated. Of this, only ten percent is being irrigated using properly engineered systems with the remainder dependent on traditional irrigation methods, some of these based on run-offs from or use of aquifers that are being degraded by deep water wells and insufficient investment in recharge basins. Significant donor funded investment has gone into rehabilitating damaged or degraded irrigation systems, but little has been done in terms of making new investments the structures needed to increase efficiency in water use. There is a lack of resources needed to improve water management, including a lack of skilled human resources. Information systems are now being reconstituted, but there is a lack of reliable hydrological, meteorological, geo-technical and water quality data. The infrastructure and equipment needed to efficiently conserve and utilize water resources is insufficient. There are limited data on ground water resources and information indicating that un-regulated deep well drilling may be depleting aquifers that are essential to water supplies and traditional irrigation systems (Karezes and springs). There is a lack of economic mechanisms regulating water use and investments for water supply, sanitary systems, irrigation, and hydropower generation.

The efficient management of Afghanistan's water resources is essential for social and economic development and is an area where there is a great need for public sector involvement. Both government and donor efforts have under-invested in better water resource management that will have a major impact on the productive capacity of the economy and the lives of the people. Within the water resources sector, feasibility studies will be completed and investments will be made in the needed storage facilities, recharge basins, multi-purpose dams, irrigation systems required to improve water sector management for both agricultural and non-agricultural uses. These efforts will augment on-going efforts to rehabilitate and improve management in existing systems. Over time there will be a movement away from a project by project focus on rehabilitation to an Integrated Water Resource Management (IWRM) system geared to the five major river basins in the country, with an eventual devolution of responsibilities down to independent River Basin authorities.

TRANSPORT

The ANDS strategic goal for the transport sector is to have a safe, integrated transportation network that ensures connectivity and that enables low-cost and reliable movement of people and goods domestically as well as to and from foreign destinations. The strategy will contribute to achieving the following targets established in the Afghanistan Compact. (i) Afghanistan will have a fully upgraded and maintained ring road, as well as roads connecting the ring road to neighboring countries by end-2008 and a fiscally sustainable system for road maintenance by end-2007; (ii) By end2010, Kabul International Airport and Herat Airport will achieve full International Civil Aviation Organization compliance; Mazar-i-Sharif, Jalalabad and Kandahar will be upgraded with runway repairs, air navigation, fire and rescue and communications equipment; seven other domestic airports will be upgraded to facilitate domestic air transportation; and air transport services and costs will be increasingly competitive with international market standards and rates; and (iii) By end2010 Afghanistan and its neighbors will achieve lower transit times through Afghanistan by means of cooperative border management and other multilateral or bilateral trade and transit agreements.

The Government continues to give high priority to rehabilitate a badly damaged road system. This includes: (i) completion of a fully upgraded and maintained ring road and connector roads to neighboring countries, (ii) improving 5,334 km of secondary (national and provincial) roads and (iii) improving and building 6,290 km of rural access roads as a key to raising rural livelihoods and reducing poverty and vulnerability in rural areas. Better rural roads will improve market access and opportunities for rural households. The actual allocation of resources amongst these three areas of planned activity will depend on the estimated rates of return from analysis of proposals put forward for funding by the international community or by the ministries involved in implementing the transport sector strategies.

The ANDS: An Overview

A Transport Sector Inter-Ministerial Working Group will be formed that will coordinate the ministries in the sector to assure that investments are properly coordinated to obtain the highest returns and greatest impact on the poverty reduction goals. Careful consideration will be given to increasing employment opportunities, and assuring that the local resources or funds channeled through local communities are effectively used to maintain the rural roads established as part of this strategy.

INFORMATION AND COMMUNICATIONS TECHNOLOGY

In early 2003, Afghanistan had fewer than 15,000 functioning telephone lines for a population of approximately 25 million, one of the lowest telephone penetration rates in the world. The Government with donor assistance adopted major policy reforms for the ICT sector, moving rapidly to establish the legal framework and regulatory arrangements to promote private sector investment, resulting in a competitive environment and the rapid growth of mobile phone use from almost nothing to a present subscriber base of over five million. This development is one of the major success stories of in the implementation of the private sector based development strategy. Greater efforts will be made during ANDS period to adopt a similar investor friendly regulatory framework for development of natural resources and infrastructure. With respect to telecommunications, the ANDS strategic objective is to expand access to mobile phone service to 80 percent of the country and greatly increase access and use of the internet by consumers, the private sector and the Government.

URBAN DEVELOPMENT

The ANDS strategic objective for urban development is to greatly improve the management of urban areas through a devolution of authority and responsibilities to municipalities in a way that improves urban infrastructure and services, reduces urban poverty and allows urban residents to live safe, healthy and productive lives and cities to grow and prosper. Effective management of the rapid urbanization process will make a significant contribution to the recovery of the country. As of 2005 nearly a quarter of Afghanistan's population lived in urban areas. Outcomes will include: (i) strengthened municipal capacity to manage urban development and deliver services; (ii) improved institutional coordination and monitoring of key urban indicators; (iii) increased access to basic services for urban households;

(iv)

phased regularization of tenure for 50 percent of households living in informal settlements; (v) upgrading public services and facilities, including new urban area development;

(vi)

increased availability of affordable shelter, including a 50 percent increase in numbers of housing units and 30 percent increase in area of serviced land on the market, coupled with access to affordable finance; and (vii) improved urban environment with green areas and open spaces

More is now being done under the ANDS to devolve authority to municipalities. The urban development strategy is designed to improve urban governance through: (i) decentralization, participatory processes, market-based approaches, and improved regulations; (ii) capacity building at all levels of urban governance;

(iii) establishing a clear national land policy, including urban informal settlement policy; (iv) improved revenue generation in cities through direct cost recovery for and economic pricing of urban services, property-based taxes, and use of computer systems; (v) expanding urban upgrading pilots, including phased regularization of informal settlements, and programs to meet the immediate housing, tenure security and service needs of the poor and vulnerable people; (vi) increasing the supply of serviced land by developing new urban areas, especially within the cities, to meet the present and future housing needs of the people; (vii) improving city-wide basic infrastructure and services, in particular water supply, sanitation, roads and green areas; and (viii) rehabilitation of urban heritage facilities and sites.

EDUCATION

Efforts to improve education, which started in 2002, were focused on getting 1.5 million children into the primary/secondary school system. There are now over 6 million children at primary and secondary school. In addition universities have reopened and there are increasing opportunities for vocational training. There are now 52,200 students at higher education institutions. Although the expansion of education has been impressive, there is an urgent need to improve the quality of education.

Afghanistan National Development Strategy (ANDS)

This is one area where programs designed to meet benchmarks defined in terms of enrolment or coverage fail to give adequate consideration to the quality of the service being provided. Increased priority will be given to teacher training and other mechanisms to encourage private sector investment in educational activities.

Vocational training will become an increasing focus of attention. There is an urgent need to address problems in the vocational education sector that include staff shortages, overbuilding, lack of standardization in training courses, and qualifications that are difficult for potential employers to assess. A new organization, the National Vocational Education and Training Authority (NVETA), will be established and will: (i) manage, but not operate, all vocational training institutions; (ii) set minimum core competencies for courses, carry out accreditation, and inspect vocational institutions, to ensure that they meet minimum standards; and

(iii) call for tenders by ministries or by the private sector to operate vocational training facilities owned by the Government.

The potential role of the private sector has been expanded considerably in this strategy. In the primary and secondary education area there will be an expansion in private and NGO schools, encouraged by a more accommodating regulatory environment. In higher education the university cooperation plans that have already commenced will allow universities in Afghanistan to interact and be supported by recognized foreign universities. NVETA will contract with private sector groups or NGOs for provision of educational services. Some areas will be left to the private sector, including preschool education.

CULTURE, MEDIA AND YOUTH

The ANDS strategic objective for this sector is:

(i) to create awareness and foster a sense of pride in the country's history, future, culture and achievements; (ii) to document and preserve cultural artifacts and heritage sites; (iii) to ensure an independent and pluralistic media that contributes to an open and democratic society; and (iv) to foster a sense of confidence among the young that they can contribute to and benefit from a stable and prosperous the country. An accessible and well maintained cultural artifacts data base and the cultural artifacts collection held by the Ministry will be expanded. In the longer term, museums will be established and or expanded and historical or heritage sites will be protected. Media legislation will be enacted to provide a stable and predictable environment in which a largely privately run and independent media can operate. Media will be employed as an educational tool in addition to entertainment. Key priorities include a country-wide coverage of public Afghan media (radio and television), an increased number of hours of public broadcasting, and improved quality of programming. At this stage in its post-war development, state-owned media will be used to promote and convey information on gender policies, public health and national security. Extensive reforms have been introduced within the education strategy that is designed to assist youth. These include expansion of the education system; rehabilitation programs for young people whose education may have been limited because of the security situation; and reforms to vocational education to provide youth with marketable skills and better employment opportunities.

HEALTH AND NUTRITION SECTOR STRATEGY

By all measures, the people of Afghanistan suffer from poor health. The country's health indicators are near the bottom of international indices, and fare far worse, in terms of their health, than any other country in the region. Life expectancy is low, infant, under-five and maternal mortality is very high, and there is an extremely high prevalence of chronic malnutrition and widespread occurrence of micronutrient deficiency diseases. Substantial improvements in the health system and the health status of the people of Afghanistan have been achieved in recent years, but there are a number of challenges and constraints that must be addressed if continued progress is to be made, including: (i) inadequate financing for many of the key programs; (ii) reliance on external sources of funding; (iii) inadequately trained health workers; (iv) lack of qualified female health workers in rural areas; (v) dispersed population, geographical barriers and a lack of transportation infrastructure; (vi) low levels of utilization for certain health services, especially preventive services; (viii) variable levels of service quality; (ix) insecurity in some provinces, making it difficult for program implementation, recruitment and retention of staff, expan-

sion of service coverage and monitoring by the provincial and central levels; (x) lack of effective financial protection mechanisms for poor households to receive the care they need without experiencing financial distress; and (xi) lack of mechanisms for effective support to and regulation of for-profit private sector clinics and pharmacies.

Programs have been designed to expand and improve the system and to try and target vulnerable groups with preventive or curative programs. The Ministry of Public Health (MoPH) will review and develop relevant legal and regulatory mechanisms, such as accreditation systems, that govern health and health related work in the public and private sectors. The goal of the regulatory system will be to facilitate competitive and cost effective provision of services, carrying out its broader mandate to not only contract out service provision to civil and private groups but also to facilitate growth of the 'for profit' sector. The MoPH will review, develop and enforce relevant legal and regulatory instruments that govern health and health related work to safeguard the public and ensure service quality. The MoPH will work to identify, encourage, coordinate, and review and in some cases conduct relevant, useful research that can assist evidence-based decision making and the formulation of new policies, strategies and plans.

AGRICULTURE AND RURAL DEVELOPMENT

The ANDS strategic objective for the agriculture and rural development sector is to jointly use private investment and public sector support for efforts to transform agriculture into a source of growth and means of livelihood for the rural poor. The sector strategy articulates a road map for the way forward in which poverty reduction through economic regeneration is the central objective Some of the focus will be on the transformation of agriculture in a number of well defined zones where the conditions for growth are most favorable.

Agriculture has traditionally been the main activity for much of Afghanistan's population, particularly in the most remote and vulnerable areas. While non-farming activities account for large amounts of time, many of these are related to processing, transporting or marketing agricultural goods. The agriculture and rural development strategy establishes ambitious plans for a series of programs that are designed to achieve an improved quality of life for rural citizens – one in which food security is assured, basic services are provided, incomes increase with households actively engaged in legal activities, employment opportunities expand and where people live in a safe and secure environment. Activities are grouped into two main components of the strategy: a Comprehensive Agriculture and Rural Development (CARD) and the Agricultural and Rural Development Zone (ARDZ) initiative.

The CARD strategy articulates a road map for the way forward in which poverty reduction through economic regeneration is the central objective. The overall focus is to support the poorest and most vulnerable segments of rural society. Proposed interventions will provide a range of measures that will differ between groups and between regions, but all are designed to help diversify incomes, including income support, direct provision of assets, skills training and market opportunities.

The second main component of the strategy, the Agriculture and Rural Development Zones (ARDZ) program, is the Government's approach to expanding commercial activities and increasing agricultural productivity. The ARDZ recognizes that geographic priorities have to be set in support of the development of commercial agriculture. These geographic priorities will be used to target infrastructure, utilities and other support by various ministries. The Government will release publicly held land to increase private sector investment through a competitive bidding process. Further, the Government will continue to investigate and implement measures to increase financial and technical support that can be utilized by private firms to expand operations. This will ensure the process of transforming underutilized state land into commercially viable agro-processing enterprises will be as fast and efficient as possible.

SOCIAL PROTECTION

The ANDS strategic objective for social protection is to assure that the benefits of growth reach the poor and vulnerable, either through the attention to these groups in the design of programs and projects aimed at stimulating growth or through well targeted support programs. The social protection sector has signifi-

cantly improved since 2002 in all areas: social support, pension distribution and disaster preparedness. Cash transfer benefits have been established for martyr's families and the disabled as the main instrument of the social support and national solidarity with the victims of the war. The MoLSAMD has established its departments in all provinces and strengthen its capacity for targeting and cooperating with NGOs and donors. Around 2.5 million people have been covered with some type of public arrangement for social protection. Efforts will now focus on: (i) improving efficiency of public arrangements for social risk management; (ii) diversifying market-based arrangements for social risk management; (iii) strengthening informal arrangements for social risk management (iv) capacity building and restructuring in the MoLSAMD; and (vi) improving partnership with civil society and NGOs to enhance aid coordination. The main principle for future social support will be to enhance fiscal sustain-ability by focusing on the most vulnerable and supporting the "poorest of the poor". Finally, strengthening the public/NGOs/private sector partnership will support the Government's intention to remain mainly in the area of policy making and providing regulations and having the private sector and NGOs increasingly involved in service delivery.

REFUGEES, RETURNEES AND INTERNALLY DISPLACED PERSONS (IDPS)

The ANDS strategic objective with respect to refugees, returnees and IDP's is to efficiently manage the voluntary return of refugees and IDPs and their reintegration into productive participation in society. World-wide experience has indicated that large, unplanned, and essentially involuntary returns which have to be managed as emergency influxes generate a range of negative consequences. Therefore the planned and voluntary return of refugees and IDPs return is the guiding principle for the sector strategy.

More than five million persons have returned to their homes since 2002. Their reintegration into society has been challenging but there has no been no pattern of discrimination against returnees. There is some evidence of secondary migration of returnees from places of origin to cities and back to the neighboring countries. The latter occur most noticeably from border provinces. Population movements have largely normalized with socio-economic factors largely replacing security and politics as the key drivers. The numbers of IDPs has also fallen significantly since 2002. Currently there are an estimated 129,000 IDPs displaced by past drought and conflict and an additional 29,000 more recently displaced by recent fighting in the southern provinces. The majority of the one million IDPs identified in 2002 have returned to their homes. During 2007 there was some rise in local internal displacement in the southern provinces of Helmand and Uruzgan due to clashes with terrorist groups. Within the region, the principle legal and operational framework governing voluntary repatriation is provided by the Tripartite Agreements (TA) signed between Afghanistan, UNHCR, Iran and Pakistan respectively. These agreements are serviced by regular meetings of Tripartite Commissions at both Ministerial and working level.

It is very probable that high levels of mass and voluntary repatriation are over. The refugees' long stay in exile, poverty, and dissuasive conditions in many parts of Afghanistan are likely to prove difficult obstacles to overcome in the future. Security, lack of economic opportunities (employment) and social services (health and education) continue to limit return and reintegration. The most significant challenges for future will be: (i) ensuring peace and security in areas of refugee origin; (ii) improving the Government's abilities to negotiate effectively with its neighbors on refugee, displacement and migration issues; (iii) improving the political, economic, social and organizational absorption capacities in key sectors and areas; and (iv) developing an implementation plan and supporting resources executed over a number of years.

CROSS-CUTTING ISSUES

Since 1383, the Government has given considerable attention to a set of issues that cut across all the sectors, motivated by the belief that the overall success of the ANDS will be in jeopardy if these issues are not effectively addressed. These cross cutting issues involve (i) regional cooperation; (ii) counter-narcotics; (iii) anticorruption; (iv) gender equality; (v) capacity development; and (vi) environmental management..

The ANDS: An Overview

The regional cooperation initiatives are intended to increase access to power; generate revenues through transit trade; reduce impediments to trade and expand both import and export opportunities; increase investment and contribute to improved employment and business opportunities; facilitate the free flow of goods, services, and technology; allow the costs or benefits of development of common resources to be shared; reduce regional tensions and facilitate regional efforts to reduce cross border crime and terrorism; and facilitate the voluntary return of refugees.

Counter-narcotics programs are designed to;

(i) disrupt the drugs trade; (ii) strengthen and diversify legal rural livelihoods; (iii) reduce the demand for illicit drugs and improve treatment for drug users; and (iv) strengthen state institutions combating the drug scourge within central and provincial governments. Provincial governors will be responsible and accountable for the process of control and management of counter narcotics intervention in their jurisdiction with support from MCN.

The National Anti-Corruption Strategy is based on the following key goals: (i) enhancing government anti-corruption commitment and leadership; (ii) raising awareness of corruption and evaluating the effectiveness of anticorruption measures; (iii) mainstreaming anticorruption into government reforms and national development; and (iv) strengthening the legal framework for fighting corruption and building an institutional capacity for effective implementation of the United Nations Convention Against Corruption (UNCAC).

The ANDS goal for gender equality is an Afghanistan where women and men enjoy security, equal rights and equal opportunities in all spheres of life. The National Action Plan for Women focuses on three main outcomes: (i) government entities embracing 'gender equality' in their employment, promotion, policy making and budgetary allocations; (ii) measurable improvements in women's status as evidenced by reduced illiteracy; higher net enrollment ratio in educational and training programs; equal wages for equal work; lower maternal mortality; increasing leadership and participation in all spheres of life; greater economic opportunities and access to and control over productive assets and income; adequate access to equal justice; reduced vulnerability to violence in public and domestic spheres; and

(iii) greater social acceptance of gender equality as evidenced by increased participation by women in public affairs and policy discussions.

The ANDS capacity development objective is to assure that the skills needed to effectively implement programs and projects included in the ANDS exist or can be developed within the required time frame for implementation. The institutional responsibility will be with Inter-ministerial Commission for Capacity Development (ICCD) that will serve as a single reporting point for both government and donors. ICCD will provide a coordinated approach to support the effective management of funds and aid flows, to cut down on duplication and to ensure that critical capabilities for program and project implementation are well defined and (most importantly) that capacity development and technical assistance programs are properly focused on meeting these critical needs.

Environmental protection efforts are geared to: restoration and sustainable use of rangelands and forests; conservation of biodiversity; preservation of Natural and Cultural Heritage sites or resources; encouragement to community based natural resource management, prevention and/or abatement of pollution; and improved environmental management, education and awareness. Throughout all sectors, any environmental costs will be fully accounted for in appraisals aimed at ensuring that benefits of proposed programs or projects.

ENHANCING AID EFFECTIVENESS AND AID COORDINATION

The Government has implemented processes to increase the monitoring of aid-funded activities and to improve the efficiency of implementation. The Aid Coordination Unit in the Ministry of Finance has responsibility for issues related to the delivery and monitoring of external assistance. The Government would like to see increased core budget support (direct budget support), giving greater ownership and enabling a more effective allocation of resources based on needs and priorities. Channeling aid through established trust funds is also effective, with the Government able to access funds on an as needed basis. Pooling of donor funds also significantly reduces the duplication of efforts and leads to better coordination, management, and effectiveness of aid. This is especially so with technical assistance grants.

Efforts to increase capacity to implement the Core Development Budget more efficiently will result in higher donor contributions, aiding coordination. Equally important is the Government's accountability to Afghan citizens on how aid funds have been spent. The MoF's Public Expenditure Financial Accountability (PEFA) framework is crucial to this process. The ANDS provides the framework for priority aid delivery. Aid delivery will be greatly improved where Government, civil society and the international community align expenditures with the ANDS priorities. Further, the Government will work with civil society organizations and Provincial Reconstruction Teams to ensure that these activities are also aligned with the ANDS priorities and goals.

The success of the ANDS depends on effective implementation. The National Budget is the central tool for implementing the ANDS. Given this, all line ministries will first develop or align their programs and projects with the ANDS Sector Strategies; sector program and projects will then be costed and re-prioritized against the medium-term budget ceilings. Based on this, the ANDS Public Investment Program (PIP) will be prepared to enable the full integration of the ANDS into the medium term budget in accordance with the MoF's ongoing activities to introduce program budgeting. Furthermore, the Government will improve its absorption capacity and fiduciary practices to encourage donors to implement their projects through the National (Core) Budget or, if this is not possible, to assure that programs or projects implemented through the external budget are aligned with the ANDS objectives and priorities.

At the national level, the following structures will link policy, planning, budgeting and monitoring of the ANDS: The National Assembly is responsible for legislating an enabling environment for security, economic growth and poverty reduction. The Council of Ministers headed by the President is the highest level decision-making body, providing overall policy guidance and direction under existing legislation. The ANDS Oversight Committee (OSC), composed of senior ministers, will oversee and coordinate the overall ANDS implementation process. Line ministries and other government agencies will also be responsible for implementation itself. The MoF will play an important role by making sure that the program and projects of the line ministries are costed, prioritized and integrated into the National Budget. The OSC will play a key role in coordinating overall efforts to implement the ANDS. Moreover, the Ministry of Economy will strengthen this mechanism by coordinating the work of the line ministries at the operational level. The Joint Coordination and Monitoring Board will remain the highest Government-donor mechanism in charge of coordination and monitoring, which will cover not only the Afghanistan Compact but the entire ANDS. The Consultative and Working Groups will continue to be the key forums for improving aid coordination and ensure alignment of the donor programs and projects with the ANDS.

PROVINCIAL DEVELOPMENT PLANS (PDPS)

As part of the ANDS PDPs were developed for all 34 provinces of Afghanistan to provide a coordinated framework for the Government and the international community to undertake sector programs and projects at the sub-national level. The linking of consultation to the provincial based planning process has allowed local communities to prioritize, sequence, plan and be involved in the implementation of projects. The PDPs developed through the Sub National Consultations ensure that the priorities in the ANDS reflect the best interests of the Afghan people and are the product of the three rounds of Sub-National Consultations that took place across Afghanistan March 2007- March 2008.

The PDPs have informed policy formulation, articulated goals and needs of the people and provided strategic direction to the sector strategies and the overall ANDS. During the Sub National Consultations (SNCs), preparation and input for the PDPs was based on the following inputs:

line ministry strategies and plans;

priorities of rural communities including those set out in Community and District Development Plans;

priorities of urban communities, including those set out in Urban Plans;

priorities of vulnerable social groups including Kuchis, refugees, returnees and Internally Displaced Persons (IDP) and the disabled; and

priorities of women, who attended the consultations with an average of 47 percent participation.[12]

Development of Provincial Profiles

The PDPs contain a profile of each province using information from both the National Risk and Vulnerability Assessment (NRVA) and UNFPA's Socio-Economic and Demographic Profiles, providing a geographic, poverty-based and social picture of the province and perspectives on the state of provincial development. Opportunities for poverty alleviation have been included with the agreed goals and needs for each pillar. This provides a guide to potential development in each province; especially for the most urgent local needs.

[12] A nomad woman from Balkh province stated that this was the first time she had attended the meeting on behalf of nomad women of this province in order to present her opinions for the welfare and prosperity of the country. "We would be glad if the government continues to pursue such policy. Nomads like any other people in the society would also benefit from this process". Farida Kochi, representative of Balkh' Source: ANDS Sub-national Consultation, 1386 (2007).

Priority Projects

Ten projects have been prioritized for each sector and for each province aligned with the fiscal envelope of ministries within the outreach of national programs. In total, 80 priority projects were identified for each province. The SNCs served as an opportunity for these ideas in the shape of Community Development Plans (CDPs) and District Development Plans (DDPs) to be consolidated and improved and to reach consensus on them with a wider audience from the province before being incorporated into PDPs as priority projects. Priority projects from the eight sectors across the 34 provinces therefore represent a list of activities that respond to the most urgent sectoral needs in each province. These are being mapped into the national budget process.

PRIORITIZATION AND SEQUENCING OF THE PDPS

Prioritization of the provincial priority projects, aligned with National Programs, forms the basis on which implementation of the ANDS will take place at the local level. Out of the eighty projects prioritized during the SNC process, the most critical projects were aligned with the five most crucial sectors and prioritized into tiers. Tier one projects represent the most urgent tasks. This has allowed for a logical resource allocation and prioritization process to be carried out. Provincial budgeting, as a component of the National Program Budgeting Reform Progress, is also informed by the provincial prioritization process. It aims to empower local authorities and increase the appropriateness of resource allocation. This is currently being piloted in ten provinces and will be extended to a further ten in 1387 (2008).

INTEGRATION OF THE PDPS INTO ANDS

The data from the SNCs and PDPs was fully incorporated into ANDS in the following ways:

• For each Sector Strategy; comments gathered from the SNCs from a provincial perspective on challenges for that particular sector have been a starting point for addressing the country's most urgent needs. Thus each sector can be seen to respond directly to the concerns raised by the people.

The Participatory Process

> Prioritized projects will be aligned with ministries' national programs. This will enable a more transparent provision of services and a more clearly defined implementation and monitoring mechanism.
>
> The prioritization process will assist ministries with effective resource allocation and provincial projects highlighted as the most urgent should be seen as priority action by the ministries.

OUTCOMES FROM THE PROVINCIAL DEVELOPMENT PLANNING PROCESS

One of the most valuable outcomes of the sub-national consultations was the clear indication that the 34 provinces have different development priorities. As outputs, the PDPs have formed an integral part of Government policy formation, prioritization, sequencing and needs- related resource allocation. In addition, two national overriding considerations emerged as critically important to any intervention: the importance of preserving the country's Islamic religious principles, culture and lifestyle and ensuring equity of access to resources and intervention.

Security emerged as a top priority in two thirds of the PDPs; most strongly in the south and the east of the country. In these regions, security is perceived as the fundamental basis on which all other development depends.

Key issues identified by stakeholders[13] include: the (i) lack of access to clean drinking water in all provinces, for both domestic use and throughout institutions such as schools and clinics; (ii) improvement of provincial roads, 83 percent referring specifically to the need for tertiary road services, to improve communication between villages to district and provincial centers; access to basic services such as schools and clinics; (iii) improvement in the present low quality services emerged as a key priority throughout the country, especially with respect to poorly trained teachers and doctors; (iv) lack of alternative livelihoods to poppy cultivation;

(v) lack of vocational training for returnees and

[13] For a detailed breakdown and analysis of provincial priorities, sequencing and integration into Sector Strategies see Volume iii of the ANDS.

disabled people; (vi) poor access to electricity cited in 80 percent of the PDPs; and (vii) corruption within the public administration (mentioned in 80 percent of the PDPs, particularly within the security services).

PRIORITIZATION OF THE PILLARS

Using qualitative information from the PDPs the ANDS pillars have been prioritized. This has been illustrated in two ways. Figure 2.3 shows the proportional representation of priorities within the top five sectors across the 34 provinces. Unsurprisingly, with 80 percent of the population relying on some form of agriculture, it has appeared as a national priority. Sectors such as health and social protection are also one of people's top priorities. In order, the key priorities are:

Agriculture

Security

Education

Governance

Health

Private sector

Roads

Infrastructure (energy and water) and social protection.

AFGHANISTAN: POST-TALIBAN GOVERNANCE, SECURITY, AND U.S. POLICY[2]

BACKGROUND

Afghanistan has a history of a high degree of decentralization, and resistance to foreign invasion and occupation. Some have termed it the "graveyard of empires."

FROM EARLY HISTORY TO THE 19TH CENTURY

Alexander the Great conquered what is now Afghanistan in three years (330 B.C.E. to 327 B.C.E), although at significant cost and with significant difficulty, and requiring, among other steps, marriage to a resident of the conquered territory. From the third to the eighth century, A.D., Buddhism was the dominant religion in Afghanistan. At the end of the seventh century, Islam spread in Afghanistan when Arab invaders from the Umayyad Dynasty defeated the Persian empire of the Sassanians. In the 10th century, Muslim rulers called Samanids, from Bukhara (in what is now Uzbekistan), extended their influence into Afghanistan, and the complete conversion of Afghanistan to Islam occurred during the rule of the Gaznavids in the 11th century. They ruled over the first vast Islamic empire based in what is now Ghazni province of Afghanistan.

In 1504, Babur, a descendent of the conquerors Tamarlane and Genghis Khan, took control of Kabul and then moved onto India, establishing the Mughal Empire. (Babur is buried in the Babur Gardens complex in Kabul, which has been refurbished with the help of the Agha Khan Foundation.) Throughout the 16th and 17th centuries, Afghanistan was fought over by the Mughal Empire and the Safavid Dynasty of Persia (now Iran), with the Safavids mostly controlling Herat and western Afghanistan, and the Mughals controlling Kabul and the east. A monarchy ruled by ethnic Pashtuns was founded in 1747 by Ahmad Shah Durrani, who was a senior officer in the army of Nadir Shah, ruler of Persia, when Nadir Shah was assassinated and Persian control over Afghanistan weakened.

A strong ruler, Dost Muhammad Khan, emerged in Kabul in 1826 and created concerns among Britain that the Afghans were threatening Britain's control of India; that fear led to a British decision in 1838 to intervene in Afghanistan, setting off the first Anglo-Afghan War (1838-1842). Nearly all of the 4,500-person British force was killed in that war, which ended with a final British stand at Gandamack. The second Anglo-Afghan War took place during 1878-1880.

EARLY 20TH CENTURY AND COLD WAR ERA

King Amanullah Khan (1919-1929) launched attacks on British forces in Afghanistan (Third Anglo-Afghan War) shortly after taking power and won complete independence from Britain as recognized in the Treaty of Rawalpindi (August 8, 1919). He was considered a secular modernizer presiding over a government in which all ethnic minorities participated. He was succeeded by King Mohammad Nadir Shah (1929-1933), and then by King Mohammad Zahir Shah. Zahir Shah's reign (1933-1973) is remembered fondly by many older Afghans for promulgating a constitution in 1964 that established a national legislature and promoting freedoms for women, including dropping a requirement that they cover their face and hair. However, possibly believing that he could limit Soviet support for Communist factions in

[2] Kenneth Katzman Specialist in Middle Eastern Affairs April 15, 2011 Congressional Research Service

Afghanistan, Zahir Shah also entered into a significant political and arms purchase relationship with the Soviet Union. The Soviets began to build large infrastructure projects in Afghanistan during Zahir Shah's time, such as the north-south Salang Pass/Tunnel and Bagram airfield. He also accepted agricultural and other development aid from the United States. In part, the countryside was secured during the King's time by local tribal militias called *arbokai*.

Afghanistan's slide into instability began in the 1970s when the diametrically opposed Communist Party and Islamic movements grew in strength. While receiving medical treatment in Italy, Zahir Shah was overthrown by his cousin, Mohammad Daoud, a military leader who established a dictatorship with strong state involvement in the economy. Daoud was overthrown and killed[1] in April 1978 by People's Democratic Party of Afghanistan (PDPA, Communist party) military officers under the direction of two PDPA (Khalq faction) leaders, Hafizullah Amin and Nur Mohammad Taraki, in what is called the *Saur* (April) Revolution. Taraki became president, but he was displaced in September 1979 by Amin. Both leaders drew their strength from rural ethnic Pashtuns and tried to impose radical socialist change on a traditional society, in part by redistributing land and bringing more women into government. The attempt at rapid modernization sparked rebellion by Islamic parties opposed to such moves. The Soviet Union sent troops into Afghanistan on December 27, 1979, to prevent a seizure of power by the Islamic militias, known as the *mujahedin* (Islamic fighters). Upon their invasion, the Soviets replaced Amin with another PDPA leader perceived as pliable, Babrak Karmal (Parcham faction of the PDPA), who was part of the 1978 PDPA takeover but was exiled by Taraki and Amin.

Soviet occupation forces, which numbered about 120,000, were never able to pacify the outlying areas of the country. The *mujahedin* benefited from U.S. weapons and assistance, provided through the Central Intelligence Agency (CIA) in cooperation with Pakistan's Inter-Service Intelligence directorate (ISI). The mujahedin were also relatively well organized and coordinated by seven major parties that in early 1989 formed a Peshawar-based "Afghan Interim Government" (AIG). The seven party leaders were Mohammad Nabi Mohammadi; Sibghatullah Mojaddedi; Gulbuddin Hikmatyar; Burhanuddin Rabbani; Yunus Khalis; Abd-i-Rab Rasul Sayyaf; and Pir Gaylani. Mohammadi and Khalis have died in recent years of natural causes, but the others are still active in Afghan politics and governance or, in the case of Hikmatyar, fighting the Afghan government.

The *mujahedin* weaponry included U.S.-supplied portable shoulder-fired anti-aircraft systems called "Stingers," which proved highly effective against Soviet aircraft. The United States decided in 1985 to provide these weapons to the mujahedin after substantial debate within the Reagan Administration and some in Congress over whether they could be used effectively and whether doing so would harm broader U.S.-Soviet relations. The *mujahedin* also hid and stored weaponry in a large network of natural and manmade tunnels and caves throughout Afghanistan. Partly because of the effectiveness of the Stinger in shooting down Soviet helicopters and fixed wing aircraft, the Soviet Union's losses mounted—about 13,400 Soviet soldiers were killed in the war, according to Soviet figures—turning Soviet domestic opinion against the war. In 1986, after the reformist Mikhail Gorbachev became leader, the Soviets replaced Karmal with the director of Afghan intelligence, Najibullah Ahmedzai (known by his first name). Najibullah was a Ghilzai Pashtun, and was from the Parcham faction of the PDPA. Some Afghans say that some aspects of his governing style were admirable, particularly his appointment of a prime minister (Sultan Ali Keshtmand and others) to handle administrative duties and distribute power.

GENEVA ACCORDS (1988) AND SOVIET WITHDRAWAL

On April 14, 1988, Gorbachev agreed to a U.N.-brokered accord (the Geneva Accords) requiring it to withdraw. The withdrawal was completed by February 15, 1989, leaving in place the weak Najibullah government. A warming of relations moved the United States and Soviet Union to try for a political settlement to the Afghan conflict, a trend accelerated by the 1991 collapse of the Soviet Union, which reduced Moscow's capacity for supporting communist regimes in the Third World. On September 13, 1991, Moscow and Washington agreed to a joint cutoff of military aid to the Afghan combatants.

The State Department has said that a total of about $3 billion in economic and covert military assistance was provided by the U.S. to the Afghan *mujahedin* from 1980 until the end of the Soviet occupation in 1989. Press reports say the covert aid program grew from about $20 million per year in FY1980 to about $300 million per year during FY1986-FY1990.[2] The Soviet pullout decreased the perceived strategic value of Afghanistan, causing a reduction in subsequent covert funding. As indicated in Table 11, U.S. assistance to Afghanistan remained at relatively low levels from the time of the Soviet withdrawal, validating the views of many that the United States largely considered its role in Afghanistan "completed" when Soviets troops left, and there was little support for a major U.S. effort to rebuild the country. The United States closed its embassy in Kabul in January 1989, as the Soviet Union was completing its pullout, and it remained so until the fall of the Taliban in 2001.

With Soviet backing withdrawn, Najibullah rallied the PDPAArmy and the party-dominated paramilitary organization called the *Sarandoy*, and successfully beat back the first post-Soviet withdrawal *mujahedin* offensives. Although Najibullah defied expectations that his government would immediately collapse after a Soviet withdrawal, military defections continued and his position weakened in subsequent years. On March 18, 1992, Najibullah publicly agreed to step down once an interim government was formed. That announcement set off a wave of rebellions primarily by Uzbek and Tajik militia commanders in northern Afghanistan—particularly Abdul Rashid Dostam, who joined prominent *mujahedin* commander Ahmad Shah Masud of the Islamic Society, a largely Tajik party headed by Burhannudin Rabbani. Masud had earned a reputation as a brilliant strategist by preventing the Soviets from occupying his power base in the Panjshir Valley of northeastern Afghanistan. Najibullah fell, and the *mujahedin* regime began April 18, 1992.[3] Each year, a public parade is held to mark that day. (Some major *mujahedin* figures did not attend the 2010 celebration because of a perception that they are under Afghan and international criticism of their immunity from alleged human rights abuses during the anti-Soviet war.)

Table 1.Afghanistan Social and Economic Statistics

Population	28 million +. Kabul population is 3 million, up from 500,000 in Taliban era.
Ethnicities/Religions	Pashtun 42%; Tajik 27%; Uzbek 9%; Hazara 9%; Aimak 4%; Turkmen 3%; Baluch 2%.
Size of Religious	Religions: Sunni (Hanafi school) 80%; Shiite (Hazaras, Qizilbash, and Isma'ilis) 19%;
Minorities	other 1%Christians-estimated 500-8,000 persons; Sikh and Hindu-3,000 persons;
	Bahai's-400 (declared blasphemous in May 2007); Jews-1 person; Buddhist- small
	numbers, mostly foreigners. No Christian or Jewish schools. One church.
Literacy Rate	28% of population over 15 years of age. 43% of males; 12.6% of females.
GDP and Growth Rates	$29.8 billion purchasing power parity (PPP). 109th in the world. Per capita: $1,000
(2010)	purchasing power parity. 212th in the world. Growth: about 9% for

	2010 and expected for 2011. GDP was about $10 billion (PPP) during last year of Taliban rule.
Unemployment Rate	40%
Children in School/Schools Built	6.2 million, of which 35% are girls. Up from 900,000 in school during Taliban era. 8,000 schools built; 140,000 teachers hired since Taliban era. 17 universities, up from 2 in 2002. 75,000 Afghans in universities in Afghanistan; 5,000 when Taliban was in power. 35% of university students in Afghanistan are female.
Afghans With Access to Health Coverage	65% with basic health services access-compared to 8% during Taliban era. Infant mortality down 18% since Taliban to 135 per 1,000 live births. 680 clinics built .
Roads Built	About 2,500 miles paved post-Taliban, including repaving of "Ring Road" (78% complete) that circles the country. Kabul-Qandahar drive reduced to 6 hours.
Judges/Courts	Over 1,000 judges (incl. 200 women) trained since fall of Taliban.
Banks Operating	17, including branches in some rural areas, but about 90% of the population still use hawalas (informal money transfer services). Zero banks existed during Taliban era. Some limited credit card use. Some Afghan police now paid by cell phone (E-Paisa).
Access to Electricity	15%-20% of the population. Much of its electricity imported from neighboring states.
Government Revenues (excl. donor funds)	About $1.7 billion in 2010; more than double the $720 million 2007. Total Afghan budget is about $4.5 billion, with shortfall covered by foreign donors, including through World Bank-run Afghanistan Reconstruction Trust Fund.
Financial Reserves/Debt	About $4.4 billion, up from $180 million in 2002. Includes amounts due Central Bank. $8 billion bilateral debt, plus $500 million multilateral. U.S. forgave $108 million in debt in 2004, and $1.6 billion forgiven by other creditors in March 2010.
Foreign/Private Investment	About $500 million to $1 billion per year. Four Afghan airlines: Ariana (national) plus three privately owned: Safi, Kam, and Pamir.
Mining/Minerals	Vast untapped minerals affirmed by U.S. experts (June 2010). Chinese firm mining copper in Lowgar Province. December 2010: contracts let to produce oil in Sar-I-Pol Province (north) and for private investors to mine gold in Baghlan Province.
Agriculture/Major Legal	80% of the population is involved in agriculture. Self-sufficiency in

Exports	wheat production as of May 2009 (first time in 30 years). Products for export include fruits, raisins, melons, pomegranate juice (Anar), nuts, carpets, lapis lazuli gems, marble tile, timber products (Kunar, Nuristan provinces). July 2010 Afghanistan-Pakistan trade agreement.
Oil Proven Reserves	3.6 billion barrels of oil, 36.5 trillion cubic feet of gas. Current oil production negligible, but USAID funding project to revive oil and gas facilities in the north.
World Trade	Exports: $403 million. Imports: $3.4 billion (2009). Main imports are food, energy, capital goods, textiles, autos. Top five trading partners (in descending order): Pakistan, Russia, Iran, India, United States.
Cellphones/Tourism	About 12 million cellphones, up from several hundred used by Taliban government officials. Tourism: National park opened in Bamiyan June 2009. Increasing tourist visits.

Sources: CIA, The World Factbook; various press and U.S. government official testimony.

THE *MUJAHEDIN* GOVERNMENT AND RISE OF THE TALIBAN

The fall of Najibullah exposed the differences among the *mujahedin* parties. The leader of one of the smaller parties (Afghan National Liberation Front), Islamic scholar Sibghatullah Mojadeddi, was president during April-May 1992. Under an agreement among the major parties, Rabbani became President in June 1992 with agreement that he would serve until December 1994. He refused to step down at that time, saying that political authority would disintegrate without a clear successor. Kabul was subsequently shelled by other *mujahedin* factions, particularly that of nominal "Prime Minister" Gulbuddin Hikmatyar, a Pashtun, who accused Rabbani of monopolizing power. Hikmatyar, who never formally assumed a working prime ministerial role in Kabul because of suspicions of Rabbani, was purportedly backed by Pakistan. Hikmatyar's radical faction of the Islamist Hizb-e-Islami (Islamic Party) had received a large proportion of the U.S. aid during the anti-Soviet war. (Yunus Khalis led a more moderate faction of Hizb-e-Islami during that war.)

In 1993-1994, Afghan Islamic clerics and students, mostly of rural, Pashtun origin, formed the Taliban movement. Many were former *mujahedin* who had become disillusioned with conflict among *mujahedin* parties and had moved into Pakistan to study in Islamic seminaries ("madrassas") mainly of the "Deobandi" school of Islam.[4] Some say this Islam is similar to the "Wahhabism" that is practiced in Saudi Arabia. Taliban practices were also consonant with conservative Pashtun tribal traditions.

The Taliban viewed the Rabbani government as corrupt and anti-Pashtun, and the four years of civil war (1992-1996) created popular support for the Taliban as able to deliver stability. With the help of defections, the Taliban peacefully took control of the southern city of Qandahar in November 1994. By February 1995, it was approaching Kabul, after which an 18-month stalemate ensued. In September 1995, the Taliban captured Herat province, bordering Iran, and imprisoned its governor, Ismail Khan, ally of Rabbani and Masud, who later escaped and took refuge in Iran. In September 1996, new Taliban victories near Kabul led to the withdrawal of Rabbani and Masud to the Panjshir Valley north of Kabul with most of their heavy weapons; the Taliban took control of Kabul on September 27, 1996. Taliban gunmen subsequently entered a U.N. facility in Kabul to seize Najibullah, his brother, and aides, and then hanged them.

TALIBAN RULE (SEPTEMBER 1996-NOVEMBER 2001)

The Taliban regime was led by Mullah Muhammad Umar, who lost an eye in the anti-Soviet war while fighting as part of the Hizb-e-Islami *mujahedin* party of Yunis Khalis. Umar held the title of Head of State and "Commander of the Faithful," remaining in the Taliban power base in Qandahar and almost never appearing in public, although he did occasionally receive high-level foreign officials. Umar forged a political and personal bond with bin Laden and refused U.S. demands to extradite him. Like Umar, most of the senior figures in the Taliban regime were Ghilzai Pashtuns, which predominate in eastern Afghanistan. They are rivals of the Durrani Pashtuns, who are predominant in the south.

The Taliban progressively lost international and domestic support as it imposed strict adherence to Islamic customs in areas it controlled and employed harsh punishments, including executions. The Taliban authorized its "Ministry for the Promotion of Virtue and the Suppression of Vice" to use physical punishments to enforce strict Islamic practices, including bans on television, Western music, and dancing. It prohibited women from attending school or working outside the home, except in health care, and it publicly executed some women for adultery. In what many consider its most extreme action, and which some say was urged by bin Laden, in March 2001 the Taliban blew up two large Buddha statues carved into hills above Bamiyan city, considering them idols.

The Clinton Administration held talks with the Taliban before and after it took power, but was unable to moderate its policies. The United States withheld recognition of Taliban as the legitimate government of Afghanistan, formally recognizing no faction as the government. The United Nations continued to seat representatives of the Rabbani government, not the Taliban. The State Department ordered the Afghan embassy in Washington, DC, closed in August 1997. U.N. Security Council Resolution 1193 (August 28, 1998) and 1214 (December 8, 1998) urged the Taliban to end discrimination against women. Women's rights groups urged the Clinton Administration not to recognize the Taliban government. In May 1999, the Senate-passed S.Res. 68 called on the President not to recognize an Afghan government that oppresses women.

U.S. Efforts Against Al Qaeda During Taliban Rule

The Taliban's hosting of Al Qaeda's leadership gradually became the Clinton Administration's overriding agenda item with Afghanistan. In April 1998, then U.S. Ambassador to the United Nations Bill Richardson (along with Assistant Secretary of State Karl Inderfurth and NSC senior official Bruce Riedel) visited Afghanistan, but the Taliban refused to hand over bin Laden. They did not meet Mullah Umar. After the August 7, 1998, Al Qaeda bombings of U.S. embassies in Kenya and Tanzania, the Clinton Administration progressively pressured the Taliban, imposing

U.S. sanctions and achieving adoption of some U.N. sanctions as well. On August 20, 1998, the United States fired cruise missiles at alleged Al Qaeda training camps in eastern Afghanistan, but bin Laden was not hit.[5] Some observers assert that the Administration missed several clearer opportunities to strike him, including a purported sighting of him by an unarmed Predator drone at the Tarnak Farm camp in Afghanistan in the fall of 2000.[6] Clinton Administration officials said that domestic and international support for ousting the Taliban militarily was lacking.

The "Northern Alliance" Congeals

The Taliban's policies caused different Afghan factions to ally with the ousted President Rabbani and Masud and their ally in the Herat area, Ismail Khan—the Tajik core of the anti-Taliban opposition—into a broader "Northern Alliance." In the Alliance were Uzbek, Hazara Shiite, and even some Pashtun Islamist factions discussed in Table 4. Virtually all the figures mentioned remain key players in politics in Afghanistan, sometimes allied with and at other times feuding with President Hamid Karzai:

- Uzbeks/General Dostam. One major faction was the Uzbek militia (the Junbush-Melli, or National Islamic Movement of Afghanistan) of General Abdul Rashid Dostam. Frequently referred to by some Afghans as one of the "warlords" who gained power during the anti-Soviet war, Dostam first joined those seeking to oust Rabbani during his 1992-1996 presidency, but later joined Rabbani's Northern Alliance against the Taliban. (For more information on Dostam, see CRS Report RS21922, *Afghanistan: Politics, Elections, and Government Performance*, by Kenneth Katzman.)
- Hazara Shiites. Members of Hazara tribes, mostly Shiite Muslims, are prominent in Bamiyan, Dai Kundi, and Ghazni provinces (central Afghanistan) and are always wary of repression by Pashtuns and other larger ethnic factions. The Hazaras have tended to serve in working class and domestic household jobs, although more recently they have been prominent in technology jobs in Kabul, raising their economic status. They are also increasingly cohesive politically, leading to gains in the September 2010 parliamentary elections. During the various Afghan wars, the main Hazara Shiite militia was Hizb-e-Wahdat (Unity Party, composed of eight different groups). Hizb-e-Wahdat suffered a major setback in 1995 when the Taliban captured and killed its leader Abdul Ali Mazari. One of Karzai's vice president's Karim Khalili, is a Hazara. Another prominent Hazara faction leader is Mohammad Mohaqeq.
- Pashtun Islamists/Sayyaf. Abd-i-Rab Rasul Sayyaf, later a post-Taliban parliamentary committee chairman, headed a Pashtun-dominated hardline Islamist *mujahedin* faction called the Islamic Union for the Liberation of Afghanistan during the anti-Soviet war. Even though he is an Islamic conservative, Sayyaf viewed the Taliban as selling out Afghanistan to Al Qaeda and he joined the Northern Alliance to try to oust the Taliban. He is said to eye the speakership of the lower house of parliament.

POLICY PRE-SEPTEMBER 11, 2001

Throughout 2001, but prior to the September 11 attacks, Bush Administration policy differed little from Clinton Administration policy—applying economic and political pressure while retaining dialogue with the Taliban, and refraining from militarily assisting the Northern Alliance. The September 11 Commission report said that, in the months prior to the September 11 attacks, Administration officials leaned toward such a step and that some officials also wanted to assist ethnic Pashtuns who were opposed to the Taliban. Other covert options were reportedly under consideration as well.[7] In a departure from Clinton Administration policy, the Bush Administration stepped up engagement with Pakistan to try to reduce its support for the Taliban. At that time, there were allegations that Pakistani advisers were helping the Taliban in their fight against the Northern Alliance. In accordance with U.N. Security Council Resolution 1333, in February 2001 the State Department ordered the Taliban representative office in New York closed, although Taliban representative Abdul Hakim Mujahid continued to operate informally.[8] In March 2001, Administration officials received a Taliban envoy to discuss bilateral issues.

Even though the Northern Alliance was supplied with Iranian, Russian, and Indian financial and military support—all of whom had different motives for that support—the Northern Alliance nonetheless continued to lose ground to the Taliban after it lost Kabul in 1996. By the time of the September 11 attacks, the Taliban controlled at least 75% of the country, including almost all provincial capitals. The Alliance suffered a major setback on September 9, 2001, two days before the September 11 attacks, when Ahmad Shah Masud was assassinated by Arab journalists who allegedly were Al Qaeda operatives. He was succeeded by his intelligence chief, Muhammad Fahim,[9] a veteran figure but one who lacked Masud's undisputed authority.

SEPTEMBER 11 ATTACKS AND OPERATION ENDURING FREEDOM

After the September 11 attacks, the Bush Administration decided to militarily overthrow the Taliban when it refused to extradite bin Laden, judging that a friendly regime in Kabul was needed to enable U.S forces to search for Al Qaeda activists there. United Nations Security Council Resolution 1368 of September 12, 2001, said that the Security Council expresses its readiness to take all necessary steps to respond (implying force) to the September 11 attacks.

This is widely interpreted as a U.N. authorization for military action in response to the attacks, but it did not explicitly authorize Operation Enduring Freedom to oust the Taliban. Nor did the Resolution specifically reference Chapter VII of the U.N. Charter, which allows for responses to threats to international peace and security.

In Congress, S.J.Res. 23 (passed 98-0 in the Senate and with no objections in the House, P.L. 107-40), was somewhat more explicit than the U.N. Resolution, authorizing all necessary and appropriate force against those nations, organizations, or persons he determines planned, authorized, committed, or aided the terrorist attacks that occurred on September 11, 2001 *or harbored such organizations or persons.*

Major combat in Afghanistan (Operation Enduring Freedom, OEF) began on October 7, 2001. It consisted primarily of U.S. air-strikes on Taliban and Al Qaeda forces, facilitated by the cooperation between small numbers (about 1,000) of U.S. special operations forces and CIA operatives. The purpose of these operations was to help the Northern Alliance and Pashtun anti-Taliban forces by providing information to direct U.S. air strikes against Taliban positions. In part, the U.S. forces and operatives worked with such Northern Alliance contacts as Fahim and Amrollah Saleh, who during November 2001–June 2010 served as Afghanistan's intelligence director, to weaken Taliban defenses on the Shomali plain north of Kabul (and just south of Bagram Airfield. That airfield marked the forward position of the Northern Alliance during Taliban rule). Some U.S. combat units (about 1,300 Marines) moved into Afghanistan to pressure the Taliban around Qandahar at the height of the fighting (October-December 2001), but there were few pitched battles between U.S. and Taliban soldiers. Some critics believe that U.S. dependence on local Afghan militia forces in the war subsequently set back post-war democracy building.

The Taliban regime unraveled rapidly after it lost Mazar-e-Sharif on November 9, 2001, to forces led by Dostam.[11] Other, mainly Tajik, Northern Alliance forces—the commanders of which had initially promised U.S. officials they would not enter Kabul—entered the capital on November 12, 2001, to popular jubilation. The Taliban subsequently lost the south and east to U.S.supported Pashtun leaders, including Hamid Karzai. The end of the Taliban regime is generally dated as December 9, 2001, when the Taliban surrendered Qandahar and Mullah Umar fled the city, leaving it under tribal law administered by Pashtun leaders such as the Noorzai clan.

Subsequently, U.S. and Afghan forces conducted "Operation Anaconda" in the Shah-i-Kot Valley south of Gardez (Paktia Province) during March 2-19, 2002, against 800 Al Qaeda and Taliban fighters. In March 2003, about 1,000 U.S. troops raided suspected Taliban or Al Qaeda fighters in villages around Qandahar (Operation Valiant Strike). On May 1, 2003, Secretary of Defense Rumsfeld announced an end to "major combat."

POST-TALIBAN NATION-BUILDING EFFORTS[12]

With Afghanistan devastated after more than 20 years of warfare by the time of the 2001 fall of the Taliban regime, there were questions about the extent of a U.S. and international commitment to Afghanistan. Taking the view that leaving the Afghanistan-Pakistan theater after the 1989 Soviet pullout had led Afghanistan degenerate into chaos, the decision was made by the Bush Administration to try to rebuild try to build a relatively strong central government and to assist

Afghanistan's economy. The effort, which many outside experts described as "nationbuilding,"was supported by major international institutions and U.S. partners in several post-Taliban international meetings.

The Obama Administration's strategy review in late 2009, the results of which were announced on December 1, 2009, narrowed official U.S. goals to preventing terrorism safe haven in Afghanistan and Pakistan. A 2010 review, the summary of results of which were released December 16, 2010, did not alter U.S. goals or strategy.[13] In none of these reviews or pronouncements has the Obama Administration characterized U.S. goals in Afghanistan as "nation building," but the elements of Obama Administration strategy have continued or, in some cases, expanded, the nation-building strategy put in place by the Bush Administration. The task has proved slower and more difficult than anticipated because of the devastation that years of war wrought on governing institutions, on the education system, and on the already limited infrastructure. Some observers believe the international community had unrealistic expectations of what could be achieved in a relatively short time frame.

POST-TALIBAN POLITICAL TRANSITION

Table 2 depicts, in brief, the process and events that led to the formation of the post-Taliban government of Afghanistan. The process is discussed in greater detail in CRS Report RS21922, *Afghanistan: Politics, Elections, and Government Performance.*

TABLE 2.AFGHANISTAN POLITICAL TRANSITION PROCESS

Interim Formed by Bonn Agreement. Headed by Hamid Karzai, an ethnic Pashtun, but key security

Administration positions dominated by mostly minority "Northern Alliance." Karzai reaffirmed as leader by June 2002 "emergency loya jirga." (A jirga is a traditional Afghan assembly).

Constitution Approved by January 2004 "Constitutional Loya Jirga" (CLJ). Set up strong presidency, a rebuke to Northern Alliance that wanted prime ministership to balance presidential power, but gave parliament significant powers to compensate. Gives men and women equal rights under the law, allows for political parties as long as they are not "un-Islamic"; allows for court rulings according to Hanafi (Sunni) Islam (Chapter 7, Article 15). Set out electoral roadmap for simultaneous (if possible) presidential, provincial, and district elections by June 2004. Named ex-King Zahir Shah to non-hereditary position of "Father of the Nation;" he died July 23, 2007.

Presidential Election Elections for President and two vice presidents, for 5-year term, held Oct. 9, 2004. Turnout was 80% of 10.5 million registered. Karzai and running mates (Ahmad Zia Masud, a Tajik and brother of legendary mujahedin commander Ahmad Shah Masud, who was assassinated by Al Qaeda two days before the Sept. 11 attacks, and Karim Khalili, a Hazara) elected with 55% against 16 opponents. Second highest vote getter, Northern Alliance figure (and Education Minister) Yunus Qanooni (16%). One female ran. Hazara leader Mohammad Mohaqiq got 11.7%; and Dostam won 10%. Funded with $90 million from donors, including $40 million from U.S. (FY2004 supplemental, P.L. 108-106).

First Parliamentary Elections held Sept. 18, 2005, on "Single Non-Transferable Vote" System; candidates

Elections stood as individuals, not in party list. Parliament consists of a 249 elected lower house (Wolesi Jirga, House of the People) and a selected 102 seat upper house (Meshrano Jirga,

House of Elders). 2,815 candidates for Wolesi Jirga, including 347 women. Turnout was 57% (6.8 million voters) of 12.5 million registered. Voting was for one candidate only, although number of representatives varied by province, with the most from (Kabul Province—33 seats). The body was 28% female (68 persons), above the then quota of 62 women—two per each province. Upper house appointed by Karzai (34 seats, half of which are to be women), by the provincial councils (34 seats), and district councils (remaining 34 seats). There were 23 women in that house, above the 17 required by the constitution. Because district elections (400 district councils) were not held, provincial councils selected 68 on interim basis. Funded by $160 million in international aid, including $45 million from U.S. (FY2005 supplemental appropriation, P.L. 109-13).

First Provincial Provincial elections held Sept. 18, 2005, simultaneous with parliamentary elections. Exact

Elections/ powers vague, but now taking lead in deciding local reconstruction Provincial council sizes

District Elections range from 9 to the 29 seats on the Kabul provincial council. Total seats are 420, of which 121 held by women. l3,185 candidates, including 279 women. Some criticize the provincial election system as disproportionately weighted toward large districts. District elections not held due to complexity and potential tensions of drawing district boundaries.

Second Presidential and provincial elections were held Aug. 20, 2009, but required a runoff

Presidential/Provincial because no candidate received over 50% in certified results issued October 20. Second

Elections round not held because Dr. Abdullah, pulled out of runoff. Election costs: $300 million.

Parliamentary Originally set for May 22, 2010; held September 18, 2010. Results disputed, but agreement

Elections reached for Karzai inaugurate new lower house on January 26, 2011, six days after original date, but special tribunal continues to investigate fraud in the election.. 70 women elected, two more than quota. Speaker selected on February 27, Abdul Raouf Ibrahimi, an ethnic Uzbek. For the upper house, 68 seats council are appointed to four year terms by the elected provincial councils in each of Afghanistan's 34 provinces, and remain in office. Karzai made his 34 appointments on February 19, including 18 reappointments and 16 new members. Speaker of that body is Muslim Yaar (a Pashtun), selected January 27, 2011. See CRS Report RS21922, Afghanistan: Politics, Elections, and Government Performance.

MAJOR GOVERNANCE ISSUES

Expanding and reforming Afghan governance has been consistently and widely judged to be key to the success of U.S. policy. Governance was emphasized at the two major international conferences on Afghanistan in 2010—the January 28, 2010, "London Conference" and the July 20, 2010, "Kabul Conference."[15] This issue is expected to be the focus of an international conference on Afghanistan in Bonn in December 2011 on the 10th anniversary of the Bonn Agreement that began the post-Taliban political transition. Although the issue of governance is inseparable from that of securing Afghanistan, the sections below briefly outline Afghan-generated and international community-led efforts to build Afghanistan's governing capacity.

Obama Administration policy, as articulated in the cited strategy reviews in 2009—as well as in a State Department January 2010 document entitled *Afghanistan and Pakistan Regional Stabilization Strategy*[16]—emphasizes expanding and improving Afghan governance as a long-term means of stabilizing Afghanistan. The December 16, 2010 summary of the late 2010 Administration policy review on Afghanistan did not emphasize governance issues, but did specify that "[The United States is] also supporting Afghanistan's efforts to better improve national and sub-national governance, and to build institutions with increased transparency and accountability to reduce corruption—key steps in sustaining the Afghan government.

Anti-Corruption Efforts

U.S. officials believe that rife corruption in the Afghan government has undermined U.S. domestic support for the U.S. mission in Afghanistan, and caused the Afghan population to sour on the Karzai government. Therefore, an accelerating trend in U.S. policy—and emphasized in every Obama Administration strategy review as well as by many in Congress—is to press Karzai to confront governmental corruption. U.S. anti-corruption and rule of law efforts are discussed extensively in the "Afghanistan and Pakistan Regional Stabilization Strategy" document, referenced above, and in other anti-corruption strategy documents for Afghanistan. One conclusion of the Administration in late 2010 was to focus on lower level corruption rather than investigations of senior Afghans or Afghans close to President Karzai. Doing so in 2009 and early 2010 had proved counter-productive by causing Karzai to become suspicious of U.S. intent and to ally with undemocratic elements in Afghanistan.

Two major corruption-related issues that have most recently caused tensions between the United States and the Afghan government include the scandal surrounding the Kabul Bank, and U.S. sanctions imposed on the money trading firm New Ansari Money Exchange on February 18, 2011. These and other key cases are discussed in detail in: CRS Report R41484, *Afghanistan: U.S. Rule of Law and Justice Sector Assistance*, by Liana Sun Wyler and Kenneth Katzman and in CRS Report RS21922, *Afghanistan: Politics, Elections, and Government Performance*, by Kenneth Katzman.

Expanding Local Governance

In part because building the central government has gone slowly and because official corruption is widespread, there has been a U.S. shift, predating the Obama Administration, toward promoting local governance. Some argue that, in addition to offering the advantage of bypassing an often corrupt central government, doing so is more compatible with Afghan traditions of local autonomy. Building local governance has suffered from a deficit of trained and respected local government administrators ready or willing to serve, particularly where hostilities are ongoing.

The slow pace of progress accounts for many of the uncertainties clouding the prospects for transition to Afghan security leadership by the end of 2014. Still, Joint Chiefs of Staff Chairman Michael Mullen testified on February 16, 2011 (House Armed Services Committee) that "improvements in sub-national governance ... have not kept pace with progress in improving security." However, a U.S. civilian representative for southern Afghanistan, Henry Ensher, said in January 2011 that local governance efforts—including the self-generated formation of village councils—are expanding in concert with security provided by the U.S. troop "surge."

U.S. policy has sought to use local governance efforts to support U.S. security strategy for Afghanistan. Several districts that have been promoted as "models" of district security and governance are Nawa, in Helmand Province, and Baraki-Barak, in Lowgar Province, both cleared of Taliban militants in 2009. "Operation Moshtarek" (Operation Together), launched February 13, 2010, to clear the city of Marjah of militants, had sought to make Marjah a similar model, although that process was slowed by continuing insurgent activity around Marjah. Still, the British civilian representative in Marjah said in October 2010 that central government ministry representation in Marjah is now in place and operating consistently. On March 1, 2011, Marjah held community council elections in which 75% of registered voters cast ballots. (Marjah is currently part of Nad Ali district, and is eventually to become its own district, according to Afghan observers.) With substantial infusions of U.S. development funds that put sometime insurgents to work on projects ("cash for work:" offering $5 per day to perform such tasks as cleaning irrigation canals), these districts are, by several accounts, far more stable and secure than they were in 2009.

Human Rights and Democracy/Women's Rights

The Administration and Afghan government claim progress in building a democratic Afghanistan that adheres to international standards of human rights practices. The State Department report on human rights practices for 2010 (released April 8, 2011)[17] presented a substantial list of human rights deficiencies in Afghanistan, including: extrajudiciary killings, torture, arbitrary arrest and detention, restriction on freedom of the press, limits on freedom of assembly, official corruption, violence against women, sexual abuse of children, child labor, and abuse of workers rights. Still, virtually all observers agree that Afghans are freer than they were under the Taliban. One religious freedom case, that of Said Musa who was to be executed for converting to Christianity from Islam, was resolved quietly on February 24, 2011, when he was released from prison and left Afghanistan, reportedly for Italy to seek asylum there.

A major debate is over whether gains made by women since the fall of the Taliban can be sustained as the U.S.-led coalition transitions to Afghan leadership. Women enjoy legal protections and play public roles unheard of during the Taliban era, although conservatives attitudes prevail and often undermine the intentions of formal laws and regulations. Still others note the large role played by women in the National Assembly and throughout the governing institutions. The tables at the end of this report contain figures on U.S. funding for democracy, governance, rule of law and human rights. Afghanistan's human rights record is also covered in CRS Report RS21922, *Afghanistan: Politics, Elections, and Government Performance*.

Narcotics Trafficking/Insurgent Financing[18]

Narcotics trafficking is regarded by some as a core impediment to the U.S. mission in Afghanistan by undermining rule of law and providing funds to the insurgency. It is an area on which there has been progress in recent years, although there are questions whether progress is sustainable. The trafficking is said to generate an estimated $70 million–$100 million per year for the Taliban. A UNODC report of September 2010, continued a relatively positive trend in reporting on this issue, noting that all of the 20 provinces (out of 34 provinces in Afghanistan) in the "poppy free" category remain that way. Total production in 2010 is estimated at 3,600 metric tons, a 48% decrease from 2009, although this was due to a crop disease, for the most part.[19] Some observers report that the price for opium increased dramatically in late 2010, creating the potential for many farmers to return to poppy cultivation.

The Obama Administration approach focuses on promoting legitimate agricultural alternatives to poppy growing—and that sector is discussed extensively later in this paper—in line with Afghan government preferences. In conjunction, U.S. officials announced in July 2009 that the United States would end its prior focus on eradication of poppy fields. In this view, eradication was driving Afghans into the arms of the Taliban as protectors of their ability to earn a living. The de-emphasis on eradication also put aside the long-standing differences over whether to conduct spraying of fields, particularly by air. That concept was strenuously opposed by Karzai and not implemented. Congress sided with Karzai's view; the Successive annual appropriations laws since FY2008 have prohibited U.S. counter-narcotics funding from being used for aerial spraying on Afghanistan poppy fields without Afghan concurrence. Other policies promote incentives; Helmand, for example, received about $10 million in Good Performance funding in 2009 for a 33% cut in poppy cultivation that year.

How consistently to use U.S. and NATO forces to combat narcotics has been under almost constant debate. Britain's forces, for example, focus on interdicting traffickers and raiding drug labs. The U.S. military, in support of the effort after initial reluctance, is flying Afghan and U.S. counter-narcotics agents (Drug Enforcement Agency, DEA) on missions and identifying targets; it also evacuates casualties from counter-drug operations and assists an Afghan helicopter squadron to move Afghan counter-narcotics forces around the country. To help break up narcotics trafficking networks, the DEA presence in Afghanistan is has expanded from 13 agents in 2008 to over 80 in Afghanistan by the end of 2010.

The Obama Administration has placed additional focus on the other sources of Taliban funding, including continued donations from wealthy residents of the Persian Gulf. He established a multinational task force to combat Taliban financing generally, not limited to narcotics, and U.S. officials are emphasizing with Persian Gulf counterparts the need for cooperation.

The Bush and Obama Administrations have exercised waiver provisions to required certifications of full Afghan cooperation needed to provide more than congressionally stipulated amounts of U.S. economic assistance to Afghanistan. A certification requirement (to provide amounts over $300 million) was contained in the FY2008 appropriation (P.L. 110-161); in the FY2009 regular appropriation, P.L. 111-8 ($200 million ceiling); and the FY2010 appropriation, P.L. 111-117, ($200 million ceiling). The FY2009 supplemental (P.L. 111-32) withheld 10% of State Department narcotics funding (International Narcotics Control and Law Enforcement, INCLE) pending a report that Afghanistan is removing officials involved in narcotics trafficking or gross human rights violations. No funds for Afghanistan have been held up on these grounds. Narcotics trafficking control was perhaps the one issue on which the Taliban regime satisfied much of the international community. The Taliban enforced a July 2000 ban on poppy cultivation.[20] However, cultivation flourished in provinces under Northern Alliance control, such as Badakhshan.

U.S. AND INTERNATIONAL STRUCTURE FOR POLICY IMPLEMENTATION

Building the capacity of the Afghan government, and helping it develop economically, is primarily, although not exclusively, the purview of U.S. and international civilian officials and institutions. In line with the prioritization of Afghanistan policy, in February 2009, the Administration set up the position of appointed "Special Representative for Afghanistan and Pakistan" (SRAP), occupied by Ambassador Richard Holbrooke, reporting to Secretary of State Clinton. Holbrooke died on December 13, 2010, but his team at the State Department, led as of February 2011 by former Undersecretary of State and Ambassador to Turkey Marc Grossman, remains intact. The SRAP office consists mainly of members detailed from several different agencies; several have long-term experience on Afghanistan and Pakistan affairs.

At the U.S. Embassy in Kabul, Karl Eikenberry, who served as commander of U.S. forces in Afghanistan during 2004-2005, is U.S. Ambassador. There are reports he will rotate out in August 2011. While the main focus of the civilian side of U.S. and international policy is on building governance and promoting economic development, President Obama has said he expects the civilian team to work closely with the U.S. and NATO military structure, and a U.S. civilian-military "joint campaign plan" was developed and released in mid-August 2009.[21] There is a "deputy Ambassador," and a separate Ambassador rank official (William Todd) to manage U.S. economic assistance issues. Another Ambassador-rank official handles Embassy management, and yet another official of Ambassador rank, Hans Klemm, (as of June 2010) coordinates U.S. rule of law programs. Ambassador Timothy Carney oversaw U.S. policy for the 2009 elections.

The U.S. Embassy has progressively expanded its personnel and facilities and will expand its facilities further to accommodate some of the additional civilian hires and Foreign Service officers who have been posted to Afghanistan as mentors and advisers to the Afghan government.

U.S. officials say there are more than 1,100 U.S. civilian officials in Afghanistan, as of March 2011, up from only about 400 in early 2009. Of these at least 400 serve outside Kabul as part of initiatives such as the 32 "District Support Teams" and the "District Working Groups." That is up from 67 outside Kabul in early 2009.

The tables at the end of this report include U.S. funding for State Department and USAID operations, including Embassy construction and running the "Embassy air wing," a fleet of twin-engine turboprops that ferry U.S. officials and contractors around Afghanistan. In a significant development attempting to signal normalization of certain areas of Afghanistan, in early 2010 the United States formally inaugurated U.S. consulates in Herat and Mazar-e-Sharif. In November 2010, contracts were announced for expansion of the U.S. Embassy ($511 million) and to construct the two consulates ($20 million for each facility).

Afghan Ambassador to the United States, Sayed Tayib Jawad, served as Ambassador from 2004 until his recall in August 2010. He was recalled because of complaints in Kabul about Western-style parties that were being held at the Afghan embassy in the United States, and deputy Foreign Minister Eklil Hakimi has replaced him as of February 23, 2011.

On February 7, 2010, in an effort to improve civilian coordination between the United States, its foreign partners, and the Afghan government, a NATO "Senior Civilian Representative" in Afghanistan, UK Ambassador Mark Sedwill, took office. Ambassador Sedwill works not only with U.S. military officials but with representatives of the embassies of partner countries and with a special U.N. Assistance Mission–Afghanistan (UNAMA, see Table 3). As of April 15, 2011, he has been replaced by the former British Ambassador to Iran, Sir Simon Gass.

U.N.Assistance Mission in Afghanistan (UNAMA)

The United Nations is extensively involved in Afghan governance and national building, primarily in factional conflict resolution and coordination of development assistance. The coordinator of U.N. efforts is the U.N. Assistance Mission in Afghanistan (UNAMA), headed as of March 22, 2010, by Swedish diplomat Staffan de-Mistura, replacing Norwegian diplomat Kai Eide. Mistura formerly played a similar role in Iraq. U.N. Security Council Resolution 1806 of March 20, 2008, expanded UNAMA's authority to coordinating the work of international donors and strengthening cooperation between the international peacekeeping force (ISAF, see below) and the Afghan government. In concert with the Obama Administration's emphasis on Afghan policy, UNAMA is to open offices in as many of Afghanistan's 34 provinces as financially and logistically permissible.

(The mandate of UNAMA, reviewed at one-year intervals, ran until March 23, 2010, as provided for by Resolution 1869 of March 23, 2009, and was renewed for another year on March 22, 2011 (Resolution 1974). As did Resolution 1917 the previous year, Resolution 1974 largely restated UNAMA's expanded mandate and coordinating role with other high-level representatives in Afghanistan, and election support role, while referring to UNAMA's role in facilitating the coming transition to Afghan leadership.

In keeping with its expanding role, in 2008 U.S. Ambassador Peter Galbraith was appointed as Eide's deputy, although he left Afghanistan in early September 2009 in a reported dispute with Eide over how vigorously to insist on investigating fraud in the August 20 Afghan election. Galbraith reportedly pressed Afghan and independent election bodies to be as vigorous as possible in the interests of rule of law and election legitimacy; Eide purportedly was willing to encourage an Afghan compromise to avoid a second round run-off. The split led U.N. Secretary General Ban Ki Moon to remove Galbraith from his post at UNAMA in late September 2009 on the grounds that the disharmony was compromising the UNAMA mission. The turmoil may have caused Eide to leave his post when his contract with the U.N. expired in March 2010.

UNAMA is co-chair of the joint Afghan-international community coordination body called the Joint Coordination and Monitoring Board (JCMB), and is helping implement the five-year development strategy outlined in a "London Compact," (now called the Afghanistan Compact) adopted at the January 31–February 1, 2006, London conference on Afghanistan. The priorities developed in that document comport with Afghanistan's own "National Strategy for Development," presented on June 12, 2008, in Paris. During his term, Eide urged the furnishing of additional capacity-building resources, and he complained that some efforts by international donors are redundant or tied to purchases by Western countries. In statements and press conferences, Eide continued to note security deterioration but also progress in governance and in reduction of drug cultivation, and he publicly supported negotiations with Taliban figures to end the war. His final speech before leaving criticized the U.S.-led coalition for focusing too much on military success and not enough on governance. UNAMA also often has been involved in local dispute resolution among factions, and it helps organize elections. Under a March 2010 compromise with Karzai, it nominates two international members of the five person Electoral Complaints Commission (ECC), one fewer than the three it selected under the prior election law. UNAMA was a co-convener of the January 28, 2010, and July 20, 2010, London and Kabul Conferences, respectively.

The difficulties in coordinating U.N. with U.S. and NATO efforts were evident in a 2007 proposal to create a new position of "super envoy" that would represent the United Nations, the European Union, and NATO in Afghanistan. The concept advanced and in January 2008, with U.S. support, U.N. Secretary General Ban Ki Moon tentatively appointed British diplomat Paddy Ashdown as the "super envoy." However, Karzai rejected the appointment reportedly over concerns about the scope of authority of such an envoy. Karzai might have also sought to show independence from the international community. Ashdown withdrew his name on January 28, 2008. However, the concept reportedly was floated again in late 2009, but was again suppressed by Karzai and others who say it contradicts U.S. and other efforts to promote Afghan leadership. The NATO senior civilian representative post, held by Amb. Mark Sedwill (UK), appears to represent a step in the direction of improved donor coordination in Afghanistan and streamlining of the foreign representative structure there.

SECURITY POLICY AND FORCE CAPACITY BUILDING[22]

Although the formal Obama Administration policy is to prevent Afghanistan from again becoming a safe haven for global terrorism, the U.S. definition of "success" of the stabilization mission in Afghanistan is to help build up an Afghan government and security force that can defend itself, expand governance, and develop economically. As discussed below, the Obama Administration has not significantly changed the basic pillars of U.S. and NATO security strategy that have been in place since 2001, although the blend of these components often shifts as outcomes and prospects of various initiatives are evaluated. Since the effort began in 2001, the primary U.S.-led activities have included: (1) combat operations by U.S. forces and a NATO-led International Security Assistance Force (ISAF) to "provide space" for the expansion of Afghan governance, security leadership, and economic development; (2) U.S. and NATO operation of "provincial reconstruction teams"(PRTs) to serve as enclaves to facilitate the strategy; and (3) the equipping, training, and expansion of Afghanistan National Security Forces (ANSF).

WHO ARE U.S. /NATO FORCES FIGHTING? TALIBAN, AL QAEDA, AND RELATED INSURGENTS AND THEIR STRENGTH

As noted in the Defense Department reports and statements, security is being challenged by a confluence of related armed groups who are increasingly well equipped and sophisticated in their tactics and operations, particularly by using roadside bombs.[23] There has not been agreement about the relative strength of insurgents in all of the areas where they operate, or their degree of cooperation with each other,. Press reports in December 2010, quoting U.S. military officers in Afghanistan, said there has been increasing operational cooperation among the various insurgent groups. Afghan and U.S. assessments are that there are more than 20,000 total insurgents operating in Afghanistan, up from a few thousand in 2003.

Prior to U.S.-led offensives launched since mid-2009, the Karzai government was estimated by to control about 30% of the country, while insurgents controlled 4% (13 out of 364 districts). Insurgents "influenced" or "operated in" another 30% (Afghan Interior Ministry estimates in August 2009). Tribes and local groups with varying degrees of loyalty to the central government control the remainder. Some outside groups report higher percentages of insurgent control or influence.[24] U.S. military officers in Kabul told CRS in October 2009 that the Taliban had named "shadow governors" in 33 out of 34 of Afghanistan's provinces, although many provinces in northern Afghanistan were assessed as having minimal Taliban presence.

As far as tactics, U.S. commanders increasingly worry about growing insurgent use of improvised explosive devices (IEDs), including roadside bombs. IED's are the leading cause of U.S. combat deaths, although the Joint Improvised Explosive Device Defeat Organization, a part of DOD, reported in February 2011 substantial progress finding IED's before they explode. In January 2010, President Karzai issued a decree banning importation of fertilizer chemicals (ammonium nitrate) commonly used for the roadside bombs, but there reportedly is informal circumvention of the ban for certain civilian uses, and the material reportedly still comes into Afghanistan from Pakistan. U.S. commanders have said they have verified some insurgent use of surface-to-air missiles.[25]

There were about 310 U.S. soldiers killed in 2009, nearly double the previous year, and U.S. deaths in 2010 reached a new high for the Afghan conflict of just over 500. There were about 210 soldiers from partner countries killed during 2010. According to a UNAMA report issued in December 2010, covering the fall of 2010, there was a 66% increase in security incidents as compared to the same period in 2009. However, over 80% of those deaths are purportedly caused by insurgent attacks, and criticizing insurgents—and not NATO or other coalition elements—for attacks that kill civilians, is an increasing feature of U.N. and human rights organizations.

GROUPS: THE TALIBAN ("QUETTA SHURA TALIBAN")

The core of the insurgency remains the Taliban movement centered around Mullah Umar, who led the Taliban regime during 1996-2001. Mullah Umar and many of his top advisers remain at large and are reportedly running their insurgency from their safe haven in Pakistan. They are believed to be primarily in and around the city of Quetta, according to Afghan officials, thus accounting for the term usually applied to Umar and his aides: "Quetta Shura Taliban" (QST). Some believe that Umar and his inner circle blame their past association with Al Qaeda for their loss of power and want to distance themselves from Al Qaeda. Other experts see continuing close association that is likely to continue were the Taliban movement to return to power.

Some believe that the U.S. "surge" in Afghanistan may be Taliban leaders to mull the concept of a political settlement. Umar's top deputy, Mullah Bradar, was arrested in a reported joint U.S.Pakistani operation near the city of Karachi in February 2010—Karzai considered his capture set back Afghan government-Taliban reconciliation talks, which Bradar reportedly supports. In recent years, other top Taliban figures, including Mullah Dadullah, his son Mansoor, and Mullah Usmani have been killed or captured. Some observers say that informal settlement ideas floated between the Taliban and the Karzai government may envision Umar being granted exile in Saudi Arabia. Two other purported members of the Quetta Shura, Mullah Hassan Rahmani, former Taliban governor of Qandahar, and Mullah Afghan Tayib, another spokesman, are said to have come under some Pakistani pressure to refrain from militant activities.

To address losses, Umar reportedly has replaced Bradar with younger and reputedly hardline, anti-compromise leaders Mullah Abdul Qayyum Zakir, a U.S. detainee in Guantanamo Bay, Cuba until 2007, and Akhtar Mohammad Mansoor, a logistics expert.[26] The Taliban has several official spokespersons still at large, including Qari Yusuf Ahmadi and Zabiullah Mujahid, and it operates a clandestine radio station, "Voice of Shariat" and publishes videos.

AL QAEDA/BIN LADEN WHEREABOUTS

The summary of an Administration policy review, released December 16, 2010, says that "there has been significant progress in disrupting and dismantling the Pakistan-based leadership and cadre of Al Qaeda over the past year." U.S. commanders say that Al Qaeda militants are more facilitators of militant incursions into Afghanistan rather than active fighters in the Afghan insurgency. Director of Central Intelligence Leon Panetta said on June 27, 2010, that Al Qaeda fighters in Afghanistan itself might number 50-100.[27] Contradicting those comments to some extent, NATO/ISAF officials said in October 2010, that Al Qaeda cells may be moving back into remote areas of Kunar and Nuristan provinces,[28] particularly in areas vacated by U.S.-led forces. Press reports in April 2011 added that some Al Qaeda training camps may have been established inside Afghanistan, but Gen. Petraeus tried to refute these stories on April 10 by saying that the Al Qaeda presence in Afghanistan remains small at "less than 100 or so." Some of the Al Qaeda fighters are believed to belong to Al Qaeda affiliates such as the Islamic Movement of Uzbekistan (IMU).

Despite the reports of progress against Al Qaeda in Afghanistan and Pakistan, Al Qaeda's top leadership has consistently eluded U.S. efforts. In December 2001, in the course of the post-September 11 major combat effort, U.S. Special Operations Forces and CIA operatives reportedly narrowed Osama bin Laden's location to the Tora Bora mountains in Nangarhar Province (30 miles west of the Khyber Pass), but the Afghan militia fighters who were the bulk of the fighting force did not prevent his escape. Some U.S. military and intelligence officers (such as

Gary Berntsen and Dalton Fury, who have written books on the battle) have questioned the U.S. decision to rely mainly on Afghan forces in this engagement.

Amid debate over the potential operational significance of capturing or killing bin Laden, he and his close ally Ayman al-Zawahiri have long been presumed to be on the Pakistani side of the border. CNN reported October 18, 2010, that assessments from the U.S.-led coalition now say the two are likely in a settled area near the border with Afghanistan, and not living in a very remote uninhabited area. A U.S. strike reportedly missed Zawahiri by a few hours in the village of Damadola, Pakistan, in January 2006, suggesting that there was intelligence on his movements.[29] On the ninth anniversary of the September 11 attacks, some U.S. observers said it was still significant to try to capture bin Laden if for no other reason than for symbolic value.

Among other bin Laden aides, press reports in September 2010 said that Al Qaeda's former spokesman, Kuwait-born Sulayman Abu Ghaith, may have been released from house arrest by Iran and allowed to proceed to Pakistan. Other reports in November 2010 said that another Al Qaeda senior operative, Sayf al Adl, who was believed to be in Iran during 2002-2010, may have left Iran and gone to Pakistan, and reportedly may have been elevated by bin Laden to top Al Qaeda operational commander.

As a consequence of other U.S. efforts, a January 2008 strike near Damadola killed Abu Laith al-Libi, a reported senior Al Qaeda figure who purportedly masterminded, among other operations, the bombing at Bagram Air Base in February 2007 when Vice President Cheney was visiting. In August 2008, an airstrike was confirmed to have killed Al Qaeda chemical weapons expert Abu Khabab al-Masri, and two senior operatives allegedly involved in the 1998 embassy bombings in Africa reportedly were killed by an unmanned aerial vehicle (Predator) strike in January 2009. Such aerial-based strikes have become more frequent under President Obama, indicating that the Administration sees the tactic as effective in preventing attacks. Unmanned vehicle strikes are also increasingly used on the Afghanistan battlefield itself and against Al Qaeda affiliated militants in such countries as Yemen.

Hikmatyar Faction

Another "high value target" identified by U.S. commanders is the faction of former *mujahedin* party leader Gulbuddin Hikmatyar (Hizb-e-Islami Gulbuddin, HIG) allied with Al Qaeda and Taliban insurgents. As noted above, Hikmatyar was one of the main U.S.-backed *mujahedin* leaders during the Soviet occupation era. Hikmatyar's faction received extensive U.S. support against the Soviet Union, but is now active against U.S. and Afghan forces in Kunar, Nuristan, Kapisa, and Nangarhar provinces, north and east of Kabul. On February 19, 2003, the U.S. government formally designated Hikmatyar as a "Specially Designated Global Terrorist," under the authority of Executive Order 13224, subjecting it to financial and other U.S. sanctions. It is *not* designated as a "Foreign Terrorist Organization" (FTO).

While U.S. commanders continue to battle Hikmatyar's militia, on March 22, 2010, both the Afghan government and Hikmatyar representatives confirmed they were in talks in Kabul, including meetings with Karzai. Hikmatyar has expressed a willingness to discuss a cease-fire with the Karzai government since 2007, and several of Karzai's key allies in the National Assembly are members of a moderate wing of Hikmatyar's party. The newly selected speaker of the lower house, Abdul Raouf Ibrahimi, is said to be a member of this group. In January 2010, Hikmatyar outlined specific conditions for a possible reconciliation with Karzai, including elections under a neutral caretaker government following a U.S. withdrawal. Some close to Hikmatyar apparently attended the consultative peace *loya jirga* on June 2-4, 2010, which discussed the reconciliation issue, as analyzed further below.

HAQQANI FACTION

Another militant faction, cited repeatedly as a major threat, is the "Haqqani Network" led by Jalaludin Haqqani and his eldest son, Siraj (or Sirajjudin). Jalaludin Haqqani, who served as Minister of Tribal Affairs in the Taliban regime of 1996-2001, is believed closer to Al Qaeda than to the ousted Taliban leadership in part because one of his wives is purportedly Arab. The group is active around its key objective, Khost city, capital of Khost Province. The Haqqani network has claimed responsibility for attacks on India's embassy in Kabul and other India-related targets.

U.S. officials say they are continuing to pressure the Haqqani network with military action in Afghanistan and air strikes on the Pakistani side of the border. Siraj's brother, Mohammad, was reportedly killed by a U.S. unmanned vehicle strike in late February 2010, although Mohammad was not thought to be a key militant commander. Pakistan reportedly arrested a minor family member (Nasruddin Haqqani) in December 2010—a possible indication that Pakistan senses U.S. pressure for increased action against the network. However, some doubt has been cast that an arrest took place. The Haqqani network is said to be a major driver of the reported debate within the Obama Administration over whether to authorize additional Special Operations raids across the border into Pakistan, and presumably against the Haqqani network.

Among other potential steps, in July 2010, it was reported that General Petraeus, as part of his adjustments to policy as top commander in Afghanistan, wanted the Haqqani network to be named as an FTO under the Immigration and Naturalization Act. Such a move would be intended to signal to Pakistan that it should not see the Haqqani network, as a whole, as part of a reconciled political structure in Afghanistan that would protect Pakistan's interests and work to limit the influence of India.[31] The Haqqani faction has been thought not amenable to a political settlement, although some experts question that assessment. Table 7 contains estimated numbers of Haqqani fighters.

PAKISTANI GROUPS

The Taliban of Afghanistan are increasingly linked politically and operationally to Pakistani Taliban militants. The Pakistani groups might see a Taliban recapture of Afghanistan's government as helpful to the prospects for these groups inside Pakistan or in their Kashmir struggle. A major Pakistani group, the Pakistani Taliban (Tehrik-e-Taliban Pakistan, TTP), is primarily seeking to challenge the government of Pakistan, but they facilitate the transiting into Afghanistan of Afghan Taliban and support the Afghan Taliban goals of recapturing Afghanistan. The TTP may also be seeking to target the United States, an assessment based on a failed bombing in New York City in May 2010. The State Department designated the TTP as a Foreign Terrorist Organization (FTO) under the Immigration and Naturalization Act on September 2, 2010, allegedly for having close connections to Al Qaeda.

Another Pakistani group said to be increasingly active inside Afghanistan is Laskhar-e-Tayyiba (LET, or Army of the Righteous). LET is an Islamist militant group that has previously been focused on operations against Indian control of Kashmir.

THE U.S.-LED MILITARY EFFORT: 2001-2008

To combat the insurgency, in partnership with 49 other countries and the Afghan government and security forces (see Table 24), there are nearly 100,000 U.S. troops in Afghanistan as of March 2011. The vast majority operate under NATO/ISAF command, but about 10,000 of them are part of the post-September 11 anti-terrorism mission Operation Enduring Freedom (OEF). Serving under the top U.S. and NATO/ISAF commander General Petraeus is Major General David Rodriguez, who heads a NATO-approved "Intermediate Joint Command" focused primarily on day-to-day operations. He has been in this position since mid-2009. Press reports appeared in February 2011 indicating that General Petraeus might leave the command at the end of 2011.

Many of the U.S. forces in Afghanistan are in eastern Afghanistan and lead Regional Command East of the NATO/ISAF operation. These U.S. forces belong to Combined Joint Task Force 101 (as of June 2010), which is commanded by Major General John Campbell. The most restive provinces in RC-E are Paktia, Paktika, Khost, Kunar, and Nuristan. Helmand, Qandahar, Uruzgan, Zabol, Nimruz, and Dai Kundi provinces constitute "Regional Command South (RCS)," a command formally transferred to NATO/ISAF responsibility on July 31, 2006. U.S. forces have not led RC-S; the command was rotated among Britain, the Netherlands, and Canada. The growing U.S. troop strength in RC-S prompted a May 23, 2010, NATO decision to bifurcate RCS, with the United States leading a "southwest" subdivision for Helmand and Nimruz.

Perception of "Victory" in the First Five Post-Taliban Years

During 2001-mid-2006, U.S. forces and Afghan troops fought relatively low levels of insurgent violence. The United States and Afghanistan conducted "Operation Mountain Viper" (August 2003); "Operation Avalanche" (December 2003); "Operation Mountain Storm" (March-July 2004) against Taliban remnants in and around Uruzgan province, home province of Mullah Umar; "Operation Lightning Freedom" (December 2004–February 2005); and "Operation Pil" (Elephant) in Kunar Province in the east (October 2005). By late 2005, U.S. and partner commanders appeared to believe that the combat, coupled with overall political and economic reconstruction, had virtually ended any insurgency. Anticipating further stabilization, NATO/ISAF assumed lead responsibility for security in all of Afghanistan during 2005-2006.

Contrary to U.S. expectations, violence increased significantly in mid-2006, particularly in the east and the south, where ethnic Pashtuns predominate. Reasons for the deterioration include some of those discussed above in the sections on governance: Afghan government corruption; the absence of governance or security forces in many rural areas. Other factors included the safe haven enjoyed by militants in Pakistan; the reticence of some NATO contributors to actively combat insurgents; a popular backlash against civilian casualties caused by NATO and U.S. military operations; and the slow pace of economic development. Many Afghans are said to have turned to the Taliban as a source of impartial and rapid justice, in contrast to the slow and corrupt processes instituted by the central government.

Perception of Deterioration and Growing Force Levels in 2007 and 2008

Since 2006, and particularly during 2010, the key theater of implementation of U.S. strategy has been eastern and southern Afghanistan, especially Helmand and Qandahar provinces. NATO counter-offensives during 2006-2008—such as Operation Mountain Lion, Operation Mountain Thrust, and Operation Medusa (August-September 2006, in Panjwai district of Qandahar Province)—cleared key districts but did not prevent subsequent reinfiltration because Afghan governance was not established in cleared areas. In late 2006, British forces—who believe in negotiated local solutions—entered into an agreement with tribal elders in the Musa Qala district of Helmand Province, under which they would secure the main town of the district themselves. That strategy failed when the Taliban took over Musa Qala town in February 2007, but a NATO offensive in December 2007 retook it.

As a further response, NATO and OEF forces tried to apply a more integrated strategy involving preemptive combat and increased development work. Major combat operations in 2007 included U.S. and NATO attempted preemption of an anticipated Taliban "spring offensive" ("Operation Achilles," March 2007) in the Sangin district of Helmand Province, around the Kajaki dam, and Operation Silicon (May 2007), also in Helmand. (In September 2010, Britain turned over security leadership in Sangin to U.S. forces. The district produced half of Britain's entire casualties in Afghanistan to date.)

Despite the additional resources put into Afghanistan, throughout 2008, growing concern took hold within the Bush Administration. Pessimism was reflected in such statements as a September 2008 comment by Joint Chiefs of Staff chairman Admiral Mike Mullen that "I'm not sure we're winning" in Afghanistan. Several major incidents supported that assessment, including (1) expanding Taliban operations in provinces where it had not previously been active, particularly Lowgar, Wardak, and Kapisa, close to Kabul; (2) high-profile attacks in Kabul against well-defended targets, such as the January 14, 2008, attack on the Serena Hotel in Kabul and the July 7, 2008, suicide bombing at the Indian Embassy in Kabul, killing more than 50; (3) the April 27, 2008, assassination attempt on Karzai during a military parade celebrating the ouster of the Soviet Union; and (4) a June 12, 2008, Sarposa prison break in Qandahar (several hundred Taliban captives were freed, as part of an emptying of the 1,200 inmates there).

To try to arrest deterioration, the United States and its partners decided to increase force levels. The added forces partly fulfilled a mid-2008 request by General McKiernan for 30,000 additional

U.S. troops (beyond the approximately 35,000 there at the time of the request). However, as the November 2008 U.S. presidential election approached, the decision whether to fulfill the entire request was deferred to the next Administration. U.S. troop levels started 2006 at 30,000; climbed slightly to 32,000 by December 2008; and reached 39,000 by April 2009 (shortly after President Obama took office). Partner forces were increased significantly as well, by about 6,000 during this time, to a total of 39,000 at the end of 2009 (rough parity between U.S. and non-U.S. forces). Many of the U.S. forces deployed in 2008 and 2009 were Marines that deployed to Helmand, large parts of which had fallen out of coalition/Afghan control.

OTHER POLICY COMPONENTS: BUILDING AFGHAN FORCES

Since the Taliban were ousted from power, a key tenet of U.S. and NATO policy – and the key to their "exit strategy" from Afghanistan – has been to build capable Afghan National Security Forces (ANSF), consisting of the Afghan National Army (ANA) and Afghan National Policy (ANP). Although the ANSF has expanded considerably since 2002, it has been considered a struggle to bring these forces to a level of capability that would allow for a transition from international forces in securing Afghanistan. Obama Administration strategy emphasizes expanding the ANSF and improving it through partnering and more intense mentoring and training—about 70% of Afghan units are now partnered with international forces.

On January 21, 2010, the joint U.N.-Afghan "Joint Coordination and Monitoring Board" (JCMB) agreed that, by the end of 2011, the ANA would expand to 171,600 and the ANP to about 134,000. As of August 11, 2010, both forces reached their interim size of 134,000 and 109,000 respectively (two months earlier than planned). As of April 2011, the forces total about 150,000 ANA and 120,000 ANP, and Defense Minister Wardak said on February 25, 2011, that the forces would reach their 171,600 and 134,000 established target sizes ahead of the end of 2011 date.

A Petraeus recommendation to raise the target level for both forces to 378,000 (from 305,600) was to be put to the JCMB in January 2011, but U.S. and partner country concerns about the Afghan ability to sustain so large a force put the plan on hold. However, U.S. commanders said in March 2011 that they expect the expansion to be approved in the near future. While holding to his recommendation for the 78,000 increase, Gen. Petraeus testified on March 15 and 16, 2011, that he considers the ANSF to need a minimum of 44,000 more authorized forces than the current target. This would put his minimum recommended total at about 360,000.

U.S. forces along with partner countries and contractors, train the ANSF. In February 2010, the U.S.-run "Combined Security Transition Command-Afghanistan" (CSTC-A) that ran the training was subordinated to the broader NATO Training Mission—Afghanistan (NTM-A). NTM-A is commanded by U.S. Major General William Caldwell. CSTC-A's mission was reoriented to building the capacity of the Afghan Defense and Interior Ministries, and to provide resources to the ANSF. The total number of required trainers (U.S. and partner) for these institutions is 4,750. The unfilled gap of trainers totaling about 750 was discussed in the section on Alliances above. Particular attention has been called to the need for 290 police trainers to staff five new police training centers scheduled to open in 2011.[32] A separate France-led 300-person European Gendarmerie Force (EGF) has been established to train Afghan forces out in the provinces. The European Union is providing a 190-member "EUPOL" training effort, and 60 other experts to help train the ANP. These efforts are subsumed under NTM-A.

A core element of NATO's training efforts are its mentoring teams—known as Operational Mentoring Liaison Teams (OMLTs) and Police Operational Mentoring and Liaison Teams (POMLTs). While NTM-A focuses on building institutional capacity in the ANSF and on training initial recruits, OMLTs and POMLTs are responsible for training and mentoring deployed ANSF units. OMLTs, which operate with the Afghan National Army (ANA), consist of 11-28 personnel from one or several countries. As of October 2010, there were 150 OMLTs operating in Afghanistan; 76 were staffed by the United States.[33] POMLTs, which teach and mentor the Afghan National Police (ANP), are composed of 15-20 personnel each. As of October 2010, there were 317 POMLTs, of which 279 were staffed by the United States. In addition to the training, Obama Administration strategy emphasizes expanding the ANSF and improving it through partnering—about 70% of Afghan units are now partnered with international forces.

The U.S. police training effort was first led by State Department/INL, but the Defense Department took over the lead in police training in April 2005. Much of the training is still conducted through contracts with DynCorp.

AFGHAN NATIONAL ARMY

The Afghan National Army has been built "from scratch" since 2002—it is not a direct continuation of the national army that existed from the 1880s until the Taliban era. That national army all but disintegrated during the 1992-1996 *mujahedin* civil war and the 1996-2001 Taliban period. However, some Afghan officers who served prior to the Taliban have joined the ANA.

U.S. and allied officers say that the ANA is becoming a major force in stabilizing the country and a national symbol. It now has at least some presence in most of Afghanistan's 34 provinces, working with the PRTs, and it deployed outside Afghanistan to assist relief efforts for victims of the October 2005 Pakistan earthquake. According to the Department of Defense, the ANA is able to lead a growing percentage of all combat operations, but there is substantial skepticism within the U.S. defense establishment that it can assume full security responsibility by 2014, which is the target time frame announced by Karzai. Among examples of the ANA taking overall responsibility, in August 2008, the ANA took over security of Kabul city from Italy, and it took formal control of Kabul Province in early 2009. The commando forces of the ANA, trained by

U.S. Special Operations Forces, and numbering about 5,300, are considered well-trained and are taking the lead in some operations against high-value targets, particularly against HIG elements in Nuristan province.

However, some U.S. military assessments say the force remains poorly led. It still suffers from at least a 20% desertion rate. Many officers are illiterate or poorly motivated.[34] Some accounts say that a typical ANA unit is only at about 50% of its authorized strength at any given time, and there are significant shortages in about 40% of equipment items. The high desertion rate complicates U.S.-led efforts to steadily grow the force. Some recruits take long trips to their home towns to remit funds to their families, and often then return to the ANA after a long absence. Others, according to U.S. observers, often refuse to serve far from their home towns. The FY2005 foreign aid appropriation (P.L. 108-447) required that ANA recruits be vetted for terrorism, human rights violations, and drug trafficking.

ANA battalions, or "Kandaks," are the main unit of the Afghan force. There are over 120 Kandaks. As noted, the Obama Administration strategy is to also partner the ANA with U.S. and other foreign units to enhance effectiveness. General Petraeus and others have attributed the previous lack of progress in the ANSF to the non-systematic use of the partnering concept.

The United States has built five ANA bases: Herat (Corps 207), Gardez (Corps 203), Qandahar (Corps 205), Mazar-e-Sharif (Corps 209), and Kabul (Division HQ, Corps 201, Air Corps). Coalition officers conduct heavy weapons training for a heavy brigade as part of the "Kabul Corps," based in Pol-e-Charki, east of Kabul.

Ethnic and Factional Considerations/Defense Minister Wardak

At the time the United States first began establishing the ANA, Northern Alliance figures who were then in key security positions weighted recruitment for the national army toward its Tajik ethnic base. Many Pashtuns, in reaction, refused recruitment or left the ANA program. The naming of a Pashtun, Abdul Rahim Wardak, as Defense Minister in December 2004 reduced desertions among Pashtuns (he remains in that position). U.S. officials in Afghanistan say this problem was further alleviated with better pay and more close involvement by U.S. forces, and that the force is ethnically integrated in each unit and representative. With about 41% Pashtuns, 34% Tajiks, 12% Hazaras, and 8% Uzbeks, the force is roughly in line with the broad demographics of the country, according to the April 2010 DOD report. However, U.S. commanders say that those Pashtuns who are in the force are disproportionately eastern Pashtuns (from the Ghilzai tribal confederations) rather than southern Pashtuns (mostly Durrani tribal confederations). Defense Minister Wardak said in February 2011 that a greater proportion of southern Pashtuns are being recruited to redress that imbalance somewhat. The chief of staff was General Bismillah Khan, a Tajik who was a Northern Alliance commander, although as of June 2010 he is Interior Minister.

There were press reports in April 2011 that Karzai might be planning to replace Wardak (as well as Finance Minister Omar Zakhiwal) partly because he perceives them as working too closely with their U.S. counterparts. A name that has surfaced to potentially replace Wardak is Gen. Abdul Rauf Begi, an ethnic Uzbek who is close to Abdul Rashid Dostam; his appointment would represent a Karzai move to further consolidate support from the Uzbek community, but could alienate the Pashtuns in the military.

Afghan Air Force

Equipment, maintenance, and logistical difficulties continue to plague the Afghan National Army Air Corps (Afghan Air Force). The force is a carryover from the Afghan Air Force that existed prior to the Soviet invasion, and is expanding gradually after its equipment was virtually eliminated in the 2001-2002 U.S. combat against the Taliban regime. It now has about over 3,000 personnel, including 400 pilots, as well as a total of about 46 aircraft. Afghan pilots are based at Bagram air base.

The Afghan goal is to have 61 aircraft by 2011, but it remains mostly a support force for ground operations rather than a combat-oriented Air Force. However, the Afghan Air Force has been able to make ANA units nearly self-sufficient in airlift. Afghanistan is seeking the return of 26 aircraft, including some MiG-2s that were flown to safety in Pakistan and Uzbekistan during the past conflicts in Afghanistan. U.S. plans do not include supply of fixed-wing combat aircraft such as F-16s, which Afghanistan wants, according to U.S. military officials. In 2010, Russia and Germany supplied MI-8 helicopters to the Afghan Air Force.

AFGHAN NATIONAL POLICE (ANP)

U.S. and Afghan officials believe that building up a credible and capable national police force is at least as important to combating the insurgency as building the ANA. The April 2010 and November 2010 DOD reports on Afghanistan stability reinforce a widespread consensus that the ANP substantially lags the ANA in its development. Outside assessments are widely disparaging, asserting that there is rampant corruption to the point where citizens mistrust and fear the ANP. Among other criticisms are a desertion rate far higher than that of the ANA; substantial illiteracy; involvement in local factional or ethnic disputes because the ANP works in the communities its personnel come from; and widespread use of drugs. It is this view that has led to consideration of stepped up efforts to promote local security solutions such as those discussed above.

Some U.S. commanders are more positive, saying that it is increasingly successful in repelling Taliban assaults on villages and that is experiencing fewer casualties from attacks than it was previously. Afghan police in Kabul won praise from the U.S. commanders for putting down, largely on their own and without major civilian casualties, the insurgent attack on Kabul locations near the presidential palace on January 18, 2010, and a similar attack on February 26, 2010. Bismillah Khan, the new Interior Minister, was highly respected as ANA chief of staff and has taken new steps to try to improve the police force, including through unannounced visits to ANP bases and stations around the country. Still, some Pashtuns might resent his Tajik ethnicity.

Other U.S. commanders credit a November 2009 raise in police salaries (nearly doubled to about $240 per month for service in high combat areas)—and the streamlining and improvement of the payments system for the ANP—with reducing the solicitation of bribes by the ANP. The raise also stimulated an eightfold increase in the number of Afghans seeking to be recruited. Others note the success, thus far, of efforts to pay police directly (and avoid skimming by commanders) through cell phone-based banking relationships (E-Paisa, run by Roshan cell network). At a February 14, 2011, news conference. Lt. Gen. Caldwell stated that 21,000 ANP officers have undergone NTM-A-furnished literacy training, and that 86% of the ANP can now read, at the least, on a first-grade level.

POLICE RETRAINING AND OTHER INITIATIVES

Some U.S. officials believe that the United States and its partners still have not centered on a clearly effective police training strategy. The latest training reorganization implemented since 2007 is called "*focused district development,*" which attempts to retrain individual police forces in districts, which is the basic geographic area of ANP activity. (There are about 10 "districts" in each of Afghanistan's 34 provinces.) In this program, a district force is taken out and retrained, its duties temporarily performed by more highly trained police (Afghan National Civil Order Police, or ANCOP, which number about 5,800 nationwide), and then reinserted after the training is complete. As of late 2010, police in at least 100 districts have undergone this process, although program success has been hampered by continuing governance and other problems in those districts, according to DOD reports. The ANCOP officers are being used to staff the new checkpoints being set up to better secure Qandahar.

Police training now includes instruction in human rights principles and democratic policing concepts, and the State Department human rights report on Afghanistan, referenced above, says the government and outside observers are increasingly monitoring the police force to prevent abuses. In March 2010, then-Interior Minister Atmar signed a "strategic guidance" document for the ANP, which prioritizes eliminating corruption within the ANP and winning public confidence. About 1,000 ANP are women, demonstrating some commitment to gender integration of the force.

There have been few quick fixes for the chronic shortage of equipment in the ANP. Most police are under-equipped, lacking ammunition and vehicles. In some cases, equipment requisitioned by their commanders is being sold and the funds pocketed by the police officers. These activities contributed to the failure of a 2006 "auxiliary police" effort that attempted to rapidly field large numbers of new ANP officers.

RULE OF LAW/CRIMINAL JUSTICE SECTOR

Many experts believe that an effective justice sector is vital to Afghan governance. Some of the criticisms and allegations of corruption at all levels of the Afghan bureaucracy have been discussed throughout this report. U.S. justice sector programs generally focus on promoting rule of law and building capacity of the judicial system, including police training and court construction. The rule of law issue is covered in detail in CRS Report R41484, *Afghanistan: U.S. Rule of Law and Justice Sector Assistance*, by Liana Sun Wyler and Kenneth Katzman

U.S. SECURITY FORCES FUNDING/"CERP"

Because the Afghan government has so few resources, the Afghan security sector is funded almost entirely through international donations. In December 2009, Karzai asserted that the Afghan government could not likely fund its own security forces until 2024. More than half of all U.S. assistance to Afghanistan since 2002 has gone toward building the ANSF. U.S. funds are used to cover ANA salaries as well as to equip and train them. Recent appropriations for the ANA and ANP are contained in the tables at the end of this report, which also contain breakdowns for Commanders Emergency Response Program funds, or CERP, which is used for projects that build goodwill and presumably reduce the threat to use forces. CERP has also been used for projects that are traditionally considered suitable for management by USAID, a point of contention among some observers. The tables at the end also list breakdowns for ANSF funding. As noted in the tables, as of FY2005, the security forces funding has been DOD funds, not State Department funds.

INTERNATIONAL TRUST FUND FOR THE ANSF

In 2007, ISAF set up a trust fund for donor contributions to fund the transportation of equipment donated to and the training of the ANSF. U.S. funding for the ANSF is provided separately, not through this fund. The fund is estimated to require $2 billion per year. NATO allies in Europe have contributed about $375 million to the fund.

LAW AND ORDER TRUST FUND

There is also a separate "Law and Order Trust Fund" (LOTF) for Afghanistan, run by the U.N. Development Program. The fund is used to pay the salaries of the ANP and other police-related functions. Japan's payments of ANP salaries, discussed above, run through the LOTF. Its budget for the two years September 2008—December 2010 is about $630 million. From 2002-2010, donors contributed $1.56 billion to the Fund, of which the United States contributed about $500 million, according to the November 2010 DOD report (p. 19). Japan's 2009 pledge to pay the expenses of the Afghan police for at least six months (about $125 million for each six month period) is implemented through the LOTF.

POLICY COMPONENT: PROVINCIAL RECONSTRUCTION TEAMS (PRTS)

U.S. and partner officials have generally praised the effectiveness of "Provincial Reconstruction Teams" (PRTs)—enclaves of U.S. or partner forces and civilian officials that provide safe havens for international aid workers to help with reconstruction and to extend the writ of the Kabul government—in accelerating reconstruction and assisting stabilization efforts. The PRTs, the concept for which was announced in December 2002, perform activities ranging from resolving local disputes to coordinating local reconstruction projects, although most U.S.-run PRTs and most PRTs in combat-heavy areas focus on counter-insurgency. Many of the additional U.S. civilian officials deployed to Afghanistan during 2009 and 2010 are based at PRTs, which have facilities, vehicles, and security.

The list of PRTs in operation, including lead country, is shown in Table 25. Virtually all the PRTs are now under the ISAF mission. Each PRT operated by the United States has U.S. forces; Defense Department civil affairs officers; representatives of USAID, State Department, and other agencies; and Afghan government (Interior Ministry) personnel. Most PRTs, including those run by partner forces, have personnel to train Afghan security forces. USAID officers assigned to the PRTs administer PRT reconstruction projects, although USAID observers say there is little Afghan input, either into project decision making or as contractors for facility and other construction. That lack of input has fed criticism by Karzai, most recently at his February 6, 2011, speech at a security conference in Munich, that the PRTs should be abolished and all aid funds channeled through the Afghan government. USAID spending on PRT projects is in the table on USAID spending in Afghanistan at the end of this report, and there is a database on development projects sponsored by each PRT available to CRS, information from which can be provided on request.

In the south, most PRTs are heavily focused on security. In August 2005, in preparation for the establishment of Regional Command South (RC-S), Canada took over the key U.S.-led PRT in Qandahar. In May 2006, Britain took over the PRT at Lashkar Gah, capital of Helmand Province. At the same time, the Netherlands took over the PRT at Tarin Kowt, capital of Uruzgan Province. However, the Tarin Kowt PRT has been led by Australia and the United States since the September 2010 Dutch departure.

Some aid agencies say they have felt more secure since the PRT program began, fostering reconstruction,[35] and many of the new civilian advisers arriving in Afghanistan under the new Obama Administration strategy work out of the PRTs. On the other hand, some relief groups do not want to associate with military forces because doing so might taint their perceived neutrality. Others, such as Oxfam International, argue that the PRTs are delaying the time when the Afghan government has the skills and resources to secure and develop Afghanistan on its own.

EVOLVING CIVIL-MILITARY CONCEPTS AT THE PRTS

Representing evolution of the PRT concept, some donor countries—as well as the United States—are trying to enhance the civilian component of the PRTs and change their image from mainly military institutions. There has been long been consideration to turn over the lead in the U.S.-run PRTs to civilians rather than military personnel, presumably State Department or USAID officials. That was first attempted in 2006 with the establishment of a civilian-led U.S.run PRT in the Panjshir Valley. As noted, in March 2009, the Netherlands converted its PRT to civilian lead, although that alteration has not continued with the assumption of U.S. and Australian PRT command as of July 2010. Turkey opened a PRT, in Wardak Province, on November 25, 2006, to focus on providing health care, education, police training, and agricultural alternatives in that region.

As of November 2009, the "civilianization" of the PRT concept has evolved further with the decision to refer to PRTs as Interagency Provincial Affairs (IPA) offices or branches. In this new concept—a local parallel to the Senior Civilian Representatives now assigned to each regional command—State Department officers enjoy enhanced decision-making status at each PRT.

POLICY PILLAR: COOPERATION WITH ALLIES AND BURDENSHARING[36]

Since inception, the U.S.-led mission in Afghanistan has been international, and dependent on cooperation with partners. Since 2006, the vast bulk of all U.S. troops in Afghanistan have served under the umbrella of the NATO-led "International Security Assistance Force" (ISAF). ISAF consists of all 26 NATO members states plus partner countries—a total of 50 countries including the United States. President Obama's December 1, 2009, policy speech on Afghanistan was explicit in seeking new partner troop commitments, and pledges met or exceeded what some U.S. officials expected. However, as the transition to Afghan leadership begins later in 2011, Secretary of Defense Gates has led a U.S. effort to prevent U.S. partners from "rushing to the exits" by pulling forces out before their areas of responsibility are ready for transition.

Virtually all the European governments are under pressure from their publics and parliaments to end or reduce their military involvement in Afghanistan. Several key contingents either (1) have already ended their combat missions (the Netherlands), (2) will end those missions (Canada, by the summer of 2011), or (3) are setting notional times to depart before the 2014 time frame agreed on for completing the transition to Afghan leadership (a time frame agreed to in the November 19-20, 2010, NATO summit in Lisbon). Britain has steadily increased its troop commitment in Afghanistan—mainly in high combat Helmand Province—to about 9,500 (plus 500 special forces). In line with other contributors, British official comments have indicated that Britain might want to end its mission before 2014. Britain has lost over 300 soldiers in Afghanistan. Italy, Poland, and Germany have also indicated an intent to try to wind down their involvement in Afghanistan before the end of 2014, and Germany's parliament in January 2011 only renewed the German participation for one year, although that might be reviewed in late 2011. Partner forces that continue to bear the brunt of combat in Afghanistan include Britain, Canada, Poland, France, Denmark, Romania, and Australia.

Background on NATO/ISAF Formation and U.N. Mandate

The International Security Assistance Force (ISAF) was created by the Bonn Agreement and U.N. Security Council Resolution 1386 (December 20, 2001, a Chapter 7 resolution),37 initially limited to Kabul. In October 2003, after Germany agreed to contribute 450 military personnel to expand ISAF into the city of Konduz, ISAF contributors endorsed expanding its presence to several other cities, contingent on formal U.N. approval—which came on October 14, 2003 in U.N. Security Council Resolution 1510. In August 2003, NATO took over command of ISAF— previously the ISAF command rotated among donor forces including Turkey and Britain.

NATO/ISAF's responsibilities broadened significantly in 2004 with NATO/ISAF's assumption of security responsibility for northern and western Afghanistan (Stage 1, Regional Command North, in 2004 and Stage 2, Regional Command West, in 2005, respectively). The transition process continued on July 31, 2006, with the formal handover of the security mission in southern Afghanistan to NATO/ISAF control. As part of this "Stage 3," a British/Canadian/Dutchled "Regional Command South" (RC-S) was formed. Britain is the lead force in Helmand; Canada is lead in Qandahar, and the Netherlands was lead in Uruzgan until its departure in July 2010; the three rotated the command of RC-S. "Stage 4," the assumption of NATO/ISAF command of peacekeeping in 14 provinces of eastern Afghanistan (and thus all of Afghanistan), was completed on October 5, 2006. As part of the completion of the NATO/ISAF takeover, the United States put about half the U.S. troops then operating in Afghanistan under NATO/ISAF in "Regional Command East" (RC-E).

The ISAF mission was renewed (until October 13, 2011) by U.N. Security Council Resolution 1943 (October 13, 2010), which reiterated previous resolutions' support for the Operation Enduring Freedom mission. Tables at the end of this report list contributing forces, areas of operations, and their Provincial Reconstruction Teams.

Recent Major Contingent Developments

Following the Obama Administration's March 27, 2009, policy announcement, some additional pledges came through at the April 3-4, 2009, NATO summit. Major new force pledges were issued in conjunction with the January 28, 2010, conference in London. However, some of these forces were intended to compensate for the pullouts by the Netherlands and Canada 2010 and 2011, respectively. The major recent pledges are the following:

• April 2009: NATO agreed to a new training missions for the ANSF. A NATO Training Mission—Afghanistan (NTM-A) under the command of Lt. Gen. William Caldwell has been established. Also that month, $500 million in additional Afghan civilian aid was pledged by several donors. Also that month, there was agreement for partners to deploy 3,000 troops to secure the Afghan elections and 2,000 trainers for the Afghan security forces.

- November 10, 2009: Ahead of President Obama's visit to Asia, Japan announced a pledge of $5 billion over the next five years for Afghanistan civilian development, although it suspended its naval refueling mission. Japan has been covering about half of the salary costs of the ANP (which are about $250 million total per year).
- July 2009: South Korea announced it would increase its aid contribution to Afghanistan by about $20 million, in part to expand the hospital capabilities at Bagram Air Base. In November 2009, it announced a return of about 150 engineers to Afghanistan for development missions, protected by 300 South Korean forces. The forces deployed to Parwan Province in July 2010.[38]
- December 2009-January 2010 (London conference): A total of about 9,000 forces were pledged (including retaining 2,000 sent for the August 2009 election who were due to rotate out). Several countries pledged police trainers.
- In July 2010, Malaysia became a new contributor to the Afghanistan effort, furnishing 40 military medics.
- In late 2010, partner countries pledged to help fill a gap of about 750 trainers for the Afghan National Security Forces. However, Lt. Gen. Caldwell said in February 2011 that this trainer gap remains. A commitment in February 2011 by the Netherlands to send 545 trainers to northern Afghanistan was a separate commitment that did not close the overall trainer gap.
- In March 2011, Germany said it would add 300 forces to operate surveillance systems, although this decision was related to its refusal to participate in military action against Libya rather than to an Afghanistan-specific requirement.

National "Caveats" on Combat Operations

One of the most thorny issues has been the U.S. effort to persuade other NATO countries to adopt flexible rules of engagement that allow all contributing forces to perform combat missions. NATO and other partner forces have not, as they pledged at the NATO summit in April 2008, removed the so-called "national caveats" on their troops' operations that Lt. Gen. McChrystal says limits operational flexibility. For example, some nations refuse to conduct night-time combat. Others have refused to carry Afghan personnel on their helicopters. Others do not fight after snowfall. These caveats were troubling to NATO members like Canada, with forces in heavy combat zones; such countries feel they are bearing the brunt of the fighting.

OBAMA ADMINISTRATION STRATEGY AND TROOP BUILDUP

In September 2008, the U.S. military and NATO each began strategy reviews. The primary U.S. review was headed by Lt. Gen. Douglas Lute, the Bush Administration's senior adviser on Iraq and Afghanistan (who is in the Obama NSC with responsibility for Afghanistan). These reviews were briefed to the incoming Obama Administration. The Obama Administration, which maintained that Afghanistan needed to be given a higher priority than it was during the Bush Administration, integrated the reviews into an overarching 60-day inter-agency "strategy review." It was chaired by South Asia expert Bruce Riedel and co-chaired by Ambassador Holbrooke and Under Secretary of Defense for Policy Michele Flournoy.

MARCH 27, 2009, POLICY ANNOUNCEMENT AND TROOP INCREASE, FIRST COMMAND CHANGE, AND MCCHRYSTAL ASSESSMENT

President Obama announced a "comprehensive" strategy on March 27, 2009.[39] In conjunction, he announced the deployment of an additional 21,000 U.S. forces, of which about 4,000 would be trainers. Shortly after the announcement, the Administration decided that U.S. military leadership in Afghanistan was insufficiently innovative. On May 11, 2009, Secretary of Defense Gates announced that General McKiernan would be replaced by General Stanley McChrystal, considered an innovative commander as head of U.S. special operations from 2003 to 2008. He assumed command on June 15, 2009.

General McChrystal, after assuming command, assessed the security situation and suggested a strategy in a report of August 30, 2009, and presented to NATO on August 31, 2009, [40]as follows:

- That the goal of the U.S. military should be to protect the population—and to help the Afghan government take steps to earn the trust of the population—rather than to search out and combat Taliban concentrations. Indicators of success such as ease of road travel and normal life for families are more important than are counts of numbers of enemy fighters killed.
- That there is potential for "mission failure" unless a fully resourced, comprehensive counter-insurgency strategy is pursued and reverses Taliban momentum within 12-18 months. About 44,000 additional U.S. combat troops (beyond those approved by the Obama Administration strategy review in March 2009) would be needed to have the greatest chance for his strategy's success.

SECOND HIGH-LEVEL REVIEW AND FURTHER FORCE INCREASE

The McChrystal assessment set off debate within the Administration and another policy review, taking into account the McChrystal recommendations and the marred August 20, 2009, presidential election. Some senior U.S. officials, such as Secretary of Defense Gates, were concerned that adding many more U.S. forces could create among the Afghan people a sense of "occupation" that could prove counter-productive. The high-level review included at least nine

[39] "White Paper": http://www.whitehouse.gov/assets/documents/Afghanistan-Pakistan_White_Paper.pdf. [40] Commander NATO International Security Assistance Force, Afghanistan, and U.S. Forces, Afghanistan. "Commander's Initial Assessment." August 30, 2009,

available at http://media.washingtonpost.com/wp-srv/politics/
documents/Assessment_Redacted_092109.pdf?.

high-level meetings, chaired by President Obama, and reportedly concluded on November 19, 2009. The President announced his decisions in a speech at West Point military academy on December 1, 2009.[41] The major features of the December 1 statement included the following:

- That 30,000 additional U.S. forces would be sent (bringing U.S. levels close to 100,000) to "reverse the Taliban's momentum" and strengthen the capacity of Afghanistan's security forces and government.
- That there would be a transition, beginning in July 2011, to Afghan leadership of the stabilization effort and a corresponding beginning of a drawdown of U.S. force levels. The July 2011 "deadline" caused significant controversy, as discussed below.

McChrystal Replaced by Petraeus

On June 23, 2010, President Obama accepted the resignation of General McChrystal after summoning him to Washington, DC, to discuss the comments by him and his staff to a reporter for *Rolling Stone* magazine that disparaged several civilian figures involved in Afghanistan policy. He named General Petraeus as General McChrystal's successor. In a June 23, 2010, statement, President Obama attributed the change purely to the *Rolling Stone* comments, and stated that Afghanistan policy would not change. General Petraeus was confirmed by the Senate on June 30, 2010, and assumed command on July 4, 2010.

Summary of Current U.S. Strategy as Implemented by General Petraeus

The major outlines of Obama Administration strategy have taken shape as outlined below, and Gen. Petraeus testified before the Senate and House Armed Services Committees on March 15 and 16, 2011, that U.S. strategy has "arrested" Taliban momentum in much of the country and reversed it in a number of important areas. The major tenets are:

Goals: (1) disrupt terrorist networks in Afghanistan and Pakistan to degrade their ability to launch international terrorist attacks; (2) promote a more capable, accountable, and effective government in Afghanistan; (3) develop self-reliant Afghan security forces; and (4) involve the international community to actively assist in addressing these objectives.

Strategy Definition: To "clear, hold, build, and transition"—to protect the population and allow time for Afghan governance and security forces to take leadership and for infrastructure and economic development to take root.

Limiting Civilian Casualties. To win support of Afghans by sharply limiting air strikes and some types of raids and combat that cause Afghan civilian casualties and resentment42 Some refer to the rules as the "Karzai 12," referring to the number of points of these rules of engagement. The NATO International Security Assistance Force (ISAF) and the Karzai government want to prevent any recurrence of incident such as the one that occurred near Herat on August 22, 2008, in which a NATO bomb killed up to 90 civilians, as well as the incident in September 2009 in Konduz in which Germany's contingent called in an airstrike on Taliban fighters who captured two fuel trucks; killing several civilians as well as Taliban fighters. Still, ISAF-caused civilian casualties continue and usually lead to recriminations from President Karzai.

July 2011Beginning of Transition. The Obama Administration's December 2009 emphasis on transition to Afghan security leadership beginning in July 2011 was interpreted by some

Administration officials—and by some Afghan and regional leaders—as laying the groundwork for winding down U.S. involvement in coming years.43 The time frame may have been somewhat overtaken by NATO decisions in Lisbon in November, 2010, as discussed further below. Initial areas of transition announced by Karzai on March 22.

Resources and Troops: The Administration and foreign partners assert that resource "inputs" are, as of October 2010, aligned with mission requirements. However, in January 2011, the Administration announced that an extra 1,400 U.S. troops would deploy to solidify 2010 gains prior to the start of the heavier combat likely in spring 2011. This would bring U.S. force levels to just about 100,000. A gradual U.S. drawdown is to begin in July 2011 with a purportedly small (3,000 – 5,000) force reduction.

Improving and Expanding Afghan Governance: A key strategy component is to develop Afghan institutions, particularly at the provincial and local levels. The Administration asserts that the Karzai government is being held to account for its performance, although, as noted, no specific penalties have been imposed on the Afghan government for shortfalls.

Civilian-Military Integration: There is a commitment to civilian-military integration, as outlined in a DOD-State Department joint campaign plan and the late Ambassador Holbrooke's January 2010 strategy document, referenced earlier. High-level "Senior Civilian Representatives" have been appointed in regional commands where they serve.

Reintegration and Reconciliation: As discussed later, the Administration supports Afghan efforts to provide financial and social incentives to persuade insurgents to lay down their arms and accept the Afghan constitution. The United States was at first skeptical but is now increasingly supporting Karzai's policy of negotiating with senior insurgent leaders.

Pakistan: Engagement with Pakistan and enlisting its increased cooperation is pivotal to U.S. policy. However, there reportedly is a debate over whether to step up U.S.-combat operations inside Pakistan against militant safehavens. More information is in the section on Pakistan, below, and in CRS Report RL33498, Pakistan-U.S. Relations, by K. Alan Kronstadt.

International Dimension: New international diplomatic mechanisms have been formed to better coordinate all "stakeholders" in the Afghanistan issue (NATO, Afghanistan's neighbors, other countries in Afghanistan's region, the United Nations, and other donors). Meetings such as the January 28, 2010, meeting in London and the July 20, 2010, Kabul Conference are part of that effort. Another conference is to be held in Bonn in December 2011. To date, at least 25 nations have appointed direct counterparts to the SRAP, including the UAE, Saudi Arabia, and Turkey, which meet periodically as part of a 44-nation (and growing) "International Contact Group" for Afghanistan. It has met nine times, most recently in Jeddah, Saudi Arabia, the seat of the Organization of Islamic Conference, on March 3, 2010.

Partner Contributions: Increased partner contributions of funding and troops were sought and offered. Currently, there is U.S. effort to encourage partner forces to remain in Afghanistan at least until the completion of the transition.

Metrics: The Administration will continue to measure progress along clear metrics. Many in Congress, pressing for clear metrics to assess progress, inserted into P.L. 111-32 (FY2009 supplemental appropriation) a requirement that the President submit to Congress, 90 days after enactment (by September 23, 2009), metrics by which to assess progress, and a report on that progress every 180 days thereafter. The Administration's approximately 50 metrics were reported at the website of Foreign Policy44 and reports were submitted in March and September 2010. However, the difficulty in formulating useful and clear metrics that would enable members of

Congress and officials to assess progress in the war effort was demonstrated by comments by the late Ambassador Holbrooke on August 12, 2009, saying that on defining success in Afghanistan and Pakistan: "We will know it when we see it."45 In its September 22, 2009, report on the situation in Afghanistan (A/64/364-S/2009/475), the United Nations developed its own "benchmarks" for progress.

STRATEGY AMENDMENT: JULY 2011 "DEADLINE" YIELDS TO "TRANSITION" BY 2015

The Obama Administration emphasis on transition to Afghan security leadership beginning in July 2011 has been perhaps the most widely debated aspect of policy. Debate over whether to announce such a timeframe is described in the 2010 book by Bob Woodward called *Obama's Wars*. The 2011 "deadline" was interpreted by some Administration critics—and by some Afghan and regional leaders—as laying the groundwork for winding down U.S. involvement in coming years.[46] The Administration has said it set the time frame to demonstrate to a war-weary public that U.S. military involvement in Afghanistan is not open-ended. Perhaps to address perceived criticism of such a deadline in the upper ranks of the U.S. military, in an August 31, 2010 statement, the President asserted that the pace and scope of any drawdown in 2011 would be subject to conditions on the ground.

The debate over the July 2011 drawdown abated substantially with an agreement between the United States and NATO partner forces to focus on a longer time frame for transition to Afghan leadership. At the November 19-20, 2010, NATO summit in Lisbon, it was agreed that the transition to Afghan leadership would begin in 2011 and would be completed by the end of 2014. The 2014 date is one that Karzai articulated in 2009 as a time when Afghan forces would be able to secure Afghanistan.

IMPLEMENTATION OF STRATEGY, EARLY RESULTS, AND TRANSITION BEGINS

The pace and scope of the transition will depend on assessments of how well U.S. policy is working. As discussed, Gen. Petraeus reiterated in his March 15 and 16, 2011, testimony before the two armed services committees of Congress that U.S. strategy is showing results, particularly in the provinces of focus (Helmand, Qandahar) although such gains are "fragile and reversible." That same assessment was reflected in a White House report to Congress submitted in March 2011 and covering July 2010-March 2011.[47] According to these statements and documents:

- The progress is creating a contiguous secure corridor for commerce between Helmand and Qandahar, and markets and other signs of normal life are proliferating in Helmand and Qandahar.
- U.S. commanders are receiving overtures from local insurgent leaders who have lost morale and seek to discuss possible terms for their surrender and reintegration.
- The Afghan forces are becoming increasingly large, adding 70,000 personnel since the start of the U.S. buildup in 2009, and are increasingly in the lead on operations.

Less optimistic views are based on observations that the insurgency continues to make gains in previously quiet provinces, including Baghlan, Konduz, and Faryab provinces. Still others say that Afghan governance is lagging to the point where the Afghans will not be able to hold U.S./NATO gains on their own and insurgents will be able to regroup as soon as international forces thin out. On the other hand, U.S. and British civilians officials responsible for southern Afghanistan, including State Department officer Henry Ensher and British senior representative Michael O'Neill, said in January 2011 that strides are being noticed in Afghan governance, as noted above.

Some commanders attribute the signs of progress not only to the increase in numbers of U.S. forces, but to General Petraeus' tactics, including nearly tripling Special Operations Force operations in Afghanistan and greatly increased UAV (unmanned aerial vehicle) strikes on concentrations across the border in Pakistan to try to drive insurgents to reconcile with the Karzai government and cease fighting. Some attribute progress to increased operations by U.S. Special Forces and CIA-trained Afghan special forces and militias, including Afghan "Counterterrorism Pursuit Teams." In November 2010, General Petraeus reportedly approved the deployment of about 16 M1A1 tanks for use by the Marines in southern Afghanistan in order to put further pressure on militants. To solidify gains prior to a likely upsurge of fighting in spring 2011, in January 2011, the Administration announced an extra 1,400 U.S. troops would deploy to Afghanistan.

FOCUS OF THE 2010-2011 EFFORT: HELMAND, AND QANDAHAR

Prior to the start of the transition to Afghan lead in 2011, the U.S.-led effort has focused on securing the most restive provinces of Helmand and Qandahar, and has yielded substantial gains, by most accounts. The reports of progress in Helmand represent a turnaround from earlier pessimism about the outcome of "Operation Moshtarek" (Operation Together). It consisted of about 15,000 U.S., foreign partner, and Afghan forces (about 8,000 of the total) that, beginning on February 13, 2010, sought to clear Taliban militants from Marjah city (85,000 population) in Helmand. An Afghan governing structure was identified in advance (so-called "government in a box"), the population had substantial warning, and there were meetings with regional elders just before the offensive began—all of which were an apparent effort to cause militants to flee and to limit civilian losses.[48] The city, for the most part, was declared cleared of militants as of February 26, 2010, but some militants continued to fight in and on the outskirts of Marjah and to assassinate and intimidate Afghans cooperating with U.S. and Afghan forces. That activity reportedly has diminished as of January 2011. Further progress in Helmand was noted in early January 2011. Tribal figures in highly restive Sangin district, mentioned above, agreed with U.S. commanders to help prevent Taliban reinfiltration. However, such "deals" have often been struck in the past, only to later collapse, and there were reports in February 2011 that this arrangement has frayed.

QANDAHAR

The Administration assessments of progress are based largely on views of success in Qandahar Province. In early 2010, U.S. commanders had emphasized that the Qandahar effort would focus less on combat and more on conducting consultations and *shuras* with tribal leaders and other notables to enlist their cooperation against Taliban infiltrators. U.S. commanders described the operation as more of a "process," or a slow push into restive districts by setting up Afghan checkpoints to secure the city and districts around it (particularly Arghandab, Zhari, and Panjwai)—and not a classic military offensive. Qandahar's population is far larger (about 2 million in the province), and Qandahar province and city have functioning governments, which Marjah did not. The city hosts numerous businesses and has always remained vibrant, despite some Taliban clandestine activity.

A sense of doubt about the prospects for Qandahar built in April-August 2010 as Afghan tribal and other residential resistance—expressed at local *shuras*—to any combat to secure Qandahar. However, General Petraeus increased operations by U.S. Special Operations Forces against key militants near the city[49] and subsequently expanded the U.S. force presence in partnership with Afghan forces. The strategy ended Taliban control of many neighborhoods and Afghan checkpoints have been established. Further *shuras* have been held to promote Afghan governance. As part of the effort to stabilize Qandahar U.S. officials are reportedly trying to strengthen Governor Tooryalai Wesa and balance the flow of U.S. and international funds to the various tribes and clans in the province. An unstated objective is also to weaken the influence of Karzai's brother, Ahmad Wali Karzai, chair of the provincial council, who is discussed above,[50] although it is not clear that this has been accomplished. DOD and USAID are also working to expand electricity availability in and around Qandahar by refurbishing substations, a large effort that prompted a request for the "Afghanistan Infrastructure Fund" mechanism discussed later.

Transition and U.S. Drawdown Set to Begin

Despite doubts about the durability of progress to date, the stated transition to Afghan leadership is to begin in 2011. On March 22, 2011, as expected, Karzai announced the first set of areas to be transitioned, as of June 22, 2011. They are:

- Three provinces: Kabul (except Sarobi district, which is still restive), Panjshir, and Bamiyan. The latter two are considered highly stable. In Kabul, Afghan forces have already been in the lead for at least one year.
- Four cities: Herat, Mazar-e-Sharif, Lashkar Gah, and Mehtarlam. The former two cities are widely considered stable. The latter two are in restive areas, Helmand and Laghman provinces, respectively, and the announcement of transition surprised many observers.

U.S. Drawdown

According to statements by General Petraeus, as areas are "transitioned," U.S. forces are to be withdrawn or thinned out. Some forces may be "reinvested" (redeployed) to areas where extra combat force is required. In his testimony, Gen. Petraeus said he has not yet made recommendations as to how many U.S. forces might be withdrawn from Afghanistan in July 2011, but that there will be at least some drawdown at that time. Press reports say the range of the drawdown of July 2011 is likely to be from virtually no forces, to about 5,000 personnel, including some combat forces.

Resolving Operational Differences/SOFA?

As the Afghan forces assume a larger role in operations, it is likely that the Afghan government will step up its efforts to assume a larger role in approving NATO-led operations. Such sentiments arose in 2008, when the Afghan cabinet reacted to some high-profile instances of accidental civilian deaths by demanding negotiation of a formal "Status of Forces Agreement" (SOFA). As noted earlier, differences between Karzai and the U.S. command in Afghanistan erupted again in November 2010 with Karzai calling for a decrease in the number of night raids and other operations that cause civilian unrest. Anger erupted in March 2011 over the mistaken shooting of nine young boys in Kunar Province by U.S. helicopter operations. Karzai at first rejected a direct apology by General Petraeus, but then accepted the apology from visiting Secretary Gates on March 7, 2011.

To try to avoid recriminations, a SOFA is typically negotiated to spell out the combat authorities of non-Afghan forces, and might limit the United States to airstrikes, detentions, and house raids.[52] U.S. forces currently operate in Afghanistan under relatively vague "diplomatic notes" between the United States and the interim government of Afghanistan—primarily one that was exchanged in November 2002. That agreed note gives the United States legal jurisdiction over

U.S. personnel serving in Afghanistan and states the Afghan government's acknowledgment that U.S.-led military operations were "ongoing." A draft SOFA—or technical agreement clarifying U.S./coalition authorities in Afghanistan—reportedly has been under discussion between the United States and Afghanistan since 2007.

BEYOND 2014: LONG-TERM SECURITY COMMITMENT

President Obama and other senior U.S. officials say that 2014 is not a date certain for a complete U.S. pullout, but rather for a transition to Afghan lead, with some international forces remaining after 2014 to train and mentor the Afghans. During a visit to Afghanistan ,Vice President Biden reiterated on January 10, 2011, that U.S. forces would likely be required to help secure Afghanistan after 2014. This was reiterated by Secretary Gates on his March 7, 2011, visit to Afghanistan.

The issue of a SOFA, discussed above, is related to that of a longer-term strategic partnership with Afghanistan. As noted above, some Afghan leaders perceived the Obama Administration's 2011 deadline to "begin" a transition to Afghan security leadership as a sign the Administration might want to abandon Afghanistan. In part to reassure the Afghan government, President Obama, at a May 12, 2010, press conference with visiting President Karzai, stated that the United States and Afghanistan would renew a five-year-old strategic partnership.

Some advocate that any SOFA or strategic accord with Afghanistan resemble that which was agreed with Iraq in 2008—which stipulated an end date for U.S. military involvement in Iraq. However, unlike Iraq, no major Afghan figures are calling for an end to U.S. military involvement in Afghanistan. Negotiations on a long term strategic partnership began with the February 24-28, 2011, visit to Washington, DC, of Afghan Defense Minister Wardak and Interior Minister Khan; the talks continued with the March 2011 visit to Afghanistan of a U.S. negotiating team, as stated by Secretary Gates on March 7, 2011. The Administration intent is to finalize the new strategic partnership to coincide with the beginning of the U.S. drawdown in July 2011.

The strategic partnership was first established on May 23, 2005, when Karzai and President Bush issued a "joint declaration"[53] providing for U.S. forces to have access to Afghan military facilities, in order to prosecute "the war against international terror and the struggle against violent extremism." The joint statement did not give Karzai enhanced control over facilities used by U.S. forces, over U.S. operations, or over prisoners taken during operations. Some of the bases, both in and near Afghanistan, that support combat in Afghanistan, include those in Table 8. Karzai's signing of the partnership had been blessed by Afghan representatives on May 8, 2005, when he summoned about 1,000 delegates to a consultative *jirga* in Kabul on whether to host permanent U.S. bases. That *jirga* supported an indefinite presence of international forces to maintain security but urged Karzai to delay a decision. He stated on March 22, 2011, that he would likely call another *loya jirga* to evaluate any renewal of the partnership. A FY2009 supplemental appropriation (P.L. 111-32) and the FY2010 and FY2011 National Defense Authorization Acts (P.L. 111-84 and H.R. 6523, respectively) prohibit the U.S. establishment of permanent bases in Afghanistan.

THREATS TO LONG-TERM U.S. PRESENCE: 2011 PROTESTS

If there is a decision to retain international forces in Afghanistan beyond 2014, the attitudes of the Afghan population might become a factor. The insurgent forces had always used the presence of foreign forces on Afghan soil as a rallying and recruiting point, but the vast bulk of Afghans have, in surveys, generally appreciated the need for foreign forces to secure Afghanistan. There were signs in April 2011 that the public welcome of foreign forces might be eroding. On April 1, 2011, crowds of Afghans in the northern city of Mazar-e-Sharif demonstrated against the March 2011 burning of a Quran by a Florida pastor. The demonstration turned violent, with protesters storming the U.N. compound in the city and killing 12, including 7 U.N. staff. Demonstrations in other Afghan cities followed, including anti-U.S. slogans and posters echoing the Taliban's anti-U.S., anti-Western rhetoric. The demonstrations raised questions as to whether the Afghan public has begun to see international forces as occupiers, and appeared to illustrate that a long term presence of large numbers of international forces might be opposed broadly within Afghanistan.

able 6. Operation Enduring Freedom Partner Forces

Operation Enduring Freedom continues as a separate combat track, led by the United States but joined by a few partners. The caveat issue is less of a factor with OEF, since OEF is known as a combat-intensive mission conducted in large part by special forces contingents of contributing nations. The overwhelming majority of non-U.S. forces are under the NATO/ISAF mission. Prior to NATO assumption of command in October 2006, 19 coalition countries— primarily Britain, France, Canada, and Italy contributing approximately 4,000 combat troops to OEF-Afghanistan. Now, that figure is lower as most have been rebadged to ISAF. However, several foreign contingents, composed mainly of special operations forces, including a 200 person unit from the UAE, are still part of OEF-Afghanistan. This includes about 500 British special forces, some German special forces, and other special forces units. In early 2010,

U.S. Special Forces operating in Afghanistan were brought under direct command of the top U.S. command in Afghanistan, now General Petraeus.

Under OEF, Japan provided naval refueling capabilities in the Arabian sea, but the mission was suspended in October 2007 following a parliamentary change of majority there in July 2007. The mission was revived in January 2008 when the new government forced through parliament a bill to allow the mission to resume. It was renewed again, over substantial parliamentary opposition, in December 2008, but the opposition party won September 2009 elections in Japan and reportedly has decided on an alternative to continuing the refueling mission—by increasing its financial contributions to economic development in Afghanistan. That led to an October 2009 pledge by Japan—already the third largest individual country donor to Afghanistan, providing about $1.9 billion in civilian reconstruction aid since the fall of the Taliban—to provide another $5 billion over five years. It has been requested to be a major financial donor of an Afghan army expansion, and, in March 2009, it pledged to pay the costs of the Afghan National Police for six months.

As part of OEF outside Afghanistan, the United States leads a multi-national naval anti-terrorist, anti-smuggling, anti-proliferation interdiction mission in the Persian Gulf/Arabian Sea, headquartered in Bahrain. That mission was expanded after the fall of Saddam Hussein to include protecting Iraqi oil platforms in the Gulf.

SECURITY INNOVATIONS TO FACILITATE THE TRANSITION

Despite the assessments of progress, General Petraeus and others are said to believe that a faster end to the conflict on U.S./NATO/Afghan government terms requires new approaches that convince insurgent leaders that further conflict is futile and that a negotiated settlement should be pursued. Some of the more recent strategy and policy innovations designed to shape an "end game" in Afghanistan are discussed below.

"Reintegration" and "Reconciliation" With Insurgents

The issue of reintegrating insurgent fighters into society, and reconciling with insurgent leaders, are Afghan-led processes but they are activities in which the United States and the international community is increasingly interested and involved. The issues have concerned some in the international community and Afghanistan, because of the potential for compromises with insurgents that may involve backsliding on human rights. Most insurgents are highly conservative

Islamists who agreed with the limitations in women's rights that characterized Taliban rule. Many leaders of ethnic minorities are also skeptical of the effort because they fear that it might further Pashtun political strength within Afghanistan, and enhance the influence of Pakistan in Afghan politics. General Petraeus has said that the way conflicts like the one in Afghanistan end is through a political settlement. The United States and the Karzai government agree that any settlement must involve fighters and insurgent leaders: (1) cease fighting, (2) accept the Afghan constitution, and (3) sever any ties to Al Qaeda or other terrorist groups.

REINTEGRATION/"PEACE JIRGA"

A major Afghan and U.S./NATO initiative is to provide incentives to persuade insurgents to surrender and reenter their communities. The elements included in a reintegration plan drafted by the Afghan government and presented to the peace *loya jirga* during June 2-4, 2010[54] included providing surrendering fighters with jobs, amnesty, protection, and an opportunity to be part of the security architecture for their communities. In its final declaration, the *peace jirga* backed the plan, but also called for limits in NATO-led raids and further efforts to limit civilian casualties. It also called for the release of some detained insurgents where allegations against them are weak. The day after the *jirga* concluded, Karzai sought to implement that recommendation by calling for a review of the cases of all insurgent detentions. In late June 2010, President Karzai issued a decree to implement the plan, which involves outreach by Afghan local leaders to tribes and others who are in a position to convince insurgents to lay down their arms. The of international donors formally took up the issue and backed Afghan programs to reintegrate fighters amenable to surrendering. The issue received formal international backing at the January 28, 2010, London conference and the follow-up July 20, 2010, Kabul Conference. Britain, Japan, and several other countries, including the United States, have announced a total of about $235 million in donations to a new fund to support the reintegration process, of which $134 million has been received.[55] The U.S contribution is to be about $100 million (CERP funds), of which $50 million was formally pledged in April 2011.

Although it reached some substantive conclusions, the peace *jirga* itself received mixed reviews for its inclusiveness or lack thereof. Karzai tried to bring other minority communities along in backing the peace *jirga* and the reintegration process, and to do so he appointed former leader Burhanuddin Rabbani to chair the *jirga*. However, "opposition leader" Dr. Abdullah Abdullah, Karzai's rival in the 2009 presidential election, boycotted the *jirga*.

Despite the international funding for the effort, the Afghan-led reintegration process has moved forward slowly. As of March 2011, according to Petraeus testimony, about 700 fighters have reintegrated and another 2,000 are expected to begin the process in the near future. In addition, press reports say that some Taliban fighters sought information on the September 18, 2010, parliamentary election as a possible prelude to joining the political process.

U.S. military meetings with tribal elders have, in some cases, persuaded Taliban and other insurgents in their areas to stop fighting. Some U.S. commanders are reporting some success, using Commanders Emergency Response Program (CERP) funds. The National Defense Authorization Act for FY2010 (P.L. 111-84) authorized the use of CERP funds to win local support, to "reintegrate" Taliban fighters. FY2011 budget language requested by the Administration would authorize U.S. funds to be contributed to the reintegration fund mentioned above. To help the process along from the international perspective, in November 2009, ISAF set up a "force reintegration cell" to develop additional programs and policies to accelerate the effort to cause insurgents to change sides. These strategies are similar to what was employed successfully in Anbar Province in Iraq in 2006 and 2007.

Karzai has consistently advocated talks with Taliban militants who want to end their fight. Noted above is the "Program for Strengthening Peace and Reconciliation" (referred to in Afghanistan by its Pashto acronym "PTS") headed by *Meshrano Jirga* speaker Sibghatullah Mojadeddi and former Vice President Karim Khalili, and overseen by Karzai's National Security Council. The program is credited with persuading 9,000 Taliban figures and commanders to renounce violence and join the political process.

RECONCILIATION WITH TALIBAN/INSURGENT LEADERS

A separate Karzai initiative—far more widely debated than reintegration—is to conduct negotiations with senior insurgent leaders. Many in the international community, and within the Obama Administration, had feared that reconciliation has the potential to result in insurgent leaders obtaining senior positions or control over some Afghan territory, and that these figures will retain ties to Al Qaeda and commit abuses similar to those under the Taliban regime. The July 20, 2010, Kabul Conference did not issue unqualified support for high-level reconciliation talks, instead endorsing establishment of an Afghan High Peace Council to build Afghan consensus on the issue. That Council was established on September 5, 2010, and its 70 members met for the first time under the leadership of Tajik leader Rabbani on October 10, 2010. Yet, the direct role of the Council in negotiations is unclear; rather, it might be asked to review and endorse any settlement that is reached. In a significant step, the leadership of the Afghan High Peace Council visited Pakistan during January 12, 2011, to discuss with senior Pakistani officials some of the issues that might promote a negotiated settlement in Afghanistan. Rabbani also attended the Contact Group meeting in Jeddah, mentioned above, on March 3, 2011.

In an apparent shift, as stated by President Obama on December 16, 2010, the United States now backs the concept of reconciliation with insurgent leaders who meet the conditions stated above. Earlier, in March 2009, President Obama publicly ruled out negotiations with Mullah Umar and his top aides because of their alignment with Al Qaeda. Others still differ on the willingness of senior insurgents to bargain in earnest. CIA director Panetta, in a June 27, 2010, interview cited earlier, and reflecting the reported view of several U.S. intelligence agencies as of late 2010, said he saw no indications that insurgent leaders are contemplating settling with the government.

Senior U.S. commanders have grown more optimistic about reconciliation as contacts between Taliban representatives and the Karzai government have continued and proliferated. In February 2011, Karzai stated that he was aware of some recent contacts between Taliban figures and NATO/ISAF personnel. However, observers say that all the discussions to date have been about modalities and an agenda for further talks. Several sets of talks were reported in October 2010, and some press accounts said that NATO/ISAF forces were facilitating the movement of insurgent representatives to these talks. Representatives of the Quetta Shura Taliban were purported to be involved, although this was placed in doubt in late November 2010 when it was revealed that one of the purported senior Taliban interlocutors was an imposter. Still, Mullah Bradar, who is close to Mullah Umar, was said by the Afghan side to have been engaged in talks with the Afghan government prior to his arrest by Pakistan in February 2010. Karzai reportedly believes that Pakistan arrested Bradar in order to be able to influence the course of any Afghan government-Taliban settlement. The Taliban as a movement was not invited to the June 2-4, 2010, consultative peace *jirga*, but some Taliban sympathizers reportedly were there. The Taliban continues to demand that (1) all foreign troops leave Afghanistan; (2) a new "Islamic" constitution be adopted; and (3) Islamic law is imposed. However, those are viewed as opening positions; the Afghan government, for its part, may have softened its position on changes to the Afghan constitution as part of a settlement.

Other talks have taken place over the past few years, although with less apparent momentum than is the case in 2010. Press reports said that Afghan officials (led by Karzai's brother Qayyum) and Taliban members had met each other in Ramadan-related gatherings in Saudi Arabia in September 2008. Another round of talks was held in January 2009 in Saudi Arabia, and there were reports of ongoing contacts in Dubai, UAE. Some of these talks apparently involved Arsala Rahmani, a former Taliban official now in parliament, and the former Taliban Ambassador to Pakistan, Abdul Salam Zaeef, who purportedly is in touch with Umar's inner circle. These same Taliban representatives may have been involved in talks in the mid-late 2010 as well. As discussed above, in advance of the peace *jirga*, the Karzai government and representatives of Hikmatyar confirmed peace talks on March 21, 2010, in which Karzai, his brother, Ahmad Wali, and several Northern Alliance figures met with the Hikmatyar representatives.

The consultative peace *jirga*, in its final declaration, supported Karzai's call for the removal of the names of some Taliban figures from U.N. lists of terrorists, lists established pursuant to Resolution 1267 and Resolution 1333 (October 15, 1999, and December 19, 2000, both pre-September 11 sanctions against the Taliban and Al Qaeda) and Resolution 1390 (January 16, 2002). Press reports before the July 20 Kabul Conference said the Afghan government has submitted a list of 50 Taliban figures it wants taken off this list as a confidence-building measure. The Conference called on Afghanistan to engage with the U.N. Security Council to provide evidence to justify such de-listings, and U.N., U.S., and other international officials said they would support considering de-listings on a case-by-case basis. On January 26, 2010, Russia, previously a hold-out against such a process, dropped opposition to removing five Taliban-era figures from these sanctions lists, including Taliban-era foreign minister Wakil Mutawwakil, who ran in 2005 parliamentary elections. Also removed was Abdul Hakim Monib, who has served Karzai as governor of Uruzgan, Abdul Hakim Mujahid, who was Taliban representative in the United States, and three others. Mujahid now is one of three deputy chairs of the High Peace Council. "Mullah Rocketi," not on the sanctions list, is a former Taliban commander who ran for president in the August 2009 elections.

LOCAL SECURITY EXPERIMENTS: AFGHAN PROVINCIAL PROTECTION PROGRAM (APPP), AFGHAN LOCAL POLICE (ALP), AND RELATED INITIATIVES

Until mid-2008, U.S. military commanders opposed assisting local militias anywhere in Afghanistan for fear of creating rivals to the central government. The urgent security needs in Afghanistan caused reconsideration and General Petraeus has expanded local security experiments, based on successful experiences in Iraq. Press reports in July 2010 say he succeeded, after several of his first meetings with Karzai, in overcoming Karzai's reticence to them by assuring him that any local security organs would be under the administration of the Ministry of Interior.

AFGHAN LOCAL POLICE

The newest initiative is the "Afghan Local Police" (ALP) initiative, in which local security organs are formed from local recruits who want to defend their communities. The local units are under the control of district police chiefs and each fighter is vetted by a local shura as well as Afghan intelligence (Petraeus testimony, March 15 and 16, 2011). As of early 2011, the initiative has recruited a total of about 2,000—3,000 ALP, who purportedly have protected their communities in Dai Kundi, Heart, Paktika, Paktia, Uruzgan, Konduz, and Farah provinces. In his March 2011 testimony, Gen. Petraeus said that 70 districts had been approved for the program, each with about 300 fighters, which would bring the target size of the program to about 21,000. The Defense Department notified Congress in September 2010 that it will reprogram about $35 million in Afghan security forces funding to support the initiative.

AFGHAN PROVINCIAL PROTECTION PROGRAM

The ALP initiative follows on another program begun in 2008, termed the "Afghan Provincial Protection Program" (APPP, commonly called "AP3") and is funded with DOD (CERP) funds. The APPP got under way in Wardak Province (Jalrez district) in early 2009 and 100 local security personnel "graduated" in May 2009. It has been expanded to 1,200 personnel, in a province with a population of about 500,000. U.S. commanders say that no U.S. weapons are supplied to the militias, but this is an Afghan-led program and the Afghan government is providing weapons (Kalashnikov rifles) to the local groups, possibly using U.S. funds. Participants in the program are given $200 per month. General Petraeus showcased Wardak in August 2010 as an example of the success of the APPP and similar efforts. The National Defense Authorization Act (P.L. 111-84) called for a report on the program within 120 days of the October 28, 2009, enactment.

OTHER INITIATIVES

A separate program, the Local Defense Initiative, began in February 2010 in Arghandab district of Qandahar Province. U.S. Special Forces organized about 25 villagers into a neighborhood watch group, which is armed. The program has been credited by U.S. commanders as bringing normal life back to the district. A different militia was allowed to operate in Konduz to help secure the northern approaches to that city. Problems arose when the militia began arbitrarily administering justice, fueling the concerns discussed above these local security approaches.

The local security experiments to date are not *arbokai*, which are private tribal militias. Still, some believe that the *arbokai* concept should be revived as a means of securing Afghanistan, as the *arbokai* did during the reign of Zahir Shah and in prior pre-Communist eras. Reports persist that some tribal groupings have formed *arbokai* without specific authorization.

REVERSAL OF PREVIOUS EFFORTS: DDR AND DIAG PROGRAMS

As noted, the local security programs appear to reverse the 2002-2007 efforts to disarm local sources of armed force. The main program, run by UNAMA, was called the "DDR" program—Disarmament, Demobilization, and Reintegration—and it formally concluded on June 30, 2006. The program got off to a slow start because the Afghan Defense Ministry did not reduce the percentage of Tajiks in senior positions by a July 1, 2003, target date, dampening Pashtun recruitment. In September 2003, Karzai replaced 22 senior Tajiks in the Defense Ministry officials with Pashtuns, Uzbeks, and Hazaras, enabling DDR to proceed. The major donor for the program was Japan, which contributed about $140 million. Figures for collected weapons are in and U.S. spending on the programs are in the U.S. aid tables later in the report.

The DDR program was initially expected to demobilize 100,000 fighters, although that figure was later reduced. (Figures for accomplishment of the DDR and DIAG programs are contained in Table 7) Of those demobilized, 55,800 former fighters have exercised reintegration options provided by the program: starting small businesses, farming, and other options. U.N. officials say at least 25% of these found long-term, sustainable jobs. Some studies criticized the DDR program for failing to prevent a certain amount of rearmament of militiamen or stockpiling of weapons and for the rehiring of some militiamen.[56] Part of the DDR program was the collection and cantonment of militia weapons, but generally only poor-quality weapons were collected. As one example, Fahim, still the main military leader of the Northern Alliance faction, continues to turn heavy weapons over to U.N. and Afghan forces (including four Scud missiles), although the U.N. Assistance Mission in Afghanistan (UNAMA) says that large quantities of weapons remain in the Panjshir Valley.

Despite the earlier demobilization, which affected many of the northern minorities, there are indications that some faction leaders may be seeking to revive disbanded militias. The minorities may fear increased Taliban influence as a result of the Karzai reconciliation efforts, and the minorities want to be sure they could combat any Taliban abuses that might result if the Taliban achieves a share of power.

DIAG

Since June 11, 2005, the disarmament effort has emphasized another program called "DIAG"—Disbandment of Illegal Armed Groups. It is run by the Afghan Disarmament and Reintegration Commission, headed by Vice President Khalili. Under the DIAG, no payments are available to fighters, and the program depends on persuasion rather than use of force against the illegal groups. DIAG has not been as well funded as was DDR: it has received $11 million in operating funds. As an incentive for compliance, Japan and other donors have made available $35 million for development projects where illegal groups have disbanded. These incentives were intended to accomplish the disarmament of a pool of as many as 150,000 members of 1,800 different "illegal armed groups": militiamen that were not part of recognized local forces (Afghan Military Forces, AMF) and were never on the rolls of the Defense Ministry. These goals were not met by the December 2007 target date in part because armed groups in the south say they need to remain armed against the Taliban, but UNAMA reports that 100 out of 140 districts planned for DIAG are now considered "DIAG compliant." (U.N. Secretary General Report, March 9, 2011).

Major Security-Related Indicators

Force Current Level

Total Foreign Forces in Afghanistan	About 140.000: About 99,000 U.S. and 41,000 non-U.S. partner forces. (U.S. total was: 25,000 in 2005; 16,000 in 2003; 5,000 in 2002. ISAF totals were: 12,000 in 2005; and 6,000 in 2003.) US. forces deployed at 88 bases in Afghanistan, and include 1 air wing (40 aircraft) and 1 combat aviation brigade (100 aircraft). 1,400 extra U.S. forces deployed as of January 2011.
U.S. Casualties in Afghanistan	1,423 killed, of which 1,176 by hostile action. Additional 99 U.S. deaths in other OEF theaters, including the Philippines and parts of Africa. 150 U.S. killed from October 2001-January 2003. 315 killed in 2009, and about 500 killed in 2010. Over 300 UK forces killed in Afghanistan to date.
NATO Sectors (Regional Commands-South, east, north, west, and central/Kabul)	RC-S: 35,000 (U.K. lead). RC-Southwest: 27,000 (U.S. lead); RC-E: 32,000 (U.S. lead); RC-N: 11,000 (German lead); RC-W: 6,000 (Italy lead) RC-Kabul: 5,000 (Turkey, Afghan lead).
Afghan National Army (ANA)	150,000+, close to the end goal is 171,600 by late 2011. Reached the interim October 2010 goal of 134,000 earlier than planned. About 2,000 trained per month. 5,300 are commando forces, trained by U.S. Special Forces. ANA private paid about $200 per month; generals receive about $750 per month.
Afghan National Police (ANP)	120,000+, exceeding the interim goal of 109,000 by October 2010. End goal is 134,000 by late 2011. Of the force, 14,000 are Border Police; 3,800+ counter-narcotics police; 5,300 Civil Order P olice (ANCOP). 1,000+ are female. ANP salaries raised to $240 per month in November 2009, from $120, to counter corruption. Some police paid by E-Paisa system of Roshan cell phone network.
ANSF Salaries	About $800 million per year total, paid by donor countries bilaterally or via donor trust funds
U.S. and Partner	About 4,000, with target of 4,750. Pledges to fill the 750 person gap still

Trainers	required
Armed Fighters disarmed by DDR or DIAG	63,380 demobilized by DDR—all of the pool identified for the program. 100 out of 140 districts identified for DIAG deemed "DIAG compliant" as of March 2010.
Number of Al Qaeda	"Less than 100 or so", according to Gen. Petraeus in April 2011. Also, small numbers of Lashkar-e-Tayyiba, Islamic Movement of Uzbekistan, Pakistan Taliban, others.
Number of Taliban fighters	Over 20,000 (U.S. military and Afghan estimates). Some estimates higher. Plus about 2,500 Haqqani faction and 1,000 Hikmatyar (HIG).
Insurgents Reintegrated	About 1,000 during 2010
Attacks per day (average)	1,500+ per month in 2010; compared to 800 per month in 2007; 400 in 2005.
Afghan casualties	See CRS Report R41084, Afghanistan Casualties: Military Forces and Civilians, by Susan G. Chesser.

Sources: CRS; testimony and public statements by DOD officials.

POLICY ALTERNATIVES/SUPPORT FOR REDUCED U.S. MILITARY INVOLVEMENT

Although the testimony of Gen. Petraeus in March 2011 pointed to clear positive results, there is growing discussion of alternatives to address the apparent growth of support for efforts to wind down U.S. involvement in Afghanistan. Those who support policy alternatives generally believe that the current Afghanistan effort is faltering and that it is distracting from other priorities on foreign or domestic policy.[57] Others believe that pursuing the suggested alternatives could lead to a collapse of the Afghan government, and would produce an unraveling of the economic, political, and social gains made through the international military involvement in Afghanistan since 2001.

"Counter-Terrorism" Strategy

During the late 2009 strategy review, some, purportedly including Vice President Joseph Biden, favored a more limited mission for Afghanistan designed solely to disrupt Al Qaeda in Afghanistan and Pakistan. Some believe that this might become U.S. strategy once a transition to Afghan lead is complete. There is no firm number of U.S. troops that was put forward as appropriate to pursue this strategy, although press reports and observers commonly float an informal number of about 25,000 U.S. forces.

As noted, this strategy was not adopted in 2009. However, U.S. commanders say that some of the most effective U.S. operations consist of Special Operations forces tracking and killing selected key mid-level insurgent commanders, even though such operations were not intended to be the centerpiece of U.S. strategy that was decided in 2009. Some of these operations reportedly involve Afghan commandos trained by U.S. Special Forces and the CIA, bearing such names as the "Counterterrorism Pursuit Teams" and the "Paktika Defense Force." Some believe that there could be a decision to pursue this counter-terrorism strategy more directly, and to include raids across the border into Pakistan, as 2011 progresses.

Critics of the limited counter-terrorism strategy express the view that the Afghan government might collapse and Al Qaeda would have safe haven again in Afghanistan if there are insufficient numbers of U.S. forces there to protect the government.[58] Others believed it would be difficult for President Obama to choose a strategy that could jeopardize the stability of the Afghan government, after having defined Afghan security and stability as a key national interest. Still others say that it would be difficult to identify targets to strike with unmanned or manned aircraft unless there were sufficient forces on the ground to identify targets.

EXPAND AFGHAN FORCES/RAPID TRANSITION TO AFGHAN LEAD

Some advocate a rapid build-up of Afghan security forces and a drawdown of U.S. forces as the Afghan forces ramp up. During the Administration debate over strategy in late 2009, some members of Congress, including Senate Armed Services Committee Chairman Carl Levin, said publicly that the U.S. focus should be on expanding Afghan security forces capabilities before sending additional U.S. forces.

LEGISLATIVE INITIATIVES: DRAWDOWN PLANS

In Congress, some have expressed support for efforts, or planning, to wind down the U.S. involvement in Afghanistan. In the 111th Congress, H.Con.Res. 248, a resolution introduced by Representative Kucinich to require removal of U.S. forces from Afghanistan not later than December 31, 2010, was defeated in the House by a vote of 65 to 356 on March 10, 2010. Other legislation required the Administration to develop, by January 1, 2011, plans to wind down the U.S. military presence in Afghanistan. This provision was voted on in consideration of a FY2010 supplemental appropriation (H.R. 4899), where it failed in the Senate (May 27, 2010) by a vote of 18-80. On July 1, 2010, the House voted 162-260 to reject a plan in that bill to require the Administration to submit, by April 4, 2011, a plan and timetable to redeploy from Afghanistan. Earlier, in House consideration of a FY2010 National Defense Authorization Act (H.R. 2647), a similar provision failed on June 25, 2009, by a vote of 138-278.

In the 112th Congress, H.R. 651 requires an agreement with Afghanistan under which U.S. forces redeploy from Afghanistan within one year of entry into that agreement. Other bills requiring a withdrawal include H.Con.Res. 28, H.R. 780, H.R. 5015, and H.Con.Res. 248. The latter bill failed by a vote of 356 to 65 on March 10, 2011.

CONCEDE TO THE TALIBAN

Some experts, such as former U.S. Ambassador Robert Blackwill and members of a working group sponsored by the Century Foundation (including former negotiator Lakhdar Brahimi and former high-ranking State Dept. official Thomas Pickering), believe that a preferable strategy would be to work with Pakistan and other neighboring states to reach a political settlement that might be favorable to the Taliban. These plans might involve allowing the Taliban to control large parts of the south and east, where the insurgency is most active, and to work with the Northern Alliance to keep other parts of Afghanistan relatively peaceful. Others believe these plans amount to little more than a managed U.S. defeat and that Al Qaeda and other militants would likely take root in Taliban-controlled areas.

REGIONAL DIMENSION

Most of Afghanistan's neighbors believed that the fall of the Taliban would stabilize the region, but Islamist militants have not only continued to challenge the Afghan government but have also battled the government of Pakistan and have conducted acts of terrorism in India and elsewhere in the region. The Obama Administration announcement of a beginning of a "transition" to Afghan leadership in July 2011 has led some regional powers to plan for what they believe might be a post-U.S. presence scramble for influence in Afghanistan—or at least for the ability to deny their rivals influence there. Iran, which shares with India a fear of any return of radical Taliban (Sunni

Muslim) extremism in Afghanistan, has begun over the past year to engage more substantively on the future of Afghanistan with other regional countries and, to a lesser extent ,with other international actors. These maneuverings, to some extent, cast doubt on the commitment of Afghanistan's six neighbors to a non-interference pledge (Kabul Declaration) on December 23, 2002.

At the same time, Afghanistan has been re-integrating into regional security and economic organizations that reflect an effort to conduct relatively normal commerce and diplomatic relationships and which could make Afghanistan the Central Asia-South Asia trading hub that has been long discussed. In November 2005, Afghanistan joined the South Asian Association for Regional Cooperation (SAARC), and Afghanistan has observer status in the Shanghai Cooperation Organization, which is discussed below. U.S. officials have sought to enlist both regional and greater international support for Afghanistan through the still-expanding 44-nation "International Contact Group," which held its latest meeting in Jeddah on March 3, 2011.

Several regional summit meeting series have been established involving Afghanistan, including summit meetings between Afghanistan, Pakistan, and Turkey; and between Iran, Afghanistan, and Pakistan. The fifth of the Turkey-led meetings occurred on December 24, 2010, and resulted in a decision for joint military exercises in March 2011 between Turkey, Afghanistan, and Pakistan, and support from Karzai for the Taliban to set up an office in Istanbul for conducting reconciliation talks. Russia has put together two "quadrilateral summits," the latest of which was on August 18, 2010, among Pakistan, Russia, Afghanistan, and Tajikistan, and focused on counter-narcotics and anti-smuggling

Other regional collaborations include the Regional Economic Cooperation Conference on Afghanistan, which was launched in 2005. Another is a UNAMA-led "Kabul Silk Road" initiative, to promote regional cooperation on Afghanistan. As shown in the table below, cooperation from several of the regional countries are crucial to U.S. and ISAF operations and resupply in Afghanistan.

PAKISTAN/PAKISTAN-AFGHANISTAN BORDER

Pakistan's apparent determination to retain influence over Afghanistan is heavily colored by fears of historic rival India. Pakistan viewed the Taliban regime as providing Pakistan strategic depth against rival India, and Pakistan apparently remains wary that the current Afghan government may come under the sway of India. Numerous militant groups, such as LET (Laskhar-e-Tayyiba, or Army of the Righteous) were formed in Pakistan to challenge India's control of part of the disputed territories of Jammu and Kashmir. Some observers believe Pakistan wants to retain the ability to stoke these militants against India, even though these militants may be aiding Islamist groups challenging Pakistan's stability. Pakistan says India is using its Embassy and four consulates in Afghanistan (Pakistan says India has nine such consulates) to train and recruit anti-Pakistan insurgents, and is using its reconstruction funds to build influence there.

The Obama Administration strategy reviews in 2009 and 2010 all emphasized the linkage between militants present in Pakistan and the difficulty stabilizing Afghanistan. The December 2010 U.S. policy review said that greater cooperation with Pakistan is necessary to address militant safehavens there, but that denial of safehavens also requires effective development strategies inside Pakistan. The Administration report on progress in Afghanistan, released April 5, 2011, cited earlier, noted that Pakistan has, in some ways, been deficient in pursuing militants and eliminating safehavens on its side of the border.

Part of the U.S. concern could reflect Pakistan's efforts to secure its interests in any settlement between the Afghan government and the insurgent leadership. Pakistan has done so by purportedly protecting certain Afghan militant factions, such as the Haqqani network, that might play a role in a post-settlement Afghanistan. As part of its efforts to engage Karzai on the shape of any conflict-ending settlement, during 2010 there has been a growing pattern of meetings between Karzai and Pakistan's army chief of staff General Ashfaq Kiyani and with the head of Pakistan's Inter Services Intelligence Directorate (ISI), General Ahmad Shuja Pasha. Through meetings such as these, Pakistan has sought to rebut allegations that its Inter-Service Intelligence (ISI) directorate is supporting the Haqqani faction and others.[60]

INCREASED DIRECT U.S. ACTION AGAINST AFGHAN MILITANTS IN PAKISTAN[61]

The Obama Administration has tried to combat Afghanistan-focused militants in Pakistan without directly violating Pakistan's restrictions on the U.S. ability to operate "on the ground" in Pakistan. The Obama Administration has significantly increased the use of Predator and Reaper unmanned aircraft to strike militant targets in Pakistan as compared to the Bush Administration. Such a strike reportedly was responsible for the death of Beitullah Mehsud, and some militant websites say the strikes are taking a major toll on their operations and networks. The *New York Times* reported on February 23, 2009, that there are about 70 U.S. military advisers on the ground in Pakistan but they are there to help train Pakistani forces to battle Al Qaeda and Taliban militants. However, a U.S. raid over the border, which killed two Pakistani Frontier Corps soldiers in early October 2010, caused Pakistan to close off for several days the northern border crossing through with much of NATO/ISAF's supplies flow.

PAKISTAN'S COOPERATION AGAINST AL QAEDA

Pakistani cooperation against Al Qaeda has been more consistent than has cooperation against Afghan militants. During 2001-2006, the Bush Administration praised then President Pervez Musharraf for Pakistani accomplishments against Al Qaeda, including the arrest of over 700 Al Qaeda figures since the September 11 attacks.[62] After the attacks, Pakistan provided the United States with access to Pakistani airspace, some ports, and some airfields for OEF. Others say Musharraf acted against Al Qaeda only when it threatened him directly; for example, after the December 2003 assassination attempts against him. Musharraf resigned in August 2008, and the civilian government is led by the party of the late Pakistani secular leader Benazir Bhutto. Her widower, Asif Ali Zardari, is President.

U.S. criticism of Pakistan's approach increased following a *New York Times* report (February 19, 2007) that Al Qaeda had reestablished some small terrorist training camps in Pakistan, near the Afghan border. This possibly was an outgrowth of a September 5, 2006, compromise between Pakistan and tribal elders in this region. That, and subsequent compromises were criticized, including a 2008 "understanding" with members of the Mehsud tribe, among which is Tehrik-e-Taliban (TTP, Pakistan Taliban) leader Baitullah Mehsud (killed in a U.S. strike in August 2009). As noted, the TTP was named a Foreign Terrorist Organization on September 2, and some of its leaders (Hakimullah Mehsud) were named as terrorism supporting entities that day.

PAKISTAN-AFGHANISTAN RELATIONS

The U.S. mission in Afghanistan also depends on healthy, consistent, and operationally significant cooperation between Pakistan and Afghanistan. However, Afghanistan-Pakistan relations have tended to fluctuate. Many Afghans fondly remember Pakistan's role as the hub for U.S. backing of the mujahedin that forced the Soviet withdrawal in 1988-89, but some Afghan leaders resent Pakistan as the most public defender of the Taliban movement when it was in power. (Pakistan was one of only three countries to formally recognize it as the legitimate government; Saudi Arabia and the United Arab Emirates are the others).

Since 2008, the end of the Musharraf era, there has been a dramatic improvement in Afghanistan-Pakistan relations. Karzai attended the September 9, 2008, inauguration of Zardari. A "peace *jirga*" process—a series of meetings of notables on each side of the border—was launched at a September 28, 2006, dinner hosted by President Bush for Karzai and Musharraf, and meetings of 700 Pakistani and Afghan tribal elders were held in August 2007 and again in October, 2008. Zardari visited Kabul on January 9, 2009, where he and Karzai signed a joint declaration against terrorism that affects both countries. (A September 2010 meeting between them appeared to be a rededication of this declaration.) Afghan and Pakistani ministers jointly visited Washington, DC, during February 23-27, 2009, to participate in the first Obama Administration strategic review. As noted above, Karzai and Zardari conducted a joint visit to Washington, DC, in May 2009.

In April 2008, in an extension of the Tripartite Commission's work, the three countries agreed to set up five "border coordination centers" (BCCs) - which include networks of radar nodes to give liaison officers a common view of the border area. These centers build on an agreement in May 2007 to share intelligence on extremists' movements. Four have been established to date, including one near the Torkham Gate at the Khyber Pass, but all four are on the Afghan side of the border. The White House report released April 5, 2011, said that Pakistan had not fulfilled its pledge (May 2009) to establish one on the Pakistani side of the border. In June 2008, Pakistan ended a six-month suspension in attendance at meetings of the Tripartite Commission under which NATO, Afghan, and Pakistani military leaders meet regularly on both sides of the border.

Regarding the long-term relationship, Pakistan wants the government of Afghanistan to pledge to abide by the "Durand Line," a border agreement reached between Britain (signed by Sir Henry Mortimer Durand) and then Afghan leader Amir Abdul Rahman Khan in 1893, separating Afghanistan from what was then British-controlled India (later Pakistan after the 1947 partition). The border is recognized by the United Nations, but Afghanistan continues to indicate that the border was drawn unfairly to separate Pashtun tribes and should be renegotiated. As of October 2002, about 1.75 million Afghan refugees have returned from Pakistan since the Taliban fell, but as many as 3 million might still remain in Pakistan, and Pakistan says it plans to expel them back into Afghanistan in the near future.

AFGHANISTAN-PAKISTAN TRADE AGREEMENT

Pakistan has also sought to control Afghanistan's trade, particularly with India, leading to U.S. efforts to persuade Pakistan to forge a "transit trade" agreement with Afghanistan. That effort bore success with the signature of a trade agreement between the two on July 18, 2010, allowing for an easier flow of Afghan products, which are mostly agricultural products that depend on rapid transit. The two are estimated to do about $2 billion in trade per year. The agreement could also represent a success for the Canada-sponsored "Dubai Process" of talks between Afghanistan and Pakistan on modernizing border crossings, new roads, and a comprehensive border management strategy to meet IMF benchmarks. In early January 2011, Secretary of Homeland Security Janet Napolitano visited Afghanistan and announced a future tripling (from 25 to 77) of the number of U.S. customs agents that will train Afghan border and customs officers. The Afghanistan-Pakistan trade agreement comes after earlier signs of growing cooperation, including Afghan agreement to send more Afghan graduate students to study in Pakistan, and a June 2010 Afghan agreement to send small numbers of ANA officers to undergo training in Pakistan.[63]

IRAN

There are mixed views on how influential Iran is in Afghanistan; most experts appear to see Iran as relatively marginal player, particularly compared to Pakistan. The Obama Administration initially saw Iran as potentially helpful to its strategy for Afghanistan. Ambassador Holbrooke had advocated a "regional" component of the strategy, which focuses primarily on Pakistan but also envisioned cooperation with Iran on Afghanistan issues. However, as Iran-U.S. relations worsened in 2010 over Iran's nuclear program, the Obama Administration became more critical of Iran's activities in Afghanistan. Still, press reports in September 2010 indicated that the view within the Administration that Iran can contribute to stabilizing Afghanistan may be returning, and the Administration reported to be considering a U.S.-Iran dialogue in Kabul on Afghan issues.[64] Iran's attendance of the October 18, 2010, International Contact Group" meeting in Rome, including a briefing by General Petraeus, might be an indication of more U.S.-Iran engagement on the Afghanistan issue. As a member of the OIC, an Iranian representative attended the March 3, 2011, Contact Group meeting at OIC headquarters in Jeddah.

Early in the Administration, Secretary of State Clinton made a point of announcing that Iran would be invited to the U.N.-led meeting on Afghanistan at the Hague on March 31, 2009. At the meeting, the late SRAP Holbrooke briefly met the Iranian leader of his delegation to the meeting, and handed him a letter on several outstanding human rights cases involving Iranian-Americans. At the meeting, Iran pledged cooperation on combating Afghan narcotics and in helping economic development in Afghanistan—both policies Iran is already pursuing to a large degree. The United States and Iran took similar positions at a U.N. meeting in Geneva in February 2010 that discussed drug trafficking across the Afghan border. Iran did not attend the January 28, 2010, international meeting in London, but it did attend the July 28, 2010, international meeting in Kabul (both discussed above).

IRANIAN MATERIAL SUPPORT TO MILITANTS IN AFGHANISTAN

A U.S.-Iran dialogue on Afghanistan would presumably be intended to address the U.S. concerns about Iran's support for groups that operate against U.S. forces. Iran may be arming groups in Afghanistan to try to pressure U.S. forces that use Afghanistan's Shindand air base,[65] which Iran fears the United States might use to attack or conduct surveillance against Iran. Or, Iran's policy might be to gain broader leverage against the United States by demonstrating that Iran is in position to cause U.S. combat deaths in Afghanistan. Yet, the Iranian aid is not at a level that would make Iran a major player in the insurgency in Afghanistan. U.S. officials, including General Petraeus in his August 2010 press meetings, has called Iranian influence in Afghanistan, including its support for armed groups, "modest." Others are puzzled by Iran's support of Taliban fighters who are Pashtun, because Iran has traditionally supported Persian-speaking non-Pashtun factions in Afghanistan.

The State Department report on international terrorism for 2009, released August 5, 2010, said the Qods Force of the Revolutionary Guard of Iran continues to provide training to the Taliban on small unit tactics, small arms, explosives, and indirect weapons fire, as well as ships arms to "selected Taliban members" in Afghanistan. Weapons provided, according to the State Department report, include mortars, 107mm rockets, rocket-propelled grenades, and plastic explosives. On March 9, 2011, NATO said it had seized 48 Iranian-made rockets in Nimruz Province, bound for Afghan militants; the 122mm rockets, have a range (13 miles) greater than those previously provided by Iran. On August 3, 2010, the Treasury Department, acting under Executive Order 13224, named two Qods Force officers as terrorism supporting entities (freezing assets in the United States, if any). They are: Hossein Musavi, Commander of the Qods Force Ansar Corps, which is the key Qods unit involved in Afghanistan, and Hasan Mortezavi, who is a Qods officer responsible for providing funds and materiel to the Taliban, according to the Treasury Department.[66]

BILATERAL AFGHAN-IRANIAN RELATIONS

Iran, like President Karzai, is concerned about how any reduction in U.S. involvement in Afghanistan might improve the prospects for a Taliban return to power. Iran's interest in a broad relationship with Karzai has not, to date, been affected by Iran's continued support for Taliban and other militants in Afghanistan. Aside from its always tense relations with the United States, Iran perceives its key national interests in Afghanistan as exerting its traditional influence over western Afghanistan, which Iran borders and was once part of the Persian empire, and to protect Afghanistan's Shiite and other Persian-speaking minorities. Karzai has, at times, called Iran a "friend" of Afghanistan; in March 2010 he met with Iranian President Mahmoud Ahmadinejad on two occasions, possibly to signal to the United States that he might realign with regional actors if the United States continues to criticize his leadership. One of the meetings was just after the departure of visiting Defense Secretary Gates. Previously, Karzai received Ahmadinejad in Kabul in August 2007, and he visited Tehran at the end of May 2009 as part of the tripartite diplomatic process between Iran, Pakistan, and Afghanistan. During a visit to the United States in May 2009, Karzai said he had told both the United States and Iran that Afghanistan must not become an arena for the broader competition and disputes between the United States and Iran.[67]

Iran's pledged assistance to Afghanistan has totaled about $1.164 billion since the fall of the Taliban, mainly to build roads, schools, and electricity lines in Herat Province, near the Iranian border.[68] Iranian funds have also been used to construct mosques in the province, as well as pro-Iranian theological seminaries in Shiite districts of Kabul. Iran also offers scholarships to Afghans to study in Iranian universities, and there are consistent allegations that Iran has funded Afghan provincial council and parliamentary candidates who are perceived as pro-Tehran.[69] A controversy arose in late October 2010 when Karzai acknowledged accepting about $2 million per year in cash payments from Iran, via his chief of Staff Mohammad Daudzai. On the other hand, in December 2010, Iran suddenly ceased shipping fuel into Afghanistan, causing some spot dislocations in Afghanistan, including in Kabul. The move could be related to reported shortages of gasoline inside Iran, which are a result of U.S. sanctions imposed on sales of gasoline to Iran in July 2010. As of February 2011, Iran may still be allowing only a small number of deliveries (3040 trucks per day).

Many Afghans look fondly on Iran for helping them try to oust the Taliban regime when it was in power. Iran saw the Taliban regime, which ruled during 1996-2001, as a threat to its interests in Afghanistan, especially after Taliban forces captured Herat in September 1995. Iran subsequently drew even closer to the ethnic minority-dominated Northern Alliance than previously, providing its groups with fuel, funds, and ammunition.[70] In September 1998, Iranian and Taliban forces nearly came into direct conflict when Iran discovered that nine of its diplomats were killed in the course of the Taliban's offensive in northern Afghanistan. Iran massed forces at the border and threatened military action, but the crisis cooled without a major clash, possibly out of fear that Pakistan would intervene on behalf of the Taliban. Iran offered search and rescue assistance in Afghanistan during the U.S.-led war to topple the Taliban, and it also allowed U.S. humanitarian aid to the Afghan people to transit Iran. Iran helped construct Afghanistan's first post-Taliban government, in cooperation with the United States—at the December 2001 "Bonn Conference." In February 2002, Iran expelled Karzai-opponent Gulbuddin Hikmatyar, but it did not arrest him. At other times, Afghanistan and Iran have had disputes over Iran's efforts to expel Afghan refugees. About 1.2 million remain, mostly integrated into Iranian society, and a crisis erupted in May 2007 when Iran expelled about 50,000 into Afghanistan. About 300,000 Afghan refugees have returned from Iran since the Taliban fell.

INDIA

The interests and activities of India in Afghanistan are almost the exact reverse of those of Pakistan. India's goal is to deny Pakistan "strategic depth" in Afghanistan, and to deny Pakistan the ability to block India from trade and other connections to Central Asia and beyond. Some believe India is increasingly concerned that any negotiated settlement of the Afghanistan conflict will give Pakistan preponderant influence in Afghanistan, and India, which supported the Northern Alliance against the Taliban in the mid-1990s, is said to be stepping up its contacts with those factions to discuss possible contingencies in the event of an Afghan settlement deal.

Many of the families of Afghan leaders have lived in India at one time or another and, as noted above, Karzai studied there. India saw the Taliban's hosting of Al Qaeda as a major threat to India itself because of Al Qaeda's association with radical Islamic organizations in Pakistan dedicated to ending Indian control of parts of Jammu and Kashmir. Some of these groups have committed major acts of terrorism in India, and there might be connections to the militants who carried out the terrorist attacks in Mumbai in November 2008.

Pakistan accuses India of using its four consulates in Afghanistan (Pakistan says there are nine such consulates) to spread Indian influence in Afghanistan. However, many U.S. observers believe India's role in Afghanistan is constructive, and some would support an Indian decision to deploy more security forces in Afghanistan to protect its construction workers, diplomats, and installations. India reportedly decided in August 2008 to improve security for its officials and workers in Afghanistan, but not to send actual troops there. Yet, Tajikistan, which also supported the mostly Tajik Northern Alliance against the Taliban when it was in power, allows India to use one of its air bases.

India is the fifth-largest single country donor to Afghan reconstruction, funding projects worth over $1.2 billion. Indian officials assert that all their projects are focused on civilian, not military, development and are in line with the development priorities set by the Afghan government. India, along with the Asian Development Bank, financed a $300 million project, mentioned above, to bring electricity from Central Asia to Afghanistan. It has also renovated the well-known Habibia High School in Kabul and committed to a $25 million renovation of Darulaman Palace as the permanent house for Afghanistan's parliament. India financed the construction of a road to the Iranian border in remote Nimruz province, and it is currently constructing the 42 megawatt hydroelectric Selwa Dam in Herat Province at a cost of about $80 million. This will increase electricity availability in the province. India is also helping the IDLG with its efforts to build local governance organizations, and it provides 1,000 scholarships per year for Afghans to undergo higher education in India. Some Afghans want to enlist even more Indian assistance in training Afghan bureaucrats in accounting, forensic accounting, oversight, and other disciplines that will promote transparency in Afghan governance.

RUSSIA, CENTRAL ASIAN STATES, AND CHINA

Some neighboring and nearby states take an active interest not only in Afghan stability, but in the

U.S. military posture that supports U.S. operations in Afghanistan. The region to the north of Afghanistan is a growing factor in U.S. efforts to secure new supply lines to Afghanistan. Some of these alternative lines have begun to open, at least to non-lethal supplies.

Russia

Russia wants to reemerge as a great power and to contain U.S. power in Central Asia, including Afghanistan. Its hosting of the "quadrilateral summits" mentioned above, the first in July 2009 and the latest on August 18, 2010, could represent stepped up efforts by Russia to exert influence on the Afghanistan issue. Still, Russia supports U.S. efforts to combat militants in the region who have sometimes posed a threat to Russia itself. Previously, Russia had kept a low profile in the country because it still feels humiliated by its withdrawal in 1989 and senses some Afghan resentment of the Soviet occupation. In November 2010, in its most significant intervention in Afghanistan since its occupation, Russian officers reportedly joined U.S. and Afghan forces attempting to interdict narcotics trafficking in Afghanistan; the move reportedly prompted a complaint by President Karzai because he was not consulted about the inclusion of the Russians. In June 2010, Russia said more economic and social assistance is needed for Afghanistan. Russia reportedly is considering investing $1 billion in Afghanistan to develop its electricity capacity and build out other infrastructure. Included in those investments are implementation of an agreement, reached during a Karzai visit to Moscow on January 22, 2011, for Russia to resume long dormant Soviet occupation-era projects such as expanding the Salang Tunnel connecting the Panjshir Valley to Kabul, hydroelectric facilities in Kabul and Baghlan provinces, a customs terminal, and a university in Kabul. Russia expressed readiness to Since 2002, Russia has been providing some humanitarian aid to Afghanistan.

Russian cooperation is crucial to the U.S. effort in Afghanistan. In February 2009, Russia resumed allowing the United States to ship non-lethal equipment into Afghanistan through Russia (following a suspension in 2008 caused by differences over the Russia-Georgia conflict). In July 2009, following President Obama's visit to Russia, it announced it would allow the transit to Afghanistan of lethal supplies as well. Russia reportedly is being urged by NATO (as evidenced in a visit by NATO Secretary General Anders Fogh Rasmussen to Russia in December 2009) to provide helicopters and spare parts to the Afghan forces (which still make heavy use of Russian-made Hind helicopters) as well as fuel.

During the 1990s, Russia supported the Northern Alliance against the Taliban with some military equipment and technical assistance in order to blunt Islamic militancy emanating from Afghanistan.[71] Although Russia supported the U.S. effort against the Taliban and Al Qaeda in Afghanistan out of fear of Islamic (mainly Chechen) radicals, Russia continues to seek to reduce the U.S. military presence in Central Asia. Russian fears of Islamic activism emanating from Afghanistan may have ebbed since 2002 when Russia killed a Chechen of Arab origin known as "Hattab" (full name is Ibn al-Khattab), who led a militant pro-Al Qaeda Chechen faction. The Taliban government was the only one in the world to recognize Chechnya's independence, and some Chechen fighters fighting alongside Taliban/Al Qaeda forces have been captured or killed.

Central Asian States

These states are crucial to U.S. strategy in Afghanistan. As discussed in the chart, Uzbekistan, Turkmenistan, Tajikistan and Kazakhstan are pivotal actors in U.S. efforts to secure supply routes into Afghanistan that avoid Pakistan. They are also becoming crucial to Afghanistan's strategy to attempt to emerge as a trade crossroads between South and Central Asia—a strategy that could net Kabul substantial customs duties and other economic benefits. The possible revival of a longstanding plan to establish Afghanistan as a transit hub for Central Asian natural gas is discussed later in this paper under long term economic development opportunities.

During Taliban rule, Russian and Central Asian leaders grew increasingly alarmed that radical Islamic movements were receiving safe haven in Afghanistan. Uzbekistan, in particular, has long asserted that the group Islamic Movement of Uzbekistan (IMU), allegedly responsible for four simultaneous February 1999 bombings in Tashkent that nearly killed President Islam Karimov, is linked to Al Qaeda.[72] One of its leaders, Juma Namangani, reportedly was killed while commanding Taliban/Al Qaeda forces in Konduz in November 2001. Kazakhstan and Kyrgyzstan do not directly border Afghanistan, but IMU guerrillas transited Kyrgyzstan during incursions into Uzbekistan in the late 1990s.

Uzbekistan, a sponsor of Afghan faction leader Abdul Rashid Dostam, an ethnic Uzbek, allowed use of Karshi-Khanabad air base by OEF forces from October 2001 until a rift emerged in May 2005 over Uzbekistan's crackdown against riots in Andijon, and U.S.-Uzbek relations remained largely frozen. Uzbekistan's March 2008 agreement with Germany for it to use Karshi-Khanabad air base temporarily, for the first time since the rift in U.S.-Uzbek relations developed in 2005, suggests that U.S.-Uzbek cooperation on Afghanistan and other issues might be rebuilt. Renewed

U.S. discussions with Uzbekistan apparently bore some fruit with the Uzbek decision in February 2009 to allow the use of Navoi airfield for shipment of U.S./NATO goods into Afghanistan. The late Ambassador Holbrooke visited in February 2010, indicating further warming.

Central Asian Activities During Taliban Rule

In 1996, several of the Central Asian states banded together with Russia and China into a regional grouping called the Shanghai Cooperation Organization to discuss the Taliban threat. It includes China, Russia, Uzbekistan, Tajikistan, Kazakhstan, and Kyrgyzstan. Reflecting Russian and Chinese efforts to limit U.S. influence in the region, the group has issued statements, most recently in August 2007, that security should be handled by the countries in the Central Asia region. Despite the Shanghai Cooperation Organization statements, Tajikistan allows access primarily to French combat aircraft, and Kazakhstan allows use of facilities in case of emergency. In April 2010, it also agreed to allow U.S. overflights of lethal military equipment to Afghanistan, allowing the United States to use polar routes to fly materiel directly from the United States to Bagram Airfield. A meeting of the Shanghai Cooperation Organization to discuss Afghanistan was held in Moscow on March 25, 2009, and was observed by a U.S. official, as well as by Iran.

Of the Central Asian states that border Afghanistan, only Turkmenistan chose to seek close relations with the Taliban leadership when it was in power, possibly viewing engagement as a more effective means of preventing spillover of radical Islamic activity from Afghanistan. It saw Taliban control as facilitating construction of a natural gas pipeline from Turkmenistan through Afghanistan (see below). The September 11 events stoked Turkmenistan's fears of the Taliban and its Al Qaeda guests and the country publicly supported the U.S.-led war. No U.S. forces have been based in Turkmenistan.

China

China's involvement in Afghanistan policy appears to be growing. China reportedly is considering contributing some People's Liberation Army (PLA) forces, possibly in a non-combat role, to helping secure Afghanistan. A communiqué from the Obama visit to China in November 2009 implied a possible larger role for China to help stabilize Afghanistan. In late 2009, China allocated an additional $75 million in economic aid to Afghanistan, bringing its total to close to $1 billion since 2002. On March 20, 2010, ahead of a visit to China by Karzai, China called for more international support for Afghanistan. During the visit, China stressed that its investments in Afghanistan would continue.

Chinese delegations continue to assess the potential for new investments in such sectors as mining and energy,[74] and a $3.4 billion deal was signed in November 2007 for China Metallurgical Group to develop the Aynak copper mine south of Kabul, and build related infrastructure. Actual work at the mine was long stalled due to security concerns, the presence of mines, and lack of road infrastructure to ship the copper out of Afghanistan, but is now reportedly under way. U.S. forces do not directly protect the project, but U.S. forces are operating in Lowgar province, where the project is located, and provide general stability there. China is also a major contender to develop the Hajji Gak iron ore mine near Kabul.

A major organizer of the Shanghai Cooperation Organization, China has a small border with a sliver of Afghanistan known as the "Wakhan corridor." As noted in the U.N. report on Afghanistan of December 10, 2010, Afghanistan is increasingly involved in Shanghai Cooperation

Organization affairs. China had become increasingly concerned about the potential for Al Qaeda to promote Islamic fundamentalism among Muslims in China. In December 2000, sensing China's increasing concern about Taliban policies, a Chinese official delegation met with Mullah Umar. China did not enthusiastically support U.S. military action against the Taliban, possibly because China was wary of a U.S. military buildup nearby. In addition, China has been allied to Pakistan in part to pressure India, a rival of China.

PERSIAN GULF STATES: SAUDI ARABIA AND UAE

The Gulf states are, according to Ambassador Holbrooke, a key part of the effort to stabilize Afghanistan. As noted, Ambassador Holbrooke has focused increasing U.S. attention—and has formed a multilateral task force—to try to curb continuing Gulf resident donations to the Taliban in Afghanistan. Holbrooke has said these donations might be a larger source of Taliban funding than is the narcotics trade.

Saudi Arabia has a role to play in Afghanistan in part because, during the Soviet occupation, Saudi Arabia channeled hundreds of millions of dollars to the Afghan resistance, primarily Hikmatyar and Sayyaf. Drawing on its reputed intelligence ties to Afghanistan during that era, Saudi Arabia worked with Taliban leaders to persuade them to suppress anti-Saudi activities by Al Qaeda. Some press reports indicate that, in late 1998, Saudi and Taliban leaders discussed, but did not agree on, a plan for a panel of Saudi and Afghan Islamic scholars to decide bin Laden's fate. A majority of Saudi citizens practice the strict Wahhabi brand of Islam similar to that of the Taliban, and Saudi Arabia was one of three countries to formally recognize the Taliban government. The Taliban initially served Saudi Arabia as a potential counter to Iran, but Iranian-Saudi relations improved after 1997 and balancing Iranian power ebbed as a factor in Saudi policy toward Afghanistan.

Saudi Arabia has played a role as a go-between for negotiations between the Karzai government and "moderate" Taliban figures. This role was recognized at the London conference on January 28, 2010, in which President Karzai stated in his opening speech that he sees a role for Saudi Arabia in helping stabilize Afghanistan. As noted, some reports say that a political settlement might involve Mullah Umar going into exile in Saudi Arabia.

According to U.S. officials, Saudi Arabia cooperated extensively, if not publicly, with OEF. It broke diplomatic relations with the Taliban in late September 2001 and quietly permitted the United States to use a Saudi base for command of U.S. air operations over Afghanistan, but it did not permit U.S. airstrikes from it.

The United Arab Emirates, the third country that recognized the Taliban regime, is emerging as another major donor to Afghanistan. Its troop contribution was discussed under OEF, above. At a donors conference for Afghanistan in June 2008, UAE pledged an additional $250 million for Afghan development, double the $118 million pledged by Saudi Arabia. That brought the UAE contribution to Afghanistan to over $400 million since the fall of the Taliban. Projects funded include housing in Qandahar, roads in Kabul, a hospital in Zabol province, and a university in Khost. There are several daily flights between Kabul and Dubai emirate.

U.S. AND INTERNATIONAL AID TO AFGHANISTAN AND ECONOMIC DEVELOPMENT ISSUES

Some experts have long believed that accelerating economic development would do more to improve the security situation than any amount of combat. This belief appears to constitute a major element of Obama Administration policy, although some believe the link between economic development and security is unproved. The United States and partner countries provide large amounts of assistance, but many economic sectors are developing with private investment, including by wealthy or well-connected Afghans who have founded companies. Afghanistan's economy and society are still fragile after decades of warfare that left about 2 million dead, 700,000 widows and orphans, and about 1 million Afghan children who were born and raised in refugee camps outside Afghanistan. More than 3.5 million Afghan refugees have since returned, although a comparable number remain outside Afghanistan. The U.N. High Commission for Refugees (UNHCR) supervises Afghan repatriation and Afghan refugee camps in Pakistan. The literacy rate is very low and Afghanistan lacks a large pool of skilled labor, particularly of middle managers and accountants.

There are debates over almost all aspects of international aid to Afghanistan, including amounts, mechanisms for providing it, coordination among donors, and how aid is distributed within Afghanistan. For example, some of the more stable provinces, such as Bamiyan and Balkh, are complaining that U.S. and international aid is flowing mostly to the restive provinces in an effort to quiet them, and ignoring the needs of poor Afghans in peaceful areas. Later in this report are tables showing U.S. appropriations of assistance to Afghanistan, and Table 23 lists U.S. spending on all sectors for FY2001-FY2009.

U.S. ASSISTANCE TO AFGHANISTAN

During the 1990s, the United States became the largest single provider of assistance to the Afghan people. During Taliban rule, no U.S. aid went directly to that government; monies were provided through relief organizations. Between 1985 and 1994, the United States had a cross-border aid program for Afghanistan, implemented by USAID personnel based in Pakistan. Citing the difficulty of administering this program, there was no USAID mission for Afghanistan from the end of FY1994 until the reopening of the U.S. Embassy in Afghanistan in late 2001.

For all of FY2002-FY2010, the United States has provided about $54.5 billion in assistance, including military "train and equip" for the ANA and ANP (which is about $30 billion of these funds). The figures in the tables do not include costs for U.S. combat operations. Including those costs, the United States spent about $105 billion for FY2010 and expects to spend about $120 billion for FY2011. A total of $118 billion in DOD funds is requested for FY2012 for *both* Afghanistan and Iraq. For further information on combat costs, see CRS Report RL33110, *The Cost of Iraq, Afghanistan, and Other Global War on Terror Operations Since 9/11*, by Amy Belasco.

AID OVERSIGHT

Still heavily dependent on donors, Karzai has sought to reassure the international donor community by establishing a transparent budget and planning process. Some in Congress want to increase independent oversight of U.S. aid to Afghanistan; the conference report on the FY2008 defense authorization bill (P.L. 110-181) established a "special inspector general" for Afghanistan reconstruction, (SIGAR) modeled on a similar outside auditor for Iraq ("Special Inspector General for Iraq Reconstruction," SIGIR). Funds provided for the SIGAR are in the tables below.

On May 30, 2008, Major General Arnold Fields (Marine, ret.) was named to the position. His office has filed several reports on Afghan reconstruction, which include discussions of SIGAR staffing levels and activities, as well as several specific project audits. However, he acknowledged that criticisms in a July 2010 "peer review" of SIGAR operations by the Inspectors General of several U.S. agencies were valid, attributing many of the shortcomings to slow pace of fully funding his office.[75] One recent SIGAR report noted deficiencies in the ability of the Afghan government's Central Audits Office to monitor how funds are used. Another (January 2011) assesses the degree of coordination in U.S. programs to help women and girls. Some members of Congress criticized the SIGAR for ineffective oversight and called for his replacement; General Fields (ret) announced his resignation in January 2011. His deputy, Herb Richardson, has replaced him on an acting basis as of February 3, 2011.

AID AUTHORIZATION: AFGHANISTAN FREEDOM SUPPORT ACT

A key post-Taliban aid authorization bill, S. 2712, the Afghanistan Freedom Support Act (AFSA) of 2002 (P.L. 107-327, December 4, 2002), as amended, authorized about $3.7 billion in U.S. civilian aid for FY2003-FY2006. The law, whose authority has now expired, was intended to create a central source for allocating funds; that aid strategy was not implemented. However, some of the humanitarian, counter-narcotics, and governance assistance targets authorized by the act were met or exceeded by appropriations. No Enterprise Funds authorized by the act have been appropriated. The act authorized the following:

- $60 million in total counter-narcotics assistance ($15 million per year for FY2003-FY2006);
- $30 million in assistance for political development, including national, regional, and local elections ($10 million per year for FY2003-FY2005);
- $80 million total to benefit women and for Afghan human rights oversight ($15 million per year for FY2003-FY2006 for the Afghan Ministry of Women's Affairs, and $5 million per year for FY2003-FY2006 to the Human Rights Commission of Afghanistan);
- $1.7 billion in humanitarian and development aid ($425 million per year for FY2003-FY2006);
- $300 million for an Enterprise Fund;
- $550 million in drawdowns of defense articles and services for Afghanistan and regional militaries. (The original law provided for $300 million in drawdowns. That was increased by subsequent appropriations laws.)

A subsequent law (P.L. 108-458, December 17, 2004), implementing the recommendations of the 9/11 Commission, contained "The Afghanistan Freedom Support Act Amendments of 2004." The subtitle mandated the appointment of a U.S. coordinator of policy on Afghanistan and requires additional Administration reports to Congress.

AFGHAN FREEDOM SUPPORT ACT REAUTHORIZATION

In the 110th Congress, H.R. 2446, passed by the House on June 6, 2007 (406-10), would have reauthorized AFSA through FY2010. A version (S. 3531), with fewer provisions than the House bill, was not taken up by the full Senate. AFSA reauthorization was not reintroduced in the 111th Congress. H.R. 2446 would have authorized about $1.7 billion in U.S. economic aid and $320 in military aid (including drawdowns of equipment) per fiscal year. It also would have authorized a pilot program of crop substitution to encourage legitimate alternatives to poppy cultivation; and a cut off of U.S. aid to any Afghan province in which the Administration reports that the leadership of the province is complicit in narcotics trafficking.

DIRECT AID AND BUDGET SUPPORT TO THE AFGHAN GOVERNMENT

Although the Afghan government has been increasing its revenue (about $1.7 billion for 2010) and is covering about one third of its overall budget of about $4.5 billion, USAID provides funding to help the Afghan government meet gaps in its operating budget. As shown in the tables below, some U.S. funds are provided both directly and through a U.N.-run multi-donor Afghan Reconstruction Trust Fund (ARTF) account, run by the World Bank.

Currently, only about 20% of all donated aid funds disbursed are channeled through the Afghan government. The United States views only four ministries as sufficiently transparent to handle donor funds, although more might be qualified as 2011 progresses. The Kabul Conference (July 20, 2010) communiqué endorsed a goal of increasing that to about 50% and for 80% of all funds to align with Afghan government priorities. Karzai has long complained about the high percentage of donor aid not channeled through the Afghan government and this criticism of what he calls a "parallel government" was emphasized in his February 6, 2011, speech at a Munich security conference.[76]

National Solidarity Program

Through the ARTF, the United States is trying to support an Afghan government program that promotes local decision making on development—the "National Solidarity Program" (NSP). The program provides block grants of about $60,000 per project to local councils to implement their priority projects, most of which are water projects. The Afghan implementer is the Ministry of Rural Rehabilitation and Development. It is widely hailed as a highly successful, Afghan-run program.

U.S. funds for the program are drawn from a broad category of ESF for "good governance." A FY2009 supplemental request asked about $85 million for the ARTF account, of which much of those funds would be used to fill a $140 million shortfall in the NSP program. P.L. 111-32, the FY2009 supplemental discussed above, earmarks $70 million to defray the shortfall. The FY2010 consolidated appropriation (P.L. 111-117) earmarked another $175 million in ESF for the program. A total of almost $800 million in good governance funds are requested for FY2012, meaning that the NSP funding provided by the U.S. will likely meet prior years' levels, if the funds are appropriated. The FY2010 National Defense Authorization Act (P.L. 111-84) authorizes the use of some CERP funds, controlled by the U.S. military, to supplement the funding for the NSP. However, this authorization, if implemented, incurred opposition from some international NGOs who are opposed to combining military action with development work.

Major Reporting Requirements

Several provisions require Administration reports on numerous aspects of U.S. strategy, assistance, and related issues:

- P.L. 108-458, The Afghanistan Freedom Support Act Amendments required, through the end of FY2010, an overarching annual report on U.S. strategy in Afghanistan. Other reporting requirements expired, including required reports: (1) on long-term U.S. strategy and progress of reconstruction; (2) on how U.S. assistance is being used; (3) on U.S. efforts to persuade other countries to participate in Afghan peacekeeping; and (4) a joint State and Defense Department report on U.S. counter-narcotics efforts in Afghanistan.
- P.L. 110-181 (Section 1230), FY2008 Defense Authorization Act requires a quarterly DOD report on the security situation in Afghanistan; the first was submitted in June 2008. It is required by that law through FY2011. Section 1231 requires a report on the Afghan National Security Forces through the end of FY2010.
- Section 1229 of the same law requires the quarterly report of the Special Inspector General for Afghanistan Reconstruction (SIGAR).
- P.L. 111-8 (Omnibus Appropriation, explanatory statement) required a State Department report on the use of funds to address the needs of Afghan women and girls (submitted by September 30, 2009).

- P.L. 111-32, FY2009 Supplemental Appropriation (Section 1116), required a White House report, by the time of the FY2011 budget submission, on whether Afghanistan and Pakistan are cooperating with U.S. policy sufficiently to warrant a continuation of Administration policy toward both countries, as well as efforts by these governments to curb corruption, their efforts to develop a counter-insurgency strategy, the level of political consensus in the two countries to confront security challenges, and U.S. government efforts to achieve these objectives. The report was released with a date of September 30, 2010.
- The same law (Section 1117) required a report, by September 23, 2009, on metrics to be used to assess progress on Afghanistan and Pakistan strategy. A progress report measured against those metrics is to be submitted by March 30, 2010, and every six months thereafter, until the end of FY2011.
- Section 1228 of the FY2010 National Defense Authorization Act (P.L. 111-84) required a report, within 120 days, on the Afghan Provincial Protection Program and other local security initiatives. Section 1235 authorized a DOD-funded study of U.S. force levels needed for eastern and southern Afghanistan, and Section 1226 required a Comptroller General report on the U.S. "campaign plan" for the Afghanistan (and Iraq) effort.
- The FY2011 National Defense Authorization Act (H.R. 6523,P.L. 111-383) provides for:: (Section 1231) a one year extension—through FY2012—on the security situation in Afghanistan that was begun in P.L. 11-181: a two year extension (Section 1232) in the reporting requirement—through FY 2012—on the Afghan National Security Forces; (Section 1535) a report within six months of enactment on U.S. economic strategy for Afghanistan and a plan, to be submitted concurrent with the FY2012 budget submission, to transition the duties of the Task Force for Business and Stability Operations in Afghanistan to the Department of State; and a report by State, DOD, and USAID on the use of contractors in Afghanistan.

INTERNATIONAL RECONSTRUCTION PLEDGES/NATIONAL DEVELOPMENT STRATEGY

International (non-U.S.) donors have pledged over $30 billion in assistance to Afghanistan since the fall of the Taliban. When combined with U.S. aid, this by far exceeds the $27.5 billion for reconstruction identified as required for 2002-2010. The major donors, and their aggregate pledges to date, are listed in Table 9, and some of the more recent major pledges were discussed in the section on Alliances and Burdensharing" above. Major pledges have been made primarily at donor conferences suich as: Tokyo (2002), Berlin (April 2004), Kabul (April 2005), London (February 2006), Paris (June 2008, and London (January 2010). The following was pledged at the January 2010 London Conference:[77] France ($45 million); Saudi Arabia ($150 million over three years); Australia ($40 million); China ($75 million). Other pledges were made for Taliban reintegration, as noted above. The Afghanistan Compact generally endorses the view of Afghan leaders that a higher proportion of the aid (50%) be channeled through the Afghan government, a policy adopted by the United States.

Among multilateral lending institutions, in May 2002, the World Bank reopened its office in Afghanistan after 20 years. Its projects have been concentrated in the telecommunications and road and sewage sectors. The Asian Development Bank (ADB) has also been playing a major role in Afghanistan, including in financing railway construction. Another of its projects in Afghanistan was funding the paving of a road from Qandahar to the border with Pakistan, and as noted above, it is contributing to a project to bring electricity from Central Asia to Afghanistan. On the eve of the London conference on January 28, 2010, the IMF and World Bank announced $1.6 billion in Afghanistan debt relief.

RESULTS OF U.S. AND INTERNATIONAL AID IN KEY SECTORS

Efforts to build the legitimate economy are showing some results, by accounts of senior U.S. officials, including expansion of roads and education and health facilities constructed. The following are some key sectors and what has been accomplished with U.S. and international donor funds:

Roads. Road building is considered a U.S. priority and has been USAID's largest project category there, taking up about 25% of USAID spending since the fall of the Taliban. Roads are considered key to enabling Afghan farmers to bring legitimate produce to market in a timely fashion, and former commander of U.S. forces in Afghanistan General Eikenberry (now Ambassador) said "where the roads end, the Taliban begin." The major road, the Ring Road, is nearly all repaved. Among other major projects completed are a road from Qandahar to Tarin Kowt, (Uruzgan province) built by U.S. military personnel, inaugurated in 2005; and a road linking the Panjshir Valley to Kabul. In several provinces, U.S. funds (sometimes CERP funds) are being used to build roads that link up farming communities to the market for their products. Another key priority is building a Khost-Gardez road, under way currently.

Bridges. Afghan officials are said to be optimistic about increased trade with Central Asia now that a new bridge has opened (October 2007) over the Panj River, connecting Afghanistan and Tajikistan. The bridge was built with $33 million in (FY2005) U.S. assistance. The bridge is helping what press reports say is robust reconstruction and economic development in the relatively peaceful and ethnically homogenous province of Panjshir, the political base of the Northern Alliance.

Education. Despite the success in enrolling Afghan children in school since the Taliban era (see statistics above), setbacks have occurred because of Taliban attacks on schools, causing some to close. In addition, Afghanistan's university system is said to be woefully underfunded, in part because Afghans are entitled to free higher education by law, and this is impeding the development of a large enough pool of skilled workers for the Afghan government. Afghanistan requires

about $35 million to operate its universities and institutes for one year; USAID has requested $20 million to help fund those activities for FY2012.[78]

Health. The health care sector, as noted by Afghan observers, has made considerable gains in reducing infant mortality and giving about 65% of the population at least some access to health professionals. In addition to U.S. assistance to develop the health sector's capacity, Egypt operates a 65-person field hospital at Bagram Air Base that instructs Afghan physicians. Jordan operates a similar facility in Mazar-e-Sharif.

Railways. Afghanistan does not currently have any functioning railway. However, three railway projects are under way. One, from Mazar-i-Sharif to the border with Uzbekistan, is now under construction with $165 million from the Asian Development Bank. Another portion is funded by Japan, and another segment, from the Tajikistan border down to Konduz, is to be built by China as part of its contract to develop the Aynak Copper Mine discussed below. The various segments are eventually to link up and parallel the Ring Road that circles Afghanistan. The railway will integrate Afghanistan to the former Soviet railway system in Central Asia, increasing Afghanistan's economic integration in the region.

ELECTRICITY SECTOR

At least 10% of USAID funds for Afghanistan have been spent on power projects, although that percentage is rising in 2010 and 2011. The Afghanistan Compact states that the goal is for electricity to reach 65% of households in urban areas and 25% in rural areas by 2010, a goal that has not been met. However, severe power shortages in Kabul, caused in part by the swelling of Kabul's population to about 3 million, up from half a million when the Taliban was in power, are fewer now than two years ago. Power to the capital has grown due to the Afghan government's agreements with several Central Asian neighbors to import electricity, as well as construction of new substations. Many shops in Kabul are now lit up at night, as observed by CRS in October 2009. As noted above, in January 2011, Russia pledged to resume work on some long dormant hydroelectric projects in Afghanistan that were suspended when Soviet troops withdrew in 1989.

A major USAID and DOD focus is on power projects in southern Afghanistan. The key longterm project is to expand the capacity of the Kajaki Dam, located in unstable Helmand Province. USAID has allocated about $500 million to restore and expand the capacity of the dam. As of October 2009, two turbines were operating—one was always working, and the second was repaired by USAID contractors. This has doubled electricity production in the south and caused small factories and other businesses to come to flourish. USAID plans to further expand capacity of the dam by installing a third turbine (which there is a berth for but which never had a turbine installed.) In an operation involving 4,000 NATO troops (Operation Ogap Tsuka), components of the third turbine were successfully delivered to the dam in September 2008. It was expected to be operational in mid-late 2009 but technical and security problems, such as inability to secure and build roads leading to the dam, have delayed the project and there is no public estimate as to when the third turbine will be completed. In the interim, the U.S. military and USAID have agreed on a plan to focus on smaller substations and generator projects that can bring more electricity to Qandahar and other places in the south quickly. For this and other power projects, the Administration is requesting legislative authority for an "Infrastructure Fund" to be funded by DOD ($500 million is requested for FY2012) but controlled jointly by DOD and USAID. That authority is provided in the FY2011 DOD authorization bill (P.L. 111-383).

Solar Power

There is also an apparent increasing emphasis on providing electricity to individual homes and villages through small solar power installations. A contractor to USAID, IRG, is providing small solar powered-electricity generators to homes in several districts of Afghanistan, alleviating the need to connect such homes to the national power grid. However, there are technical drawbacks, including weather-related inconsistency of power supply and the difficulty of powering appliances that require substantial power. The U.S. broadcasting service to Afghanistan, Radio Azadi, run by Radio Free Europe/Radio Liberty, has given out 20,000 solar-powered radios throughout Afghanistan, according to RFE/RL in December 2010.

Agriculture Sector

With about 80% of Afghans living in rural areas, the agriculture sector has always been key to Afghanistan's economy and stability. The late Ambassador Holbrooke, including in his January 2010 strategy document, has outlined U.S. policy to boost Afghanistan's agriculture sector not only to reduce drug production but also as an engine of economic growth. Prior to the turmoil that engulfed Afghanistan in the late 1970s, Afghanistan was a major exporter of agricultural products.

USAID has spent about 15% of its Afghanistan funds on agriculture (and "alternative livelihoods" to poppy cultivation), and this has helped Afghanistan double its legitimate agricultural output over the past five years. One emerging "success story" is growing Afghan exports of high-quality pomegranate juice called Anar. Other countries are promoting not only pomegranates but also saffron rice and other crops that draw buyers outside Afghanistan. Another emerging success story is Afghanistan's November 2010 start of exports of raisins to Britain.[79] Wheat production was robust in 2009 because of healthy prices for that crop, and Afghanistan is again self-sufficient in wheat production. According to the SRAP January 2010 strategy document reference earlier, 89 U.S. agricultural experts (64 from U.S. Department of Agriculture and 25 from USAID) are in Afghanistan. Their efforts include providing new funds to buy seeds and agricultural equipment, and to encourage agri-business.

U.S. strategy has addressed not only crop choice but also trying to construct the entirety of the infrastructure needed for a healthy legitimate agriculture sector, including road building, security of the routes to agriculture markets, refrigeration, storage, transit through Pakistan and other transportation of produce, building legitimate sources of financing, and other aspects of the industry. U.S. officials in Kabul say that Pakistan's restrictions on trade between Afghanistan and India have, to date, prevented a rapid expansion of Afghan pomegranate exports to that market. Dubai is another customer for Afghan pomegranate exports. A key breakthrough on this issue was reached with the July 18, 2010, signing of a transit trade agreement between Afghanistan and Pakistan, reportedly brokered by the United States. It will allow for more rapid transit of Afghan and Pakistani trucks through each others' territories, ending a requirement that goods be offloaded at border crossings.

To help Afghanistan develop the agriculture sector, the National Guard from several states (Texas, for example) is deploying "Agribusiness Development Teams" in several provinces to help Afghan farmers with water management, soil enhancement, crop cultivation, and improving the development and marketing of their goods.

There is a vibrant timber industry in the northeast provinces. However, the exports are illegal. Deforestation has been outlawed because of the potential for soil erosion and other economic and environmental effects.

PRIVATE SECTOR-LED DEVELOPMENT

Some sectors, discussed below, are being developed primarily (although not exclusively) with private investment funding. There has been substantial new construction, particularly in Kabul, such as the Serena luxury hotel (opened in November 2005); a $25 million Coca Cola bottling factory (opened in September 2006); and numerous apartment complexes, marriage halls, office buildings, and other structures. The bottling factory is located near the Bagrami office park (another private initiative), which includes several other factories. The Serena was built by the Agha Khan foundation, a major investor in Afghanistan; the Agha Khan is a leader of the Isma'ili community, which is prevalent in northern Afghanistan. The foundation has also funded the successful Roshan cellphone company. An arm of the Defense Department, called the Task Force for Business and Stability Operations, headed by deputy undersecretary Paul Brinkley, is attempting to facilitate the investment. On the other hand, that Task Force reportedly has seen many of its personnel depart because of a provision of the FY2011 Defense Authorization Act (P.L. 111-383) that the Task Force be folded into State/USAID-led assistance structures by the end of FY2011. Others say that private investment could be healthier if not for the influence exercised over it by various faction leaders and Karzai relatives.

- Telecommunications and Transportation. Several Afghan telecommunications firms have been formed, including Afghan Wireless (another cell phone service, which competes with Roshan) and Tolo Television. The 52-year-old national airline, Ariana, is said to be in significant financial trouble due to corruption that has affected its safety ratings and left it unable to service a heavy debt load, but there are new privately run airlines, such as Pamir Air, Safi Air (run by the Safi Group, which has built a modern mall in Kabul), and Kam Air. Major new buildings include several marriage halls in Kabul city, as observed by CRS in October 2009. U.S. funds are being used to supplement the private investment; a $4 million U.S. grant, in partnership with the Asia Consultancy Group, is being used to construct communication towers in Bamiyan and Ghor provinces.

- Mining and Gems. Afghanistan's mining sector has been largely dormant since the Soviet invasion. Some Afghan leaders complain that not enough has been done to revive such potentially lucrative industries as minerals mining, such as of copper and lapis lazuli (a stone used in jewelry). The issue became more urgent in June 2010 when a Defense Department development team announced, based on surveys, that Afghanistan may have untapped minerals worth over $1 trillion.
- General Petraeus, in an interview with NBC News on August 15, 2010, said the amount could be in the "trillions." Although copper and iron are the largest categories by value, there are believed to also be significant reserves of such minerals as lithium in western Afghanistan—lithium is crucial to the new batteries being used to power electric automobiles.

A major project, signed in November 2007, is with China Metallurgical Group for the company to invest $3.4 billion to develop Afghanistan's Aynak copper field in Lowgar Province. The agreement, viewed as generous to the point where it might not be commercially profitable for China Metallurgical Group, includes construction of two coal-fired electric power plant (one of which will supply more electricity to Kabul city); a segment of railway (discussed above); and a road from the project to Kabul. As noted above, work on the mine reportedly has been slowed by various factors, including the need to clear mines in the area.

On December 14, 2010, with involvement of the DOD Task Force for Business and Stability Operations, 10 outside investors announced $50 million in investment in a gold mine in Baghlan Province. There is another gold mine operating in neighboring Takhar Province. Bids are being accepted for another large mining project, the Haji Gak iron ore mine (which may contain 60 billion tons of iron ore) near Kabul. China Metallurgy, as well as companies from India, are said to be finalists for the project.

• Hydrocarbons and Pipelines. Afghanistan has no hydrocarbons energy export industry and a small refining sector that provides some of Afghanistan's needs for gasoline or other fuels. Almost all of Afghanistan's fuel comes from neighboring states. As noted, Afghanistan has had virtually no operational hydrocarbon energy sector. However, Afghanistan's prospects in this sector appeared to brighten by the announcement in March 2006 of an estimated 3.6 billion barrels of oil and 36.5 trillion cubic feet of gas reserves. Experts believe these amounts, if proved, could make Afghanistan relatively self-sufficient in energy and able to export energy to its neighbors. In a major development, on December 15, 2010, the Afghan government let a six-month contract to a local firm, Ghazanfar Neft Gas, to collect and market crude oil from the Angot field in northern Afghanistan (part of a field that may contain 80 million barrels of oil), initially producing at the low rate of 800 barrels per day. However, the sector is expected to expand to more fields in the Amu Darya basin (northern Afghanistan), and a tender will be offered to develop a larger oil field in Balkh Province, estimated to hold 1.8 billion barrels of oil. Separately, USAID is funding a test project to develop gas resources in northern Afghanistan.

TAPI (Turkmenistan-Afghanistan-Pakistan-India) Gas Pipeline Project . Another major energy project remains under consideration. During 1996-1998, the Clinton Administration supported proposed natural gas and oil pipelines through western Afghanistan as an incentive for the warring factions to cooperate. A consortium led by Los Angeles-based Unocal Corporation proposed a $7.5 billion Central Asia Gas Pipeline that would originate in southern Turkmenistan and pass through Afghanistan to Pakistan, with possible extensions into India.[81]

The deterioration in U.S.-Taliban relations after 1998 suspended hopes for the pipeline projects, but prospects for the project improved in the post-Taliban period. In a summit meeting in late May 2002 between the leaders of Turkmenistan, Afghanistan, and Pakistan, the three countries agreed to revive the project. Sponsors held an inaugural meeting on July 9, 2002, in

Turkmenistan, signing a series of preliminary agreements. Turkmenistan's leadership (President Gurbanguly Berdimukhamedov, succeeding the late Saparmurad Niyazov) favors the project as well. Yet another agreement in principle to implement the project was signed among Karzai and other regional leaders on December 12, 2010, in the Turkmenistan capital Ashkabad. Disagreements remain over the proportion of gas supplied to the line by individual countries, and over pricing, but Afghan officials say the Asian Development Bank has agreed to finance the project, removing what had been a major hurdle. U.S. officials view this project as a superior alternative to a proposed gas pipeline from Iran to India, transiting Pakistan.

TRADE INITIATIVES/RECONSTRUCTION OPPORTUNITY ZONES

The United States is trying to build on Afghanistan's post-war economic rebound with trade initiatives. In September 2004, the United States and Afghanistan signed a bilateral trade and investment framework agreement (TIFA). These agreements are generally seen as a prelude to a broader and more complex bilateral free trade agreement, but negotiations on an FTA have not yet begun. On December 13, 2004, the 148 countries of the World Trade Organization voted to start membership talks with Afghanistan. Another initiative supported by the United States is the establishment of joint Afghan-Pakistani "Reconstruction Opportunity Zones" (ROZ's) which would be modeled after "Qualified Industrial Zones" run by Israel and Jordan in which goods produced in the zones receive duty free treatment for import into the United States. For FY2008, $5 million in supplemental funding was requested to support the zones, but P.L. 110-252 did not specifically mention the zones.

Bills in the 110th Congress, S. 2776 and H.R. 6387, would have authorized the President to proclaim duty-free treatment for imports from ROZ's to be designated by the President. In the 111th Congress, a version of these bills was introduced (S. 496 and H.R. 1318). President Obama specifically endorsed passage of these bills in his March 2009 strategy announcement. H.R. 1318 was incorporated into H.R. 1886, a Pakistan aid appropriation that is a component of the new U.S. strategy for the region, and the bill was passed by the House on June 11, 2009, and then appended to H.R. 2410. However, another version of the Pakistan aid bill, S. 1707, did not authorize ROZ's; it was passed and became law (P.L. 111-73).

Major International (Non-U.S.) Pledges to Afghanistan Since January 2002

(as of March 2010; $ in millions)

Japan	6,900
Britain	2,897
World Bank	2,803
Asia Development Bank	2,200
European Commission (EC)	1,768
Netherlands	1,697
Canada	1,479
India	1,200
Iran	1,164
Germany	1,108
Norway	977
Denmark	683
Italy	637
Saudi Arabia	533

Spain	486
Australia	440
Total Non-U.S. Pledges	30,800
(including donors not listed)	

Sources: Special Inspector General for Afghanistan Reconstruction. October 2008 report, p. 140; various press announcements. Figures include funds pledged at April 2009 NATO summit and Japan's October 2009 pledge of $5 billion over the next five years.

Note: This table lists donors pledging over $400 million total.

Table 11. U.S.Assistance to Afghanistan, FY1978-FY1998 ($ in millions)

Fiscal Year	Devel. Assist.	Econ. Supp. (ESF)	P.L. 480 (Title I and II)	Military	Other (Incl. Regional Refugee Aid)	Total
1978	4.989	—	5.742	0.269	0.789	11.789
1979	3.074	—	7.195	—	0.347	10.616
1980	—	(Soviet invasion-December 1979)			—	—
1981	—	—	—	—	—	—
1982	—	—	—	—	—	—
1983	—	—	—	—	—	—
1984	—	—	—	—	—	—
1985	3.369	—	—	—	—	3.369
1986	—	—	8.9	—	—	8.9
1987	17.8	12.1	2.6	—	—	32.5
1988	22.5	22.5	29.9	—	—	74.9
1989	22.5	22.5	32.6	—	—	77.6
1990	35.0	35.0	18.1	—	—	88.1
1991	30.0	30.0	20.1	—	—	80.1
1992	25.0	25.0	31.4	—	—	81.4
1993	10.0	10.0	18.0	—	30.2	68.2
1994	3.4	2.0	9.0	—	27.9	42.3
1995	1.8	—	12.4	—	31.6	45.8
1996	—	—	16.1	—	26.4	42.5
1997	—	—	18.0	—	31.9a	49.9
1998	—	—	3.6	—	49.14b	52.74

Source: Department of State.

a. Includes $3 million for demining and $1.2 million for counternarcotics.

b. Includes $3.3 million in projects targeted for Afghan women and girls, $7 million in earthquake relief aid, 100,000 tons of 416B wheat worth about $15 million, $2 million for demining, and $1.54 for counternarcotics.

Table 19. U.S.Assistance to Afghanistan, FY2009

Regular Appropriation (P.L. 111-8)		Bridge Supplemental (P.L. 110-252)	FY2009 Supplemental (P.L. 111-32)	Total
ANSF Funding		2,000	3,607	5,607
CERP (DOD funds)		683		683
Detainee ops (DOD)		4		4
Counternarcotics (C-N) (DOD)	24	150	57	232
C-N (DEA)	19			19
C-N—Alternative. Livelihoods (INCLE)	100	70	87	257
C-N—Eradication, Interdiction (INCLE)	178	14	17	209
IMET	1.4			1.4
ARTF (Incl. National Solidarity Program)	45	20	85	150
Governance building	100	68	115	283
Civil Society promotion	8	4		12
Election Support	93	56	25	174
Strategic Program Development			50	50
Rule of Law Programs (USAID)	8	15	20	43
Rule of Law (INCLE)	34	55	80	169
Roads (ESF)	74	65		139
Power (ESF)	73	61		134
Agriculture (ESF and DA)	25		85	110
PRTs/Local Governance (ESF)	74	55	159	288
Education	88	6		94
Health	61	27		88
Econ Growth/"Cash for Work"	49	37	220	306
Water, Environment, Victims Comp.	31	3		34
Karzai Protection (NADR)	32		12	44
Food Aid (P.L. 480, Food for Peace)	14	44		58
Migration, Refugee Aid		50	7	57
State Ops/Embassy Construction	308	131	450	889
USAID Programs and Ops	18	2	165	185
State/USAID IG/SIGAR	3	11	7	20
Cultural Exchanges, International Orgs	6	10		16
Totals	1,463	3,640	5,248	10,352

Notes: P.L. 111-32 (FY2009 supplemental): provides requested funds, earmarks $70 million for National Solidarity Program; $150 million for women and girls (all of FY2009); ESF over $200 million subject to narcotics certification; 10% of supplemental INCLE subject to certification of Afghan government moves to curb human rights abuses, drug involvement.

Table 20. FY2010 Assistance (Includes Supplemental) ($ in millions)

Afghan Security Forces Funding (DOD funds)	9,162 (6,563 appropriated plus 2,600
	supplemental request)
CERP (DOD funds)	1,000
Counternarcotics (DOD)	361
INCLE: all functions: interdiction, rule of law,	620 (420 regular approp. plus 200
alternative livelihoods	supplemental request)
IMET	1.5
Global Health/Child Survival	92.3
Afghanistan Reconstruction Trust Fund (Incl.	200
National Solidarity Program) (ESF)	
Governance building (ESF)	191
Civil Society promotion (ESF)	10
Election Support (ESF)	90
Strategic Program Development (ESF)	100
USAID Rule of Law Programs (ESF)	50
Roads (ESF)	230
Power (ESF)	230
Agriculture (ESF)	230
PRT programs/Local governance (ESF)	251
Education (ESF)	95
Health (ESF)	102
Econ Growth/"Cash for Work" (ESF)	274
Water, Environment, Victim Comp. (ESF)	15
Karzai Protection (NADR)	58
Food Aid (P.L. 480, Food for Peace)	16
Refugees and Migration	11
State Ops/Embassy Construction	697 (486 regular plus 211 supplemental)
Cultural Exchanges	6
SIGAR	37 (23 regular plus 14 supp request)
FY2010 supplemental ESF request (for ESF	1,576
programs above)	
Total Appropriated (Incl. Supplemental)	15,700

Laws derived: FY2010 foreign aid appropriation in Consolidated Appropriation (P.L. 111-117), which earmarks: $175 million (ESF and INCLE) for programs for women and girls, and $175 million (ESF) for the National Solidarity Program. The FY2010 Defense Appropriation (P.L. 111-118), which cut $900 million from the requested amount for the ANSF (regular defense appropriation). FY2010 supplemental funds appropriated by H.R. 4899 (P.L. 111-212)

Table 21. FY2011 ($ in millions)

Program/Area	Request/Enacted in April 2011 Budget Agreement
Afghan National Security Forces (DOD funds)	11,600
	(enacted, as requested)
CERP	900
	(of which 400 is for Afghanistan Infrastructure Fund. CERP request was for 1,300)
Economic Support Funds (ESF)	3,316.3 (req)
Global Health/ Child Survival	71.1 (req)
INCLE	450 (req)
Karzai Protection (NADR funds)	69.3 (req)
IMET	1.5 (req)
State Dept. Operations (not incl. security)	754 (req)
SIGAR	24+
	35.3 (req)
Total Request	17,000 (approx)

Budget agreement is H.R. 1473. The Administration requested to authorize an "Afghanistan Infrastructure Fund," to contain mostly DOD funds, beginning with $400 million in FY2011, was authorized in H.R 6523, the National Defense Authorization Act for FY2011, P.L.111383). Funds were appropriated. The fund will be used mostly for electricity projects, including an ongoing major electricity project for Qandahar, but could be used for other infrastructure projects later on, such as roads.

Table 22. FY2012 ($ in millions)

Program/Area Request

ANSF Funding 12,800

Economic Support Funds 2,804

(incl.: $227 m for health, $115 m for education, $790 m (of which 1,216 is Overseas for "good governance,"$185 m for agriculture, $66 m for Contingency Operations "private sector competitiveness") funding)

Health and Child Survival (State) 0.5 Health and Child Survival (USAID) 0.5 Food For Peace Title II 15.5 INCLE (counter-narcotics, rule of law) 324 NADR funds (Karzai protection, explosives removal,

66.2 counter-terrorism) IMET 2.4 Diplomatic and Consular (embassy construction, 758personnel) Diplomatic and Consular (security) 190 SIGAR 44 CERP (regular) 400 CERP (contribution to Afghan Infrastructure Fund) 500 CERP (Taskforce for Business) 150 Total 18,050

Figures do not include about $100 billion in U.S. military operations costs

TABLE 23.TOTAL OBLIGATIONS FOR MAJOR PROGRAMS: FY2001-FY2010

(From SIGAR quarterly report, July 2010. $ in millions. Some sector breakdowns not available as of FY2010, as shown)

Security Related Programs (mostly DOD funds)

Afghan National Security Forces (incl. FMF, and train and equip)	26,746
Commander Emergency Response Program (CERP)	2,639
Karzai Protection (NADR funds)	371.6
Counter-Narcotics (INCLE, DoD, DEA)	4,237.4
De-Mining Operations (Halo Trust, other contractors)	98.53
International Military Education and Training Funds (IMET)	8.3
Afghanistan Freedom Support Act (defenses article drawdown under AFSA)	550
Humanitarian-Related Programs	
Food Aid (USDA and USAID: P.L. 480 Title 1 and II; Food for Progress, 416(b), Food for Education)	961.1
Migration and Refugee aid (including emergency)	614
Debt Relief for Afghan government	11
Economic Support Funds (ESF) and Development Assistance (DA)	10,625
Afghan government budget support	81+ FY2010
Good Governance	1,951
Afghan Reconstruction Trust Fund (for National Solidarity Program, etc)	305+ FY2010
Civil Society programs	54
Election support	600 + FY2010
Rule of Law and Human Rights (incl. some INCLE funds)	935
Roads	1,908 + FY2010
Power/Electricity	934.4 + FY2010
Education	683.6
Health Sector	706.3
Water	128 + FY2010
Agriculture	903.3
PRT projects	698 + FY2010
Private Sector Development/Econ. Growth (incl IT, communications)	882
Embassy Operations, Construction, Aid Oversight	3,720.9
Other Aid:	
Child Survival and Health	486.4
Commodity Credit Corporation (CCC)	25.87
Treasury Technical Assistance	3.5
USAID (other)	31.37
Total (including minor amounts not included in table)	51,501.8

Provincial Reconstruction Teams

Location (City)		Province/Command
U.S.-Lead (all under ISAF banner)		
1. Gardez		Paktia Province (RC-East, E)
2. Ghazni		Ghazni (RC-E). with Poland.
3. Jalalabad		Nangarhar (RC-E)
4. Khost		Khost (RC-E)
5. Qalat		Zabol (RC-South, S). with Romania.
6. Asadabad		Kunar (RC-E)
7. Sharana		Paktika (RC-E). with Poland.
8. Mehtarlam		Laghman (RC-E)
9. Jabal o-Saraj		Panjshir Province (RC-E), State Department lead
10. Qala Gush		Nuristan (RC-E)
11. Farah		Farah (RC-SW)
Partner Lead (most under ISAF banner)		
PRT Location	Province	Lead Force/Other forces
12. Qandahar	Qandahar (RC-S)	Canada (seat of RC-S)
13. Lashkar Gah	Helmand (RC-S)	Britain. with Denmark and Estonia
14. Tarin Kowt	Uruzgan (RC-S)	Australia (and U.S.) (Replaced Netherlands in August 2010)
15. Herat	Herat (RC-W)	Italy (seat of RC-W)
16. Qalah-ye Now	Badghis (RC-W)	Spain
17. Mazar-e-Sharif	Balkh (RC-N)	Sweden
18. Konduz	Konduz (RC-N)	Germany (seat of RC-N)
29. Faizabad	Badakhshan (RC-N)	Germany. with Denmark, Czech Rep.
20. Meymaneh	Faryab (RC-N)	Norway. with Sweden.
21. Chaghcharan	Ghowr (RC-W)	Lithuania. with Denmark, U.S., Iceland
22. Pol-e-Khomri	Baghlan (RC-N)	Hungary
23. Bamiyan	Bamiyan (RC-E)	New Zealand (not NATO/ISAF).
24. Maidan Shahr	Wardak (RC-C)	Turkey
25. Pul-i-Alam	Lowgar (RC-E)	Czech Republic
26. Shebergan	Jowzjan (RC-N)	Turkey
27. Charikar	Parwan (RC-E)	South Korea (Bagram, in Parwan Province, is the base of RC-E)

Note: RC = Regional Command.

Major Factions/Leaders in Afghanistan

Party/ Leader	Leader	Ideology/ Ethnicity	Regional Base
Taliban	Mullah (Islamic cleric) Muhammad Umar (still at large	Ultra-	Insurgent
	possibly in Afghanistan. Umar, born in Tarin Kowt, Uruzgan	orthodox	groups, mostly
	province, is about 65 years old.	Islamic,	in the south and

		Pashtun	east.
Haqqani	Jalaludin and Siraj Haqqani. Allied with Taliban and Al Qaeda.	Same as	Paktia, Paktika,
Network	Said to be heavily influenced by elements within Pakistani	above	Khost, Kabul
	military intelligence.		
Islamic Society	Burhannudin Rabbani/ Yunus Qanooni (speaker of lower	Moderate	Much of
(leader of	house)/Muhammad Fahim/Dr. Abdullah Abdullah (Foreign	Islamic,	northern and
"Northern	Minister 2001-2006). Ismail Khan, a so-called "warlord,"	mostly Tajik	western
Alliance")	heads faction of the grouping in Herat area. Khan, now		Afghanistan,
	Minister of Energy and Water, visited United States in March		including Kabul
	2008 to sign USAID grant for energy projects.		
National	Abdul Rashid Dostam. During OEF, impressed U.S.	Secular,	Jowzjan, Balkh,
Islamic	commanders with horse-mounted assaults on Taliban	Uzbek	Faryab, Sar-i-Pol,
Movement of	positions at Shulgara Dam, south of Mazar-e-Sharif, leading		and Samangan
Afghanistan	to the fall of that city and the Taliban's subsequent collapse.		provinces.
	Was Karzai rival in October 2004 presidential election, then		
	his top "security adviser."		
Hizb-e-	Composed of Shiite Hazara tribes from central Afghanistan.	Shiite,	Bamiyan, Ghazni,
Wahdat	Karim Khalili is Vice President, but Mohammad Mohaqiq is	Hazara	Dai Kundi
	Karzai rival in 2004 presidential election and parliament.	tribes	province
	Generally pro-Iranian. Was part of Rabbani 1992-1996		
	government, and fought unsuccessfully with Taliban over		
	Bamiyan city. Still revered by Hazara Shiites is the former		
	leader of the group, Abdul Ali Mazari, who was captured and		
	killed by the Taliban in March 1995.		
Pashtun	Various regional governors and local leaders in the east and	Moderate	Dominant in the
Leaders	south; central government led by Hamid Karzai.	Islamic,	south and east
		Pashtun	
Hizb-e-Islam	Mujahedin party leader Gulbuddin Hikmatyar.	Orthodox	Small groups in

	Was part of		
Gulbuddin	Soviet-era U.S.-backed "Afghan Interim Government" based	Islamic,	Nangarhar,
(HIG)	in Peshawar, Pakistan. Was nominal "prime minister" in	Pashtun	Nuristan, and
	1992-1996 mujahedin government but never actually took		Kunar provinces
	office. Lost power base around Jalalabad to the Taliban in		
	1994, and fled to Iran before being expelled in 2002. Still		
	allied with Taliban and Al Qaeda in operations east of Kabul,		
	but open to ending militant activity. Leader of a rival Hizb-e-		
	Islam faction, Yunus Khalis, the mentor of Mullah Umar, died		
	July 2006.		
Islamic Union	Abd-I-Rab Rasul Sayyaf. Islamic conservative, leads a pro	orthodox	Paghman
	Karzai faction in parliament. Lived many years in and	Islamic,	(west of Kabul)
	politically close to Saudi Arabia, which shares his "Wahhabi"	Pashtun	
	ideology. During anti-Soviet war, Sayyaf's faction, with		
	Hikmatyar, was a principal recipient of U.S. weaponry.		
	Criticized the U.S.-led war against Saddam Hussein after		
	Iraq's invasion of Kuwait.		

Source: CRS.

RESIDUAL ISSUES FROM PAST CONFLICTS

A few issues remain unresolved from Afghanistan's many years of conflict, such as Stinger retrieval and mine eradication.

STINGER RETRIEVAL

Beginning in late 1985 following internal debate, the Reagan Administration provided about 2,000 man-portable "Stinger" anti-aircraft missiles to the *mujahedin* for use against Soviet aircraft. Prior to the ouster of the Taliban, common estimates suggested that 200-300 Stingers remained at large, although more recent estimates put the number below 100.[82] The Stinger issue resurfaced in conjunction with 2001 U.S. war effort, when U.S. pilots reported that the Taliban fired some Stingers at U.S. aircraft. No hits were reported. The danger of these weapons has become apparent on several past occasions. Iran bought 16 of the missiles in 1987 and fired one against U.S. helicopters in the Persian Gulf. India claimed that it was a Stinger supplied to Islamic rebels in Kashmir by sympathizers in Afghanistan, that shot down an Indian helicopter over Kashmir in May 1999.[83] Soviet-made SA-7 "Strella" man-portable launchers, which allegedly have been used in the past by Al Qaeda, including against an Israeli passenger jet in Kenya on November 30, 2002, were discovered in Afghanistan by U.S. forces in December 2002.

In 1992, after the fall of the Russian-backed government of Najibullah, the United States reportedly spent about $10 million to buy the Stingers back, at a premium, from individual *mujahedin* commanders. The *New York Times* reported on July 24, 1993, that the buy back effort failed because the United States was competing with other buyers, including Iran and North Korea, and that the CIA would spend about $55 million in FY1994 in a renewed effort. On March 7, 1994, the *Washington Post* reported that the CIA had recovered only about 50 or 100 at-large Stingers. In February 2002, the Afghan government found and turned over to the United States "dozens" of Stingers.[84] In January 2005, Afghan intelligence began buying Stingers back, at a reported cost of $150,000 each.[85] Any Stingers that remain in Afghanistan likely pose little threat, in part because of deteriorating components. No recent uses are reported.

MINE ERADICATION

Land mines laid during the Soviet occupation constitute one of the principal dangers to the Afghan people. The United Nations estimates that 5 million to 7 million mines remain scattered throughout the country, although some estimates are lower. U.N. teams have destroyed one million mines and are now focusing on de-mining priority-use, residential and commercial property, including lands around Kabul. Amounts contributed by the United States to the de-mining effort are shown in the tables above. Most of the funds have gone to HALO Trust, a British organization, and the U.N. Mine Action Program for Afghanistan. The Afghanistan Compact adopted in London in February 2006 states that by 2010, the goal should be to reduce the land area of Afghanistan contaminated by mines by 70%.

[82] Saleem, Farrukh. "Where Are the Missing Stinger Missiles? Pakistan," *Friday Times*. August 17-23, 2001. [83] "U.S.-Made Stinger Missiles—Mobile and Lethal." Reuters, May 28, 1999. [84] Fullerton, John. "Afghan Authorities Hand in Stinger Missiles to U.S." Reuters, February 4, 2002. [85] "Afghanistan Report," Radio Free Europe/Radio Liberty. February 4, 2005.

U.S. AND INTERNATIONAL SANCTIONS LIFTED

Virtually all U.S. and international sanctions on Afghanistan, some imposed during the Soviet occupation era and others on the Taliban regime, have now been lifted.

P.L. 108-458 (December 17, 2004, referencing the 9/11 Commission recommendations) repealed bans on aid to Afghanistan outright. On October 7, 1992, President George H.W. Bush had issued Presidential Determination 93-3 that Afghanistan is no longer a Marxist-Leninist country, but the determination was not implemented before he left office. Had it been implemented, the prohibition on Afghanistan's receiving Export-Import Bank guarantees, insurance, or credits for purchases under Section 8 of the 1986 Export-Import Bank Act, would have been lifted. In addition, Afghanistan would have been able to receive U.S. assistance because the requirement would have been waived that Afghanistan apologize for the 1979 killing in Kabul of U.S. Ambassador to Afghanistan Adolph "Spike" Dubs. (Dubs was kidnapped in Kabul in 1979 and killed when Afghan police stormed the hideout where he was held.)

U.N. sanctions on the Taliban imposed by Resolution 1267 (October 15, 1999), Resolution 1333 (December 19, 2000), and Resolution 1363 (July 30, 2001) have now been narrowed to penalize only Al Qaeda (by Resolution 1390, January 17, 2002). Resolution 1267 banned flights outside Afghanistan by Ariana, and directed U.N. member states to freeze Taliban assets. Resolution 1333 prohibited the provision of arms or military advice to the Taliban (directed against Pakistan); ordered a reduction of Taliban diplomatic representation abroad; and banned foreign travel by senior Taliban officials. Resolution 1363 provided for monitors in Pakistan to ensure that no weapons or military advice was provided to the Taliban.

On January 10, 2003, President Bush signed a proclamation making Afghanistan a beneficiary of the Generalized System of Preferences (GSP), eliminating U.S. tariffs on 5,700 Afghan products. Afghanistan had been denied GSP on May 2, 1980, under Executive Order 12204 (45 F.R. 20740).

On April 24, 1981, controls on U.S. exports to Afghanistan of agricultural products and phosphates were terminated. Such controls were imposed on June 3, 1980, as part of the sanctions against the Soviet Union for the invasion of Afghanistan, under the authority of Sections 5 and 6 of the Export Administration Act of 1979 [P.L. 96-72; 50 U.S.C. app. 2404, app. 2405].

In mid-1992, the George H.W. Bush Administration determined that Afghanistan no longer had a "Soviet-controlled government." This opened Afghanistan to the use of U.S. funds made available for the U.S. share of U.N. organizations that provide assistance to Afghanistan.

On March 31, 1993, after the fall of Najibullah in 1992, President Clinton, on national interest grounds, waived restrictions provided for in Section 481 (h) of the Foreign Assistance Act of 1961 mandating sanctions on Afghanistan, including bilateral aid cuts and suspensions, including denial of Ex-Im Bank credits; the casting of negative U.S. votes for multilateral development bank loans; and a non-allocation of a U.S. sugar quota. Discretionary sanctions included denial of GSP; additional duties on exports to the United States; and

curtailment of air transportation with the United States. Waivers were also granted in 1994 and, after the fall of the Taliban, by President Bush.

On May 3, 2002, President Bush restored normal trade treatment to the products of Afghanistan, reversing the February 18, 1986, proclamation by President Reagan (Presidential Proclamation 5437) that suspended most-favored nation (MFN) tariff status for Afghanistan (51 F.R. 4287). The Foreign Assistance Appropriations for FY1986 [Section 552, P.L. 99-190] had authorized the denial of U.S. credits or most-favored-nation (MFN) status for Afghanistan.

On July 2, 2002, the State Department amended U.S. regulations (22 C.F.R. Part 126) to allow arms sales to the new Afghan government, reversing the June 14, 1996, addition of Afghanistan to the list of countries prohibited from importing

U.S. defense articles and services. Arms sales to Afghanistan had also been prohibited during 1997-2002 because Afghanistan had been designated under the Antiterrorism and Effective Death Penalty Act of 1996 (P.L. 104-132) as a state that is not cooperating with U.S. anti-terrorism efforts.

On July 2, 2002, President Bush formally revoked the July 4, 1999, declaration by President Clinton of a national emergency with respect to Taliban because of its hosting of bin Laden. The Clinton determination and related Executive Order 13129 had blocked Taliban assets and property in the United States, banned U.S. trade with Taliban-controlled areas of Afghanistan, and applied these sanctions to Ariana Afghan Airlines, triggering a blocking of Ariana assets (about $500,000) in the United States and a ban on U.S. citizens' flying on the airline. (The ban on trade with Taliban-controlled territory had essentially ended on January 29, 2002, when the State Department determination that the Taliban controls no territory within Afghanistan.)

TRAVEL TO AFGANISTAN

US STATE DEPARTMENT SUGGESTIONS

TRAVEL WARNING: The Department of State warns U.S. citizens against travel to Afghanistan. We continue to receive threats from terrorists, including Usama Bin Laden, who is based in Afghanistan, that do not distinguish between American military and civilian targets. U.S. citizens who are in Afghanistan or considering traveling there should be aware that the U.S. Government reserves the right to retaliate against the facilities of those who harbor terrorists, as well as the terrorists themselves.

The Department of State urges Americans who decide to remain in Afghanistan in spite of this warning to exercise extreme caution, monitor their security situation closely and make plans for responding to a sudden deterioration in security conditions. All U.S. personnel at the U.S. Embassy in Kabul were evacuated in 1989, and no other diplomatic mission represents U.S. interests or provides consular services.

President Clinton signed an Executive Order effective July 6, 1999, imposing financial and commercial sanctions against the Taliban in Afghanistan, a faction that currently exercises de facto control over much of the country, for their support of Usama bin Ladin and his terrorist network.

In addition, frequent military operations continue in various regions of Afghanistan, sometimes involving intense fighting. Americans remain vulnerable to politically and criminally motivated attacks and violence, including robbery, kidnapping and hostage-taking. The estimated 5-7 million landmines scattered throughout the countryside pose a danger to all residents and visitors to Afghanistan.

U.S. citizens who decide to enter Afghanistan in spite of the Travel Warning are strongly urged to register and obtain updated security information at the American Embassy in Islamabad, Pakistan, or the U.S. Consulate in Peshawar, Pakistan, at the following addresses:

U.S. Embassy, Diplomatic Enclave, Ramna 5, Islamabad, telephone (92-51) 2080-0000, consular section (92-51) 2080-2700, fax (92-51) 822-632

U.S. Consulate Peshawar, 11 Hospital Road, Peshawar Cantonment, telephone (92-91) 279-801, fax (92-91) 276-712

TRAVELLING TO AFGHANISTAN

Flight Operations UNOCHA/UNDP Islamabad
Tel: +92 (51) 211451-5
Fax: +92 (51) 211450
E-mail: unocha@undpafg.org.pk

Boy, if you hate crowded hiking trails and booked hotels, have we got a place for you. Although the U.S. State department says don't go, the Talibs say don't go and the north says don't go, Afghanistan is number one with a bullet for people who want to visit dangerous places. There is no U.S. embassy at the moment (hell, there's no anything at the moment), The NGOs keep their bags packed and no one quite knows who's in charge at any one time. The Talibs are here to stay, but that doesn't mean there is an long-term sense or logic regarding their entry policy for foreigners.

Journos and scribes are officially welcomed by the Taliban and then never given visas to enter. The Red Cross needs Talib approval for all journos before you can book a flight. Same goes for the UN. There are a number of restrictions, advance notice and permission requirements so contact:

Once inside journos have to comply with a two page list of do's and don'ts, which oddly enough includes having your picture taken in a place where taking pictures of living things is forbidden. Being beaten every time you whip out a camera does put a damper on bringing in a Betacam crew. If you are sponsored by an NGO you must only cover the activities of that group. If you somehow get it just to look around, you must stay at the Intercontinental, hire a guide and a driver who maintains his lonely vigil in the lobby. Figure on doubling the rate when you go to the front lines. Strangely, if you are not a journalist there are no laws to restrict your movement. And techncially, once outside Kabul you are free to do what you like (other than photograph people or, as a male, interview women). In the north, you must register in Mazar and stay at the UN guesthouse, whereas journos are forbidden from staying with the UN in Kabul. You will find the Taliban both pleasurable, exasperating and sometimes brutal, depending on circumstances.

DP called the embassy to get the latest travel stats. Apparently, Afghanistan is where all the journos were headed to earn their spurs. When asked who is going to Afghanistan, our contact replied, "Lots of journalists." The embassy needs $60, a couple of photos and a letter from your company saying why you want to be Afghanistan bound. If you enter from Peshawar, don't forget you need to arrange a double or multiple entry visa, a Khyber Pass permit and a gunman from the Khyber Tribal Agency office in Peshawar to get to Torkham. For some odd reason going back doesn't require this. You also need an exit visa (which can eat up half a day) if you leave from Kabul.

Pleasure tourists may find their visa request turned down unless they are truly persuasive. or bum a ride with an NGO car. The border crossings are as mercurial as they are dangerous. DP narrowly missed being caught up in a shootout at Torkham between slack-jawed Talib boy-guards and veddy British and veddy nervous Pakistani border guards. After the Talibs rocketed the top of the Pakistani post and shot through a demining vehicle, calm was restored and the Talibs went back to whipping urchins with their steel cables.

The Taliban-friendly U.S. embassy (locked in their usual time warp) told us that Massoud was getting support from "Russia and the Soviet Union" and when pressed for advice on how to stay safe, they came up with "Don't steal anything." Any other advice? "Well, you might have to grow a beard, or if you are a woman you might have to wear the chador, well no, now that I think of it, I guess Diane Sawyer didn't have to." We assume he meant the chador not the beard.

The London Afghan Embassy is run by Massoud's brother Wali. He can get you a journo visa for the north but can't do much about arranging a flight in. Tajikistan and Pakistan are your only safe bets for getting into the north. But just getting into and out of Tajikistan is its own nightmare (see the "Tajikistan" chapter).

All border crossings except Termez in Uzbekistan are technically open, but the embassy recommends that travelers use the crossings from Pakistan, Iran and Tajikistan only. The best way into the north and the south is from Pakistan. The intrepid can stroll into Afghanistan over the many mountain trails that connect the two countries in the north and along the Khyber Pass. Since these are usually drug smuggling routes, all travelers will be suspect. A few years ago the

DEA (via the Pakistani antidrug agency) was actually offering tribesmen a bounty on any gringos caught buying drugs, so shop for souvenirs with caution.

Afghans are quite hospitable and will offer food and whatever lodging they have. You are expected to reciprocate with some type of gift or remembrance. Photos of your family are great icebreakers and gifts like flashlights, medicine or even clothes are received well. Make sure you pick the right guide, one on good terms with the tribes who control the regions you will be passing through. You will probably be the only tourist in Afghanistan. Camels can be rented to carry heavy gear for US$10 dollars a day, and guides go for about US$20 a day, plus baksheesh (a tip). Travelers would be ill-advised to go gem hunting or arms collecting in the hills at this time due to the prevalence of land mines-still the number-one killer and maimer of humans and other living things-and the propensity of Afghans to kidnap foreigners for a few quick dollars.

Most of the country is in the hands of the Taliban, who also control the entry and movement of all outsiders.The northwest is in the hands of the Tajiks and the Wahkan corridor is a no-man's-land under any condition due to the mountainous terrain and drug smuggling. Those who want to meet the Taliban can also contact them in Pakistan.

DANGER OF KIDNEPPING FOR FOREIGNERS

Traditionally and historically the Afghans are among the most hospitable people in the world. Today their "hospitality" can go extreme. Foreigners can be just kidnapped. Kidnapping is actually a tribal tradition that goes back before recorded time. Recently, kidnapping has been a means to bring attention to tribal disputes or grievances. Locals, expats and tourists are routinely kidnapped in Afghanistan and near the border with Pakistan. Ransoms run from US$2,000 up to US$50,000 and more for foreign workers.

The positive side to this is that if you're traveling under the protection of one tribe and are kidnapped by another, your host tribe has an obligation to free you. The people in the greatest danger are foreign workers who travel in a predetermined route or stay in a fixed place.
http://travel.state.gov/afghanistan_warning.html
Any foreigner is going to be considered a suspect spy and enemy.

LAND MINES

The Russians buried and dropped about 12 million mines in the ground. Some say at the current removal rate it will take 20,000 years to remove all the mines. HALO figures that 640,000 mines have been laid since 1979. In 1998 they cleared 100,000 individual items of unexploded ordnance, or UXO. HALO has 1,300 Afghan deminers working under the supervision of only two expats clearing the towns and countryside. They are working feverishly to demine the 95 percent of the country under peace so that more than 3 million Afghans can return to their formerly mined villages. There are currently 300,000 Afghans waiting to rebuild or move back into their homes in Kabul.

Most deminers will tell you privately that the UN estimate is a little over the top but makes them look good when they do it faster. There are more than 50 different kinds of mines, and not just Russian made. There are RAP-2s from Zimbabwe, and even NR-127s made in Belgium. There are neat battery-powered multicensored mines that blow up when they feel vibration. According to the UN, 162 of AfghanistanOs 356 districts are affected by mines. The most dangerous areas for mines are Helmand with 5 major fields, Kandahar with 47, Paktia with 118, Logar with 53 and Herat with 86. The areas affected are grazing land, irrigation systems, agricultural land and cities.

Both the Taliban (who promised me they didnOt and wouldnOt use mines back in the bad old days) and the northern alliance is busy putting new ones in as you read this.

The UN estimates it needs $185 million to carry out all its programs, including demining. Afghanistan currently has the worldOs largest demining program and in seven years has destroyed over 200,000 devices, but has cleared only 80 square kilometers. The most heavily mined areas are security zones around the major cities along the Iranian and Pakistani borders (Herat, Kandahar, Jalalabad and Khost). Follow the basic rules and you will survive: Do not wander off hard surface (even when taking a leak). Learn to squat at the edge of the road to urinate like the locals do. Do not travel in snow. Land mines were laid in strength along mountain passes and can be more sensitive with ice and snow cover. Do not turn over or pick up any items, do not inspect abandoned military vehicles, do not run up a hill to get a better vantage point . . . and the list goes on.

http://www.un.org/Depts/Landmine/program/Afghan/partners.htm

What were people in Afghanistan doing when they were killed or injured by a land mine.
Fetching water 20 percent
Traveling 15 percent
Fighting 13 percent
Playing with a mine 8 percent
Demining 4 percent

EVERYDAY LIFE INFORMATION

Electricity (when you can find it) is 220v/50Hz. The official languages are Pashtu (mostly in the south and east) and Dari Persian (in the north and west). Many people speak English and some Russian. The money is the Afghani and the black market is the only real place you can exchange notes. Figure on a U.S. dollar getting you 44,360 afghanis. Be forewarned that there are two afghanis. One, called Dostum money, is used in the north and is one-tenth of the value of the Talib afghani used in the south. They look identical except for the spacing between the type on the front. The way to remember is the type of the northern or Dostum money is "allied" or together and the south is apart.

The money changers are fair since this is how all people change money. Try not to use U.S. $100 bills printed before 1993 since many money changers won't take them. When shops are open they start at 8 a.m. and close between noon and 1 p.m. and then reopen until 4:30 p.m. Some shops are closed Wednesday and Friday. Traffic drives on the right and the normally paved roads are full of potholes from shells and disrepair. Jalalabad is the main smuggling area for cars, electronic goods and drugs into Pakistan, so be judicious when asking questions or taking photographs.

Web Sites: http://www.agora.stm.it/politic/afghanistan.htm

Even though things are settling down, medical care is not Afghanistan's strong point. Health care is available in the major cities through aid groups. Many prescription drugs and antibiotics (not opiates) can be bought over the counter. They will be old and dusty and we do not recommend self-medication. A traveler with a serious condition should seek help in Pakistan or Iran. Better yet, take the next flight home or to London. Expect that the most basic medical care is limited or nonexistent with war wounded and children getting priority treatment. Malaria (primarily the benign vivax form) is present below 2,000 meters (6,562 feet) between May and November in the southern area and falciparcium strain occurs in the warmer south. Chloroquine-resistant falciparcium has been reported. Rabies, tick-borne relapsing fever and cutaneous leishmaniasis are present.

THE TALIBAN EVERYDAY LIFE RULES

Men must grow beards
No 24-hour All Mullah, All the Time, Talibvision
No Afghan space program
No book reading
No coed cheerleading
No drinking
No flying kites
No foreigners with Afghan women
No movies
No music
No paper bag jokes
No paper bags
No photography
No recycling the Koran
No schooling for females
No sneaking Colt 45s in a bag
No soccer
No theater
No TV
No videos
No Internet
No white socks for females

In Taliban areas, soccer, volleyball and even chess have been banned because they cause youths to miss some of their five daily prayers. Women must wear the burqa, a kind of shmoo-sack slash veil that covers the entire body, and men must have long beards, something that shocks naive journos but is quite normal outside of Kabul. Western pleasures like trashy novels, MTV, movies, beer and Nintendo are all forbidden. The idea is to not divert people's minds from God and family. Come to think of it, these guys might be on to something. To contact the Taliban stateside get ahold of:

Mulawi Abdul Hakeem Mujahid or Noorullah Zadran
55/16 Main Street
Flushing, NY
Tel.: (718) 359-0457
News Hotline: (718) 762-8095
Fax: (718) 661-2721
Web site: www.taleban.com
E-mail: AMujahid@aol.com
Nonofficial site:
http://www.ummah.net/Taliban/

GETTING OUT

The bus system still operates, taxis are cheap (DP paid $25 to go the 200 miles from Torkham to Kabul) and depending on how many crashes Ariana has there are airliners flying in and out of the southern cities. Last time we checked the one-way fare from Kabul to Dubai was $175. Ariana, which was once run by Pan Am, now has three Boeing 727s, three Antonov 24s and is buying a wide-bodied Boeing 747 from Kuwait Airlines. The airport at Kabul is blown to bits but open.

Ariana flies a lot of unknown cargo to Dubai, so it's hard for foreigners to buy tickets. Most journos drive in or fly on the Peshawar-based Red Cross and Islamabad-based UN flights.

Ariana Airlines
3rd Floor, Dudley House,
169 Piccadilly
London W1V9DD, UK
Tel.:+44-171-4931411
Fax:+44-171-6291611
Web site: http://fly.to/ariana
E-mail: arianaaf@brain.net.pk

DANGEROUS PLACES IN AFGHANISTAN

DRUGS

Despite the don't askDdon't tell antidrug stance of the Taliban, Afghanistan is the major poppy growing nation in the world (after Myanmar) and a major transporter. The latest word on the street is that bin Laden is buying up raw opium and using it to fight a second front in his war against the West. About $350 of opium gum can be refined into herioin worth a street price of $70,000 in New York. Farmers in Helmand and Nangarhar provinces grow poppies, which are cut to ooze gum. The gum is gathered and send to the 60 or so labs in the southeast and east of Afghanistan. Wrapped tightly in plastic or in glass jars it is shipped to Pakistan across Iran or through Turkmenistan to Turkey or north to Tajikistan, where the Russian military expedites its shipment to Moscow.

Afghanistan is the largest grower of poppies (4,600 tonnes in 1999 compared to 1,300 tonnes from Myanmar) and the largest exporter of hashish in the world. Up to 14 metric tons of hashish have been seized by the border states of Uzbekistan, Turkmenistan, Kyrgystan, Tajikistan and Kazakhstan. Badakhshan borders Tajikistan, where Russia has deployed 25,000 troops to help fight antigovernment Islamic guerrillas believed to have bases in Afghanistan. Strangely, Osama's efforts to corner the market has pushed the price down to $37 a kilo (2.2 lbs.) from $60.

http://www.afghan-politics.org/Reference/Drugs/drugs_main.htm

MILITARY TRAINING CAMPS

Afghanistan has always had training camps for mujahedin. We know this because the United States paid for them to be built and expanded back in the '80s. So it wasn't that hard to cruise missile them on August 20, 1998, and it wasn't that hard to rebuild them in Khost and outside Jalalabad, Kabul and Kunduz by December, five months later. Osama, the son of a Saudi construction maven from Yemen, just can't stop building. He has about 3,000 people on the payroll in Afghanistan and is building everything from mosques to government buildings. Tomahawk missiles also hit Jamiatul Mujahideen and Harkatul Ansar camps, both run by Pakistanis, almost 21 kilometers away from Osama's exclusively Arab camp in Khost. The Salman Farsi camp and the Badar 1 and Badar 2 are for the training of Arabs, while the Pakistani-run camps of Pakistani-based Harkatul Mujahideen (former Harakatul Ansar or HUA) and Harkatul Jihad Al-Islami. Osama is one of the benefactors of the Harkatul Mujahideen who teach volunteers from as far away as North America, the Phillipines, Bosnia and Algeria to fight low-intensity terrorist wars.

Missiles also hit the ten-year-old Jamiatul Mujahideen camp commanded by the Kashmiri Mufti Bashir. This camp was for training up to 250 volunteers from Kashmir and Pakistan to fight in Kashmir, a war the Pakistani ISI funds and provides training for.

TRIBAL AREAS

The Khyber Pass is still controlled by tribal chiefs who make a living by shipping drugs, taking money from truck drivers and kidnapping people that visit this historic route. Robbery, shootouts, murder, extortion and/or kidnapping are an everyday occurrence for the unwary, and it has only been the lack of foreigners that have kept this region out of the headlines.

http://www.javed.com.pk/Peshawar.html

OUTFEET

Females have become the latest pawns in the war in Afghanistan. Reacting to a report by DP's co-resident at the UNICA guesthouse Zohra Rasekh, the Physicians for Human Rights and other junket journos have declared war on the Afghan people. By focusing on the burqa as a symbol of evil (something Zohra, a woman, forgets to mention she didn't have to wear in Kabul), she has demonized Afghan culture and blamed it on the Taliban. Any visitor to the north will tell you that the burqa is a part of Afghan life except in once-cosmopolitan Kabul.

The report goes on to clinically document the lack of health care for women as if the author has comparable statistics from Afghan women in Rochester, Minnesota. "PHR explored the reasons for decreased access to health care services. Of the 40 women interviewed, 87% (33 of 38) reported a decrease in their access to health services. The reasons given included: no chaperone available (27%), restrictions on women's mobility (36%), hospital refused to provide care (21%), no female doctor available (48%), do not own a burqa (6%), and economics (61%)." Taken the other way DP finds it amazing that 52% of afghan women had access to any doctor male or female. Women and their rights are being used as a pawn in this war but the endgame is they have lost either way. The lack of aid because of the way their unelected government treats them and another generation lost to poverty and hopelessness.

http://www.rawa.org/

http://www.phrusa.org/campaigns/af_exec1.html

WEAPONS IN AFGHANISTANS

Taday, Afghanistan has more guns per capita than anywhere else on earth. England allowed the Pathans to manufacture their own guns 200 years ago, and the CIA delivered enough weapons to keep the region swimming in weaponry for years to come. But this was all dwarfed by the stockpiles of weapons the Russians abandoned or lost in the ten years of warfare.

The Affridi tribe of Afghanistan and Pakistan still produce about 900 to 1,200 copies of modern weapons a day in its gun factories in Darra Adam Khel.

The best place to buy guns is actually just outside Afghanistan in Pakistan. Anyone can hire a gunman for about $20 a day, but if you want to shop for that special hard-to-please someone, take along an Afghan guide and go visit the Smugglers Bazaar (20 minutes east of Peshawar) in Darra (about 40 minutes south of Peshawar). Although Darra has been officially closed for two years to outsiders you can still buy a worn but serviceable AK-47 for $200. Pros know to buy the short Chinese-made assault versions, since their barrels don't heat up as much and they can be concealed under your shwaler qamiz. These go for about $375D$1,000 Chinese- and Russian-made pistols are between $10D$100, with the Pakistani-made knockoffs at the low end of the price spectrum.

Anyone can buy Chinese and Russian rocket launchers for just under a grand and rockets by the case for 400 rupees (US$125) each. Grenades are a bargain at US$3 each. Perfect for that kidnap scenario when you threaten to pull the pin. Other items for sales at bargain basement prices include land mines, antiaircraft guns, bazookas, Stalin OrganDstyle rocket launchers (the self-propelled kind) and even lovely used Russian T-55 tanks.

Wanna-bes who don't want to be arrested in Darra can head north of Peshawar to Sakahot and see guns being made from cheap pig iron. Lookee loos who appreciate the smell of cordite and the sound of tinnitus can arrange to fire automatic weapons in the nearby gorge. One banana clip of 30 bullets will set you back about ten bucks. Cheap, even by Coney Island standards. The hottest selling items are still the pen guns that fire a single bullet and can be used to write ransom notes. They are a measly six dollars. Naturally, you will need a complete Soviet eraDuniform, bayonets, combat gear, watches, boxes of uncirculated rubles (wrapped and still in serial number order) and medals to complete your Cold War GI Joe play kit.

GETTING AROUND

Afghanistan is sort of an Adventureland notch for journos-a place where you can take a cab to the front lines and be home in time to shop for carpets on Chicken street. The Talibs view most journos with a jaundiced eye since the rash of gender junkets trashed their ideas on women's fashion and law and order.

Although they told me that DP was the first North American the Taliban had talked to long ago, I am sure the thrill has long worn off as everyone from National Geographic to Dateline does their prerequisite Afghan Taliban adventure story. Areas under Talib control are safe but expect major league hassles from Talibs who want to know what your business is. Try taking pictures of them and you may end up walking like a chicken. The north is still wild and wooly and the last time I tried to get around on a fuel convoy I was told that I might be stopped by brigands and "teased" like one of their drivers was a while back. I learned later that this is a polite way of saying sodomized. Soooeii.

The favored modes of travel are by minibus (cheap and available in all small towns), private car (not as available) and pack animals, which are slow and a great way to see what land mines can do. There is no law inside Afghanistan other than the Taliban's industrial-strength version of sharia, usually mixed in with a little local tribal law and whatever the local commander feels like doing with you that night. If he wants you to watch a Ned Beatty movie with him decline, politely. (no more Deliverance jokes from here on in.)

It is helpful if Westerners understand Afghan culture and have a basic understanding of the Pakhtun (Pathan) language. Most important is knowledge of the customs of Islam. Despite what you read in the press most Afghans (and not just the Taliban) are devout Muslims and adopt traditional dress and customs. Currently, there is little animosity toward Westerners, but you will be lectured continuously on Islam and considered an oddity for not embracing what is essentially the only religion in Afghanistan. Any major affront to Islam could result in severe punishment or a sound beating. Travel only with the permission of each local commander and be prepared to drink a lot of tea.

Abdul Hakeem Mujahid is your man if you want to get into Talib-held areas. The Taliban's ambassador in Pakistan now works out of a small office in a third-floor walkup in Queens, New York.

EMBASSY LOCATIONS

Because there is no U.S. embassy in Afghanistan and no country represents U.S. interests here, the U.S. government is unable to provide normal protective services to U.S. citizens in Afghanistan (as if they would even if they had an embassy). The nearest U.S. embassies and consulates are in Pakistan and Tajikistan. The telephone number for the (very helpful if you want reasons to stay out of Afghanistan) but under siege U.S. embassy in Islamabad, Pakistan, is: [92] (51) 826-161/179. There is little they can do for you once you are in Afghanistan.

U.S. Consulate in Peshawar, Pakistan
Tel: [92] (521) 279-801/2/3
U.S. Embassy in Tashkent, Uzbekistan
Tel: (3712) 771-407/771-081
U.S. Embassy in Dushanbe, Tajikistan
Tel: (3772) 21-0356/-0360/-0457
U.S. Embassy in New Delhi, India
Tel: [91] (11) 600-651

BUSINESS TRAVEL

BUSINESS CUSTOMS

Business meetings are usually conducted in Dari, Pashto or English in the principal's office. Green or black tea, nuts and raisins are served to greet guests. The form of greeting is "Asalam Aleikum" (Peace be with you), followed by a firm handshake and then, for courtesy and to pay homage to the host (you don't necessarily have to), briefly place your right hand over your heart. It is best to take a few minutes initially to engage in pleasantries about each other's country, rather than going straight to business. Afghan interlocutors may appear vague and non-committal during meetings. In order to build trust and "get to yes," be patient, share meals and other social events and discuss matters other than business. Capture the essence of your business meetings and agreements in a follow up letter to your Afghan interlocutor. Be clear about what you have committed yourself or your U.S. firm to do, or in many cases, have not committed to do. A promise to "look into" or "research" an issue, quote, or pricing policy may be interpreted as a firm commitment.

DO'S and DON'TS in Afghan Culture
Don't show impatience if your interlocutor isn't giving you direct answers. Afghans like to elaborate and want to be clear in communicating.

Don't panic. Afghanistan's government can be bureaucratic. It may take you several days to get a simple authorization signed. Keep in mind that Afghanistan's government is undergoing a reform process.

Don't call an Afghan "Afghani." Afghani is the currency, Afghans are the people of Afghanistan.

Don't drink alcohol in front of an Afghan.

Do greet everyone when entering a room. Shake hands with the men, but not with a woman unless she extends her hand first.

Do eat with your right hand as much as possible.

Do dress modestly.

Do accept a chair if someone brings you one to sit on, even if you would rather stand. This is a sign of respect.

Do read about the country's history, culture, and people before you come, as this will be treated as a sign of respect for Afghanistan.

TRAVEL ADVISORY

While the U.S. Embassy in Kabul encourages U.S. companies to review business opportunities in Afghanistan, it is important to keep in mind the volatile security situation in the country. Travelers should consult the State Department Travel web site http://travel.state.gov prior to any travel and review both the Consular Information Sheet and Travel Warning for Afghanistan. These documents can be found at: http://travel.state.gov/travel/cis_pa_tw/cis/cis_1765.html

VISA REQUIREMENTS

A passport and valid visa are required to enter and exit Afghanistan. Afghan entry visas are not available at Kabul International Airport. American citizens who arrive without a visa are subject to confiscation of their passport and face heavy fines and difficulties in retrieving their passport and obtaining a visa, as well as possible deportation from the country. Americans arriving in the country via military air usually have considerable difficulties if they choose to depart Afghanistan on commercial air because their passports do not receive stamps showing they entered the country legally. Those coming on military air should move quickly after arrival to legalize their status if there is any chance they will end up departing on anything other than military air.

For the most updated requirements to obtain an Afghan visa, please contact the Embassy of Afghanistan located at 2341 Wyoming Ave., NW, Washington, DC 20008, phone 202-483-6410, fax 202-483-6488), http://www.embassyofafghanistan.org

U.S. companies that require travel of foreign businesspersons to the United States should know that it could take weeks or months for an Afghan citizen to receive a visa to visit the United States. The U.S. Embassy in Afghanistan currently does not process visas for Afghan citizens. Please see the U.S. Embassy website for information on how Afghan citizens may apply in Islamabad, Pakistan.

State Department Visa Website: http://travel.state.gov/visa/index.html

United States Visas.gov: http://www.unitedstatesvisas.gov

U.S. Embassy in Afghanistan: http://kabul.usembassy.gov

TELECOMMUNICATIONS

Local telephone networks do not operate reliably. Most people rely on satellite or cellular telephone communications even to make local calls. Cellular phone service is available in Kabul with coverage extending to 23 provinces . Teledensity is 3.5 percent of the population. There are currently two wireless service providers : (i) Afghan Wireless Communications Company (AWCC) (44% market share), a joint venture between U.S.-based Telephone Systems International and the Afghan Ministry of Communications and (ii) Telephone Development Company Afghanistan (TDCA) (56% market share), operating under the brand name Roshan. TDCA is an international consortium led by the Aga Khan Fund for Economic Development. A third provider, Investcom, is scheduled to begin operations in 2006. The country has multiple internet service providers.

TRANSPORTATION

Several commercial airlines serve Afghanistan at Kabul International Airport. Pakistan International Airlines has three weekly flights to and from Islamabad. Azerbaijan Airways has twice weekly flights to and from Baku. Indian Airlines flights three times a week to and from Delhi. Kam Air has flights daily to Dubai . The U.S. Embassy does not recommend use of Ariana Afghan Airlines to any destination or Kam Air flights to and from destinations other than Dubai because existing civil aviation regulations in Afghanistan do not meet international aviation standards. Please see the State Department's Consular Information Sheet at http://travel.state.gov/travel/cis_pa_tw/cis/cis_1056.html for more information.

Taxis around Kabul should range between Afs 50 to 100 ($1 or $2 depending on where you are going) per trip, but a dedicated car and driver is recommended. For travel within Kabul, a car and driver (no English) will run up to US$30 to $100 per day. Public buses are not recommended.

LANGUAGE

Dari and Pashto are the official languages of the country. Few native Afghans speak English, but many returning expatriate Afghans speak English or German. Rates vary widely; a reliable interpreter fluent in English, Dari and Pashto may earn anything between $150 - $3,000 per month.

HEALTH

The weather in Afghanistan is very dry, with summer highs into the 100s F and winter lows into the 20s F with snow. Kabul is very dusty, and shoes and clothes are difficult to maintain.

Well-equipped medical facilities are few and far between throughout Afghanistan. European and American medicines are available in limited quantities and may be expensive or difficult to locate. There is a shortage of standard medical supplies. Basic medicines manufactured in Iran, Pakistan, and India are available, but their reliability can be questionable. Travelers should bring all necessary medications, both prescription and over-the-counter.

A couple of western-style private clinics have opened in Kabul in recent months: the DK-German Medical Diagnostic Center (http://www.medical-kabul.com), and CURE International Hospital (ph. 0799-883-830) offer a variety of basic and routine-type care; Americans seeking treatment should request American or Western health practitioners. American travelers may seek emergency medical services at the International Security Assistance Forces (ISAF) medical facilities in the Kabul area, but routine care is not available. The ISAF German Hospital, located about 10 kilometers from Kabul on Jalalabad Road (a road often off-limits to official Americans because of security concerns), and the combined forces ISAF clinic, adjacent to Kabul International Airport, may provide medical care to American citizens who can show a passport and request emergency care. Shino Zada Private Hospital located in Microrayon 4, opposite the central heating center, provides general surgery, maternity care, ambulance and pharmacy facilities 24 hours a day. Imran Clinic, across from the Ministry of Interior, has limited laboratory and x-ray facilities.

Afghan public hospitals should be avoided. Individuals without government licenses or even medical degrees often operate private clinics; there is no public agency that monitors their operations. Travelers will not be able to find Western-trained medical personnel in most parts of the country outside of Kabul, although there are some international aid groups temporarily providing basic medical assistance in various cities and villages. For any medical treatment, payment is required in advance. Commercial medical evacuation capability from Afghanistan is limited.

Information on vaccinations and other health precautions, such as safe food and water precautions and insect bite protection, may be obtained from the Centers for Disease Control and

Prevention's hotline for international travelers at 1-877-FYI-TRIP (1-877-394-8747) or via the CDC's Internet site at http://www.cdc.gov/travel. For information about outbreaks of infectious diseases abroad consult the World Health Organization's website at http://www.who.int/en. Further health information for travelers is available at http://www.who.int/ith.

LOCAL TIME, BUSINESS HOURS, AND HOLIDAYS

Local time is GMT +4.5.

Afghanistan observes a five and a half day workweek, with Thursday afternoon and Friday as the days off. Business hours are typically 8 AM to 4 PM. Commercial shops keep longer but varying hours, usually from 7am to 11pm.

Holidays vary year to year and are determined by the Islamic Calendar and the visibility of the lunar crescent. Holidays include three days for Eid-ul-Qurban in January, three days for Eid-Al-Fitr in December, one day for the Prophet's Birthday in May, February 9 (10 th of Maharam), March 21 (Nawrooz) and August 18 (Independence Day.)

TEMPORARY ENTRY OF MATERIALS AND PERSONAL BELONGINGS

Afghan customs authorities may enforce strict regulations concerning temporary importation into or export from Afghanistan of items such as firearms, alcoholic beverages, religious materials, antiquities, medications, and printed materials. American travelers have faced fines and/or confiscation of items considered antiquities upon exiting Afghanistan. It is advisable to contact the Embassy of Afghanistan in Washington for specific information regarding customs requirements.

WEB RESOURCES

U.S. Department of State Travel Website http://travel.state.gov

U.S. Department of State Consular Information Sheets and Travel Warnings http://travel.state.gov/travel/cis_pa_tw/cis/cis_1765.html

U.S. Department of State Visa Website http://travel.state.gov/visa/index.html

United States Visas http://www.unitedstatesvisas.gov

U.S. Embassy in Afghanistan http://kabul.usembassy.gov

Embassy of Afghanistan in the U.S. http://www.embassyofafghanistan.org

Center for Disease Control http://www.cdc.gov/travel

World Health Organization http://www.who.int/en and http://www.who.int/ith

SUPPLEMENT

IMPORTANT CONTACTS

U.S. GOVERNMENT CONTACTS

U.S. Department of Commerce
Jana Nelhybel
Afghanistan Investment and Reconstruction Task Force
Washington D.C. 20230
Tel: (202) 482-1812
Fax: (202) 482-0980
Email: afghaninfo@ita.doc.gov
http://www.export.gov/afghanistan

U.S. Embassy Kabul
Great Masood Road
Tel: +93 (20) 230-0436, +93 (0) 70-108-001, +93 (0) 70-108-002
http://kabul.usembassy.gov

Ronald Neumann, Ambassador
Richard Norland, Deputy Chief of Mission
Douglas Climan, Economic/Commercial Counselor
Rian Harris, Commercial Officer, HarrisRH@state.gov , Ext. 8364
Economic/Commercial Assistant, Ext. 8395

U.S. Agency for International Development
Great Masood Road
Tel: +93 (0) 70-234-236
Alonzo Fulgham, Mission Director
Grace Agana, Assistant to the Director, gagana@usaid.gov , Ext. 4445
http:// www.usaid.gov/afghanistan

Note: Phone and fax communications in Afghanistan can be accessed. However, e-mail is the most reliable form of communication

USAID Washington Office
1300 Pennsylvania Avenue, NW
Ronald Reagan Building
Washington, D.C. 20523-1000
Sepideh Keyvanshad, Afghanistan Desk Officer
Tel: (202) 712-0324
Email: skeyvanshad@usaid.gov

U.S. Embassy Islamabad
Consular Section
Ramna 5, Diplomatic Enclave
Islamabad, Pakistan
Tel: +92 (51) 208-02700
Fax: +92 (51) 282-2632
http://usembassy.state.gov/pakistan/consular.htm

U.S. Trade & Development Agency (USTDA)
Dan Stein
Regional Director for Europe and Eurasia
Suite 1600
1000 Wilson Boulevard
Arlington, VA 22209
Tel: (703) 875-4357
Fax: (703) 875-4009
Email: dstein@ustda.gov
http:// www.ustda.gov

Overseas Private Investment Corporation (OPIC)
John Aldonas
1100 New York Avenue NW
Washington, DC 20527
Tel: (202) 336-8400
Fax: (202) 408-9859
Email: jaldo@opic.gov
http://www.opic.gov

Export-Import Bank (Exlm)
811 Vermont Avenue, N.W.
Washington, DC 20571
Tel: (202) 565-3946 (EXIM) or (800) 565-3946 (EXIM)
G rayson Wolfe
Tel: (202) 565-3450
Email: grayson.wolfe@exim.gov
http://www.exim.gov

INTERNATIONAL FINANCIAL INSTITUTIONS

World Bank
Alastair J. Mckechnie, Country Director for Afghanistan
House 19, Street 15, Wazir Akbar Khan
Kabul, Afghanistan
Contact:: Abdul Raouf Zia
Tel: +93 (0) 70280800
Email: azia@worldbank.org

Mr. William Center, Senior Commercial Officer
U.S. Commercial Liaison to the World Bank in Washington
Tel: (202) 458-0120
Fax: (202) 477-2967
Email: WCenter@worldbank.org
http://www.worldbank.org/af

Asian Development Bank
Afghanistan Resident Mission
Bryan Fawcett, Country Director
126, Street 2, Haji Yaqoub Round About
Shahar-e-Now,
P. O. Box 3070
Kabul, Afghanistan
Tel: +93 (20) 210-3602

Email: afrm@adb.org
http://www.adb.org/afrm

AFGHAN GOVERNMENT CONTACTS

Afghan Investment Support Agency (AISA)
Tel: +93 (20) 210 3404
Email: info@aisa.org.af, invest@aisa.gov.af
http://www.aisa.org.af/
Mr. Omar Zakhilwal
President & CEO
Cellular Phone: +93 (0) 799 322-735
Email: zakhilwal@aisa.org.af
Mr. Suleman Fatimie
Vice President
Cellular Phone: +93 (0) 799 336-616
Email: fatimies@aisa.org.af, invest@aisa.gov.af

Ms. Masouda Delawar
Secretary to the President
Cellular Phone: +93 (0) 70 293-173
Email: M.H.A@aisa.org.af

Mr. Mohammad Sharif
Investment Manager (Agriculture, Livestock, Water and Power, Banking and Environment)
Cellular Phone: +93 (0) 799 336-529
Email: sharif@aisa.org.af

Mr. Salam Zahid
Investment Manager (Manufacturing, Industry, Trade, Transport, and Industrial Parks)
Cellular Phone: +93 (0) 799 336-527
Email: ZahedA@aisa.org.af

Mr. Naseem Akbar
Investment Manager (Public Health, Education, Media and Services)
Cellular Phone: +93 (0) 799 336-529
Email: NaseemA@aisa.org.af

Mr. Abdul K. Safi
Investment Manager (Information Technology and Construction Projects)
Cellular Phone: +93 (0) 799 336-552
Email: Abdulksafi@aisa.org.af

Embassy of Afghanistan
Mariam Nawabi, Economic and Commercial Counselor
Economic, Trade and Investment Department
2341 Wyoming Avenue, N.W.
Washington D.C. 20006
Tel: (202) 483-6410
Fax: (202) 483-6487
Email: contact@afghanistanembassy.org, commerce@embassyofafghanistan.org
http://www.embassyofafghanistan.org/, http://www.afghanistan.business-gateways.com/

Afghanistan Reconstruction and Development Service (ARDS)
Email: procurement@afghanistangov.org

http://www.eafghanistan.gov.af/procurement/

Ministry of Commerce
Tel: +93 (20) 210-2365
Email: info@commerce.gov.af
http://www.commerce.gov.af/

Ministry of Finance
Tel: +93 (20) 210-3272
Email: info@mof.gov.af
http://www.mof.gov.af/

OTHER USEFUL CONTACTS

Afghanistan International Chamber Of Commerce (AICC)
Azarakhsh Hafizi, Chairman
House #91, Street 2, Shash Darak
Kabul, Afghanistan
Tel: +93 (0) 70-033-799, 0799-014-493,
Email: chairmanaicc@yahoo.com & hafizi@yahoo.com
http://www.en.aicc-online.org

Afghan-American Chamber of Commerce (AACC)
Atiq Panjshiri, President
8201 Greensboro Drive, Suite #103
McLean, VA 22102
Tel: (U.S) (703) 658-2929
Fax: (U.S.) (703) 658-9103
Email: apanjshiri@a-acc.org
http://www.a-acc.org

Afghanistan Builders Association (ABA)
Abdullah Nadi, President
Tel: + 93 (0) 70-286-103
Email: AbdullahNadi@aol.com

AFGHAN EMBASSIES

Australia

Consulate of the Islamic State of Afghanistan
GPO Box 88
Canberra ACT 2601
Tel.: 612-62868445 Fax: 612-62868446
E-mail: admin@afghanconsulate.net
Website: www.afghanconsulate.net
Honorary Consul: Mr. Mahmoud SAIKAL

Austria

Embassy of the Islamic State of Afghanistan
Kaiserstrasse 84/1/3
A-1070 Wien
Tel.: 431-5247806 Fax: 431-5247807
E-mail: afg.emb.vie@chello.at
Charge d' Affaires: Mr. Farid AMIN

(non-Resident Ambassador to Hungary & Bosnia)

Bangladesh (People's Republic of)

Embassy of the Islamic State of Afghanistan
House No. CWN (C) - 2A
Road No. 24, Culshan
Dhaka
Tel.: 8802-9884767 Fax: 8802-9884767
Charge d'Affaires: Mr. Ghulam Mohammad SOKHAN-YAR

Bulgaria (Republic of)

Embassy of the Islamic State of Afghanistan
61 "Boryana" Street
Bl. 216-A App. 15, Ovcha Kupel
1618 Sofia
Tel.: 3592-8708394 Fax: 3592-9559986
Charge d' Affaires: Mr. Mohammad Fazel SAIFI

China (People's Republic of)

Embassy of the Islamic State of Afghanistan
8 Tung Chih Men Wia
Chao Yang District
Peking
Tel.: 8610-65321622 Fax: 8610-65322269
Charge d'Affaires: Mr. Abdul Bassir HOOTAK

Czech Republic

Embassy of the Islamic State of Afghanistan
Nakazance 634/7
17100 Praha 7 – Troja
Tel.: 4202-8544228 Fax: 4202-7650732
Charge d' Affaires: Mr. Mohammad Zahir SALJOOQI

Egypt (Arab Republic of)

Embassy of the Islamic State of Afghanistan
59 El-Orouba Street, Heliopolis
Cairo
Tel.: 202-4177236 Fax: 202-4177238
Ambassador: Mr. Sayed Fazlullah FAZIL

France

Ambassade de l'Etat Islamique d'Afghanistan
32 Avenue Raphael
75016
Tel.: 331-45250529 Fax: 331-45250529
E-mail: ambassade.afg@worldonline.fr Website: www.ambafghane.com
Charge d' Affaires: Mr. Mehrabuddin MASTAN

Germany

Die Botschaft des Islamischen Staates Afghanistan
Wilhemstrasse 65
10117 Berlin
Tel.: 4930-2292612 Fax: 4930-2291510

Charge d' Affaires: Mr. Amrullah JAYHOON

Generalkonsulate des Islamischen Staates Afghanistan
Uckesdorf, Liebfrauenweg 1A
53125 Bonn
Tel.: 4922-8251927 Fax: 4922-8255310
General Consul:

India

Embassy of the Islamic State of Afghanistan
Plat No. 5, Block 50F, Shantipath, Chanakyapuri
New Delhi 110021
Tel.: 9111-6882191 Fax: 9111-6875439
E-mail: Afghanspirit@yahoo.com
Ambassador: Mr. Masood KHALILI

Indonesia (Republic of)

Embassy of the Islamic State of Afghanistan
15 Jalan DR Kuskmas Atmaja
Jakarta
Tel.: 6221-335390 Fax: 6221-335390
Charge d'Affaires: Fat'h Mohammad SHERZAI

Iran (Islamic Republic of)

Embassy of the Islamic State of Afghanistan
Dr. Beheshti Avenue, 4th Street
Tehran
Tel.: 9821-625040, 625600 Fax: 9821-8735600
Consulate Section: 9821-8737531
Ambassador: Mr. Mohammad KHAIR-KHAWH

Consulate of the Islamic State of Afghanistan
Imam Khomeini Avenue, Doshahid Street
Sevom Isfand Sq.
Mashad
Tel.: 9851-827544 Fax: 9851-44404, 814797
Consul: Mr. Abdul RAHIM

Iraq

Embassy of the Islamic State of Afghanistan
Shareh Al-Maghreb
Aldifaeih Waziria 27/1/12
Baghdad
Tel.: 9641-5569508 Fax: 9641-5560331
Charge d'Affaires: Mr. Sayed Sharif YOUSEFI

Italy

Embassy of the Islamic State of Afghanistan
Via Nomentana 120
00161 Rome
Tel.: 3906-86216111 Fax: 3906-86322939
Charge d'Affaires: Mr. Hamidullah NASSER-ZIA

Kazakhstan (Republic of)

Embassy of the Islamic State of Afghanistan
Mir 12
Alma-Ata
Tel.: 73272-247660, 338711 Fax: 73272-323729
Charge d'Affaires: Mr. Abdul AZIZ

Kuwait (State of)

Surra, Block 6, Surra Street
Across Surra Co-op Society
House No. 16
P.O. Box 33186, Rawdah, 73452
Tel.: 965-5329461, 5328156 Fax: 965-5326274
E-mail: afg_emb_kuw@hotmail.com
Charge d'Affaires: Dr. Naseer Ahmad NOOR

Kyrgyzstan (Republic of)

Trading Representation in Bishkek
Tel.: 996332-284826 Fax: 996332-284826
Trade Attache: Habibullah MAHSHAR

Malaysia

Embassy of the Islamic State of Afghanistan
No. 1, Lorong Ru Kedua
Off Jalan Ampang,
55000 Kuala Lumpur Malaysia
Tel.: 603-4565199 Fax: 603-4564933
E-mail: murad1@tm.net.my Website: www.afghanembassy.homepage.com
Charge d'Affaires: Mr. Abdulsattar MURAD

Poland

Embassy of the Islamic State of Afghanistan
Ul. Staroscinska 1 lok. 25
02-516 Warszawa
Tel.: 4822-6460314 Fax: 4822-8480280
Ambassador: Mr. Abdul Hai HAIDAR

Russian Federation

Embassy of the Islamic State of Afghanistan
Sverchkov Per 3/2
Moscow
Tel.: 7095-9287278, 9217094 Fax: 7095-9240478, 9219563
Ambassador: Mr. Abdulwahab ASSEFI

Sudan (Republic of)

Embassy of the Islamic State of Afghanistan
Madinatol Riyadh
Shareol Moshtal,
Square 10, House No. 81
Khartoum
Tel.: 24911-221852, 221827 Fax: 24911-222059
Charge d'Affaires: Mr. Enatullah KHALIL

Switzerland

Permanent Mission of the Islamic State of Afghanistan to the UN
Consulate of the Islamic State of Afghanistan
63 Rue de Lausanne
1202 Geneva (CH)
Tel.: 4122-7311616 Fax: 4122-7314510
Charge d'Affaires: Mr. Homayoun TANDAR

Syria (Arab Republic of)

Embassy of the Islamic State of Afghanistan
Mozzo, West Villas
Juber Ben Hayan Bus Station
Damascus
Tel.: 96311-6667527, 6133783 Fax: 96311-6133595
Charge d'Affaires: Mr. Abdullah MOHSENI

Tajikistan (Republic of)

Embassy of the Islamic State of Afghanistan
Ul. Pushkina, House 34
Dushanbe
Tel.: 73772-062057 Fax: 73772-276061
Charge d'Affaires: Mr. Ibrahim HIKMAT

Turkey

Embassy of the Islamic State of Afghanistan
Cinnah Caddesi, No. 88 Cankaya
Ankara
Tel.: 90312-4381121 Fax: 90312-4387745
Charge d'Affaires: Mr. Ilmorad ARGHOON

Turkmenistan

Embassy of the Islamic State of Afghanistan
14 Gerogli Street
Ashgabat 744000
Tel.: 99312-395820 Fax: 99312-395821
Charge d'Affaires: Mr. Shah MARDANQOL

Ukraine

Embassy of the Islamic State of Afghanistan
Krasnozvyozdny Ave. 48
Kiev, 25037
Tel.: 738044-2448649 Fax: 738044-2448649
Charge d'Affaires: Mr. Sayed Mahmood FARANI

United Kingdom

Embassy of the Islamic State of Afghanistan
31 Prince Gate
London SW7 1QQ
Tel.: 44171-5898891, 5898892 Fax: 44171-5813452
Charge d'Affaires: Mr. Ahmad Wali MASUD

United States of America

Permanent Mission of the Islamic State of Afghanistan to the UN
360 Lexington Avenue, 11th Floor
New York, NY 10017
Tel. 212-9721212, 9721213, 9721221 Fax: 212-9721216
E-mail: AfgWatan@aol.com
Ambassador: Dr. Abdul Ghafoor Ravan FARHADI

Consulate-General of the Islamic State of Afghanistan in New York
360 Lexington Avenue, 11th Floor
New York, NY 10017
Tel.: 212-9722276, 9722277 Fax: 212-9729046
E-mail: Consulate@aol.com
General Consul: Mr. Abdul Habib SERAJ

Representative Office in Washington

1021 Arlington Blvd. Suite 1120
Arlington, VA 22209
Tel.: 703-469-3946, 362-9246 Fax: 703-469-3859
E-mail: mohammadseshaq@aol.com
Representative: Mohammad ES'HAQ

Uzbekistan (Republic of)

Embassy of the Islamic State of Afghanistan
Ul. Gogol, House 73
Tashkent 700047
Tel.: 99871-2354112 Fax: 99871-2342634
Charge d'Affaires: Mr. Hasham SA'AD

A CHRONOLOGY OF RECENT AFGHAN HISTORY

1973	President Mohammed Daoud assumes the Presidency of Afghanistan after a military coup and abolishes the monarchy. King Zahir Shah sent into exile.
1974-1978	Opposition to Daoud increases among a range of Islamic and Communist factions.
April 1978	Daoud assassinated and replaced by a junta led by Hafizullah Amin.
December 1979	Soviet troops invade Afghanistan, install friendly government
1980	Armed tribal groups begin a *jihad* against the Soviet-installed government
1980-1989	Armed *mujahedin* groups fight Soviet and government forces; hundreds of thousands of Afghans die in the struggle, and millions more become refugees.
1986	President Mohammed Najibullah takes office
1988	Geneva Accords signed, outlining a plan for the withdrawal of Soviet troops
February 1989	Soviet troops complete withdrawal
February 1989 to	Increased conflict between government and opposition forces

April 1992	
April 1992	President Najibullah is replaced by a four-member council under a UN plan
Late April 1992	An interim government led by Professor Sebghatollah Mojadedi takes power
June 1992	An interim government led by Borhannudin Rabbani takes office
December 1992	Borhannudin Rabbani is elected President, Gulbuddin Hekmatyar Prime Minister, and Ahmad Shah Massoud Minister of Defense
1992 to early 1995	Fighting spreads to all major cities as the *Shura-e Nezar* (Supervisor Council) and the *Shura-e Hamahangi* (Supreme Coordination Council) compete for control.
Late 1994	The *Taliban* emerges as a major force.
September 27, 1996	The *Taliban* gains control of Kabul
Late 1996 – early 1997	Militia leaders Dostum and Rabbani, along with the *Hezb-e Wahdat* and *Harrakat-e Islami* factions form the Northern Alliance to resist the Taliban. The Taliban, however, continues to make gains and conquer Kandahar, Herat, and Jalalabad.
May 1997	Dostum goes into exile in Turkey for four months following the defection of General Malik, a leading commander, to the Taliban. Pakistan, Saudi Arabia, and the UAE recognize the Taliban.
September 1997	Dostum returns to his stronghold in Mazar-e Sharif with strong backing from Uzbekistan.
March 1998	UN withdraws international workers from southern Afghanistan, citing physical abuse by Pakistan.
April 1998	Ambassador Richardson visits the region and discusses Afghanistan, reaching an agreement among key parties to negotiate their differences. The Taliban breaks the agreement in May.
August 8,1998	Taliban forces capture key Northern Alliance stronghold of Mazar-e Sharif
August 20, 1998	US cruise missile strikes on Afghanistan in response to terrorist attacks by Usama Bin Laden on U.S facilities in Tanzania and Kenya.
August 1998.	Continued Taliban military advances. Iranian Revolutionary Guards deploy along Afghan border following killing of Iranian diplomats in Afghanistan and mass killings of ethnic Hazaras by Taliban troops.
September 1998 - present	The Taliban captures Bamian. Forces led by Massoud shell Kabul and continue resisting Taliban advances. Massoud's forces later recapture Bamian, and fighting continues.

February 1999	The Taliban rules out 'Usama bin Laden's extradition. The Taliban subsequently claims he is missing.

MAJOR FACTIONS IN AFGHANISTAN

Faction	Leader (s)	Ethnicity/ Ideology	Areas of Control
Taliban	Mullah Muhammad Omar	Radical Islam; Pashtun dominated	All major cities; greatest area of support is in southeastern Afghanistan
Jamiat-e Islamic	Burhannudin Rabbani (political leader) and Ahmad Shah Masoud (military leader)	Tajik; moderate Islamic	Panjshir Valley, small parts of northeast Afghanistan
Hizb-e Wahdat	Abd-al Karim Khalili	Shi'a Hazaras; movement divided internally	In August 1998 lost control of strongholds to the Taliban
Harrakat-e Islami	**SHEIK MOHSENI**	Shi'a	Shamali (regions to the north of Kabul), Takhar, Sarre Pul and Samangan
Junbesh-e-Milli-e Afghanistan	**RASHID DOSTUM**	Uzbek; nominally socialist	Lost last stronghold of Mazar-e Sharif in northwest Afghanistan to the Taliban in August 1998

BASIC TITLES ON AFGHANISTAN

IMPORTANT!
All publications are updated annually!
Please contact IBP, Inc. at ibpusa3@gmail.com for the latest ISBNs and additional information

Title
Afghanistan A "Spy" Guide - Strategic Information and Developments
Afghanistan Business and Investment Opportunities Yearbook
Afghanistan Business and Investment Opportunities Yearbook Volume 1 Strategic Information and Opportunities
Afghanistan Business Intelligence Report - Practical Information, Opportunities, Contacts
Afghanistan Business Intelligence Report - Practical Information, Opportunities, Contacts
Afghanistan Business Law Handbook - Strategic Information and Basic Laws
Afghanistan Business Law Handbook - Strategic Information and Basic Laws
Afghanistan Business Law Handbook - Strategic Information and Basic Laws
Afghanistan Business Law Handbook - Strategic Information and Basic Laws
Afghanistan Constitution and Citizenship Laws Handbook - Strategic Information and Basic Laws
Afghanistan Country Study Guide - Strategic Information and Developments
Afghanistan Country Study Guide - Strategic Information and Developments
Afghanistan Country Study Guide - Strategic Information and Developments Volume 1 Strategic Information and Developments
Afghanistan Customs, Trade Regulations and Procedures Handbook
Afghanistan Customs, Trade Regulations and Procedures Handbook
Afghanistan Diplomatic Handbook - Strategic Information and Developments
Afghanistan Diplomatic Handbook - Strategic Information and Developments
Afghanistan Ecology & Nature Protection Handbook
Afghanistan Ecology & Nature Protection Handbook
Afghanistan Ecology & Nature Protection Laws and Regulation Handbook
Afghanistan Energy Policy, Laws and Regulation Handbook
Afghanistan Foreign Policy and Government Guide
Afghanistan Foreign Policy and Government Guide
Afghanistan Healthcare Sector Organization, Management and Payment Systems Handbook - Strategic Information, Programs and Regulations
Afghanistan Immigration Laws and Regulations Handbook - Strategic Information and Basic Laws
Afghanistan Insolvency (Bankruptcy) Laws and Regulations Handbook - Strategic Information and Basic Laws
Afghanistan Investment and Business Guide - Strategic and Practical Information
Afghanistan Investment and Business Guide - Strategic and Practical Information
Afghanistan Investment and Business Guide - Strategic and Practical Information
Afghanistan Investment and Business Guide - Strategic and Practical Information
Afghanistan Labor Laws and Regulations Handbook - Strategic Information and Basic Laws
Afghanistan Land Ownership and Agriculture Laws Handbook
Afghanistan Mineral & Mining Sector Investment and Business Guide - Strategic and Practical Information
Afghanistan Mineral & Mining Sector Investment and Business Guide - Strategic and Practical

Title
Information
Afghanistan Mining Laws and Regulations Handbook
Afghanistan Recent Economic and Political Developments Yearbook
Afghanistan Recent Economic and Political Developments Yearbook
Afghanistan Recent Economic and Political Developments Yearbook
Afghanistan Reconstruction Handbook
Afghanistan Reconstruction Handbook
Afghanistan Taxation Laws and Regulations Handbook
Afghanistan Transportation Policy and Regulations Handbook
Afghanistan: How to Invest, Start and Run Profitable Business in Afghanistan Guide - Practical Information, Opportunities, Contacts

WORLD COUNTRY STUDY GUIDES LIBRARY

Strategic political, geographic, economic, business information, contacts and important developments

Price: $99.95 each

1.	Abkhazia (Republic of Abkhazia) A "Spy" Guide Volume 1 Strategic Information, Security and Political Developments
2.	Afghanistan A "Spy" Guide Volume 1 Strategic Information, Security and Political Developments
3.	Aland A "Spy" Guide Volume 1 Strategic Information, Security and Political Developments
4.	Albania A "Spy" Guide Volume 1 Strategic Information, Security and Political Developments
5.	Algeria A "Spy" Guide Volume 1 Strategic Information, Security and Political Developments
6.	Andorra A "Spy" Guide Volume 1 Strategic Information, Security and Political Developments
7.	Angola A "Spy" Guide Volume 1 Strategic Information, Security and Political Developments
8.	Anguilla A "Spy" Guide Volume 1 Strategic Information, Security and Political Developments
9.	Antigua and Barbuda A "Spy" Guide Volume 1 Strategic Information, Security and Political Developments
10.	Antilles (Netherlands) A "Spy" Guide Volume 1 Strategic Information, Security and Political Developments
11.	Argentina A "Spy" Guide Volume 1 Strategic Information, Security and Political Developments
12.	Armenia A "Spy" Guide Volume 1 Strategic Information, Security and Political Developments
13.	Aruba A "Spy" Guide Volume 1 Strategic Information, Security and Political Developments
14.	Australia A "Spy" Guide Volume 1 Strategic Information, Security and Political Developments
15.	Austria A "Spy" Guide Volume 1 Strategic Information, Security and Political Developments
16.	Azerbaijan A "Spy" Guide Volume 1 Strategic Information, Security and Political Developments
17.	Bahamas A "Spy" Guide Volume 1 Strategic Information, Security and Political Developments
18.	Bahrain A "Spy" Guide Volume 1 Strategic Information, Security and Political Developments
19.	Bangladesh A "Spy" Guide Volume 1 Strategic Information, Security and Political Developments
20.	Barbados A "Spy" Guide Volume 1 Strategic Information, Security and Political Developments
21.	Belarus A "Spy" Guide Volume 1 Strategic Information, Security and Political Developments
22.	Belgium A "Spy" Guide Volume 1 Strategic Information, Security and Political Developments
23.	Belize A "Spy" Guide Volume 1 Strategic Information, Security and Political Developments
24.	Benin A "Spy" Guide Volume 1 Strategic Information, Security and Political Developments
25.	Bermuda A "Spy" Guide Volume 1 Strategic Information, Security and Political Developments
26.	Bhutan A "Spy" Guide Volume 1 Strategic Information, Security and Political Developments
27.	Bolivia A "Spy" Guide Volume 1 Strategic Information, Security and Political Developments
28.	Bosnia and Herzegovina A "Spy" Guide Volume 1 Strategic Information, Security and Political Developments
29.	Botswana A "Spy" Guide Volume 1 Strategic Information, Security and Political Developments
30.	Brazil A "Spy" Guide Volume 1 Strategic Information, Security and Political Developments
31.	Brunei A "Spy" Guide Volume 1 Strategic Information, Security and Political Developments
32.	Bulgaria A "Spy" Guide Volume 1 Strategic Information, Security and Political Developments
33.	Burkina Faso A "Spy" Guide Volume 1 Strategic Information, Security and Political Developments
34.	Burundi A "Spy" Guide Volume 1 Strategic Information, Security and Political Developments

35.	Cambodia A "Spy" Guide Volume 1 Strategic Information, Security and Political Developments
36.	Cameroon A "Spy" Guide Volume 1 Strategic Information, Security and Political Developments
37.	Canada A "Spy" Guide Volume 1 Strategic Information, Security and Political Developments
38.	Cape Verde A "Spy" Guide Volume 1 Strategic Information, Security and Political Developments
39.	Cayman Islands A "Spy" Guide Volume 1 Strategic Information, Security and Political Developments
40.	Central African Republic A "Spy" Guide Volume 1 Strategic Information, Security and Political Developments
41.	Chad A "Spy" Guide Volume 1 Strategic Information, Security and Political Developments
42.	Chile A "Spy" Guide Volume 1 Strategic Information, Security and Political Developments
43.	China A "Spy" Guide Volume 1 Strategic Information, Security and Political Developments
44.	Colombia A "Spy" Guide Volume 1 Strategic Information, Security and Political Developments
45.	Comoros A "Spy" Guide Volume 1 Strategic Information, Security and Political Developments
46.	Congo A "Spy" Guide Volume 1 Strategic Information, Security and Political Developments
47.	Congo, Democratic Republic A "Spy" Guide Volume 1 Strategic Information, Security and Political Developments
48.	Cook Islands A "Spy" Guide Volume 1 Strategic Information, Security and Political Developments
49.	Costa Rica A "Spy" Guide Volume 1 Strategic Information, Security and Political Developments
50.	Cote d'Ivoire A "Spy" Guide Volume 1 Strategic Information, Security and Political Developments
51.	Croatia A "Spy" Guide Volume 1 Strategic Information, Security and Political Developments
52.	Cuba A "Spy" Guide Volume 1 Strategic Information, Security and Political Developments
53.	Cyprus A "Spy" Guide Volume 1 Strategic Information, Security and Political Developments
54.	Czech Republic A "Spy" Guide Volume 1 Strategic Information, Security and Political Developments
55.	Denmark A "Spy" Guide Volume 1 Strategic Information, Security and Political Developments
56.	Djibouti A "Spy" Guide Volume 1 Strategic Information, Security and Political Developments
57.	Dominica A "Spy" Guide Volume 1 Strategic Information, Security and Political Developments
58.	Dominican Republic A "Spy" Guide Volume 1 Strategic Information, Security and Political Developments
59.	Ecuador A "Spy" Guide Volume 1 Strategic Information, Security and Political Developments
60.	Egypt A "Spy" Guide Volume 1 Strategic Information, Security and Political Developments
61.	El Salvador A "Spy" Guide Volume 1 Strategic Information, Security and Political Developments
62.	Equatorial Guinea A "Spy" Guide Volume 1 Strategic Information, Security and Political Developments
63.	Eritrea A "Spy" Guide Volume 1 Strategic Information, Security and Political Developments
64.	Estonia A "Spy" Guide Volume 1 Strategic Information, Security and Political Developments
65.	Ethiopia A "Spy" Guide Volume 1 Strategic Information, Security and Political Developments
66.	Falkland Islands A "Spy" Guide Volume 1 Strategic Information, Security and Political Developments
67.	Faroes Islands A "Spy" Guide Volume 1 Strategic Information, Security and Political Developments
68.	Fiji A "Spy" Guide Volume 1 Strategic Information, Security and Political Developments
69.	Finland A "Spy" Guide Volume 1 Strategic Information, Security and Political Developments
70.	France A "Spy" Guide Volume 1 Strategic Information, Security and Political Developments
71.	Gabon A "Spy" Guide Volume 1 Strategic Information, Security and Political Developments
72.	Gambia A "Spy" Guide Volume 1 Strategic Information, Security and Political Developments
73.	Georgia A "Spy" Guide Volume 1 Strategic Information, Security and Political Developments
74.	Germany A "Spy" Guide Volume 1 Strategic Information, Security and Political Developments
75.	Ghana A "Spy" Guide Volume 1 Strategic Information, Security and Political Developments
76.	Gibraltar A "Spy" Guide Volume 1 Strategic Information, Security and Political Developments
77.	Greece A "Spy" Guide Volume 1 Strategic Information, Security and Political Developments
78.	Greenland A "Spy" Guide Volume 1 Strategic Information, Security and Political Developments
79.	Grenada A "Spy" Guide Volume 1 Strategic Information, Security and Political Developments
80.	Guam A "Spy" Guide Volume 1 Strategic Information, Security and Political Developments
81.	Guatemala A "Spy" Guide Volume 1 Strategic Information, Security and Political Developments
82.	Guernsey A "Spy" Guide Volume 1 Strategic Information, Security and Political Developments
83.	Guinea A "Spy" Guide Volume 1 Strategic Information, Security and Political Developments
84.	Guinea-Bissau A "Spy" Guide Volume 1 Strategic Information, Security and Political Developments

85. Guyana A "Spy" Guide Volume 1 Strategic Information, Security and Political Developments
86. Haiti A "Spy" Guide Volume 1 Strategic Information, Security and Political Developments
87. Honduras A "Spy" Guide Volume 1 Strategic Information, Security and Political Developments
88. Hungary A "Spy" Guide Volume 1 Strategic Information, Security and Political Developments
89. Iceland A "Spy" Guide Volume 1 Strategic Information, Security and Political Developments
90. India A "Spy" Guide Volume 1 Strategic Information, Security and Political Developments
91. Indonesia A "Spy" Guide Volume 1 Strategic Information, Security and Political Developments
92. Iran A "Spy" Guide Volume 1 Strategic Information, Security and Political Developments
93. Iraq A "Spy" Guide Volume 1 Strategic Information, Security and Political Developments
94. Ireland A "Spy" Guide Volume 1 Strategic Information, Security and Political Developments
95. Israel A "Spy" Guide Volume 1 Strategic Information, Security and Political Developments
96. Italy A "Spy" Guide Volume 1 Strategic Information, Security and Political Developments
97. Jamaica A "Spy" Guide Volume 1 Strategic Information, Security and Political Developments
98. Japan A "Spy" Guide Volume 1 Strategic Information, Security and Political Developments
99. Jersey A "Spy" Guide Volume 1 Strategic Information, Security and Political Developments
100. Jordan A "Spy" Guide Volume 1 Strategic Information, Security and Political Developments
101. Kazakhstan A "Spy" Guide Volume 1 Strategic Information, Security and Political Developments
102. Kenya A "Spy" Guide Volume 1 Strategic Information, Security and Political Developments
103. Kiribati A "Spy" Guide Volume 1 Strategic Information, Security and Political Developments
104. Korea, North A "Spy" Guide Volume 1 Strategic Information, Security and Political Developments
105. Korea, South A "Spy" Guide Volume 1 Strategic Information, Security and Political Developments
106. Kosovo A "Spy" Guide Volume 1 Strategic Information, Security and Political Developments
107. Kurdistan A "Spy" Guide Volume 1 Strategic Information, Security and Political Developments
108. Kuwait A "Spy" Guide Volume 1 Strategic Information, Security and Political Developments
109. Kyrgyzstan A "Spy" Guide Volume 1 Strategic Information, Security and Political Developments
110. Laos A "Spy" Guide Volume 1 Strategic Information, Security and Political Developments
111. Latvia A "Spy" Guide Volume 1 Strategic Information, Security and Political Developments
112. Lebanon A "Spy" Guide Volume 1 Strategic Information, Security and Political Developments
113. Lesotho A "Spy" Guide Volume 1 Strategic Information, Security and Political Developments
114. Liberia A "Spy" Guide Volume 1 Strategic Information, Security and Political Developments
115. Libya A "Spy" Guide Volume 1 Strategic Information, Security and Political Developments
116. Liechtenstein A "Spy" Guide Volume 1 Strategic Information, Security and Political Developments
117. Lithuania A "Spy" Guide Volume 1 Strategic Information, Security and Political Developments
118. Luxembourg A "Spy" Guide Volume 1 Strategic Information, Security and Political Developments
119. Macao A "Spy" Guide Volume 1 Strategic Information, Security and Political Developments
120. Macedonia,A "Spy" Guide Volume 1 Strategic Information, Security and Political Developments
121. Madagascar A "Spy" Guide Volume 1 Strategic Information, Security and Political Developments
122. MadeiraA "Spy" Guide Volume 1 Strategic Information, Security and Political Developments
123. Malawi A "Spy" Guide Volume 1 Strategic Information, Security and Political Developments
124. Malaysia A "Spy" Guide Volume 1 Strategic Information, Security and Political Developments
125. Maldives A "Spy" Guide Volume 1 Strategic Information, Security and Political Developments
126. Mali A "Spy" Guide Volume 1 Strategic Information, Security and Political Developments
127. Malta A "Spy" Guide Volume 1 Strategic Information, Security and Political Developments
128. Man A "Spy" Guide Volume 1 Strategic Information, Security and Political Developments
129. Marshall Islands A "Spy" Guide Volume 1 Strategic Information, Security and Political Developments
130. Mauritania A "Spy" Guide Volume 1 Strategic Information, Security and Political Developments
131. Mauritius A "Spy" Guide Volume 1 Strategic Information, Security and Political Developments
132. Mayotte A "Spy" Guide Volume 1 Strategic Information, Security and Political Developments
133. Mexico A "Spy" Guide Volume 1 Strategic Information, Security and Political Developments
134. Micronesia A "Spy" Guide Volume 1 Strategic Information, Security and Political Developments
135. Moldova A "Spy" Guide Volume 1 Strategic Information, Security and Political Developments
136. Monaco A "Spy" Guide Volume 1 Strategic Information, Security and Political Developments
137. Mongolia A "Spy" Guide Volume 1 Strategic Information, Security and Political Developments

138. Monserrat A "Spy" Guide Volume 1 Strategic Information, Security and Political Developments
139. Montenegro A "Spy" Guide Volume 1 Strategic Information, Security and Political Developments
140. Morocco A "Spy" Guide Volume 1 Strategic Information, Security and Political Developments
141. Mozambique A "Spy" Guide Volume 1 Strategic Information, Security and Political Developments
142. Myanmar A "Spy" Guide Volume 1 Strategic Information, Security and Political Developments
143. Nagorno-Karabakh Republic A "Spy" Guide Volume 1 Strategic Information, Security and Political Developments
144. Namibia A "Spy" Guide Volume 1 Strategic Information, Security and Political Developments
145. Nauru A "Spy" Guide Volume 1 Strategic Information, Security and Political Developments
146. Nepal A "Spy" Guide Volume 1 Strategic Information, Security and Political Developments
147. Netherlands A "Spy" Guide Volume 1 Strategic Information, Security and Political Developments
148. New Caledonia A "Spy" Guide Volume 1 Strategic Information, Security and Political Developments
149. New Zealand A "Spy" Guide Volume 1 Strategic Information, Security and Political Developments
150. Nicaragua A "Spy" Guide Volume 1 Strategic Information, Security and Political Developments
151. Niger A "Spy" Guide Volume 1 Strategic Information, Security and Political Developments
152. Nigeria A "Spy" Guide Volume 1 Strategic Information, Security and Political Developments
153. Niue A "Spy" Guide Volume 1 Strategic Information, Security and Political Developments
154. Northern Cyprus (Turkish Republic of Northern Cyprus)
155. Northern Mariana Islands A "Spy" Guide Volume 1 Strategic Information, Security and Political Developments
156. Norway A "Spy" Guide Volume 1 Strategic Information, Security and Political Developments
157. Oman A "Spy" Guide Volume 1 Strategic Information, Security and Political Developments
158. Pakistan A "Spy" Guide Volume 1 Strategic Information, Security and Political Developments
159. Palau A "Spy" Guide Volume 1 Strategic Information, Security and Political Developments
160. Palestine (West Bank & Gaza) A "Spy" Guide Volume 1 Strategic Information, Security and Political Developments
161. Panama A "Spy" Guide Volume 1 Strategic Information, Security and Political Developments
162. Papua New Guinea A "Spy" Guide Volume 1 Strategic Information, Security and Political Developments
163. Paraguay A "Spy" Guide Volume 1 Strategic Information, Security and Political Developments
164. Peru A "Spy" Guide Volume 1 Strategic Information, Security and Political Developments
165. Philippines A "Spy" Guide Volume 1 Strategic Information, Security and Political Developments
166. Pitcairn Islands A "Spy" Guide Volume 1 Strategic Information, Security and Political Developments
167. Poland A "Spy" Guide Volume 1 Strategic Information, Security and Political Developments
168. Polynesia French A "Spy" Guide Volume 1 Strategic Information, Security and Political Developments
169. Portugal A "Spy" Guide Volume 1 Strategic Information, Security and Political Developments
170. Qatar A "Spy" Guide Volume 1 Strategic Information, Security and Political Developments
171. Romania A "Spy" Guide Volume 1 Strategic Information, Security and Political Developments
172. Russia A "Spy" Guide Volume 1 Strategic Information, Security and Political Developments
173. Rwanda A "Spy" Guide Volume 1 Strategic Information, Security and Political Developments
174. Sahrawi Arab Democratic Republic Volume 1 Strategic Information, Security and Political Developments
175. Saint Kitts and Nevis A "Spy" Guide Volume 1 Strategic Information, Security and Political Developments
176. Saint Lucia A "Spy" Guide Volume 1 Strategic Information, Security and Political Developments
177. Saint Vincent and The Grenadines A "Spy" Guide Volume 1 Strategic Information, Security and Political Developments
178. Samoa (American) A A "Spy" Guide Volume 1 Strategic Information, Security and Political Developments
179. Samoa (Western) A "Spy" Guide Volume 1 Strategic Information, Security and Political Developments
180. San Marino A "Spy" Guide Volume 1 Strategic Information, Security and Political Developments
181. Sao Tome and Principe A "Spy" Guide Volume 1 Strategic Information, Security and Political Developments
182. Saudi Arabia A "Spy" Guide Volume 1 Strategic Information, Security and Political Developments
183. Scotland A "Spy" Guide Volume 1 Strategic Information, Security and Political Developments
184. Senegal A "Spy" Guide Volume 1 Strategic Information, Security and Political Developments

185. Serbia A "Spy" Guide Volume 1 Strategic Information, Security and Political Developments
186. Seychelles A "Spy" Guide Volume 1 Strategic Information, Security and Political Developments
187. Sierra Leone A "Spy" Guide Volume 1 Strategic Information, Security and Political Developments
188. Singapore A "Spy" Guide Volume 1 Strategic Information, Security and Political Developments
189. Slovakia A "Spy" Guide Volume 1 Strategic Information, Security and Political Developments
190. Slovenia A "Spy" Guide Volume 1 Strategic Information, Security and Political Developments
191. Solomon Islands A "Spy" Guide Volume 1 Strategic Information, Security and Political Developments
192. Somalia A "Spy" Guide Volume 1 Strategic Information, Security and Political Developments
193. South Africa A "Spy" Guide Volume 1 Strategic Information, Security and Political Developments
194. Spain A "Spy" Guide Volume 1 Strategic Information, Security and Political Developments
195. Sri Lanka A "Spy" Guide Volume 1 Strategic Information, Security and Political Developments
196. St. Helena A "Spy" Guide Volume 1 Strategic Information, Security and Political Developments
197. St. Pierre & Miquelon A "Spy" Guide Volume 1 Strategic Information, Security and Political Developments
198. Sudan (Republic of the Sudan) A "Spy" Guide Volume 1 Strategic Information, Security and Political Developments
199. Sudan South A "Spy" Guide Volume 1 Strategic Information, Security and Political Developments
200. Suriname A "Spy" Guide Volume 1 Strategic Information, Security and Political Developments
201. Swaziland A "Spy" Guide Volume 1 Strategic Information, Security and Political Developments
202. Sweden A "Spy" Guide Volume 1 Strategic Information, Security and Political Developments
203. Switzerland A "Spy" Guide Volume 1 Strategic Information, Security and Political Developments
204. Syria A "Spy" Guide Volume 1 Strategic Information, Security and Political Developments
205. Taiwan A "Spy" Guide Volume 1 Strategic Information, Security and Political Developments
206. Tajikistan A "Spy" Guide Volume 1 Strategic Information, Security and Political Developments
207. Tanzania A "Spy" Guide Volume 1 Strategic Information, Security and Political Developments
208. Thailand A "Spy" Guide Volume 1 Strategic Information, Security and Political Developments
209. Timor Leste (Democratic Republic of Timor-Leste) A "Spy" Guide Volume 1 Strategic Information, Security and Political Developments
210. Togo A "Spy" Guide Volume 1 Strategic Information, Security and Political Developments
211. Tonga A "Spy" Guide Volume 1 Strategic Information, Security and Political Developments
212. Trinidad and Tobago A "Spy" Guide Volume 1 Strategic Information, Security and Political Developments
213. Tunisia A "Spy" Guide Volume 1 Strategic Information, Security and Political Developments
214. Turkey A "Spy" Guide Volume 1 Strategic Information, Security and Political Developments
215. Turkmenistan A "Spy" Guide Volume 1 Strategic Information, Security and Political Developments
216. Turks & Caicos A "Spy" Guide Volume 1 Strategic Information, Security and Political Developments
217. Tuvalu A "Spy" Guide Volume 1 Strategic Information, Security and Political Developments
218. Uganda A "Spy" Guide Volume 1 Strategic Information, Security and Political Developments
219. Ukraine A "Spy" Guide Volume 1 Strategic Information, Security and Political Developments
220. United Arab Emirates A "Spy" Guide Volume 1 Strategic Information, Security and Political Developments
221. United Kingdom A "Spy" Guide Volume 1 Strategic Information, Security and Political Developments
222. United States A "Spy" Guide Volume 1 Strategic Information, Security and Political Developments
223. Uruguay A "Spy" Guide Volume 1 Strategic Information, Security and Political Developments
224. Uzbekistan A "Spy" Guide Volume 1 Strategic Information, Security and Political Developments
225. Vanuatu A "Spy" Guide Volume 1 Strategic Information, Security and Political Developments
226. Vatican City (Holy See) A "Spy" Guide Volume 1 Strategic Information, Security and Political Developments
227. Venezuela A "Spy" Guide Volume 1 Strategic Information, Security and Political Developments
228. Vietnam A "Spy" Guide Volume 1 Strategic Information, Security and Political Developments
229. Virgin Islands, British A "Spy" Guide Volume 1 Strategic Information, Security and Political Developments
230. Wake Atoll A "Spy" Guide Volume 1 Strategic Information, Security and Political Developments
231. Wallis & Futuna A "Spy" Guide Volume 1 Strategic Information, Security and Political Developments

232. Western Sahara A "Spy" Guide Volume 1 Strategic Information, Security and Political Developments
233. Yemen A "Spy" Guide Volume 1 Strategic Information, Security and Political Developments
234. Zambia A "Spy" Guide Volume 1 Strategic Information, Security and Political Developments
235. Zimbabwe A "Spy" Guide Volume 1 Strategic Information, Security and Political Developments

TITLE
Chile Recent Economic and Political Developments Yearbook
China Recent Economic and Political Developments Yearbook
Colombia Recent Economic and Political Developments Yearbook
Comoros Recent Economic and Political Developments Yearbook
Congo Recent Economic and Political Developments Yearbook
Congo, Democratic Republic Recent Economic and Political Developments Yearbook
Cook Islands Recent Economic and Political Developments Yearbook
Costa Rica Recent Economic and Political Developments Yearbook
Cote d'Ivoire Recent Economic and Political Developments Yearbook
Croatia Recent Economic and Political Developments Yearbook
Cuba Recent Economic and Political Developments Yearbook
Cyprus Recent Economic and Political Developments Yearbook
Czech Republic Recent Economic and Political Developments Yearbook
Denmark Recent Economic and Political Developments Yearbook
Djibouti Recent Economic and Political Developments Yearbook
Dominica Recent Economic and Political Developments Yearbook
Dominican Republic Recent Economic and Political Developments Yearbook
Ecuador Recent Economic and Political Developments Yearbook
Egypt Recent Economic and Political Developments Yearbook
El Salvador Recent Economic and Political Developments Yearbook
Equatorial Guinea Recent Economic and Political Developments Yearbook
Eritrea Recent Economic and Political Developments Yearbook
Estonia Recent Economic and Political Developments Yearbook
Ethiopia Recent Economic and Political Developments Yearbook
Falkland Islands Recent Economic and Political Developments Yearbook
Faroes IslandsRecent Economic and Political Developments Yearbook
Fiji Recent Economic and Political Developments Yearbook
Finland Recent Economic and Political Developments Yearbook
France Recent Economic and Political Developments Yearbook
Gabon Recent Economic and Political Developments Yearbook
Gambia Recent Economic and Political Developments Yearbook
Georgia Recent Economic and Political Developments Yearbook
Germany Recent Economic and Political Developments Yearbook
Ghana Recent Economic and Political Developments Yearbook
Gibraltar Recent Economic and Political Developments Yearbook
GlobalRecent Economic and Political Developments Yearbook
Greece Recent Economic and Political Developments Yearbook
Greenland Recent Economic and Political Developments Yearbook
Grenada Recent Economic and Political Developments Yearbook
Guam Recent Economic and Political Developments Yearbook
Guatemala Recent Economic and Political Developments Yearbook
Guernsey Recent Economic and Political Developments Yearbook
Guinea Recent Economic and Political Developments Yearbook
Guinea-Bissau Recent Economic and Political Developments Yearbook
Guyana Recent Economic and Political Developments Yearbook
Haiti Recent Economic and Political Developments Yearbook
Honduras Recent Economic and Political Developments Yearbook
Hungary Recent Economic and Political Developments Yearbook
Iceland Recent Economic and Political Developments Yearbook
India Recent Economic and Political Developments Yearbook

TITLE
Indonesia Recent Economic and Political Developments Yearbook
InternationalRecent Economic and Political Developments Yearbook
Iran Recent Economic and Political Developments Yearbook
Iraq Recent Economic and Political Developments Yearbook
Ireland Recent Economic and Political Developments Yearbook
Israel Recent Economic and Political Developments Yearbook
Italy Recent Economic and Political Developments Yearbook
Jamaica Recent Economic and Political Developments Yearbook
Japan Recent Economic and Political Developments Yearbook
Jersey Recent Economic and Political Developments Yearbook
Jordan Recent Economic and Political Developments Yearbook
Kazakhstan Recent Economic and Political Developments Yearbook
Kenya Recent Economic and Political Developments Yearbook
Kiribati Recent Economic and Political Developments Yearbook
Korea, North Recent Economic and Political Developments Yearbook
Korea, South Recent Economic and Political Developments Yearbook
KosovoRecent Economic and Political Developments Yearbook
KurdistanRecent Economic and Political Developments Yearbook
Kuwait Recent Economic and Political Developments Yearbook
Kyrgyzstan Recent Economic and Political Developments Yearbook
Laos Recent Economic and Political Developments Yearbook
Latvia Recent Economic and Political Developments Yearbook
Lebanon Recent Economic and Political Developments Yearbook
Lesotho Recent Economic and Political Developments Yearbook
Liberia Recent Economic and Political Developments Yearbook
Libya Recent Economic and Political Developments Yearbook
Liechtenstein Recent Economic and Political Developments Yearbook
Lithuania Recent Economic and Political Developments Yearbook
Luxembourg Recent Economic and Political Developments Yearbook
Macao Recent Economic and Political Developments Yearbook
Macedonia,Recent Economic and Political Developments Yearbook
Madagascar Recent Economic and Political Developments Yearbook
MadeiraRecent Economic and Political Developments Yearbook
Malawi Recent Economic and Political Developments Yearbook
Malaysia Recent Economic and Political Developments Yearbook
Maldives Recent Economic and Political Developments Yearbook
Mali Recent Economic and Political Developments Yearbook
Malta Recent Economic and Political Developments Yearbook
Man Recent Economic and Political Developments Yearbook
Marshall Islands Recent Economic and Political Developments Yearbook
Mauritania Recent Economic and Political Developments Yearbook
Mauritius Recent Economic and Political Developments Yearbook
Mayotte Recent Economic and Political Developments Yearbook
Mexico Recent Economic and Political Developments Yearbook
Micronesia Recent Economic and Political Developments Yearbook
Moldova Recent Economic and Political Developments Yearbook
Monaco Recent Economic and Political Developments Yearbook
Mongolia Recent Economic and Political Developments Yearbook
Monserrat Recent Economic and Political Developments Yearbook
Morocco Recent Economic and Political Developments Yearbook

TITLE
Mozambique Recent Economic and Political Developments Yearbook
Myanmar Recent Economic and Political Developments Yearbook
Namibia Recent Economic and Political Developments Yearbook
Nauru Recent Economic and Political Developments Yearbook
Nepal Recent Economic and Political Developments Yearbook
Netherlands Recent Economic and Political Developments Yearbook
New Caledonia Recent Economic and Political Developments Yearbook
New Zealand Recent Economic and Political Developments Yearbook
Nicaragua Recent Economic and Political Developments Yearbook
Niger Recent Economic and Political Developments Yearbook
Nigeria Recent Economic and Political Developments Yearbook
Niue Recent Economic and Political Developments Yearbook
Northern Mariana Islands Recent Economic and Political Developments Yearbook
Norway Recent Economic and Political Developments Yearbook
OffshoreRecent Economic and Political Developments Yearbook
Oman Recent Economic and Political Developments Yearbook
Pakistan Recent Economic and Political Developments Yearbook
Palau Recent Economic and Political Developments Yearbook
Palestine Recent Economic and Political Developments Yearbook
Panama Recent Economic and Political Developments Yearbook
Papua New Guinea Recent Economic and Political Developments Yearbook
Paraguay Recent Economic and Political Developments Yearbook
Peru Recent Economic and Political Developments Yearbook
Philippines Recent Economic and Political Developments Yearbook
Pitcairn Islands Recent Economic and Political Developments Yearbook
Poland Recent Economic and Political Developments Yearbook
Polynesia French Recent Economic and Political Developments Yearbook
Portugal Recent Economic and Political Developments Yearbook
Qatar Recent Economic and Political Developments Yearbook
Romania Recent Economic and Political Developments Yearbook
Russia Recent Economic and Political Developments Yearbook
Rwanda Recent Economic and Political Developments Yearbook
Saint Kitts and Nevis Recent Economic and Political Developments Yearbook
Saint Lucia Recent Economic and Political Developments Yearbook
Saint Vincent and The Grenadines Recent Economic and Political Developments Yearbook
Samoa (American) A Recent Economic and Political Developments Yearbook
Samoa (Western) Recent Economic and Political Developments Yearbook
San Marino Recent Economic and Political Developments Yearbook
Sao Tome and Principe Recent Economic and Political Developments Yearbook
Saudi Arabia Recent Economic and Political Developments Yearbook
Scotland Recent Economic and Political Developments Yearbook
Senegal Recent Economic and Political Developments Yearbook
SerbiaRecent Economic and Political Developments Yearbook
Seychelles Recent Economic and Political Developments Yearbook
Sierra Leone Recent Economic and Political Developments Yearbook
Singapore Recent Economic and Political Developments Yearbook
Slovakia Recent Economic and Political Developments Yearbook
Slovenia Recent Economic and Political Developments Yearbook
Solomon Islands Recent Economic and Political Developments Yearbook
Somalia Recent Economic and Political Developments Yearbook

TITLE
South Africa Recent Economic and Political Developments Yearbook
Spain Recent Economic and Political Developments Yearbook
Sri Lanka Recent Economic and Political Developments Yearbook
St. Helena Recent Economic and Political Developments Yearbook
St. Pierre & Miquelon Recent Economic and Political Developments Yearbook
Sudan Recent Economic and Political Developments Yearbook
Suriname Recent Economic and Political Developments Yearbook
Swaziland Recent Economic and Political Developments Yearbook
Sweden Recent Economic and Political Developments Yearbook
Switzerland Recent Economic and Political Developments Yearbook
Syria Recent Economic and Political Developments Yearbook
Taiwan Recent Economic and Political Developments Yearbook
Tajikistan Recent Economic and Political Developments Yearbook
Tanzania Recent Economic and Political Developments Yearbook
Thailand Recent Economic and Political Developments Yearbook
Togo Recent Economic and Political Developments Yearbook
Tonga Recent Economic and Political Developments Yearbook
Trinidad and Tobago Recent Economic and Political Developments Yearbook
Tunisia Recent Economic and Political Developments Yearbook
Turkey Recent Economic and Political Developments Yearbook
Turkmenistan Recent Economic and Political Developments Yearbook
Turks & Caicos Recent Economic and Political Developments Yearbook
Tuvalu Recent Economic and Political Developments Yearbook
Uganda Recent Economic and Political Developments Yearbook
Ukraine Recent Economic and Political Developments Yearbook
United Arab Emirates Recent Economic and Political Developments Yearbook
United Kingdom Recent Economic and Political Developments Yearbook
United States Recent Economic and Political Developments Yearbook
Uruguay Recent Economic and Political Developments Yearbook
Uzbekistan Recent Economic and Political Developments Yearbook
Vanuatu Recent Economic and Political Developments Yearbook
Vatican City Recent Economic and Political Developments Yearbook
Venezuela Recent Economic and Political Developments Yearbook
Vietnam Recent Economic and Political Developments Yearbook
Virgin Islands, British Recent Economic and Political Developments Yearbook
Wake Atoll Recent Economic and Political Developments Yearbook
Wallis & Futuna Recent Economic and Political Developments Yearbook
Western Sahara Recent Economic and Political Developments Yearbook
Yemen Recent Economic and Political Developments Yearbook
Zambia Recent Economic and Political Developments Yearbook
Zimbabwe Recent Economic and Political Developments Yearbook

GLOBAL ARMY, DEFENSE, INTELLIGENCE, COUNTERINTELLIGENCE, NATIONAL SECURITY HANDBOOK LIBRARY

(PRICE $149.95 each)

Ultimate handbooks on army, defense policy, intelligence, counterintelligence, national security and related operation, conducted by specific countries. National security and intelligence agencies operations and structure

TITLE
1. Albania Army, National Security and Defense Policy Handbook
2. Argentina Intelligence & Security Activities & Operations Handbook
3. Australia Army, National Security and Defense Policy Handbook
4. Australia Intelligence & Security Activities & Operations Handbook
5. Bangladesh Army, National Security and Defense Policy Handbook
6. Bulgaria and NATO Handbook
7. Bulgaria Department of Defense Handbook
8. Canada Intelligence & Security Activities & Operations Handbook
9. Canadian Security Intelligence Service (CSIS) Handbook
10. China Army, National Security and Defense Policy Handbook
11. Cuba Army, National Security and Defense Policy Handbook
12. Czech Republic Army, National Security and Defense Policy Handbook
13. Estonia Army, National Security and Defense Policy Handbook
14. Estonia Intelligence & Security Activities & Operations Handbook
15. EUROPOL – EUROPEAN POLICE OFFICE Handbook
16. Finland Army, National Security and Defense Policy Handbook
17. Finland Intelligence & Security Activities & Operations Handbook
18. France Army, National Security and Defense Policy Handbook
19. German Intelligence & Security Activities & Operations Handbook
20. Germany Army, National Security and Defense Policy Handbook
21. Global Counter-Terrorism Handbook
22. Global National Intelligence and Security Agencies Handbook
23. Global Terrorism Attacks Encyclopedic Handbook
24. Greece Army, National Security and Defense Policy Handbook

TITLE
25. Greece Intelligence & Security Activities & Operations Handbook
26. Hungary Army, National Security and Defense Policy Handbook
27. Hungary Intelligence & Security Activities & Operations Handbook
28. India Army, National Security and Defense Policy Handbook
29. India Intelligence & Security Activities & Operations Handbook
30. Iraq Economic Sanctions, Customs, Trade Regulations and Procedures Handbook
31. Ireland Army, National Security and Defense Policy Handbook
32. Ireland Intelligence & Security Activities & Operations Handbook
33. Israel Army, National Security and Defense Policy Handbook
34. Israel Intelligence & Security Activities & Operations Handbook
35. Italy Intelligence & Security Activities & Operations Handbook
36. Japan Army, National Security and Defense Policy Handbook
37. Japan Intelligence & Security Activities & Operations Handbook
38. Jordan Intelligence & Security Activities & Operations Handbook
39. Korea North Army, National Security and Defense Policy Handbook
40. Korea South Army, National Security and Defense Policy Handbook
41. Korea South Intelligence & Security Activities & Operations Handbook
42. Latvia Army, National Security and Defense Policy Handbook
43. Lebanon Army, National Security and Defense Policy Handbook
44. Lithuania Army, National Security and Defense Policy Handbook
45. Macedonia National Security, Army and Defense Policy Handbook
46. Malaysia Army, National Security and Defense Policy Handbook
47. Myanmar Army, National Security and Defense Policy Handbook
48. New Zealand Army, National Security and Defense Policy Handbook
49. New Zealand Intelligence & Security Activities & Operations Handbook
50. Norway Army, National Security and Defense Policy Handbook
51. Pakistan Army, National Security and Defense Policy Handbook
52. Pakistan Intelligence & Security Activities & Operations Handbook
53. Philippines Army, National Security and Defense Policy Handbook
54. Poland Army, National Security and Defense Policy Handbook
55. Portugal Intelligence & Security Activities & Operations Handbook
56. Romania Army, National Security and Defense Policy Handbook
57. Romania Intelligence & Security Activities & Operations Handbook
58. Russia Army, National Security and Defense Policy Handbook
59. Russia Intelligence & Security Activities & Operations Handbook
60. Russian KGB Handbook: Past and Present
61. Russian Navy Handbook: History and Modern Situation

TITLE
62. Russia-NATO Cooperation Handbook
63. Singapore Army, National Security and Defense Policy Handbook
64. Slovak Republic Army, National Security and Defense Policy Handbook
65. South Africa Army, National Security and Defense Policy Handbook
66. South Africa Intelligence & Security Activities & Operations Handbook
67. Sri Lanka Army, National Security and Defense Policy Handbook
68. Starting Business (Incorporating) in India Encyclopedic Guide
69. Sweden Intelligence & Security Activities & Operations Handbook
70. Switzerland Army, National Security and Defense Policy Handbook
71. Switzerland Intelligence & Security Activities & Operations Handbook
72. Taiwan Army, National Security and Defense Policy Handbook
73. Taiwan Intelligence & Security Activities & Operations Handbook
74. Thailand Royal Army, National Security and Defense Policy Handbook
75. The French Foreign Legion Handbook
76. The INTERPOL Handbook
77. The United Stated Ambassadors Yearbook
78. Turkey Army, National Security and Defense Policy Handbook
79. Turkey Intelligence & Security Activities & Operations Handbook
80. UK Department of Trade and Industry (DTI) Handbook
81. UK Intelligence & Counterintelligence Handbook
82. UK Intelligence & Security Activities & Operations Handbook
83. UK Intelligence and Security Policy Handbook
84. UK MI5 Security Service Handbook
85. UK Military Intelligence Handbook
86. UK National Intelligence Service Handbook
87. UK National Police Handbook
88. UK Royal Air force Handbook
89. UK Royal Army Handbook
90. UK Royal Navy Handbook
91. Ukraine Army, National Security and Defense Policy Handbook
92. Ukraine Intelligence & Security Activities & Operations Handbook
93. United Kingdom Army, National Security and Defense Policy Handbook
94. US Arms Sales to Foreign Countries Handbook
95. US Business Intelligence Handbook
96. US Counterintelligence Operations against Cuba Handbook
97. US Defense Policy Handbook
98. US Federal Depository Libraries Directory

TITLE
99. US Federal Government Directory
100. US Federal Grant Management Handbook
101. US Military Intelligence Handbook
102. US Ocean Transportation Companies Directory
103. US Political Intelligence Handbook
104. US War Against International Terrorism Handbook
105. US War Against Iraq Handbook: Political Strategy and Operations
106. US-Russia Cooperation Against Terrorism Handbook
107. US-Russia Economic & Financial Cooperation Handbook
108. US-Russia Military Cooperation Handbook
109. US-Russia Political Cooperation Handbook
110. US-Russia Scientific & Technological Cooperation Handbook
111. US-Russia Space Cooperation Handbook

www.ingramcontent.com/pod-product-compliance
Ingram Content Group UK Ltd.
Pitfield, Milton Keynes, MK11 3LW, UK
UKHW051509290926
15471UKWH00008B/1514

9 781433 000041